Provoking Religion

Provoking Religion

Sex, Art, and the Culture Wars

ANTHONY M. PETRO

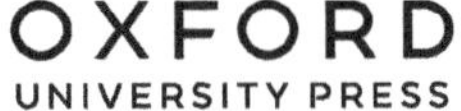

OXFORD
UNIVERSITY PRESS

Oxford University Press is a department of the University of Oxford.
It furthers the University's objective of excellence in research, scholarship,
and education by publishing worldwide. Oxford is a registered trade mark of
Oxford University Press in the UK and in certain other countries.

Published in the United States of America by Oxford University Press
198 Madison Avenue, New York, NY 10016, United States of America.

CIP data is on file at the Library of Congress

ISBN 9780190938437

DOI: 10.1093/9780190938468.001.0001

Printed by Integrated Books International, United States of America

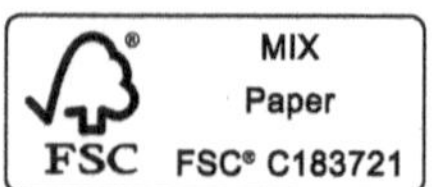

Contents

Detailed Contents

Illustrations

Acknowledgments

This book has been a decade in the making, which means I have had the privilege to learn from many people. Librarians and archivists make everything possible–my sincere appreciation goes to the wonderful people at Boston University Mugar Library, the One Archives, New York University Fales Library and Special Collections, the New York Public Library, the Stanford University Archives, the Schlesinger Library, Berkeley's Bancroft Library, and the Archives of American Art. I am ever thankful to the many artists and activists who inspired this book, some of whom have passed. Thanks especially to Isaac Alpert, Judy Chicago, Renée Cox, Cat Gund, Sheree Rose, Sarah Schulman, Amar Singh, Fred Scruton, and Riche Sorensen for providing image permissions, making archives available, or offering generous feedback.

Much of my research and writing took place at the Institute for Advanced Study in Princeton, where Yves Alain-Bois generously invited me to join and learn from a wonderful group of art historians—my deepest thanks to them. BU's Center for the Humanities provided two semester-long fellowships; my thanks to fellow fellows for suffering early drafts. Eleanor Heartney's work models how to think about contemporary art and religion, and I was thrilled that she kindly served as my mentor for the Art Writing Workshop. I remain grateful for her keen insight. My thanks to Alexandra Bayer, Tara Madhav, and Josh Smith for crucial research assistance. BU's Office of Diversity and Inclusion, the BU Dean of Arts and Sciences, the BU Center for the Humanities, and the American Academy of Religion provided critical funding.

I am grateful to Theo Calderara, once again, and to Meredith Taylor at Oxford University Press for their incredible insight and support. My thanks also to Suruthi Manogarane, for seeing this book through production. The anonymous reviewers offered invaluable feedback that improved this book throughout. Shelby Brewster performed miracles in early copyediting and later proofreading. My thanks, too, to Elise Davies for her copyediting. Many generous colleagues have invited me to present research from this project or have provided crucial feedback or other support over the years, including

Kecia Ali, Debbie Bazarsky, Andrea Berlin, Brooke Blower, Caitlin Bruce, Tim Burnside, Stephen Bush, Heath Carter, Elizabeth Castelli, Cati Connell, Rosemary Corbett, Rachel Corbman, Wendy Czik, Jamil Drake, Jodi Eichler-Levine, Cynthia Eller, Curtis Evans, Molly Farneth, Matthew Feliz, Juliet Floyd, Christienna Fryar, Kira Ganga Kieffer, Lynne Gerber, Kathryn Gin Lum, Philip Goff, Jennifer Graber, Willie Granston, Margarita Guillory, Luke Habberstad, Kyna Hamill, Kali Handelman, Laura Harrington, Cooper Harriss, Amy Hollywood, Katie Holscher, Haley Iliff, Sarah Imhoff, Janet Jakobsen, Andrea Jain, Paul Johnson, Mark Jordan, Hillary Kaell, Paula Kane, Martin Kavka, Siobhan Kelly, Jonathan Klawans, Rachel Kranson, Greta LaFleur, Aaron Lecklider, Laura McTighe, Katherine Mitchell, Susan Mizruchi, Andrew Monteith, Chad Moore, Erin Murphy, Cody Musselman, Amanda Napior, Elayne Oliphant, Bob Orsi, Ann Pellegrini, Seth Perry, Carrie Preston, Sally Promey, Teena Purohit, Jed Samer, Leigh Schmidt, Will Schultz, Adam Seligman, Adam Shear, Susanne Sreedhar, Ronit Stahl, Austin Steelman, William Stell, Kira Thurman, Daniel Vaca, Stephen Vider, Andrew Walker-Cornetta, Tisa Wenger, Peng Yin, Michael Zank, and Angela Zito. My thanks to the BU grad students in religion for workshopping an early chapter and to the Afternoon Words crew and "pom" folks who helped me push through.

I'm particularly grateful for the amazing colleagues, friends, and mentors who have challenged my thinking and supported this work in numberless ways over the last many years, including Courtney Bender, Wallace Best, Gillian Frank, David Frankfurter, Marie Griffith, Zach Herz, April Hughes, Deeana Klepper, Katie Lofton, Steve Prothero, Mark Robinson, Moulie Vidas, Judith Weisenfeld, Heather White, and Melissa Wilcox. Samira Mehta read the whole manuscript and saved me from making religious history mistakes more times than I can count. Nathan Ha reminded me without fail to be a better historian and to use my voice. Talia Dan-Cohen heard way more about this book than she bargained for but always found ways to make my thinking better.

My enduring love and gratitude go to my mother, my late father, and my brothers for sticking with me and my professorial ramblings. I wrote much of this book with one whippet (Shelby) curled in my lap and another (Truvy) laying by my side; they are the best and the worst writing assistants. Patrick McKelvey is, simply, the best.

* * *

An earlier version of chapter one appeared in *American Religion*, and an earlier version of chapter four and parts of the afterword appeared in the *Journal of the American Academy of Religion*. I appreciate the opportunity to use that material here.

Introduction

Inventing the Culture Wars

The best place for *Piss Christ* is in a church.[1]

—Andres Serrano

I like beautiful things, not modern art.[2]

—Senator Jesse Helms

Something funny happened in the 1980s and 1990s. Religious and political conservatives in the United States became increasingly interested in visual and performance art dealing with themes of gender, sexuality, race, and religion—and especially in the work of feminist and queer artists. Take North Carolina Senator Jesse Helms, who became so fixated on photographer Robert Mapplethorpe's interracial homoerotic nudes that he kept copies on hand to show people. Sometimes the Southern Baptist right-winger even requested that reporters view these images before he would grant an interview.[3] Helms was just one of many political and religious firebrands who fanned the flames of the modern culture wars by publicly denouncing such work as pornographic or sacrilegious—even as they (however ironically) became key archivists and curators of its aesthetic imaginary. I started researching the history of these debates over art because I wanted to understand how such a peculiar spectacle could arise—one that saw conservatives denounce feminist and queer art as obscene even as they publicized it, often in vivid detail, through right-wing direct-mail campaigns or across the headlines of major newspapers and television programs. And I wanted to understand how we have told this history of the culture wars.

What I found was that the way news media and even scholarly accounts have narrated this enduring history seemed strikingly limited—and curiously conservative. One typical script for this culture wars narrative pits

Provoking Religion. Anthony M. Petro, Oxford University Press. © Oxford University Press 2025.
DOI: 10.1093/9780190938468.003.0001

religious conservatives against secular progressives. But this framing misses how frequently religious iconography has animated the work of many progressive and radical artists—and to various ends.[4] I wondered if there was a way to tell this history without presuming that religion only appears on one side of the partisan divide. A second culture wars script grounds this history almost solely in the terms of its conservative participants, conflating the rhetoric of right-wing culture warriors with the culture wars themselves. This approach barely questions how or why conservatives characterize so much of this art as anti-Christian or pornographic. Of course, narratives of the culture wars often marry these scripts.

In retelling this history, *Provoking Religion* instead draws us into the rich, complicated worlds of feminist and queer artists, worlds saturated with religious imagery and theological implications, in ways that resist caricature. At the same time, this history pays attention to the habits of interpretation and the tactics of attack through which conservative Christians came to understand and oppose such work. I propose starting this story, then, not with conservatives versus progressives, but with culture warriors and artists. I hope the affordances of this recasting for shifting how we see the culture wars will become clear in the pages to follow.

Act One—The Culture Warrior

Patrick Buchanan may not have started the culture wars, but he provided one of its most strident voices. Speaking at the 1992 Republican National Convention, the former White House communications director lauded the greatness of the 1980s, when "Ronald Reagan made us proud to be American again."[5] But, he insisted, Americans had their work cut out for them in the new decade, and the 1992 presidential election would decide the nation's future. Buchanan, a longtime political commentator and traditionalist Catholic, recited what had become something of a sacred litany of the conservative culture wars. If Democrat Bill Clinton was elected, he warned, the country would witness "unrestricted abortion on demand," the elevation of "militant" lesbians and gay men to positions of national leadership, the expansion of "homosexual rights," discrimination against private Christian schools, and unbridled support for "radical feminism."[6]

Despite these threats, Buchanan found two causes for hope. The first was Reagan's defeat of communism. For the other, Buchanan brought up "the bloody riot" that had erupted in Los Angeles the previous spring. He recalled meeting only months before with "an officer of the 18th Cavalry" who had come with his troops to Los Angeles, with "M-16s at the ready," to quell the violence overtaking the city. Buchanan did not mention Rodney King, the Black motorist who was beaten by four white officers, or that their acquittal on April 29 sparked the unrest. His vision of America brooked little interest in the long history of anti-Black racism. He looked instead to the "19-year-old boys ready to lay down their lives to stop a mob." The invocation of the military was no mere happenstance. "There is a religious war going on in our country for the soul of America," Buchanan declared: "It is a cultural war, as critical to the kind of nation we will one day be as was the Cold War itself."[7] Elevating the "culture war" to a "religious war" raised the stakes: voters were no longer choosing between Republicans and Democrats but between good and evil, between national salvation and god's damnation.[8]

Communism, abortion on demand, militant homosexuality, anti-Christian discrimination, radical feminism, Black protest—these bogeymen of the right, especially the Christian Right, fueled the culture wars of the 1980s and 1990s.[9] These battles were, in many ways, symbolic struggles. "The right wing is deeply committed to symbolic politics," writes anthropologist Carol Vance, "both in using symbols to mobilize public sentiment and in understanding that, because images do stand in for and motivate social change, the arena of representation is a real ground for struggle."[10]

Indeed, images themselves would take center stage in this struggle for the soul of the country, as debates arose over what kinds of images ought to be permitted or censored, funded or banned. Culture warriors like Buchanan readily invoked some images to represent the US American public (such as the young soldiers putting their lives on the line in LA), while ignoring others (like the police brutality against Rodney King). Alternatively, as conservatives understood, some negative images could prove powerful for separating good Americans from dangerous ones, as seen in George H. W. Bush's dog-whistling invocations of William "Willie" Horton during the 1988 presidential campaign. Horton had committed violent crimes, including raping a woman, while on a temporary release from prison in Massachusetts, where Democratic presidential hopeful Michael Dukakis served as governor.[11] Bush's campaign kept Horton's name—and photo—in the news to stoke white fears of sexualized Black criminality. Like Bush, Buchanan understood that images could foster cultural corruption as much as they could feed the symbolic politics of the right.

By the late 1980s, much of this debate over images—over representation, including claims to national representation—focused specifically on the role of the National Endowment for the Arts (NEA).[12] Founded in 1965, the NEA was created to support the arts and arts education. It did so by providing grants to artists and arts institutions awarded through a peer review process, one goal of which was to prevent direct intervention from Congress into the awarding of grants. The NEA has frequently come under scrutiny, especially from conservatives who have occasionally proposed eliminating it altogether. It has also become a common trope to compare the relatively small amount of funding the NEA has received to other federal programs. In 2016, for instance, Congress allocated $148 million in total to the NEA, while the Department of Defense earmarked nearly $500 million for military bands alone in that same year.[13]

State funding for art raises critical questions: What kind of art, if any, ought the federal government to support? And to what idea of "the public" does or should this art appeal? Before the 1990s, only a tiny proportion of NEA grants had raised concern—a couple dozen out of more than eighty-five thousand grants that had been awarded. But suddenly, in the late 1980s, the funding of artists became fodder for national spectacle.[14]

Buchanan joined a chorus of conservative voices denouncing the NEA for funding elitist and "decadent" artists making work they considered offensive. In 1992, he penned a column in DC's conservative *Washington Times* bemoaning how "the left has been quietly seizing all the commanding heights of America art and culture." "A nation absorbs its values through its art," he insisted: "A corrupt culture will produce a corrupt people, and vice versa."[15] And this, he opined, was bad for the United States.

Indeed, the NEA would play a starring role in Buchanan's own (ultimately failed) bid for the GOP presidential nomination leading up to the 1992 election. That spring, his campaign ran an ad before the primaries in Georgia, Texas, and Mississippi attacking George H. W. Bush for continuing to fund the NEA. He accused the president of wasting taxpayer money to support "pornographic and blasphemous art too shocking to show."[16] Or maybe it was too shocking *not* to show. The thirty-second spot included footage that featured leather-clad white gay men dancing and carrying on during San Francisco's Folsom Street Fair, an annual celebration of the city's queer BDSM and leather subcultures. "This so-called art," the ad announced, "has glorified homosexuality, exploited children and perverted the image of Jesus Christ."[17]

That footage was pulled from Marlon Riggs's fifty-five-minute experimental documentary film *Tongues Untied* (1989). The nonlinear, lyrical film, Riggs explained, "unabashedly celebrates the struggles, lives and loves of black gay men in America."[18] *Tongues Untied* includes song, poetry, and even a lesson in "snap!thology"—how to snap one's fingers like the best diva queens. It also includes scenes that represent racism and homophobia, including the voice of a Southern man spewing anti-Black and homophobic epithets and Black Christian pastors denouncing homosexuality as an abomination. *Tongues Untied* includes nudity and scenes of Black men kissing, but no children or images of Christ appear explicitly in the film, as Buchanan's ad suggested.

Act Two—The Artist

"He's black, he's homosexual, and he's federally funded!" That's how a 1992 *Washington Post* profile described the Emmy Award–winning filmmaker Marlon Riggs, whom it also dubbed "a proud leftist insurgent in the Culture Wars."[19] This language is playful, but it captures the all too serious battles over religion, sexuality, race, and art in which Riggs had recently found himself enlisted, willingly or not. Riggs had first entered the sights of the culture wars when the Public Broadcasting Station (PBS) decided to screen his film *Tongues Untied* as part of its *POV* (Point of View) series in the summer of 1991. The backlash was swift.

Opponents attacked PBS for piping gay pornography into people's homes, penetrating that sacred space of heterosexual domesticity. A writer for the *Washington Times* claimed the film would turn "TV rooms into gay-strip film houses" and was better left to the "bawdy leather bars" of San Francisco and New York.[20] Over two hundred PBS stations eventually refused to show the film, as leaders of the Christian Right quickly joined the chorus of complaint. They criticized both PBS for scheduling the film and the NEA for funding it. Riggs had indirectly received a five-thousand-dollar grant from the NEA, which also separately funded *POV*. The American Family Association's Donald Wildmon issued a press release detailing the film's presumed offenses against decency. The Methodist pastor-turned-culture warrior had made a name for himself by trying to ban material he considered offensive. But, in an unusual turn, this time he called for a wide release of *Tongues Untied*. "This will be the first time millions of Americans will have an opportunity to see the kinds of things their tax money is being spent on," he reasoned.[21] Ralph Reed, the executive director of the right-wing Christian Coalition, sent a letter to members of the US House of Representatives also complaining about NEA funding for the film. He requested their support for an amendment proposed by Sen. Jesse Helms to prohibit federal funding for exhibits that are "patently offensive or explicitly depict sexual or excretory activity or organs." The letter included a seven-minute excerpt of scenes from *Tongues Untied*, which, it explains, "graphically depicts homosexual activity."[22] Buchanan's team also re-edited footage from Riggs's film for his campaign ad, so that the scenes deemed offensive would line up with the ad's strongest language.[23]

Riggs snapped back. In a *New York Times* editorial, he knocked the Christian Coalition for reducing his film to "seven, disjointed, highly sensationalized minutes."[24] And he called Buchanan's commercial an "outrageous distortion" that added "anti-gay bigotry to race-baiting."[25] Riggs said it made him into "the new Willie Horton"—the latest negative symbol in yet another episode of "the ruthless exploitation of race and sexuality to win high public office."[26] Buchanan's ad perversely proved all the more offensive because it featured only shots of white gay men. In the context of *Tongues Untied*, the footage pulled for Buchanan's ad was meant to demonstrate how difficult it was for Black gay men to negotiate predominantly white gay spaces. The choice by Buchanan's team to use the very few images of white gay men, rather than those of Black men loving Black men, was targeted, to say the least.[27] But Riggs was no wilting flower. He threatened to sue. His attorney served legal notice to Buchanan that his campaign had violated copyright law and instructed the presidential hopeful to stop showing the ad and to destroy all copies.[28]

Riggs also countered claims that his film was inappropriate for public television or failed to meet "community standards," including decency standards imposed by Congress on NEA grant winners. "Implicit in the much overworked rhetoric about 'community standards,'" he wrote, "is the assumption of one privileged community (mythically patriarchal, heterosexist and *usually* white) and one overarching culture (ditto)." Minority voices—especially those of Black gay men—were too often deemed obscene automatically and thus unfit for the imagined straight, white public. For Riggs, the debate over airing *Tongues Untied* surfaced pressing questions. "Who is to have access to the so-called 'public' media, and on what terms?" he asked. And who gets to decide what constitutes "innocuous 'diversity'" rather than "unacceptable 'deviance'?"[29]

Conservative culture warriors offered one take: they opposed what they considered the homosexual obscenity and sacrilege of *Tongues Untied* to their own Christian morality. But theirs were not the only voices in this debate. In July 1991, around four hundred people flooded into the Eno River Unitarian Universalist Fellowship Church in Durham, North Carolina, to watch the PBS screening of *Tongues Untied*. On their way in, they witnessed about twenty-five protestors standing outside—mostly men, both Black and white—holding up signs with Bible quotes and statements like "God Created Male and Female to Multiply."[30] Space inside the church was limited, and about fifty attendees were directed to a courtyard to contain the overflow. Most viewers applauded the film and balked at the debate over showing it. "It's not porn," said one: "It's just a point of view." "I've seen more graphic details on *Young and the Restless*," balked another.[31] For these attendees, *Tongues Untied* was nothing if not fit for public consumption.

Sex, Art, and the Modern Culture Wars

The tussle between Buchanan and Riggs surfaces many of the key themes examined in this book. A conservative culture warrior invoked images of homosexual decadence and depravity, drawn from the work of an NEA-funded artist, to stoke the fears and frustrations of potential voters (or donors)—fears that the United States they loved was headed toward destruction.[32] The only hope was to make Christian America great again. These conservatives and their supporters imagined the nation in particular terms—not the moral or religious values of those people filing into the Durham church to watch *Tongues Untied*, but rather the visions of the largely white, politically conservative evangelical and Catholic Christians nostalgic for an earlier moment in US history. Culture warriors in the 1980s and 1990s looked back to the postwar United States, before the assassination of John F. Kennedy, as a high point.[33] It was a time, they claimed, when the ideal "traditional" family reigned—a husband, his wife, and their obedient children living the American dream in quaint suburbs. But that dream—deliberately white, heterosexual, and God-centered—would soon turn into a nightmare.[34]

At the heart of the Christian Right's story of decline in the latter half of the twentieth century were the intersecting and ever-shifting cultural politics of race, gender, and sexuality. For one, many conservative Christians felt they were under attack. The Supreme Court's strike against "separate but equal" in 1954's *Brown v Board of Education* was one turning point. Many white Christians who opposed desegregation and the civil rights movement worried that interracial socializing—if legally and eventually culturally embraced, especially in schools—would lead to interracial relationships, sparking the racist threat of "miscegenation." In the theological worlds of many Southern white Christians, segregation was not merely about upholding white power; it was about sticking to God's plan for moral order and racial purity. The fight for Black equality—not to mention the Black Power movement (alongside movements for Chicano and Red Power)—risked upending this divine order.[35]

The feminist and queer movements of the 1960s and 1970s likewise threatened the conservative vision of the ideal suburban family. Women sought equality, not only in the home, but also in their ability to forge careers, to open their own bank accounts and credit lines, and to divorce their husbands, whether because they experienced abuse or for a myriad of other reasons. Feminists questioned normative assumptions about gender that restricted women's freedoms and presumed they had to be submissive caregivers rather than assertive artists, politicians, or business leaders. Some challenged marriage itself as a patriarchal institution. By the 1970s, Congress was on the cusp of ratifying the Equal Rights Amendment (ERA), which was decades in the making and had broad, bipartisan support for enshrining equal rights regardless of sex into the US Constitution. That bipartisan support collapsed when the Eagle Forum's Catholic founder Phyllis Schlafly discovered her raison d'être in mobilizing fellow conservatives, especially women, to oppose the amendment. And, of course, many Catholics (and later evangelicals) considered the legalization of abortion in 1973's *Roe v. Wade* a negative turning point in the moral outlook of the United States.[36]

Meanwhile, the modern LGBTQ rights movement challenged entrenched homophobia and transphobia. Activists disputed the very notion of the "ideal" family that many presumed unquestionable, even natural. For conservatives, this movement made sexual sin into a political platform and replaced moral duty to God and family with sexual libertinism. Many hardly knew what to think of queer women, but they still worried that radical feminism risked making lesbians of all their daughters. Transgender activists, though frequently overlooked in the history of struggles for LGBTQ recognition and social justice, would be cast in a starring role in the political dramas of the culture wars much more recently, as conservatives worried that recognition of the value and beauty in trans lives would undermine the very order of all existence: the ostensibly natural and God-given heterosexual cisgender couple.[37] Just as feminist arguments that gender was socially constructed shook normative assumptions about the roles of men and women, queer and trans movements denaturalized seemingly universal and God-given assumptions about sex and sexual desire. They revealed the natural and the universal to be particular and contingent. In the language of the culture wars, this was no less than the evil specter of moral relativism.[38] And it was spread through music, film, television, and even art—sometimes supported by taxpayers themselves.

The United States boasts a long history of debate over cultural production, ranging from popular music to high art. In the late twentieth century alone, Americans fretted over the supposed dangers of disco, punk rock, and the "degenerate lyrics of rap music," as failed Supreme Court nominee Robert Bork put it in thinly veiled racist terms.[39] The Christian Right assailed films like *The Last Temptation of Christ* as sacrilegious and attacked television shows like *Murphy Brown* as unfit for broad audiences. Plays like Terrence McNally's *Corpus Christi* (1998) and even games like Dungeons and Dragons have come under fire. Much of the heated rhetoric has turned to issues of sexuality and sacrilege in the work of visual and performance artists—especially those receiving funding from the federal government. Conservative criticism of the NEA would come to a head in the late 1980s and early 1990s, sparked by a series of public outcries over what Supreme Court Justice Sandra Day O'Connor dubbed "provocative" art.[40]

Piss Christ, Porn, and the NEA

Two controversies consumed the mainstream news media and reverberated through the halls of government during the spring and summer of 1989. It all started with a tip from Donald Wildmon, Methodist minister and director of the American Family Association. He sent a mailer to Congressional leaders blasting the NEA for supporting the work of artist Andres Serrano.[41] The specific piece in question was *Piss Christ* (1987), for which the artist photographed a cheap crucifix submerged in urine. Serrano had received a $15,000 grant from the Southeastern Center for Contemporary Art, which had itself received NEA funding. Weeks later, Wildmon raised the alarm again—this time over a retrospective on the art of photographer Robert Mapplethorpe called *The Perfect Moment*. The show included the artist's classically posed, explicitly sexual images of Black and white gay men (sometimes posed together), photos of flowers, celebrity portraits, and two images of nude or partially nude children taken with the permission of their parents.[42] The University of Pennsylvania had received $30,000 from the NEA to fund the Mapplethorpe exhibition, which traveled to several museums. In light of these controversies, conservative Christians, like the Eagle Forum's Phyllis Schlafly and Pat Robertson of the Christian Broadcasting Network, joined Wildmon to mobilize their bases to oppose what they labeled state-funded blasphemy and pornography.

Congress responded. New York Senator Alfonse D'Amato dramatically ripped up the exhibition catalogue containing *Piss Christ*, staging his gestural and material denunciation on the Senate floor. Jesse Helms, by then nicknamed "Senator No," called Serrano "a jerk" during public debate, and he had little good to say about Mapplethorpe. Helms told one reporter that he had shown the Mapplethorpe catalogue to his wife, Dorothy, who responded, "Lord have mercy, Jesse, I'm not believing this," before slamming it shut.[43] Under mounting political pressure, Congress cut the NEA's budget for the following year and enacted an amendment declaring that no NEA funds "may be used to promote, disseminate, or produce materials which in the judgment of [the NEA] may be considered obscene, including but not limited to, depictions of sadomasochism, homoeroticism, the sexual exploitation of children, or individuals engaged in sex acts and which, when taken as a whole, do not have serious literary, artistic, political, or scientific value."[44] This amendment would be overturned in federal district court in 1991, but in anticipation of that decision, members of Congress had already debated alternative measures. Members of the House dismissed a proposal to dismantle the NEA altogether, but Congress adopted a bipartisan compromise in 1990 that included a "decency clause." The key language appears in Section 954(d)(1): "Artistic excellence and artistic merit are the criteria by which applications are judged, taking into consideration general standards of decency and respect for the diverse beliefs and values of the American public." Many in the arts community and beyond worried about the vagueness of these "standards of decency."[45] Whose standards? How does one define decency? And how does one weigh the demand for decency against the freedom of expression?

In the heat of the art wars, conservative opposition worked in two directions. On the one hand, it brought a great deal of attention to a very small subset of artists, quickly elevating the financial value of their work, if nothing else. But it also had a chilling effect on art grappling with themes of gender and sexuality, especially work by feminist and queer artists. That same summer in 1989, the Corcoran Gallery in Washington, DC, canceled their showing of Mapplethorpe's *The Perfect Moment* only weeks before it was set to open. Museum leaders worried that exhibiting his work would lead to further funding cuts to the NEA or to their own institution. In 1990, law enforcement in Cincinnati, Ohio, shut down the Contemporary Art Center's exhibition of *The Perfect Moment* and put the museum and its director on trial for obscenity. Both were later acquitted—the jury was not convinced Mapplethorpe's work lacked "artistic merit." But these events sounded the alarm of censorship that would reverberate across the country for the next several years.

Indeed, leaders of the Christian Right have readily exploited such drama for their cause, adding new artists to their lists of blasphemers and pornographers. A few instances capture the trend:

- In *The Schlafly Report*, Phyllis Schlafly recounted her testimony to the US Senate in 1990 on "these items of alleged 'art' [which] include materials which deliberately insult people of certain religions and the God they worship, or deliberately display obscenity and even child pornography." She also denounced the "arrogance" of artists who demand NEA funding.[46]
- In the pages of *USA Today*, California's GOP Rep. Dana Rohrabacher listed several projects he considered "obscene, indecent or sacrilegious," in addition to those of Serrano and Mapplethorpe, that received NEA funding. They included the work of artist David Wojnarowicz, sexologist and performance artist Annie Sprinkle, and performance art duo Bob Flanagan and Sheree Rose.[47]
- The Heritage Foundation—co-founded by Paul Weyrich, one of the architects of the Religious Right—issued a report on the "misuse" of NEA funding. An appendix to the report catalogued controversial projects that received money. It lists only four funded projects from before the 1980s, including Judy Chicago's *The Dinner Party* (1972) and the "Gay Sunshine Press" (1977). In the 1980s, the number multiplies, including awards to feminist artist Cheri Gaulke, Mapplethorpe, Serrano, the National Gay and Lesbian Task Force, Southern Exposure (for a series of work that included performance artists Flanagan and Rose), Wojnarowicz, and many others.[48]

- In his 1996 screed *Slouching Towards Gomorrah*, Robert Bork argued that conservative criticisms of the misuse of taxpayer money did not go far enough, "as if taxpayers should never be required to subsidize things they don't like." "If that were the case," he quipped, the "government would have to close down altogether." To focus on taxes, he continued, is "to cheapen a moral position," which is that work by Serrano and Mapplethorpe would be just as offensive and immoral if it were wholly privately funded. "We seem too timid," he insisted, "to state that Mapplethorpe's and Serrano's pictures should not be shown in public, whoever pays for them."[49]
- In 1999, and again in 2001, New York Mayor Rudy Giuliani and the Catholic League's Bill Donohue blasted the Brooklyn Museum for hosting exhibitions that featured sacrilegious or anti-Catholic art. The pieces in question, both by Black artists, included Chris Ofili's painting *Holy Virgin Mother* (from the 1999 *Sensation* exhibition) and Renée Cox's photomontage *Yo Mama's Last Supper* (from 2001's *Committed to the Image* show). Lesbian Latina artist Alma López would also come under fire in 2001, as the leadership of the Archdiocese of Santa Fe denounced *Our Lady*, her take on the Virgin of Guadalupe, as anti-Catholic.[50]
- In 2010, the Smithsonian shelved plans to show a short film by Wojnarowicz for the exhibition *Hide/Seek* when it came under attack from Donohue's Catholic League, which denounced an image of a crucifix with ants crawling over it as anti-Catholic hate speech.

Some patterns emerge. First, we see an abiding concern with issues of gender, sexuality, and race. Those concerns—we could call them anxieties—arose from conservatives themselves. While the left is often criticized for its supposed obsession with "identity politics," right-wing activists have for decades projected a distorted form of this politics of identity—and obsessions with sexuality and race—onto feminist, queer, Black, and Latinx people, as well as other people of color, while at the same time largely centering their own movement on white Christian heterosexual identity. Second, we see how charges of obscenity often conflated sexual immorality, pornography, and sacrilege. This rhetoric figures homosexuality and feminism as necessarily obscene, indecent, and anti-Christian. Finally, we see right-wing activists casting feminist and queer artists as characters in a drama. They often scripted artists—conflated with homosexuals and feminists—as entitled, obstinate, and elitist snobs looking down on the common person.[51] This rhetorical drama also contributes to the racial history of the culture wars, often cast in Black and white; the way racial politics figures into these battles over art is notable.

Black feminist critic Michele Wallace has argued that culture wars battles of the 1980s and 1990s most often pitted white conservatives against white artists. One reason for this, she explains, is that the racism of the art world prevented many Black artists from ascending the ranks of art fame. They were less likely to receive the financial support, much less the attention or market prices for their work, that their white counterparts enjoyed. Such barriers meant there were fewer high-profile Black artists to start with. And when their work was seen, white liberals and conservatives alike viewed it through a racializing and racist lens.[52] I want to add another reason. Culture wars conservatives were also invested in representing feminist and queer artists (and activists) as white precisely to underscore their supposed elitism and arrogance. We see both of these moves at play in the way Buchanan's campaign used only the footage of white gay men from Riggs's film, which contributed to the historical and ongoing erasure of Black artists and Black queer life while also portraying white gay men as decadent sexual elites flaunting their immorality in public.

Provoking Religion

Keeping such patterns in focus, *Provoking Religion* tracks these pitched battles over sex, art, and the sacred in the United States from the 1970s into the twenty-first century. When I started this research, I wanted to understand how artistic production became a key site for cultural collisions over the politics of religion and sex—both for conservatives alarmed by challenges to social norms rooted in the liberation movements of the 1960s and 1970s and for progressive and radical artists confronting sexism, homophobia, and racism.[53] I began with three guiding questions:

1. *Why were feminist and queer artists disproportionately targeted by culture wars conservatives, especially those within the Christian Right, who attacked their work as blasphemous, anti-Christian, or pornographic?*

2. *How did conservative Christians leading these attacks understand this artistic work—that is, what habits of interpretation shaped their attacks?*

3. Why do so many of the artists who got in trouble—and who are often presumed secular, if not anti-Christian—draw so frequently on religious iconography in their work? And to what ends?

What I learned was that answering these questions required pushing back on the entrenched narratives of the modern culture wars themselves. Too frequently, both in news media and in much of our scholarship, we uncritically adopt a conservative framing of these battles—I call this the culture wars narrative.[54]

Inventing the Culture Wars Narrative (and Its Discontents)

In its simplest form, the culture wars narrative pits religious conservatives against secular progressives. This framing emerges from a longer history of modern secularism that places moral conservatism at the heart of what we think of as religion, which is often reduced to propositional beliefs about God and to moral codes, especially those having to do with gender and sexuality. This approach takes a particular kind of religion—conservative Protestantism—as a template for religion writ large. In this story, religion restricts gender and sexual freedom, while secularization lets it go free. On whichever side of the dividing line one falls, religion and sexuality are positioned against one another—and yet, perhaps ironically, obsessively linked to one another.[55] It becomes difficult, within this narrative, to consider how religious traditions, texts, or art might foster sexual pleasures, even alongside sexist or homophobic strictures; and it makes it hard to see how secular ideas and norms also come to govern sexual desires and expressions. Historians of religion and sexuality have begun chipping away at this narrative that sets religion against sexuality, but it continues to haunt the ways we understand the modern culture wars.[56]

Sociologist of religion James Davison Hunter offered a more nuanced approach in his 1991 bestseller *Culture Wars: The Struggle to Define America*, which has probably done more than any other scholarly work to popularize the "culture wars" framework. For Hunter, the modern culture wars centered on a debate over "moral authority," about which he discerned two diverging impulses. The "orthodox" impulse grounds moral authority in an unchanging external or transcendent source, such as God, the Bible, or the Torah. The "progressivist" impulse, by contrast, roots moral authority in "the spirit of the modern age, a spirit of rationalism and subjectivism."[57] Hunter tracked these polarized impulses across debates over education, law, politics, the family, and art. His book resisted a simple religious versus secular dichotomy, even noting how culture wars battles over art had emerged from tensions "between two fundamentally different conceptions of the sacred."[58]

But Hunter's approach introduced a new problem, one that has haunted scholarship on the culture wars: it privileges the orthodox or conservative impulse in its initial framing of the culture wars. Consider how his starting point for assessing the culture wars—"moral authority"—already foregrounds the language of conservatives.[59] It is not that liberals or leftists have nothing to say about morality or authority. But if we look at the history of progressive movements in the United States, we are far more likely to find people using languages of social justice and freedom. In Hunter's account, though, progressivist approaches to authority tend to dissolve into either scientific authority or relativism. This is not because progressivists are all relativists or that they merely adopt whatever view of the world scientists espouse (as if all scientists would agree), as Hunter sometimes claims, but rather because questions of moral authority are the wrong starting point. What would it look like to revise the culture wars narrative by grounding it instead in debates over liberation and social justice—to ask, for instance, what impulses for understanding liberation (rather than moral authority) have grounded orthodox versus progressivist stances? Or what would it look like if we resisted pigeonholing either pole into the privileged languages of the other, especially since the notion of one central bifurcation is, itself, more sociological fiction than a reflection of the lived experience of this history?[60] Hunter offered a powerful heuristic, but one that perhaps has hidden more than it has revealed.[61]

The Art of the Culture Wars Narrative

The problems with this culture wars narrative become apparent in Hunter's discussion of art. Two observations. First, his account hews too closely to the way conservatives have narrated battles over art by folding older criticisms of modernist art into newer caricatures of radical artists trying to undermine Christian America by peddling immorality and nihilism. Consider, for instance, how Hunter described the tendency for the progressivist side "to value novelty and the avant-garde *for their own sake*."[62] In the modernist vision, art need not reflect beauty or the sublime; instead, modernist art often plays with form, foregrounding the materiality and medium of art itself.

This is a way of looking inward, an intellectualist approach. And modernist art privileged abstraction over representation. In doing so, it gained many detractors, even before the culture wars of the 1980s and 1990s. From the first years of the NEA, Republicans and Democrats alike worried that too much federal funding was used for the seemingly meaningless work of modernist artists rather than the representational art better suited in their eyes to common tastes. In 1973, for instance, Democratic Senator Claiborne Pell expressed his discomfort during an appropriations hearing for the Senate Subcommittee on the Arts and Humanities when he asked whether paintings funded by the NEA were "realistic"—like the work of Andrew Wyeth and Norman Rockwell—or just "doodles and swirls."[63] My point here is not to defend (or attack) modernist art but rather to surface older and enduring criticisms that it was pretentious yet meaningless.

Hunter takes the criticisms further. The modernist avant-garde tests "the limits of social acceptability," he explains, by embracing "what the prevailing social consensus would have called 'perverse' and 'irreverent.'"[64] This occurred not only in visual art, Hunter continues, but also in "rap music and in television programming" that challenges social norms through "excessive sex and violence" as well as in films like Scorsese's *The Last Temptation of Christ* that "demythologize" "ancient Christian belief."[65] Note how this gloss reproduces the way conservatives conflated criticisms of modernist art (the "art for art's sake" people) with forms of cultural production emerging from artists and activists seeking to challenge stifling normative conventions of US society, which are reduced to something like "perversity" and "irreverence" *for their own sake* or simply to *test the limits*. Moreover, Hunter characterizes the progressivist definition of art as either whatever experts say is art or as "symbolically represent[ing] an individual personal quest to understand and interpret one's experience in the world."[66] Here, art becomes purely subjective, even solipsistic, a characterization eerily close to the way Illinois's GOP Congressman Henry Hyde put it: "art detached from the quest for truth and goodness is simply self-expression and ultimately self-absorption."[67] For conservative culture warriors—and for Hunter, too, it seems—the depiction of elitist artists of the avant-garde merged all too easily with images of self-obsessed, entitled radical feminist and homosexual artists acting out for the sake of causing trouble.

A second observation: when Hunter attempts to step outside of these conservative interpretations to characterize the progressivist position, the results disappoint. For conservatives, he writes, "the sacred is obvious enough." But for progressives it proves harder to discern.[68] Hunter writes that, in the context of censorship, progressives made freedom of expression itself a sacred value. There is truth to this claim, but it says little about the content of the expression whose freedom progressives have sought to protect. Hunter's other answer to what progressives hold sacred is more of a resignation than an argument: that art itself became "the religion of the educated classes."[69] He gets this argument from Tom Wolfe, a longtime critic of modernist art.[70] The problem is not so much that art could take on religious qualities, but that this characterization shields an implicit slight—that art as religion is the sad vestige of the educated elite. Moreover, Hunter's framing leaves no room to distinguish between "the establishment" and most working artists, who hardly belonged to the wealthy or educated elite. It does no good to conflate artists with art critics, museum curators, or arts brokers, much less the very small subset of wealthy patrons buying fine art. The mission of the NEA, in fact, was to make art *more* accessible, more democratic—for makers and public audiences alike. But conservatives sought to score points by portraying contemporary artists themselves as decadent snobs—the fantasied feminist and queer elite pulling one over on the common taxpayer. Hunter too readily reproduces this conservative script.

What we do not see in Hunter's narrative of the culture wars is how contemporary artists caught up in these fights were themselves often pushing against trends in modernist art, including the elitism of the avant-garde, the privileging of form over content, and the notion that art should be buffered from political concerns.[71] Nor do we get a sense for how artists themselves understood their work or what their many audiences made of it. It would stretch credulity to say that Serrano created *Piss Christ* simply to exercise his devotion to free expression. Likewise, it would make no sense to reduce that photograph, using the language of critics of modernist art, to "art for art's sake" or to mere "doodles and swirls." Wendy Steiner, a scholar of literary and visual studies, argues that the photography of artists like Serrano and Mapplethorpe troubles the "formalist aesthetics" often presumed in these culture wars diatribes; they instead "force us toward an aesthetics of content."[72] She thus observes a "tension between literalism and symbolism" that arises in Serrano's work dealing with vital fluids, including blood, milk, and urine—a tension that emerges as much from Catholic forms.[73]

Serrano often described how Catholicism shaped his work. "The best place for *Piss Christ* is in a church," he explained, noting that many Catholics, especially outside of the United States, appreciated his work, including how it engages Christian theologies of Incarnation—that Christ was both fully divine and fully human, God embodied, with all the ways bodies work. And many have seen the use of the cheap crucifix in this work as an important criticism of the ways religion and spirituality have been commodified. "One thing that always bothered me," he continued, "was the fundamentalist labeling of my work as 'anti-Christian bigotry.' As a former Catholic, and as someone who even today is not opposed to being called a Christian, I felt I had every right to use the symbols of the Church."[74] Serrano's version of the sacred may be harder to discern—and more open to interpretation—than the vision put forward by the orthodox side, but Hunter's approach barely scratches the surface, resting more on conservative caricature than careful analysis.

Beyond the Culture Wars Narrative

This book seeks to tell the story of the culture wars differently. *Provoking Religion* takes an episodic approach, with each chapter focusing on a case study of an artist or artists who got in trouble with the Christian Right.[75] Active from the 1960s to the historical present, these artists have worked across performance, film, sculpture, painting, and photography, often surfacing themes of gender, sexuality, and religion. Since most discussions of art and the culture wars center Serrano and Mapplethorpe, I focus on a broader range of artists who "got in trouble" to unravel additional layers of these debates. Chapter one sets out a theoretical approach for the analysis that follows by exploring how religious forms (in this case Catholic ones) animate the artistic and political visions of performance artists Bob Flanagan and Sheree Rose. The remaining chapters work historically. Chapter two tracks the creation and public reception of artist Judy Chicago's *The Dinner Party* from its roots in 1970s feminist spirituality and Jewish cultural forms to its rebirth, amid culture wars debate in the 1990s, as literalized and explicit pornography. Chapter three uses the occasion of artist David Wojnarowicz filing a lawsuit against the Christian Right's Donald Wildmon for misrepresenting his work to explore diverging histories of interpretation and visual culture. Chapter four underscores the convergence of Catholic and queer camp sensibilities in video collective DIVA TV's film *Like a Prayer*, focusing on artist and AIDS activist Ray Navarro. Chapter five turns to the public debate over photographer Renée Cox's *Yo Mama's Last Supper* and the racialized politics of offense it ignited among conservative Catholic and political leaders. Taken together, these chapters offer two main interventions.

Making Culture Wars Work Explicit

First, *Provoking Religion* shows how the culture wars narrative itself operates as a powerful hermeneutic, one that draws upon an assortment of rhetorical techniques for reading, dismissing, or exploiting visual and performance art deemed obscene or sacrilegious. "No work of art is blasphemous in and of itself," writes visual studies scholar S. B. Rodriguez-Plate: "it must be deemed so from within religious and/or political power structures, whether small or large scale."[76] We need to better understand how this political categorization works, including what assumptions about gender, sexuality, religion, race, and art stand behind it. The conventional culture wars narrative itself, we have seen, is already one such tactic, even when translated into the seemingly disinterested language of sociology or history. Other techniques I have found at play recur across the various episodes charted in this book and receive greater attention in specific chapters. They include: despiritualizing feminist and queer art (chapters two and four); invoking the rise of a "new" anti-Catholicism (chapters four and five); exploiting the curious politics of offense (chapter five); racializing sex and sexuality, both by casting feminist and queer artists as white and by figuring Black women's bodies as sexually explicit (this introduction and chapters one and five); conjuring conservative fantasies through the power of censorship itself (chapters two, three, and five); and employing what I call a Christian aesthetics of literalism (chapters two and three).[77] This final technique requires some explanation.

I refer to an "aesthetics of literalism" to underscore how this approach brings together assumptions and reading practices regarding visual culture, language, and taste. Steeped in a Protestant hermeneutic of images—and a long history of Scottish commonsense realism—the aesthetics of literalism names a style of reading visual culture that transforms images into words, seeking to fix meaning in place, in order to prevent the slippage of sentiment into sensuality that images too often risk. I want to make two points clear from the start. First, literalness is not uniquely conservative. We all appeal to literal claims, and many progressive artists discussed here employed literalism to creative or didactic effects. Literalism, as a way of understanding language, nonetheless unravels, because it is the nature of language (and much more so images) to exceed the fixity that literalism desires. Second, I am trying to capture how conservatives *literalized* visual and performance art—how they applied not just a literal but a literal*ist* lens to work that often resisted such readings. A literalist interpretation insists on one possible meaning—and more, on a reading that denies its very status as interpretation. Literalist interpretation in this sense insists there is no interpretation at all—just obvious meaning. In this context, the visual image ostensibly makes the reading explicit. Literalizing art in this way became a key tactic in culture wars politics.[78]

By highlighting this range of culture wars practices, I hope this book expands how we think about the practices of conservative Christian reading, interpretation, and dismissal as *work*. This book insists that it is not obvious or a given that the visual and performance art that conservative Christians opposed was obscene or anti-Christian—such readings take work, and the chapters that follow make that labor visible, including the habits that form this particular way of seeing and the contexts that made them viable. But that is only half the story.

The Feminist and Queer Arts of Religion

Provoking Religion also demonstrates how these artists were no mere provocateurs or anti-Christian secularists—nor simply moral relativists or nihilists. Sometimes they were those things. But often they were visionaries and myth-makers, transgressors and prophets. After spending years reading in the archives of these artists and observing their work, I have found that, far more often than simply mocking Christianity, they strived to express legitimate criticism of conservative religious institutions and leaders and to foster new political and spiritual visions, from Bob Flanagan's crip Catholicism to Renée Cox's Black female Jesus.

By focusing on specific artists and the debates surrounding them, this book brings into view the wide range of religious imagery and thinking from which these artists drew—and often to very different ends. Roman Catholic imagery features most prominently, and this is no mere coincidence. Roman Catholicism boasts especially rich visual and material traditions that are well represented, if not dominant, across histories of Euro-American and Latin American art. Artists have long been drawn to the ways Catholicism foregrounds the body—particularly the incarnational body—as well as the porous boundaries between sacred and profane, spiritual and material. Many contemporary feminist and queer artists have found in Catholicism a deep well of sexism and homophobia, but they have also discovered rich sources for sacralizing women's flesh, rescripting Jesus as mother, and envisioning homoerotic possibilities.[79] As art critic Eleanor Heartney has noted, many artists who grew up within Roman Catholicism, and who have drawn upon this rich tradition in their work, have disproportionately come under attack in the modern culture wars. Their focus on "flesh and sex," she explains, conflicts with the dominant Protestant culture of the United States, which is "deeply uncomfortable with Catholicism's essential carnality."[80]

While Catholicism is central to the story this book tells, I also emphasize how artists drew from feminist spirituality, transcendentalist and New Age currents, and progressive Judaism—often in various combinations—in ways that reveal ongoing historical struggles to define the relationship between the sacred and the political in public culture. Just as importantly, many onlookers took up these works of art, not as instances of sacrilege or public pornography, but as sites for "visual piety," as historian of religion and art David Morgan calls the devotional use of images.[81] To better understand this history, we need to look at how feminist and queer artists and their audiences frequently subverted, appropriated, or ironized religious and spiritual forms, often using humor, parody, and camp.

Scholars and lay observers of religion alike often assume that whatever it is we call "religion" ought to be serious and sincere (or at least it should result from performed earnestness, as in the case of hugely popular televangelists, who tap into longer histories of dramatic evangelical affect).[82] Even the US Supreme Court places a premium on religious beliefs being "sincerely held" when confronted with challenges to religious freedom.[83] Scholars of religion have rightly countered assumptions that reduce religion to sincere belief in God or adherence to various creeds, by foregrounding not only what religious people say and believe but also what they do. We often call this "lived religion."[84] But even this approach tends to privilege sincere actors working from the best of intentions and figures religion as a category of personal identity.[85] Alternatively, scholars sometimes try to explain away religious motivations that appear contrived, perhaps presuming that some "real" intention having to do with economics or politics drives religious behavior or, relatedly, that religious people are acting in "bad faith," merely exploiting religious language for specific needs.[86] Sometimes these approaches—foregrounding religious sincerity or bad faith—make sense.[87] But the reigning assumption that religious actors are either sincere or dissembling makes it hard to see how religion can be taken up in ways that are ambivalent, ironic, or humorous—and to see those relations to religion as "real" ways of doing religion that scholars should take seriously.

In this book, I try to avoid some of these assumptions by considering how religion works like language. To say that religion *is* language would be reductive; it is much more, including not only practice but also ways of seeing and being seen, of hearing, feeling, smelling, touching, moving. But I find it helpful to consider how religion works like a language in some respects. Like language, in many cases religion is not something that we freely choose, even though it becomes one of the tools for our expression, for how we act, even for how we think of ourselves as selves. It happens around us and to us, often from childhood. It creates our worlds. Thinking of religion like language also helps avoid interpretive traps, such as attempting to categorize various artists as insiders versus outsiders of any given tradition. Although many of the artists in this book were raised in Catholic households, for instance, many no longer identified with those traditions by the time they were adults. But this does not mean they stopped thinking and seeing and creating through Catholic languages and ways of existing in the world. Likewise, Jewish artists like Judy Chicago and Sheree Rose already had to contend with Christianity, which remains demographically and culturally dominant in the United Stated, the country in which they grew up and have lived. From the standpoint of identity, they are not Christians. But if we think of Christianity as operating much like language—and as a culturally pervasive one—then we begin to see how the question of insider versus outsider misses dynamics of power that become all too important in the history of the culture wars, which is no less than a historical effort to forge (or restore) a particular vision of Christian America.

Thinking of religion like language also reminds us that no such endeavors—linguistic, religious, or artistic—are singular; even the most individualistic act of spiritual or artistic creation depends on the existence of broader social collectives. Though I foreground individual artists in this book, I hope it is obvious in the chapters that follow how each drew from expansive communities. Feminist and queer art is often characterized as relativist, individualist, or even nihilist, not only because conservatives do not see their own values reflected there, but also because they want to deny—to refuse to see—the friendships, the families, the communities, indeed the full humanity that stands behind this work. And I want to underline the plural form of communities here. There is no "feminist and queer community" or even "LGBT community"—any more than there is a "straight community" or "cis community." There are many feminist and queer and trans communities. Often, they overlap, in membership and in political and aesthetic commitments. They just as frequently diverge or even come into open conflict. The fiction of a singular feminist or queer community serves as a tactic to homogenize and to domesticate their very plurality, to reduce it to the terms of the orthodox impulse.

At its core, *Provoking Religion* seeks new visual and symbolic languages to understand the modern culture wars and to intervene in the prevailing ways we write about feminist and queer artists. Too often, these artists pop up as instigators of dispute, or fuel for right-wing fires. But they are rarely considered on their own terms. More often, they are characterized as defenders of free expression, at best, if not reduced to right-wing caricatures. The effect of this move is not only to overlook the voices and visions of progressives and radicals, including how religion permeates the political and spiritual imagination of the left, but once again to make feminists and fairies into ornaments of national spectacle rather than key participants in our public culture.

I should be clear that my goal here is not simply to champion the feminist and queer artists considered here over leaders of the Christian Right. I have aspired to treat fairly and accurately all of the historical actors that arise in the following pages, though it would be misguided not to admit that I often find my sympathies gravitating more to the artists. Of course, I do not profess to agree with every idea or vision they put forward. Nor do I see my role as that of an art critic, which I reserve for the professionals. But I hope that by encountering the richness of these artists' lives, work, and communities—so often sidelined in histories of religion, art, and the culture wars—we may begin to see and to understand better some of what they saw and what they invite us to see.

1

The Queer Lives of Religious Forms: Bob Flanagan's Crip Catholicism

You could say that was a symbolic castration, or a symbolic eating of the body of Christ. It was a joke, too—we weren't saying you were going to be saved, not at all. But there was that spiritual structure, which I enjoyed playing with.[1]

—Sheree Rose

I arrange things in a Catholic way.[2]

—Robert Mapplethorpe

Bob Flanagan is something of a poster boy for transgression, a position cemented by the release of Kirby Dick's 1997 documentary *Sick: The Life and Death of Bob Flanagan, Supermasochist*. The film brought Flanagan national attention, as it chronicled the final years of his life, including his artistic and romantic partnership with Sheree Rose.[3] Together, they explored the conjunctions of performance art, disability, and sadomasochism—and Catholicism.

The attention gained through Dick's film wasn't altogether new. Flanagan had served as an actual poster boy for the North Orange County chapter of the National Cystic Fibrosis Research Foundation.[4] Born into an Irish-American Catholic family in 1952, he grew up with cystic fibrosis, a genetic disorder that most acutely affects the lungs. Few people with cystic fibrosis in this period lived past their teenage years, and Flanagan never expected to live into adulthood. But he was one of the oldest living people with cystic fibrosis before he died in 1996 at the age of 44. He had met Sheree Rose in 1980. Born in 1941 and raised in Los Angeles, she was a "divorced housewife" who, while earning a master's degree at California State University Northridge, became in involved in the Feminist Socialist Network. Her commitments to feminism

Provoking Religion. Anthony M. Petro, Oxford University Press. © Oxford University Press 2025.
DOI: 10.1093/9780190938468.003.0002

and to sex positivity (and to Judaism) would shape her life as a photographer and performance artist and her creative ventures with Flanagan, including their explorations in sadomasochism (S/M).[5]

Flanagan often rehearsed how childhood and adolescent experiences with cystic fibrosis, including frequent encounters with painful medical tests, shaped his taste for sexual masochism. Cystic fibrosis can impact eating and digestion, making it difficult to keep on weight and causing chronic stomach pain. "One way of alleviating pain," Flanagan recalled in a 1990 interview, "was rubbing my stomach up against the sheets, which turned into masturbating, which connected pain and sexual relief." Moreover, he continued, "when you're sick a lot, all these doctors probe you, and there's a lot of humiliation. There are issues of authority, there's piercing thrown in, and so on."[6] As a teenager, Flanagan experimented with combining sexual acts with self-inflicted pain; his examples included beating himself with a paddle and suspending himself from a ceiling. Such acts became erotic rituals of self-control. This play, he explained, offered one way to take back the power he had lost to this disease and to the medical establishment. In adulthood, these rituals also became the basis for a series of public performances with Sheree Rose that thematized the intersections of disability, pain, and eroticism. These performances displayed the power of transgression through which Flanagan would subvert the poster boy image, even becoming "the poster child from hell," as queer and disability studies scholar Robert McRuer puts it.[7]

In "Seeing the Disabled," a canonical essay in disability studies, Rosemarie Garland-Thomson likewise characterized Flanagan as a transgressor *par excellence*. She gets to the point when describing how he "became famous for pounding a nail through his penis in one of his performances."[8] This genital crucifixion takes center stage in Garland-Thomson's discussion of various styles of disability representation, serving as the exemplum for what she calls the "exotic" or at times the "transgressive" approach (joining the sentimental, the wondrous, and the realist). McRuer builds upon her discussion in his field-defining *Crip Theory*, in which he underscores the queer political potential of Flanagan's transgressive "crip" stylings—the term crip emerged as a reclaimed slight (like queer) to name disability justice work.[9]

Both Garland-Thomson and McRuer are powerfully attuned to juxtapositions of disability and sexuality in Flanagan's work. For now, I want to note their agreement: that Flanagan's public performance art, much of it in partnership with Rose, enacts a certain form of transgression and participates in histories of disability representation under the sign of transgression. What he seems to be transgressing, in these analyses, are the heteronormative and ableist norms of contemporary US culture, especially as those norms have been shaped by longer histories of medical and Christian moralism. Indeed, Christian rhetoric has long been taken up in US culture to stigmatize physical and cognitive difference and to denounce forms of sexual practice and desire that stand outside the bounds of heterosexual coupling.[10] This point perhaps makes even more surprising, then, the forms through which Flanagan enacts transgression: he performs transgression not only against Christian norms but also through them.[11]

This doubleness leads to questions about how Christian forms circulate in visual and performance art that conventionally falls under the umbrella of secular, if not anti-Christian. How do we understand what work religious forms do in seemingly secular visual and performance art? And how do these forms figure into contemporary styles of iconoclasm or transgression? I should state up front that ultimately I have little interest in categorizing Flanagan or his work as secular (or religious) in any strict or essentialist way. Rather, I want to explore how he talks about religion and how religious forms animate his work. Indeed, Flanagan makes for a good poster boy for conversations about the study of religion, even if he is a poster boy from hell—or perhaps because so.

Transgressing Religion

We might start by looking to how Flanagan and Rose describe their own connections to religion. In a short unpublished essay saved in her archive, Sheree Rose describes her relationship with Flanagan like this: "Bob and I were an unlikely pair. He was 27 years old when we met. I was ten years older. He was Catholic; I, a Jew."[12] Another version found in their archive revises that last sentence: "He was a *lapsed* Catholic. I was a *cultural* Jew."[13] I want to note the revision. The movement signals some ambivalence about identification with being Catholic and Jewish. They are not *not* Catholic and Jewish, but rather certain kinds of Catholic and Jewish, respectively. There is a playfulness here, emerging even alongside the ambivalence, that carries into their performances of sadomasochism.[14]

In a 1990 interview, Flanagan narrates his S/M practice in distinctly religious terms. "For me," he explained, "S&M is more than a sexual thing, it has a religious component. It's about transcendence. It's that really crazy thing, where the lower you go the higher you get." "There's a line in the slave sonnets," he continued, referencing his 1986 book of poetry: "'Each reduction makes me all the more huge.' It's an out-of-the-body experience."[15] Flanagan searches here for the right language to describe his S/M work as "more" than sexual, ultimately finding it in the terms we reserve for mystical or ecstatic religious experiences. Note how he does not reduce sexuality to religion; nor does he simply equate them. Rather, sexual masochism becomes a meditative practice, a diminution of the self, through which transcendence becomes possible.

A somewhat different picture—though not necessarily a contradictory one—emerges in a 1994 conversation with Bob Flanagan, Sheree Rose, and arts editor Deborah Drier in the pages of *Artforum*. "There's definitely a spiritual thing going on in Bob's works," Rose remarks. "Well," responds Flanagan, "for the general population I think it's easier to enter the spiritual realm—it's something they're familiar with. But I'm not comfortable with it." Rose follows up:

> Yes, Bob likes to deny the spiritual side, but for me the idea of him lying on the bed of nails and me symbolically cutting his penis [by cutting the birthday cake that lay on his lower stomach] was spiritually significant. Part of what we've always done together is the subjugation of the male by the female. So my original idea was to have the cake, dripping with cream and raspberry jam, made in the shape of a phallus, and people would be given pieces of it to eat. You could say that was a symbolic castration, or a symbolic eating of the body of Christ. It was a joke, too—we weren't saying you were going to be saved, not at all. But there was that spiritual structure, which I enjoyed playing with.[16]

Observe the movements of the conversation. Flanagan does not deny a spiritual or religious aspect to his work but notes his discomfort with that language. Then Rose layers onto the mystical or ecstatic dimensions (that Flanagan had noted earlier) the liturgical dimensions of their work, the "spiritual structure" that draws from Catholic ritual, even as it plays with it. This play with ritual—this performance of ritual—begins to mark out the queer space of Flanagan and Rose's performance art, a space that is saturated with religious forms. But more: with Catholic ones.

This chapter looks to what religious forms Flanagan's transgression takes, what forms give it shape, make it legible, and allow it to "resonate," to borrow a term from literary scholar Wai Chee Dimock.[17] Like other artists in this book, Flanagan and Rose "got in trouble" with conservative political and religious leaders. Republican Rep. Dana Rohrabacher and leaders of The Heritage Foundation attacked their work, including Flanagan's "genital piercing," as an obscene misuse of federal funding after the duo performed in a show that had received NEA support.[18] In the following chapters, I approach such culture wars battles over art historically. Here, however, I read the work of Flanagan and Rose for the conceptual tools it affords for thinking about the role of religious symbols and ritual in contemporary visual and performance art. I move between the particular and the general. First, this chapter demonstrates how Catholicism became both a context against which—and a style through which—Flanagan and Rose performed.[19] Second, their creative work suggests the importance of attending to religious forms in the study of religion. I hope that attention to the operation of forms might expand our analytical resources, especially those drawn from ethnographic and historical inquiry, for apprehending the work of religion without privileging interiority, belief, and sincerity, notions that have long haunted scholarly and lay thinking about religion. My approach emerges partly through curiosity—how might looking to form or forms take pressure off the often humanist, and at times sentimental, practice of revealing our subjects in all their expressive, earnest, and resistant glory?[20] But this is not meant to be taken as a comprehensive theory of religion or method to study it. Rather, it is "a strategy for a situation," so to speak: an approach that I have found helpful for trying to understand how religious rites and iconography circulate in visual and performance art, but one that may travel to other contexts as well.[21] I first turn to a discussion of this approach to forms, especially Catholic ones.

The Catholic Imagination, Form, and the Study of Religion

Literary scholar Thomas Ferraro has observed that Catholics in the United States have felt more at home in the arts than in the academy.[22] This is partly a consequence of the history of anti-Catholicism in secular academia. But it is also, Ferraro insists, "because populist forms of Catholic knowing reside more in *gesture* than in explication." These "forms of Catholic knowing" appear "more in public theaters of aesthetic transformation than in the sequestered libraries of its preservation."[23] Ferraro asks what it means to have been raised Catholic and to live through what we might call "Catholic forms" outside the official bounds of the church hierarchy, if not in direct conflict with them. He offers an important proviso for this study of cultural Catholics that informs my work here. "To me," he insists, "*cultural* as a qualifier to *Catholicism* does not necessarily mean dilution or dissolution—a draining of the religious imagination into banal secularity—but can in fact signify the opposite, a form of transfigurative reenvisioning that refuses to quarantine the sacred."[24] Put differently, we should not assume the modifier "cultural" means that Catholicism is any less significant or even less religious.

Ferraro provides a framework for interpreting what art critic Eleanor Heartney calls the "incarnational consciousness" that haunts many contemporary visual and performance artists or "postmodern heretics," ranging from Andy Warhol and Linda Montano to Karen Finley and Félix González-Torres.[25] Heartney draws upon what sociologist and Roman Catholic priest Andrew Greeley called "the Catholic imagination." He describes it as a "distinctive sensibility," shared among professed and cultural Catholics alike, that ranges from Catholic high culture to low.[26] This Catholic imagination inheres in the propensity toward enchantment, to see the divine manifest in all kinds of daily doings. Greeley's argument draws from Catholic theologian David Tracy, who distinguished analogical from dialectical languages.[27] Analogical languages within Christian thought and art emphasize manifestations of Christ and his likeness to humans, whereas dialectical ones negate an easy comparison between human and divine, emphasizing instead their distance from one another.

Greeley admits his adaptation of Tracy's distinction between the analogical and the dialectical is "low level"—and we should heed these words.[28] Where Tracy sought an interpretative grounding to consider theological truths within a robust pluralism, Greeley discerned the basis for a general distinction between Catholic and Protestant sensibilities arising out of the Reformation. "Put more simply," Greeley writes, "the Catholic imagination loves metaphors; Catholicism is a verdant rainforest of metaphors. The Protestant imagination distrusts metaphors; it tends to be a desert for metaphors."[29] Saying it a little differently, Greeley argues that Catholics emphasize the similarity of things compared by metaphor, whereas Protestants stress the contrast in any analogy. Greeley is careful enough to mark his exaggeration—the distinction is not perfect, as Catholics can downplay metaphor and Protestants can revel in it. But Greeley's account calls for additional qualifications.

Aside from playing too loose with the distinction between Catholic and Protestant, Greeley suggests more unity in "the Catholic imagination" than really exists—is there one Catholic imagination, or are there many? He also slides too easily between descriptive or sociological claims and more normative, theological ones. He shifts, for instance, from an imagination that is given to rich symbolism and enchantment to "one that views the world and all that is in it as enchanted, haunted by the Holy Spirit and the presence of grace."[30] Finally, perhaps because Greeley maintains this emphasis on grace and love, his vision of the Catholic imagination remains too upbeat. It lacks a sense of the tragic, ugly, or horrific that also haunts anything we might call a Catholic imaginary and that we will see in some of the artistic work examined in this book. If we keep these qualifications in mind, though, I do find Greeley's description of the Catholic imagination useful, as he explores its manifestations across examples of space, eroticism, community, and salvation, often with a very strong inclination to witnessing the imagination at work in literature and visual art (a propensity shared by Tracy). We might also appreciate Greeley's quip that "everyone tends to be pre-modern."[31] Put differently, what we often consider part of the "modern"—the emphasis we place on reason, autonomy, progress, and secularism, whatever its various forms—remains more normative or even aspirational than descriptive of how most people live.

Greeley is also careful to admit some dissonance within the Catholic imagination when it comes to sexuality and eroticism. He notes how many Catholics, across history, have played up metaphors of God's relationship to the Church as like one between two lovers or how Catholic art draws rich comparisons between the religious and the erotic.[32] He points, for instance, to the vision of orgasmic joy many viewers have seen in Gian Lorenzo Bernini's statue *Ecstasy of Saint Theresa* (1642–52). At the same time, we cannot ignore "the Church's fear of erotic imagery" or the discomfort many Catholics take in the comparison between human and divine experiences of the erotic.[33] Jesus may be like us when he suffers on the cross, these Catholics might say, but surely he is not like us *sexually*. As a Catholic, Greeley finds this resistance troubling—even attributing it to "Catholic puritans"—as he shows how thoroughly Catholic these erotic visions are, even if most Catholics today find them "utterly unacceptable."[34]

This is one of the threads that Heartney elevates in *Postmodern Heretics*, where she explores how the Catholic imagination has shaped artistic visions of the body and eroticism for a range of contemporary artists, mostly feminist and queer. Literary scholar Paul Giles also draws upon this notion of the analogical imagination in *American Catholic Arts and Fiction*. He understands Catholicism as a "residual cultural determinant" or even as "detached, floating signifiers" haunting the literature of Flannery O'Connor and Walker Percy, the art of Andy Warhol and Robert Mapplethorpe, and the films of Alfred Hitchcock and Martin Scorsese.[35] As Ferraro, Heartney, and Giles suggest, it is not merely accidental that Catholic themes saturate so much artistic practice in post-1960s America, nor that the artists producing these works would, by and large, remain in tension with Roman Catholic orthodoxy. To dismiss such work as secular, if not anti-Catholic, though, would risk missing the shape that Catholic forms—gestures, styles, iconographies, rituals—give to this artistic work and to public life, forms neither "officially" Catholic nor merely secular. Attention to forms, which has regained currency in literary studies, helps us to understand this in-between terrain.

From Catholic Imaginations to Catholic Forms

The study of form enjoys a long but not altogether positive history. The term itself has come under fire for its almost boundless (if therein ironic) elasticity. Literary scholar Angela Leighton puts it well when she writes, "Form, which seems self-sufficient and self-defining, is restless, tendentious, a noun lying in wait for its object."[36] Raymond Williams opens his chapter on form in *Marxism and Literature* by explaining how it "acquired two major senses: a visible or outward shape, and an inherent shaping impulse."[37] Form, in other words, can describe the very essence of something or gesture to its superficiality; it can be a determining force or a mere container.[38] The various opposites cast alongside form demonstrate its chameleon-like character. Over its career, as Leighton writes, form has taken on three powerful counterparts: matter, content, and formlessness.[39] When made into a method, one that has largely fallen out of favor, formalism tends to read literary or artistic texts with little to no attention to context. Historicist readings, in contrast, reduce form to context—which could mean social or political setting, historical or contemporary—often obliterating the boundaries that form any given text and distinguish it from others. Given this fraught inheritance, one might ask: why bother with form at all?

One reason is that it offers a conceptual tool to capture something otherwise missed. My inclination to consider US religion through attention to forms is indebted to recent work in literary and cultural studies that has sought ways to analyze texts that neither dissolve them into "context" nor jump immediately to "symptomatic readings," by which most authors mean readings that reproduce a hermeneutics of suspicion, seeking to uncover deep, secret meanings waiting behind texts, usually by drawing upon psychoanalysis and Marxism.[40] I do not think the study of North American religion has suffered in the same ways as some other fields from the burden of producing symptomatic readings. But the study of US religions has had its own attachments, especially to assumptions about human agency, creativity, resistance, and the power of narrative that cannot be separated from normative definitions of religion as a form of deep, sincere, or authentic identification.[41] Attention to forms invites us to think in different directions.

Another reason is that scholars of religion in North America already draw upon the language of forms to very useful ends. Consider four instances. In *Being Muslim*, Sylvia Chan-Malik combines lived religion with the study of "racial-religious form" to understand the lives of Muslim women. She tracks three key instances of these racial-religious forms—the Islamic Terrorist, the Poor Muslim Woman, and the Radical Black Muslim—which, combined with her attention to practice, begin to articulate the conditions of "being Muslim" in the United States.[42] In *Spirit in the Dark*, Josef Sorett shows how religion shaped the African American literary visions of writers in the early to mid-twentieth century. His brilliant analysis shows how "the spiritual grammar cultivated in African American literature" remained in a relationship of ambivalence to Afro-Protestantism, as "a celebratory ambivalence apparent across the history of racial aesthetics took the form of a frequent pairing of church and spirit."[43] In "Seeing the Invisible," Hillary Kaell calls our attention to the "new forms" that religion takes in a "secularizing place like Quebec" in her provocative analysis of wayside crosses—a particular material and aesthetic form of religion that becomes "ambient," shifting between "marked" and "unmarked" in Quebec's secularizing public culture.[44] And in "Altars of Ammo," John Seitz examines how "Catholic forms such as clerical robes, altars, Eucharistic hosts, and crucifixes, as well as Catholic ritual postures and persons, such as the priest's elevation of arms and host at the high point of mass" provided a rich visual vocabulary through which "wartime image-makers" during World War II could "interject holiness into wartime settings."[45] These Catholic forms signaled "protest or lamentation" for lives lost and helped US Americans accept the pains of modern warfare.[46] In each of these cases, and we could add many more, the language of form offers a way to advance our understanding of how religious histories and material cultures work on and through the people and texts we study.[47]

Observing Forms

So how do we study forms? Two observations: form need not name something essential or unchanging, and we should emphasize forms in the plural. On both points, I follow literary theorist Caroline Levine, whose *Forms: Whole, Rhythm, Hierarchy, Network* charts a path for scholars of literary and cultural studies to analyze forms as connected to historical and political contexts, thereby joining the usually separate analyses of aesthetic and political forms. Levine defines form very broadly to mean "all shapes and configurations, all ordering principles, all patterns of repetition and difference."[48] Two points in her argument are especially helpful. First, she notes how forms work: they constrain, they differ, they overlap and intersect, they travel, and they "do political work in historical contexts."[49] Second, drawing from design theory, Levine emphasizes the "affordances" of forms, by which she means the "potential uses or actions latent in materials and designs."[50] Forms, in this casting, are both iterable and portable—they can persist over time or reappear at various moments and in numerous contexts. Forms can be malleable or durable. The iterative quality of forms means that, if they are to persist, they cannot persist without difference.[51] Yet there is something to certain forms that take shape over long periods of time, that give shape to continuing ways of living, ways of being, ways of doing religion, of doing politics, of doing racism or sexism (or trying to undo them).

While I focus on religious forms, we need not presume that religious forms exist apart from nonreligious forms or that calling a form religious imputes any intrinsic quality. Rather, it could be as simple as a shape—say, a cross—that reappears on a storefront church, in the Quebecois fields, on a highway billboard, in the logo of the American Red Cross, or in the photography of Andres Serrano. What are the affordances of this particular form? How should we understand not only its appearance in particular locations but also its patterns of recurrence? Approaching the cross as an iterable form allows us to see its circulation across conventionally secular and religious contexts without reducing these appearances to the terms of one or the other. This approach, in other words, allows us to examine the interplay of religious and secular forms—or the movement of forms across religious and secular fields—without prodding us to answer the question of whether something is or is not intrinsically religious or secular. Paying attention to forms comes at that division askance, in that its primary commitment is to the shifting presence and absence of forms themselves. This approach focuses our attention on the persistence of certain visual and material forms across time, especially as they cross between aesthetic and political registers, while insisting upon interpreting them within specific, lived contexts. It thus pushes against a radical historicism that would limit certain practices to an immediate context, or reduce them to an ungeneralizable particularity, by reminding us to consider the different valences or resonances that forms take up in new places or across time.[52]

If Ferraro is right that Catholic ways of knowing reside more in gesture than in explication, more in public theaters of aesthetic transformation than in academic libraries, then attention to forms gives us a more precise analytic language to account for gestures, for the theatrical, for the forms that images take, how they travel, how they give shape to Catholic aesthetics and ways of being in the world. It also helps us move from Catholic ways of knowing to Catholic ways of doing, seeing, and being seen. In an interview, artist Robert Mapplethorpe, a cradle Catholic from Long Island, got at what I mean when he explained, "I arrange things in a Catholic way."[53] Catholicism, in other words, comes through as much in the shape his work takes as in its obvious content; indeed, rather than read content apart from this ordering we should ask how it emerges through this ordering. Attention to religious forms helps us better understand what this might mean—how Catholicism haunts visual and material culture, including the work of high art, not so much through its doxa as through its aesthetic and ritual patterns.

To suggest the purchase of this approach, I want to return to the example of Bob Flanagan and his work with Sheree Rose. I consider how Flanagan creates his public persona, that is, how he performs himself in public, often with Rose by his side, and how they work through Catholic forms in doing so. Their artistic work centers form and representation, both forming and disforming Catholic tropes of suffering, incarnation, humor, and confession. My interest here is more in testing the limits of thinking through Flanagan's work as Catholic than in taking up Flanagan as *a* Catholic in any conventional sense, in the sense in which we fold religious identity into a longer list of possible identity markers. Much can be said about this point, but I am trying to get at something a little different here, and the language of forms helps get us there. Flanagan's work, often with Rose, offers a privileged site for envisioning particular kinds of formation and dis-formation, for thinking about the forms through which religion, sex, and disability work.

Representing Disability, Forming Flanagan

We might start by returning to Flanagan's place within representations of disability and in scholarship in disability studies.[54] In "Seeing the Disabled," Rosemarie Garland-Thomson shows how the development of photography in the 1830s and 1840s led to a new emphasis on visual forms of representation in the modern period.[55] This shift had an enormous impact on representations of disability. Long hidden from public view, disabled bodies could now be photographed for much broader public consumption. Nineteenth-century US Americans were deeply ambivalent about the disabled body. On the one hand, living in a largely Christian nation, Garland-Thomson explains, they had a long tradition of venerating the weak, disfigured body of Christ. But there was also a deep-seated discomfort about such images that was "emblemized," she suggests, "in the wounded Christ being removed from the Protestant cross."[56] This ambivalence—inherited from Christian and especially Protestant American culture—has shaped dominant ways that disability has been represented.

Garland-Thomson offers four broad categories to capture how US Americans have viewed disability in visual imagery. The "wondrous" refers to images of people with disabilities performing surprising tasks. Imagine, for example, a surgical resident overcoming autism—and fending off would-be doubters—to save the life a young boy after a very unlikely accident at an airport (this is the opening scene and main conceit of the TV series *The Good Doctor*). The "sentimental" style depicts the disabled person as helpless or pitiable, such as the poster boys and girls for organizations like the March of Dimes or Jerry Lewis telethons, or the sight of Tiny Tim in *A Christmas Carol*. The "exotic" representation shows people with disabilities as "freakish" objects for viewers to gawk at, such as images of conjoined twins or the Elephant Man. The final visual category is "realism." These images avoid making the disabled person seem different from imagined "normal" viewers. This genre allows viewers to trade places with the object of the image, to put themselves in the place—mostly, at least—of the disabled person it depicts. Such representations may seem more "truthful" than others, Garland-Thomson warns, but realism is also governed by the rules of its genre.[57]

Within this taxonomy of visual rhetoric, Garland-Thomson reads Flanagan's body of work as an example of exotic representation, though it is also a case in which the disabled person himself performs or crafts that very representation. "Creating a profane parody that fuses the cultural figures of the invisible superman, the porn star, and the sick person," she writes, "he combines cape, chains, piercings, and the oxygen mask characteristic of cystic fibrosis to discomfort viewers."[58] While Flanagan's image thus troubles cultural expectations about disability, Garland-Thompson nonetheless concludes that the "realistic mode" remains the one "most likely to encourage the work the Disability Rights movement began." This is because it depicts disability as ordinary or typical rather than unusual.[59] In *Crip Theory*, Robert McRuer appreciates the power of Garland-Thomson's taxonomy but also pushes against it (and her reading of Flanagan in particular) to the extent that it reproduces a progress narrative, even if unwittingly—one that arrives, in the end, at an ostensibly better, more realistic mode of representation. For McRuer, realism as a genre too easily collapses into realistic portrayal, which then serves as the normative political horizon for disability representation. If the realist mode remains a genre for Garland-Thomson, he argues, it is one that still enacts hope for a particular future in which normalization— indexed in the ability for substitution, for mimesis—remains an unquestioned political goal.[60]

McRuer wants to return us to the potential "crip" work of the transgressive, that is, to "call back the transgressive to consider whether it might be considered otherwise."[61] He finds Flanagan a better exemplar for disability politics than does Garland-Thomson—even, in his words, "critically queer, and radically crip." Flanagan's performance art, writes McRuer, "inhabits and explodes both the poster child and the dead-already mythologies, in some ways literally fucking the compulsory future that both portend."[62] McRuer wants to marshal the transgressive aspects of Flanagan's performance and writing toward a "crip politics," one that resists the normalizing constraints of mainstream disability politics and of lesbian and gay politics in kind. Channeling French thinker Roland Barthes, he reads Flanagan's body of images for the myth-making work of which they become a part. While these images might at times "suggest little more than 'Bob Flanagan's sick,'" McRuer argues, given the right moment, " 'some future person' or collectivity might detect in that sick message the seemingly incomprehensible way to survive, and survive well, at the margins of time, space, and representation (they might, in fact, detect that surviving well can paradoxically mean surviving sick)."[63] And more, they might find that surviving well can involve surviving as (culturally) Catholic, or at the edges of Catholicism, at the limits of Catholic forms, or through the pleasures of their affordances.

Both Garland-Thomson and McRuer offer rich, indeed indispensable, lenses to analyze the politics of disability representation and performance. But I am struck by how the languages of the religious both enter and do not enter their readings. We might ask, for instance, how the transgressive aspects of Flanagan's work are both structured and fractured by a certain Catholic imagination, through a specifically Catholic mode of boundary-making and a Catholic erotics of transgression (and a Catholic erotics of boundaries).[64] What readings open up if we take transgression not as some essential form of offense against law or rule but instead as a stylized response to a particular cultural situation? Doing so would push us to ask more questions, both about the specificity of historical or cultural context and about the stylizations of transgressive acts themselves. For Flanagan, I want to suggest, mid-twentieth century Irish-American Catholicism provides a framework both for the cultural norms he transgresses and for the forms through which his transgression is performed—through which his performance becomes transgressive.[65]

∗ ∗ ∗

Roman Catholicism has a long history of dealing with disability and illness. In *Between Heaven and Earth*, Robert Orsi captures a chapter of this history in narrating the story of his uncle Sal, who had cerebral palsy, a disability that affects muscle movement. Orsi draws upon the story of his uncle to illustrate the power of Catholic ways of thinking about disability in the mid-twentieth century, the same period when Flanagan was born and raised.[66] Approaching this topic, these Catholic ways of knowing, requires scholars to think in complicated ways about religious tradition, including what a religion such as "Catholicism" is. For scholars of lived religion, it is important to understand the history of the movement and the official theology of the church. But it is just as important to examine popular devotions, including the everyday or mundane ways that people negotiate relationships among their lives, their families, their broader culture, and the divine. This approach helps bring together representation and practice. Orsi's account of his uncle is thus instructive in terms of method and for understanding some of Flanagan's own Catholic history.

Sal kept on his desk the image of a saint—Blessed Margaret of Castello—which sat alongside pictures of his family members. Born in 1287, Margaret was small and blind and had a twisted foot and a hunched back. Catholics devoted to Saint Margaret often say that she would not have been born today, with modern medical advances. For this reason, she has been proposed as the patron saint of the unborn and unwanted.[67] Catholic culture in the mid-twentieth century identified sickness with sin and moral corruption. But it also upheld the devotional benefits of suffering and sickness, Orsi explains, which took on "the character of a sacrament," an act that could bring one closer to salvation. He describes the feeling as an "erotic" of suffering. Pain could be a sign of corruption, but it also could signal spiritual glory. This was especially true for people born with physical disabilities, who were considered "innocent"—sometimes called the "fortunate unfortunates."[68]

Devotional literature in this period called for the sick to suffer in silence and to suffer cheerfully. These "happy handicapped," as they were sometimes named in popular literature, could function as intermediaries to the divine for those who were not suffering. They were what historian Paula Kane describes as "victim souls," an idea that emerged in the late nineteenth century.[69] People with disabilities became spiritual heroes, and their devotees regarded their suffering, mimicking that of Christ, as an act of God that could help others. In this sense, Catholic culture in the mid-twentieth century represented disability as a sign of sin, but also as an occasion for deep holiness. This culture of Catholicism was formative for Flanagan, who worked within and against these Catholic devotions to suffering as much as he did Catholic disciplines of sex.

Narrating Flanagan

Flanagan's story offers up a narrative about his escape from the guilt and sexual shame imposed by his Roman Catholic upbringing. This narrative frames the 1993 collection *Bob Flanagan: Supermasochist*, assembled by Andrea Juno and V. Vale, which contains several interviews and photographs of Flanagan and Rose's work. Their co-authored introduction presents a common secularist story about overturning religious oppression. "We are still under the tight, insidious grip of the past thousand years of Judeo-Christian brainwashing," write Juno and Vale, "that runs like an unconscious river through all of our myths and belief systems."[70] Against the onslaught of this repressive religious system stands Flanagan, whose performances "force seldom-expressed conflicts such as these into discussion." "Particularly noteworthy," they insist, "is his attitude of fully living his life in the present, accepting the body he was given, and not only accepting all his desires but *owning* and *living* them."[71] Here, Flanagan's public performances refuse the sexual shame and guilt attached to Christian teachings about sexuality and disability. This is a liberation narrative—and an important one. But we can ask still other questions about Flanagan's sexual practices, his artistic work, his Catholicism and Catholic iconoclasm.

Flanagan's writing and performance art yield alternative readings, or additional readings, including some that take Catholicism as more than a source of repression or as an external domination to overcome—whether in reference to sex or to disability. Such readings might start with the records of Flanagan's more explicit references to Catholicism.

With biographical details—Flanagan described in one interview how he "got to experience Catholic guilt and confession, the Stations of the Cross, and the saintliness of suffering." He continued: "I think I related my suffering and illness to the suffering of Jesus on the cross—the idea that suffering in some way was kind of holy."[72]

With humor—On various occasions, Flanagan joked that Jesus was the first super-masochist.[73] He formed his public persona in this mold, one that might cause even Mel Gibson's passionate Christ to blush.

With testimony—In his 1985 poem "Why?," one of his most well-known works, Flanagan recited a litany of reasons for his enjoyment of sexual masochism:

> Because it feels good, because it gives me an erection, [. . .] because I was humiliated by nuns, because of Christ and the crucifixion, [. . .] because I'm a Catholic, because I still love Lent and I love my penis and in spite of it all I have no guilt, [. . .] because of the cross, [. . .] because my parents loved me even more when I was suffering, [. . .] because spare the rod and spoil the child.[74]

Flanagan's poem brings together a style of Catholic prayer with autobiographical details of his life. After his death, Rose would respond with a poem called "Why Not?" replicating this cadence. Her poem introduces references to feminist and Jewish spirituality, invoking both "the Hindu Goddess Kali" and Judith, "my ancestor," as it builds to a testament to Flanagan. It closes in Hebrew: "She-ma Yis-ro-el, adonoi elohaynu, adonoi e-chad" (Hear of Israel, the Lord our God, the Lord is One).[75]

With performance—Consider two examples. Flanagan often experimented with piercings, with running needles through his skin, including the skin of his genitals. On at least two occasions, including one captured in Kirby Dick's documentary, he would drive a nail through the flesh of his penis and into a wooden board. It was a transgressive act, but one not wholly unknown to the rich archives of Catholic mortification, in which many before him have sought to punish the flesh, to mimic the suffering of Christ on the cross, to find transcendence through the body.

The second example comes from Flanagan and Rose's performance piece *Visiting Hours*, probably their most celebrated work, which first opened at the Santa Monica Museum of Art in December of 1992. In 1993, they were invited to show it at the New Museum in New York City and then later at the School of the Museum of Fine Arts in Boston. The New York exhibition featured what Rose describes as "a very elaborate coffin like you would see in a Catholic funeral."[76] The coffin included a monitor placed where one would expect someone's head to be. It showed Flanagan's face. Running around the monitor was a Latin inscription, which read, in translation, "what you are, I once was, what I am, you will become." As an audience member got closer to read it, a camera hidden in the flowers would suddenly project their face onto the screen, rendering the coffin their own. "So if you stood three feet away, you'd see Bob lying in the coffin," Rose explained: "You had to be curious enough to want to go closer, maybe to read those Latin words, and as soon as you did that, you were caught! So it had a jokey element, like 'we got you.' We wanted to show that Bob was as human as anybody else, a person with a great sense of humour, even about death."[77]

In another segment of *Visiting Hours*, Flanagan sat in a hospital bed in a makeshift hospital room and greeted his visitors (Figure 1.1). One goal of the piece was to familiarize audience members with the hospital room itself and with a sick patient. The scene was meant to destigmatize the space of the hospital and to humanize its inhabitants. It also functioned as a confessional space. Rose described the atmosphere it created for visitors: "Some of them were crying. They had kids who had cystic fibrosis, or they had somebody who had died, and it was like a confessional." "People would come in and just open up their hearts," she continued: "There was a psychiatrist who came back three or four times. People would come back and just sit and hang out with Bob."[78]

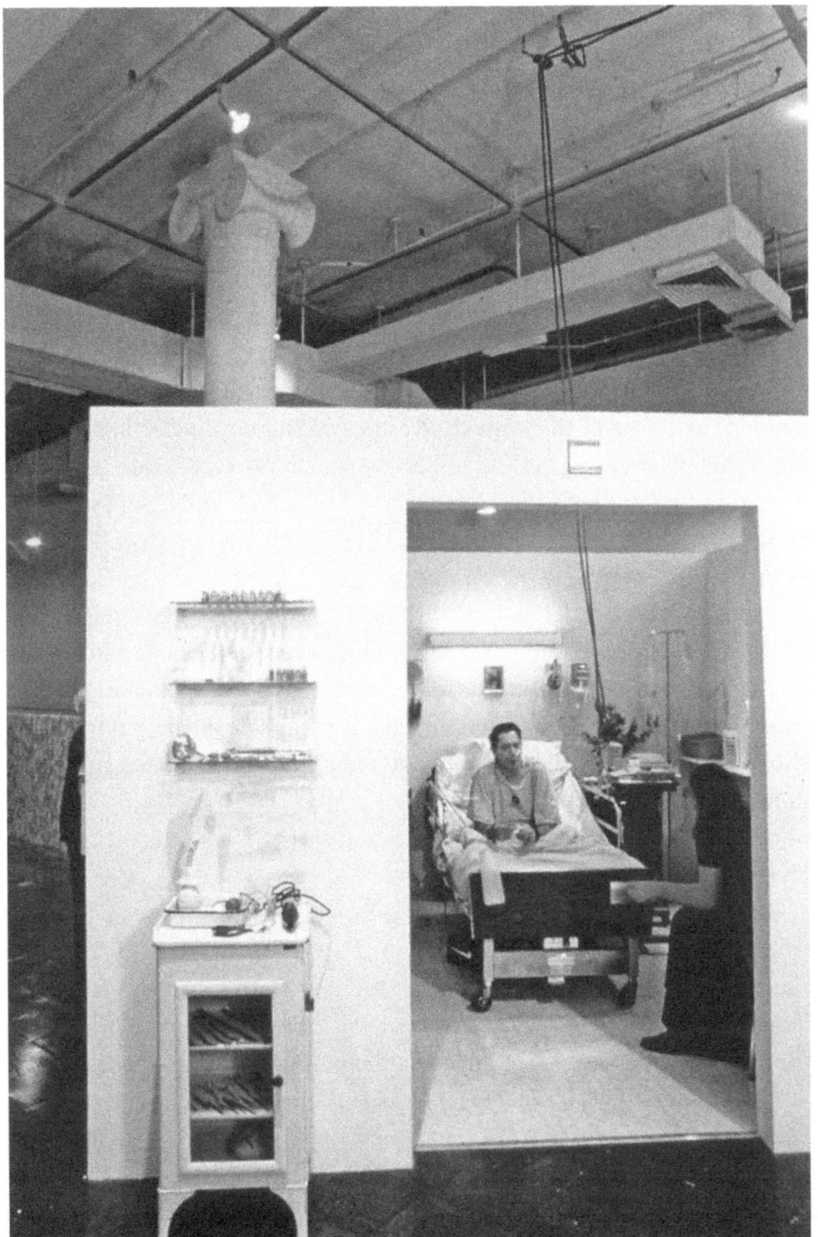

Figure 1.1 Flanagan speaking with a visitor. Bob Flanagan and Sheree Rose. Exhibition: 9/23/1994–12/31/1994, Work: 1994. Exhibition: *Visiting Hours*: An installation by Bob Flanagan in collaboration with Sheree Rose, Hospital room entryway wall installation. Photo by Fred Scruton, used with permission.

From inside, this hospital room appeared conventional. But glimpsed from the outside, one could see an external wall painted to look like a blue sky with a few wispy clouds. Periodically, usually twice a day, Rose would turn a lever behind the exhibition's main room. It tightened a strap attached to Flanagan's ankles. As she pulled, Flanagan began to rise, higher and higher, against the backdrop of the blue sky and finally beyond it. They called this scene "The Ascension" (Figure 1.2).

The scene conjures Jesus's ascension to heaven, but it also plays on another scene of Christian and theatrical history. The idea came from depictions of the death of the character Little Eva in *Uncle Tom's Cabin*, Harriet Beecher Stowe's mid-nineteenth-century blockbuster of sentimental anti-slavery literature.[79] In the novel, the white child Little Eva falls terminally ill. Before her death, she experiences a vision of heaven, which prompts other characters to turn toward the light. Early theatrical productions often supplemented Stowe's very short descriptions of Little Eva's vision and death with a much more dramatic scene. The vision was restaged in the style of a melodramatic martyrdom. After her death, Little Eva would be elevated above stage, using fishing wire, to represent her ascension to heaven. Flanagan and Rose playfully recreate this scene, with Rose performing the physical labor offstage, while Flanagan is elevated to heaven naked and upside down. But like Peter, who Catholic tradition tells us was martyred upside down, Flanagan ascends nonetheless.

Confessing Bodies

These examples draw our attention to how Catholic forms animated Flanagan's life and work, even as they raise more questions than answers. They suggest we might find religion in the modes through which Flanagan performed himself in public, especially how he performed disability and sexuality. What do we learn from the confessional gestures in his interviews, where he delighted to talk at length about his sexual practices, or from the affordances of his poem, "Why?," which reproduces the cadence of prayer or confession?

The Christian form of confession, and of public confession in particular, takes on a special valence in Flanagan's work. It has a much older history, of course. The philosopher and historian Michel Foucault became interested in how models of Catholic confession shaped various styles of the self. He

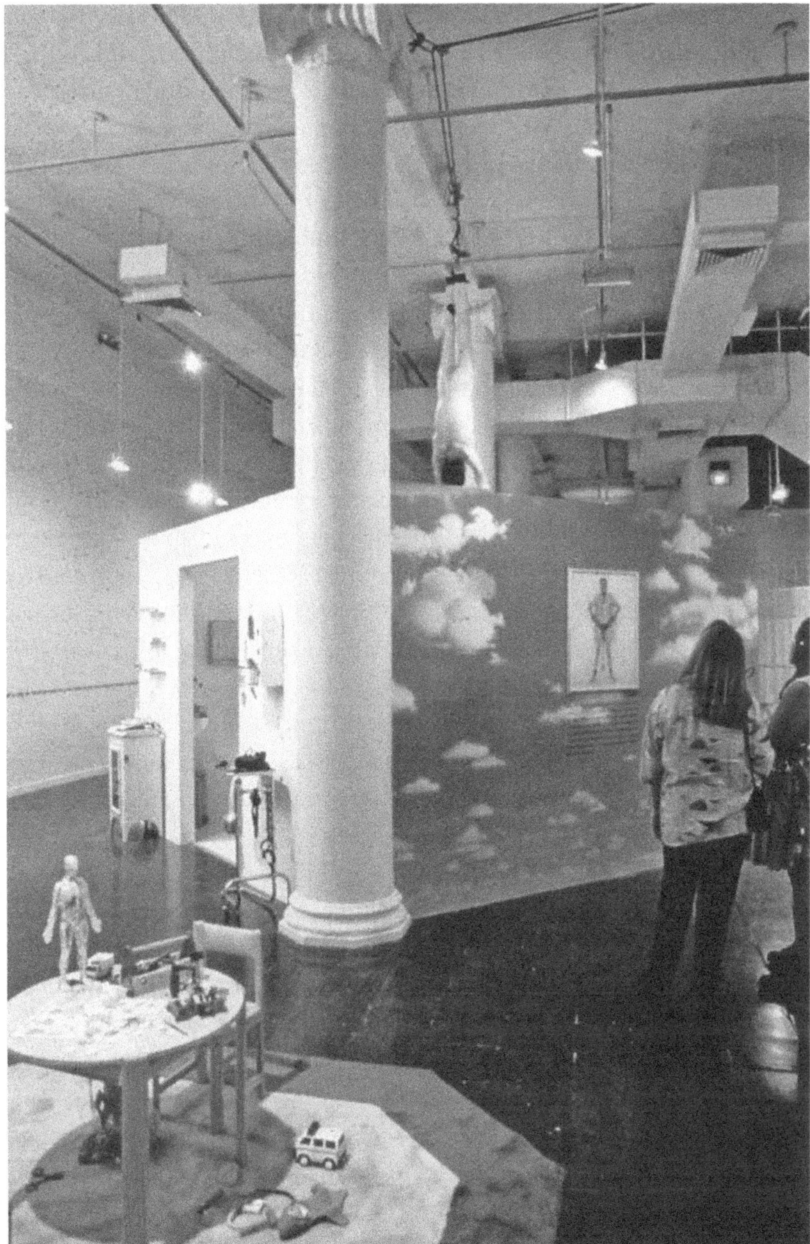

Figure 1.2 Flanagan ascending above the exhibit sky. Bob Flanagan and Sheree Rose. Exhibition: 9/23/1994–12/31/1994. Exhibition: *Visiting Hours*: An installation by Bob Flanagan in collaboration with Sheree Rose. Photo by Fred Scruton, used with permission.

was particularly concerned with what theologian Mark Jordan calls "the confession of who one is, of one's state."[80] Across Christian history, this form of confession has taken two forms. One is better known to Catholics today—it is the confession of one's sins, usually by speaking them, privately, to a priest. The other kind of confession, less familiar to modern Catholics, takes the form of a public ritual and is accomplished less through speech than through the body. It is characterized, Jordan writes, following Foucault, by a "dramatization" or "theatricalization." Foucault's key example for this confession recounts the tragic history of the fourth-century Roman matron Fabiola, who escaped a physically abusive husband and married another man. Upon the death of her second husband, Fabiola repents for her sins. It is how she repents that matters here: she does so through a dramatic act of public penance, which includes beating her face, an act that represents physically the sins she had committed. To consider this as a kind of drama, as Foucault does, should in no way undercut Fabiola's experiences of abuse—drama, in this sense, is not opposed to the serious or real. This drama is, rather, all *too* real. It marks the style of confession to which Fabiola was led. This form of confession is likened to martyrdom, Jordan explains, to the refusal of self, a refusal inscribed upon the flesh.[81]

Flanagan's performance work in many instances mimicked this form of confession. As with the example of Fabiola, it raises questions about the work of dramatization, even theatricalization, as Foucault saw it, in this older form of Christian confession. Foucault's own fascination with the dramatized ritual of Fabiola recalls for Jordan the possibilities of queer camp for offering different stylizations of the body, different relations to excess, and different uses for theatricalization. We could add: different relations to religion and different uses of religious forms. To be sure, a camp reading introduces valences of humor and irony that we do not see in Fabiola's public confession. The differences are important. But it would be a mistake to oppose humor to tragedy—or to suffering. I explore the workings of camp—and Catholic camp specifically—in chapter four of this book. For now, though, I want to suggest that such a reading, following Jordan, opens space to consider Flanagan's work—his genital crucifixion, his poem "Why?," his ascension in *Visiting Hours*—as instances of Catholic forms taken up through the mode of theatricalization.

Catholicism provides the forms, the styles, through which this work operated, offering both the occasion for humor and irony as well as the performative force of religious forms themselves. Reading for Catholic forms opens the range of work that religious references do in Flanagan's writing and performance. One of the key ironies of this work is that Flanagan enacted so many of these Catholic forms under the sign of "performance," a convention that primes viewers to read this work as insincere, acted out, or fake. A mere performance of religious forms, a dramatization of public confession. Of course, when Rose pierced his skin, he really did bleed. When she struck him during an S/M performance, he felt pain. When she hoisted him into the sky, he followed a long tradition of ascension.[82]

* * *

Consider how McRuer describes the work of religion in Flanagan's poem "Why?" Flanagan's "earnest insistence that 'Christ and the crucifixion' were responsible," he writes, "is offset by what comes next—it's difficult to sustain the importance of being earnest when Christ cavorts with Porky Pig."[83] But why should we think this reference to "Christ and the crucifixion" to be earnest? Whose earnestness is it? The author's? The reader's? The poem's? And is this earnestness sincere, if it is earnest at all? If religion, or at least normative religion, takes the form of earnestness in much of contemporary life—an inheritance from the secularization of Protestant sincerity, as some have argued—then reading Flanagan's deployment of religious forms works against this. His use of religious forms is theatrical, playful, campy. Flanagan's forms work on the surface, resisting the usual substance of true or deep religious meaning, if by true or deep we mean sincere or authentic attachment or modern forms of identity. These were not his forms.

What I want to stress here is that Flanagan's relationship to Catholicism was not simply one of rejection, liberation, or mockery; nor was it the site for religious earnestness juxtaposed to the humor of a stuttering pig. We might read it instead as a stylization, as a particular deployment of Catholic forms, that need not be attached to the sincerity too often assumed to underwrite modern religion. Following Jordan, we might read Flanagan's use of Catholic forms as a kind of camp performance that seeks to make fun and subvert meaning. In doing so, this performance works against normative definitions of religion while also illustrating the uses of religious forms in public performance, in public ritual. Camp works through habits of attachment. It works, somewhat ironically, by obeying rules, by venerating aesthetics, by exalting forms. If anything, camp might be accused of putting too much faith in forms. On one reading, perhaps what Flanagan was transgressing wasn't merely social norms regarding disability and sexuality, but also those social norms that defined him as secular and in opposition to religion—to the sacred or the transcendent.

On this reading, Flanagan's relationship to Catholicism in his performance work is not merely one of identity or belonging any more than one of transgressive liberation, but rather one of stylization. We can read him, his body, his performance, as shaped by religious power, by Catholic disciplines and aesthetics, yet also as sites through which Catholic forms become stylized toward incredible and resistant ends—which is to say, in other words, of course, toward older and newer Catholic forms, including crip Catholic forms. And if this is so, what new critiques of power—of sexual moralism, ableism, sexism, religious oppression—can these stylizations perform, not through the overthrow of power, but through its enactment otherwise?

Flanagan was right: any religious or spiritual reading of his work should make us uncomfortable. Most new forms of pedagogy do.

2

Judy Chicago's *The Dinner Party*, Feminist Myth, and the Literalism of Sex

The Dinner Party is a work of art that is women's history; women's religion; women's metaphor. It gives women something they never had—a history, a mythology, a religion, a cultural identity that is their own.[1]

—Judy Chicago

My vagina is a metaphysical question.[2]

—Judy Chicago

It started as a gesture of goodwill. In 1990, Judy Chicago, probably the best-known feminist artist working in the United States, agreed to donate *The Dinner Party* to the University of the District of Columbia (UDC), a historically Black public university in the nation's capital. First exhibited in 1979, Chicago's massively popular installation piece had become an icon of feminist art. It features thirty-nine place settings for mythical and historical women chosen to represent Western history. Each setting includes a ceramic plate painted or sculpted in the butterfly/vulvar imagery characteristic of Chicago's feminist aesthetics. The place settings are equally lined along three sides of a triangular table, each side stretching about forty-eight feet. Embroidered table runners show the name of each woman, from the Primordial Goddess to Hildegard of Bingen to Georgia O'Keeffe.[3] After several years of touring, *The Dinner Party*'s run slowed by the late 1980s, and it had been sitting in storage when Chicago began entertaining the possibility of donating it to UDC.

The university planned to house *The Dinner Party* in a new multicultural center, where it would join other works by feminist and Black artists. A known attraction, *The Dinner Party* was all but guaranteed to make back

Provoking Religion. Anthony M. Petro, Oxford University Press. © Oxford University Press 2025.
DOI: 10.1093/9780190938468.003.0003

initial money needed for necessary building upgrades to house the installation and even to raise additional funding for the cash-strapped institution. By most accounts, this was a good deal for artist and institution alike.[4] But it would soon fall apart.

UDC depended on congressional support for its funding allocations—and this opened the floodgates for political meddling. As news about the donation spread, conservative politicians and religious leaders quickly started attacking *The Dinner Party* on television, in newspapers, and on the floor of Congress. It was little more than pornography, they would claim—women's genitalia on plates. One congressman called it "weird sexual art" and questioned the "sanity" of UDC leaders who wanted to display this monument to feminist obscenity and moral decay.[5]

The Dinner Party thus became the site for one of many rhetorical battles over art, sex, and morality—one that ultimately succeeded in reversing the plan to exhibit this piece at UDC. Chicago's work would eventually find a permanent home at the Elizabeth A. Sackler Center for Feminist Art at the Brooklyn Museum, where it was installed in 2008. But this debate exceeded the question of where to house a prominent work of feminist art: it also contributed to what we might call the culture wars script, one that sets feminist or queer art against conservative visions of American morality.

And this script has endured. In 2018, the mayor of Belen, New Mexico, suggested the town create a museum to honor its most famous resident—Judy Chicago. The idea came from former Belen mayor Ronnie Torres, who was also Chicago's hairdresser and a member of the city council. Although the proposal garnered support, some residents hesitated.[6] A fellow city council member worried the museum might invite "protestors with pitchforks and torches." "Some of the art might upset the masses once they start looking up some of this stuff," he explained.[7] He was right.

Evangelical Christians in Belen mobilized against the effort to promote what one person called Chicago's "vaginas on plates." "I love fine art, but I would never want to see a vagina hanging on my wall," one resident explained. "As Christians, we are for order, justice, security and protection," said another, who continued: "I'm for protecting the eyes of the innocent, especially the children." The pastor of First Assembly of God Church in Belen raised another challenge. "We don't have a problem with freedom of expression," he explained, but he did not think tax dollars should be used to fund a museum dedicated to Chicago's work, which many locals considered pornographic.[8] This is a tried-and-true culture wars framing, positing Christianity against ostensibly secular feminist art. But if this culture wars script renders Chicago's *Dinner Party* an altar to feminist smut, others elevate it to the feminist heavens.

For many devoted fans, *The Dinner Party* has become no less than an icon of feminist art and Judy Chicago its leading prophet. One art critic writing in 1979 presciently claimed that Chicago's 1975 autobiography *Through the Flower* "has virtually become a bible," investing her work with an evangelical fervor that would only increase after the initial opening of *The Dinner Party*.[9] Over the course of the 1970s, Chicago had become a leader in the feminist art movement and what would later be called cultural feminism, a style of second-wave feminism that emphasized the particularity of women's experiences.[10] This feminist vision was largely eclipsed by the postmodern 1980s and 1990s, as critics countered the cultural and biological essentialism of cultural feminism.[11] But this spirit of feminism has nonetheless found new life.

A 2018 profile in the *New York Times* celebrated Chicago as "the Godmother," heralding her renewed "relevance" alongside a return to a kind of feminist art that had gone out of style. The profile attributed to Chicago's artistic and feminist legacy the pink "pussy hats" that have become a symbol of women's empowerment.[12] This feminist revival—and its accompanying pink hats—took shape amid Donald Trump's misogynistic presidential campaign and controversial election in November 2016, when he defeated Hillary Clinton, who many hoped would become the first woman elected to the nation's highest office. In the shadow of this stunning upset, Chicago's *Dinner Party* gave shape to the need for women to take charge of their political destiny—and maybe their spiritual destiny as well.

Indeed, this celebratory script also reveals something of *The Dinner Party*'s New Age spirituality or "specialness," to use historian of religion Ann Taves's more encompassing term to describe things "set apart."[13] Consider an example. In early March 2020, just before the COVID pandemic shut down most of the world, the Alvin Ailey School released a dance performance video commemorating the fortieth anniversary of *The Dinner Party* and celebrating International Women's Day.[14] The School—the preprofessional training program attached to the lauded Black modern choreographer's concert dance enterprise—added movement to *The Dinner Party*'s already ambitious combination of artistic media.[15] Directed by Redha Medjellekh and Katya Martín and set to music by The Stormz, the ninety-second tribute features thirty-nine dancers, one for each of *The Dinner Party*'s symbolic place settings celebrating mythical and historical women.

The Ailey piece never names feminist spirituality explicitly, but it works through a visual, embodied, and musical aesthetic that gestures in this direction. The performance has an ethereal, almost mystical quality. It works through rhythms more than words. Like much religious ritual, it collapses time and space. It commemorates Chicago's piece, but the performance also seems like it could have been assembled anytime and anywhere. The dancers offer embodied doubles for the thirty-nine women invited to the party, but they dissolve into a collective—they are individuals but go unnamed; they are Ailey dancers, but also all women, everywhere.

To say this differently, the tribute fuses the historical and the spiritual, as contemporary dancers invoke historical women like Sojourner Truth, Virginia Woolf, and Hypatia, as well as mythic goddesses of love, fertility, creation, and destruction. In this way, the performance bridges Chicago's *Dinner Party* with Ailey's aesthetic, moving between the particular and the universal—that is, between the presumed particularity of Black or feminist self-determination and the rhetoric of universalism within modernist art and dance.[16] Like *The Dinner Party* itself, the dance tribute exceeds efforts to contain it within the secular world of mere art or within a disenchanted feminist politics. In this script, *The Dinner Party* becomes feminist testimony, perhaps even a spiritual center—what historian of religion Mircea Eliade called an "axis munde," a sacred point where the heavens touch the earth, where the universal meets the particular.[17]

As these moments in the reception of *The Dinner Party* reveal, the work has lived a curious artistic, political, and spiritual life—several, in fact—since its debut in the 1970s, through its rebirths in the public spotlight in the 1990s, and more recently. Across this long career, *The Dinner Party* has been in turns lauded as a feminist masterpiece, experienced as a spiritual awakening, attacked as a relic of 1970s feminism, and lambasted as pornographic. I am interested in how these varied scripts consistently figure Chicago's work in relation to something we might want to call "religion." And to competing visions of religion. In this chapter, I don't simply want to examine how this piece got caught up in the culture wars. I want to ask: how has the same work of art that has incited accusations of obscenity also sparked feminist spiritual awakenings?

To understand these competing scripts, this chapter looks to the longer history of *The Dinner Party* and places it within the broader archives of religion in the United States. It asks how religious iconography and language have animated the cultural politics of Chicago's landmark work, which invokes not just Leonardo da Vinci's *The Last Supper*, but also the communion plate, religious mysticism, Jewish secularism, and feminist spirituality. As we will see, visitors have frequently described viewing it as a spiritual experience. But religious language has also animated critical responses, especially among feminist detractors and art critics in the 1970s and 1980s, such as one reviewer who derided it as "gaudily evangelical."[18] I read the work of this religious language alongside accusations that *The Dinner Party* is too literal, explicit, or pornographic, which also took on different meanings when Chicago's twist on the Last Supper was cast in a starring role in the culture wars politics of the 1990s.

Such accusations sometimes tapped into what I call an aesthetics of literalism (a culture wars tactic that takes center stage in chapter three). In short, this approach sees Chicago's vulvar imagery—symbolic representations—as pornography. Granted, we cannot assume that all accusations that *The Dinner Party* is pornographic are necessarily sincere (sometimes they are and sometimes they're not). But this rhetorical style has constituted the scene of much debate over feminist and queer art and leads to a series of questions: How has this politics of "seeing" this piece as "vaginas on plates" worked as a de-mythologizing and re-mythologizing tactic to incite disgust among some feminist critics and right-wing leaders alike? What does this have to do with the politics of gender that *The Dinner Party* enacts, and how have styles of religion and literalist readings shaped the work and the sexual politics viewers see enacted through it?

To answer these questions, this chapter traces *The Dinner Party*'s formation and reception, from its emergence within second-wave feminism through its arrival at the center of culture wars politics. I make three claims. First, taking up *The Dinner Party* as an object of US religious history underscores the many ways that religion has animated both the piece itself and its competing receptions. We need to understand how religion, feminism, and art came together in the decades leading up to the culture wars of the 1980s and 1990s, paying attention to the often-ignored histories of feminist spirituality. Doing so also allows us to appreciate a second claim: that conservative religious and political rhetoric has operated through a particular hermeneutics—an aesthetics of literalism—that is fundamentally reductive. It reduces feminist and queer visual art to pornography through specific pedagogies of unseeing, including unseeing the diverse religious and symbolic traditions that so often animate this artistic work. Finally, this chapter takes up Judy Chicago as no less than a mythographer—a maker of

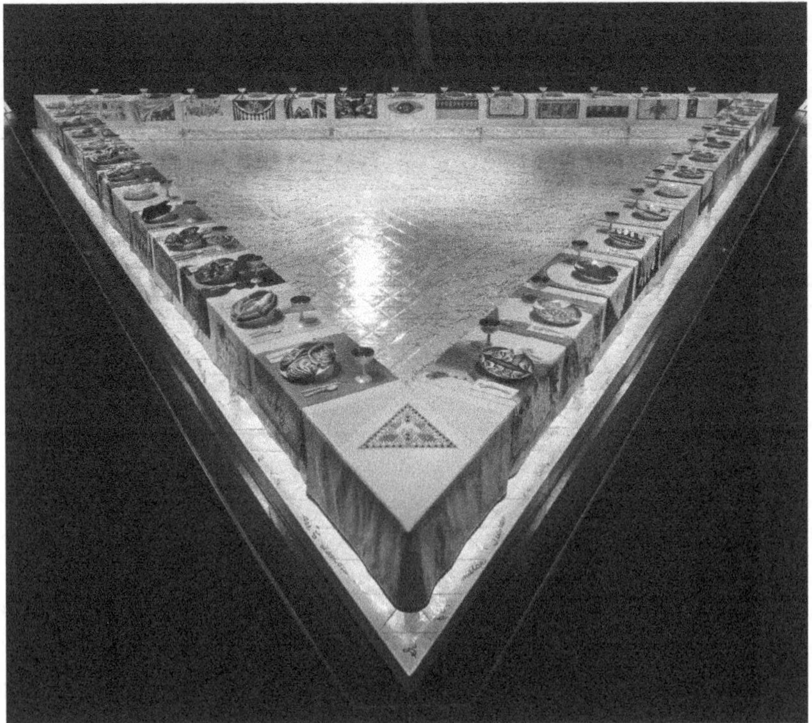

Figure 2.1 Judy Chicago, *The Dinner Party*, 1974–79. Ceramic, porcelain, textile, 576 × 576 in. (1463 × 1463 cm). Brooklyn Museum, Gift of the Elizabeth A. Sackler Foundation, 2002.10 © Judy Chicago/Artist Rights Society (ARS), New York. Photo © Donald Woodman/ARS NY.

myth—and *The Dinner Party* her most elaborate creation story. I treat *The Dinner Party* as myth not only because Chicago was herself interested in the work that myth does, but also because the analytic language of myth helps to avoid misleading tendencies to separate religion from the secular, from the artistic, and from the political.

What Is *The Dinner Party*?

The Dinner Party is many things. To start, it's a multilayered installation piece combining various artistic methods and media (Figure 2.1). But it also includes a surplus of textual components, including two books that Chicago wrote to accompany its launch. The first—titled *The Dinner Party*—tells

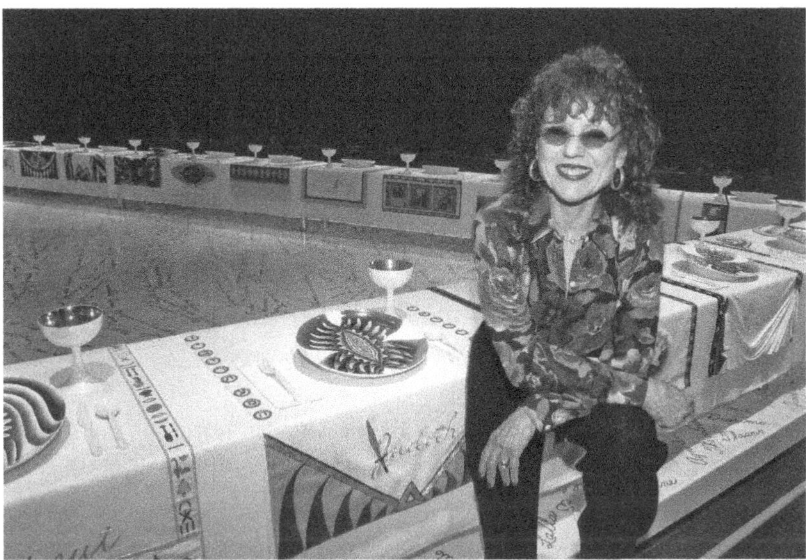

Figure 2.2 Judy Chicago with *The Dinner Party* installed in the Elizabeth A. Sackler Center for Feminist Art at the Brooklyn Museum, Brooklyn, NY, 2007. Photo © Donald Woodman/ARS NY.

its history, richly illustrates the plates, describes each guest, and includes excerpts from journals Chicago kept while working on the piece. The book also features a creation myth written by Chicago that runs across the top of every page. A second book—*Embroidering Our Heritage*—describes the rich tapestries of each place setting. But there is much more, including various *Dinner Party* gifts, commemorative reenactments, a documentary film, and even a curriculum for students called *The Dinner Party K-12*.[19]

Chicago's *Dinner Party* turns out to be a holy host of things, from the materiality of the piece itself, to the bodies and minds of the people witnessing it, to scores of texts that now accompany it, including books, interviews, and exhibition catalogues. And there is now very much written *about* Judy Chicago and *The Dinner Party*, waves of responses—criticisms and celebrations—that change with shifting political and aesthetic winds. What *The Dinner Party* is, then, remains to some degree an ongoing revelation. Although I will try to capture here some of the things that it is, focusing on the installation now housed at the Brooklyn Museum, we should also keep in mind questions about what *The Dinner Party* does, how it affects the people who encounter it, and what people do with *The Dinner Party* and why.

I first saw *The Dinner Party* at the Brooklyn Museum, where I've now taken many friends to see it with me. The exhibit begins with a short walkway decorated with six banners. Each includes a line of poetry:

> *And She Gathered All before Her*
> *And She made for them A Sign to See*
> *And lo They saw a Vision*
> *From this day forth Like to like in All things*
> *And then all that divided them merged*
> *And then Everywhere was Eden Once again*[20]

Past the hall of banners, one enters the large room featuring *The Dinner Party*'s enormous, triangular table and assorted place settings. It sits over the "Heritage Floor," which includes white tiles bearing the names of an additional 999 women in handwritten gold script.[21] The room is dark. The primary source of light illuminates the table from above, making it seem to glow. The table includes three wings, each bearing place settings for thirteen mythical or historical women. Even though *The Dinner Party* is triangular, rather than linear, one can move about the table chronologically, from prehistorical figures like Ishtar and the Snake Goddess to twentieth-century figures like Margaret Sanger and Virginia Woolf. *The Dinner Party*'s first wing moves from prehistory to classical Rome. It begins with the Primordial Goddess, a reference to the early Goddess traditions that many feminists celebrated in the 1970s. The setting includes a porcelain plate hand-painted with the butterfly/ vulvar iconography that would become a signature of Chicago's art, part of what she and fellow artist Miriam Schapiro called feminist or central core imagery. The colors combine dark reds and bright tans, recalling flesh and earth. In her book *The Dinner Party*, Chicago explains how the Primordial Goddess also represents the "Primal Vagina," the ultimate source of life and creativity, and the "Sacred Vessel," "the gateway to existence and the doorway to the abyss."[22] The plate sits atop a handwoven runner that bears a calfskin decorated with cowry shells and a coil—a common symbol of the feminine divine, Chicago explains—that recalls both pottery and women's crafts, such as basketmaking.[23] This wing, which also includes a setting for the Amazon women of Greek mythology, the ancient Egyptian pharaoh Hatshepsut, and the poet Sappho, concludes with a setting for philosopher and mathematician Hypatia of Alexandria. If the first wing celebrates feminine divinity, creativity, and brilliance, the second wing recalls darker times in Western history, after men usurped the power of the goddesses, and women struggled for equality. It moves from early Western Christianity to the Reformation, starting with a place set for Marcella, an early Christian monastic and later Catholic saint, and concludes with Anna Maria van Schurman, a Dutch poet, scholar, and champion of women's education.

The final wing presents women's rise and hope for future equality, both symbolically and literally. Symbolically, the guests in this wing demonstrate women's increasing freedom and creative potential, starting with a place set for Anne Hutchinson, the Puritan exiled from the Massachusetts Bay Colony for challenging the authority of the male clergy. She's joined by Sacagawea, the Shoshone translator who aided the Lewis and Clark expedition; Mary Wollstonecraft, who authored *A Vindication of the Rights of Woman* in 1792; abolitionist and suffragist Sojourner Truth; and women's rights leader Susan B. Anthony. The wing also includes settings for several literary and artistic lights, ending with British novelist Virginia Woolf and American painter Georgia O'Keeffe. The plates in this wing literally rise: sculptural elements emerge from the plates and crescendo into the almost muscular folds of O'Keeffe's plate. The sculptural forms represent a combination of liberation and power, the culmination of the female core imagery animating the installation more generally. Yet, in Chicago's design, even O'Keeffe's imagery ultimately remains grounded, unable to take flight from the table, a symbol of freedom yet to come.[24]

Of course, such descriptions fail to capture the full work—what it is like to experience it, to look at each individual plate and runner and the larger Heritage Floor beneath it. The piece is choreographed to appear monumental, each setting an altar and the full experience a transformative witnessing. I have observed many spectators surprised by the sheer magnitude and overwhelmed by the complexity of *The Dinner Party*. It's not obvious, without prior knowledge or paying very close attention to directions provided by the museum, how to observe it—that the logic of the piece, though triangular, moves from myth, to ancient history, to modern history. Like many observers, some of whom I've seen crack a smile or let out an unexpected laugh, I have found *The Dinner Party*'s reimagining of the Last Supper in turns funny and earnest. Its sexual politics, as much as the mix of colors, patterns, and textures, feel very grounded in its moment—the 1970s—even if its curatorial context seeks to transcend this history. So what was that moment? How do we understand *The Dinner Party* in the context of the 1970s, including the histories of religion, politics, and feminist art that shaped it?

Judy Chicago, Los Angeles Art, and Second-Wave Feminism

To situate *The Dinner Party* in the history of religion requires understanding the artistic and feminist contexts that shaped it. By the time Chicago began working on *The Dinner Party* in the mid-1970s, she had already made a name for herself as an artist and as a leading voice in US feminism—a "cult figure in the women's art movement," as one art critic maintained.[25] How did she gain this status?

Chicago, then called Judy Cohen, was born in 1939 in Chicago, Illinois. In her most recent autobiography—she has three—Chicago recalls her parents Arthur and May Cohen as "Jewish liberals" who provided her the freedom, even as a young girl, to pursue her own interests and goals. Her goal was to become an artist. And, in 1957, Chicago moved to Los Angeles to pursue this calling as a student at the University of California, Los Angeles (UCLA). She later spent a year in New York with Jerry Gerowitz, who would become her first husband in 1961, before returning to UCLA. Now Judy Gerowitz, she graduated in 1962 with a bachelor's degree in fine arts. Tragedy struck the following year, when Jerry was killed in a car accident. Amid this devastation, Chicago turned to art, and she decided to continue her education at UCLA, completing an MFA in painting and sculpture in 1964.

During these years, Chicago dove headfirst into the Los Angeles art world, which would shape her later work in significant ways. In the 1960s, this scene was becoming known for its particular aesthetic approach called the "L.A. look" or "finish fetish," which combined pop art and minimalism in very sleek, abstract, and often sculptural pieces. Art historian Laura Meyer explains that the "allure" of finish fetish arose from "its meticulous erasure of labor, which produces the illusion of casual mastery, a mastery that is the result of masculine know-how and technical prowess."[26] To fit into this male-dominated scene, Chicago learned to mimic the masculine bravado of her peers and fought to ensure that her work received the same consideration as that of male artists. She also played with masculinist aesthetics by creating "increasingly smaller and more playful works that challenged the heroic (and implicitly masculinist) pretensions of minimalism."[27]

Even as Chicago gained recognition for her abstract painting and sculpture, she bristled under the sexist culture of the LA art world and American society more broadly. In 1965, while sharing studio space with her romantic partner and fellow artist Lloyd Hamrol, Chicago recalls, artists and gallery owners would regularly drop by, only to overlook her work in favor of his. At one point, Hamrol even covered a piece of his work until a curator would look at Chicago's art first.[28] Hamrol and Chicago married later that year. This time, though, Chicago did not take her husband's last name. She instead chose a name that lacked any connection to familial patriarchy—neither her father's name nor her husband's. This is how Judy Cohen, who became Judy Gerowitz, finally emerged as Judy Chicago.

And she did not keep this early feminist act quiet. The name change was publicized in the pages of *Artforum* in an exhibition announcement for a show in 1970. Along with images of Chicago sporting short hair, a headband, and sunglasses, the announcement included a statement written in cursive: "Judy Gerowitz hereby divests herself of all names imposed upon her through male social dominance and freely chooses her own name: Judy Chicago." Chicago later recalled the unsettling irony of the situation, which was that Hamrol had to sign the papers making the change legal.[29]

Forging Feminist Art

That same year—1970—Chicago began teaching at Fresno State University (now California State University-Fresno), where she founded a cutting-edge feminist art education project. Over the next several years, Chicago grappled in her artistic practice with the long-standing elevation of aesthetic form over content, as she tried to bridge her training in abstract art with the rising concerns of second-wave feminism. During her year in Fresno, Chicago learned on the spot, alongside her students, what it meant to teach, learn, and practice feminist art. She would also begin conversations with Miriam Schapiro, who had recently moved to the newly founded California Institute of the Arts (CalArts), about bringing the feminist art program there, where she hoped it would find greater institutional support. By the fall of 1971, the Feminist Art Program at CalArts would officially launch, with Chicago and Schapiro at the helm.

The Feminist Art Program would eventually leave its stamp on the LA art world and make waves far beyond Southern California. But Chicago, Schapiro, and their students were starting from scratch. They first needed to find studio space, which was not available on campus at the start of the school year.[30] They eventually rented a dilapidated Victorian mansion in

Hollywood and worked together to repair the space, which had sat empty for decades. The demands of the renovation required students to learn presumably masculine skills related to construction and repair that at first seemed far afield of feminist education. But for Chicago this was critical. Women artists needed to learn to create their own space. Doing so would further empower them, providing trade skills but also a sense of agency and seriousness that could be applied to their art. The students also had to learn to work together, and they often drew on the feminist practices of consciousness raising and collective cooperation as part of the process.

The hard work paid off. In 1972, Chicago and Schapiro led their students in opening Womanhouse, widely regarded as the first major public exhibition of feminist art. The renovated seventeen-room mansion featured various installations—including Kathy Huberland's *Bridal Staircase*, Sandra Orgel's *Linen Closet*, and *The Dollhouse Room* by Sherrie Brodie and Miriam Schapiro—that thematized women's experiences in "the home." Chicago contributed an installation piece called *Menstruation Bathroom*, which highlighted sexist taboos around women's bodies, and wrote a play called *Cock and Cunt*, performed by Faith Wilding and Jan Lester, which satirized gender stereotypes and domestic violence. The opening of the Womanhouse exhibition proved a critical moment in the history of feminist art. In addition to its roughly ten thousand visitors, Womanhouse reached an even larger audience when it became the subject of Johanna Demetrakas's 1974 documentary film *Womanhouse*.[31] Despite this success, Schapiro and Chicago started to disagree about the future of their program. Chicago wanted to find a space for feminist art outside of male-dominated institutions like CalArts, from which she resigned at the end of her two-year contract in the spring of 1973. Her next move would again change the course of art history.

Along with graphic designer Sheila de Bretteville and art historian Arlene Raven, Chicago started the Feminist Studio Workshop, through which they would open the Los Angeles Woman's Building in the fall of 1973. It quickly became a key center for feminist visual art and performance, offering not only formal education in feminist art but also an institutional home for feminist activism and writing that would include, at various moments, key leaders such as Kate Millett, Audre Lorde, and Adrienne Rich. In 1977, Raven and Terry Wolverton founded the groundbreaking Lesbian Art Project there. In short, the Woman's Building, writes art critic Lucy Lippard, "was the capital of cultural feminism, where the spiritual and the political met and rowdily merged."[32]

Chicago's "Cunts"

For the opening of the Woman's Building, Chicago exhibited work from her *Great Ladies* series, paintings that honored women in history who "transcended" their gendered roles, including Queen Victoria, Marie Antoinette, Catherine the Great, and Christina of Sweden.[33] There were three key elements of this earlier work that Chicago would further develop for *The Dinner Party*. First, *Great Ladies* evinces Chicago's increasing interest in researching and recovering the historical and literary importance of women and her identification with women across time and space.[34] Second, in creating this series, Chicago found herself beginning to write directly onto her paintings, bringing feminist content more explicitly into her abstract imagery. "When I made abstract images of my feelings," she recalled, "many people did not know how to 'read' those images. By writing about the idea I was working with visually, perhaps the viewer would then be able to recognize the meaning of the image." In this way, Chicago explained, "I would be educating people to understand my work while they were looking at it."[35] Finally, these works share the emerging visual aesthetic, called "female core imagery" or "central core imagery," for which Chicago—and *The Dinner Party*—would be in turns lauded for recovering an essential female experience, criticized for espousing biological essentialism, and blasted for publicizing pornographic artwork. The visual language of *Great Ladies* is abstract, floral—the paintings feature geometric and wave patterns spiraling around a core with various shades of pink, blue, yellow, and orange. In *Transformation Painting–Great Ladies Transforming Themselves into Butterflies*, created in 1973, Chicago takes this visual imagery further, moving from square, to circular, to butterfly forms, as the great ladies progress toward freedom.[36]

In her 1975 autobiography, Chicago describes her journey to this new aesthetic approach, which she based on her experience as a woman. She was writing before many leading US feminists began to disarticulate sex from gender, much less to interrogate the assumptions of cisnormativity. Her language gestures both to biological or embodied experiences and to cultural experiences of femininity.[37] In aesthetic terms, Chicago recalls moving from sculptural dome shapes toward two-dimensional renderings. The rounded forms came out "blobby, undefined," which she likens to her sense of self.[38] Chicago added additional forms with darkened centers. "I felt the darkness in my stomach as a sense of wrongness," she writes, as if there was something wrong with *me*, and I knew that I was going into the place inside me that had been made to feel wrong by my experiences in a male-dominated world. I opened the forms and let them stand for my body experience. The closed forms transmuted into doughnuts, stars, revolving mounds representing cunts. . . . I chose that format to express what it was like to be organized around a central core, my vagina, that which made me a woman.[39]

Chicago directly addresses using the derogatory word "cunt" in her work. "I use the word 'cunt' deliberately," she writes, "for it embodies society's contempt for women. In turning the word around, I hope to turn society's definition of the female around and make it positive, instead of negative."[40] Many other feminists agreed, as the word became commonplace in this artistic milieu and part of what would be called "cunt art." At one point, Chicago even found herself surrounded by the "cunt cheerleaders," younger feminist artists donning cheer drag who played on the joy found in this reclamation.[41]

Chicago elaborated her aesthetic approach in "Female Imagery," a groundbreaking essay cowritten with Miriam Schapiro that appeared in the feminist magazine *Womanspace* in 1973. They survey works from several women artists—from Emily Carr and Lee Bontecou to Barbara Hepworth and Georgia O'Keeffe—to theorize the existence of a common or core female imagery. Their own work provided examples, too, including Schapiro's 1967 painting *Big Ox* and Chicago's 1971 piece *Desert Fan*. Reaching across history, they suggest a universal women's experience undergirding these aesthetics forms—a move that fits squarely within the cultural feminism of this moment. But they also resist understandings of this central female imagery as merely biological or essentialist in an anatomical way, explaining that it "must not be seen in a simplistic sense as 'vaginal or womb art.'" They draw a connection between embodiment and identity. "We are suggesting," they continue:

that women artists have used the central cavity which defines them as women as the framework for an imagery which allows for the complete reversal of the way in which women are seen by culture. That is, to be a woman is to be an object of contempt, and the vagina, stamp of femaleness, is devalued. The woman artist, seeing herself as loathed, takes that very mark of her otherness and by asserting it as the hallmark of her iconography, establishes a vehicle by which to state the truth and beauty of her identity.[42]

Here, Chicago and Schapiro describe the vagina as a "stamp of femaleness" that women artists take as a "mark" of otherness, one they can reassert in their iconography. If they sometimes employ biologically grounded claims as well, in this passage they remain more within a field of gendered meanings than one of anatomical destinies. This tension would endure.

Finally, their essay seeks to bridge "female" identity and the universality of this imagery, a universality not only among women, which would be a standard claim in essentialist feminist rhetoric, but among both male and female identities. "The central image assumes universality in these works," they explain, "because it is used to define first, the nature of female identity and then, the nature of human identity and the human dilemma. The sense of double identity, both male and female, has allowed these artists to reveal all of the contradictions of life, unified within the image of female self which becomes the house of life."[43] These lines show Chicago and Schapiro struggling to find language to describe something new to their moment, something they consider tethered to the embodied experience of ciswomen, emerging from histories of gender discrimination, and at the same time common to both male and female identities. This is not to say that the sex essentialism that later feminist, queer, and trans activists would criticize is not to be found here, too. It is there. But we can also see in this essay, and in Chicago's work generally, how unstable this essentialism was, shot through with history, contingency, and a universality not limited to women—an effort to allow "women" to stand in as the universal every bit as much as "men" have throughout history.[44]

Chicago taught in the Woman's Building for only about a year before moving back to her own studio, where she would develop many of the themes of her *Great Ladies* series—including its core imagery, feminist history, and didactic writing—into her most well-known piece of art.

Creating *The Dinner Party*

The Dinner Party took five years to create, partly because Chicago's vision for the project kept expanding. At first, she wanted to build on *Great Ladies* by transposing the idea onto a series of plates displayed on a wall to represent how women "had been swallowed up and obscured by history."[45] An early version was subtitled "Twenty-Five Women Who Were Eaten Alive," but Chicago wanted to shift the focus from women being consumed to women as models.[46] Eventually, she decided on hosting a dinner party—a play on Leonardo's all-male *Last Supper* but also a challenge to it. Where were the women at that dinner, Chicago wondered? How has women's work been ignored in history and art? Chicago wasn't the first feminist artist to reimagine Leonardo's classic. In 1972, Mary Beth Edelson created a collage, called *Some Living American Women Artists*, that replaced the faces of Christ and his disciples with images of women artists. Fittingly, Georgia O'Keeffe took center stage as the feminist host. But Chicago would take *The Last Supper* in yet another direction.

Chicago created not a last supper of men but a first dinner for women. She was drawn to the idea of inviting thirteen guests to her feminist revision, a number that mirrored not only that of Jesus and his twelve apostles but also, she explains, the number of women in a coven of witches.[47] "So the same number that is associated with masculine holiness," Chicago explained in a 1979 interview, "is associated with feminine evil!"[48] But thirteen seats at the table was still not enough. To allow for more guests, Chicago shifted to a triangular table, with thirteen spots on each side, bringing the number to thirty-nine. As it evolved, *The Dinner Party* required a massive team of assistants, mostly women, who helped with needlework, ceramics, research, fundraising, and other aspects of the project. Over a hundred members of the project offered long-term assistance, but closer to four hundred would help in some way or another. As news of *The Dinner Party* spread, so did grassroots support for the project, and visitors would often join for a day or two to lend their time and take part in the experience. Although this was a cooperative effort, Chicago remained in creative control of the project, which she saw as following the model of apprentices working with a master.[49] Though critics would later charge that Chicago exploited the women who aided with *The Dinner Party*, most expressed gratitude for the opportunity to participate.[50]

To create *The Dinner Party*, Chicago and her team researched the history of women in "Western civilization."[51] In the mid-1970s, women's history, like most programs in women's studies generally, was only just forming.[52] Researchers for *The Dinner Party* scoured available histories and catalogues for records and information about the women they hoped to include, not only the mythical goddesses and historical figures seated at the table, but also the additional 999 women named on the Heritage Floor. They also researched needlework techniques to make period-specific runners for each place setting, as detailed in Chicago's *Embroidering Our Heritage*. In doing so, Chicago centered women's crafts as art—joining artists like Faith Ringgold and Sheila Hicks, who increasingly employed such materials and methods in the 1970s and 1980s—thus subverting the longstanding sexism found in the art world's elevation of masculine art over feminized crafts.[53]

Chicago's guest list for her *Dinner Party* represented both the revolutionary efforts and the limitations of much feminist practice at the time. It does so in the ways her cultural feminism focused on separating out a space for women, even inverting masculine forms by placing women at the center, as we see in this send-up of *The Last Supper*. And it does so in the reclamation of "women" as a shared, even universal, identity that trumped other kinds of difference, including race, class, and sexuality, and that left little intentional room for trans experience or politics.[54] As Jane Gerhard explains in her wonderful history of *The Dinner Party*, "concern with establishing women as a class of people discriminated against because of their female bodies—a view articulated predominantly by white middle-class women—was woven into *The Dinner Party* while other concerns (welfare rights, women of color feminism, lesbian and gay discrimination, to name a few) were not."[55]

Several Black feminists viewing *The Dinner Party* have noted its limitations, not simply in the selection of guests but also in its visual representation. Nearly all the *Dinner Party* plates appear to feature Chicago's vulvar/butterfly imagery but two—those for Black abolitionist Sojourner Truth and white composer Ethel Smyth—though accounts vary on this point. Alice Walker penned an early critique in 1979 charging that the Truth plate was the lone exception, "the only one in the collection that shows—instead of a vagina—a face. In fact, three faces."[56] Artist Lorraine O'Grady made a similar observation, setting *The Dinner Party* within the "unseeing erasure" of Black women from popular culture to high art. "Of the 39 places at Chicago's dinner table," O'Grady writes, "38 are set with plates painted with vaginas that glow miraculously. Sojourner Truth, the only black guest, must make it without a pussy." Truth instead has a face, she continues, "and not one but three: one screaming, one smiling, and one weeping a clichéd tear."[57] Walker suggests, "perhaps white women feminists, no less than white women generally, cannot imagine black women have vaginas. Or if they can, where imagination leads them is too far to go."[58] Building on this reading, cultural theorist Hortense Spillers describes Truth's plate as no less than a "symbolic castration."[59]

While Walker, O'Grady, and Spillers singled out Truth's depiction, art critic Lucy Lippard considered the sole outlier to be Ethel Smyth's plate, which depicts a piano to honor the English composer. Lippard acknowledges Walker's criticism but nonetheless sees some semblance of Chicago's core metaphorical imagery in Truth's plate. "In fact," she writes, "the image is still there, composed of three faces–a weeping one at the left, a fierce image of masked strength at the right, and a still more schematic central image of 'hidden feelings.'"[60] My own sense is that the plates honoring both Truth and Smyth break the iconographic conventions of the other plates in curious ways, though this need not contravene the apt criticism of Truth's plate, which is also burdened to represent the only Black woman at the table.[61]

Even if Truth's plate is not the only outlier, Spillers's reading of it as a form of symbolic castration is suggestive. Her psychoanalytic figuration might also lead us to ask about the work of granting vaginal forms to some of the mythic goddesses, to ask what kinds of work this granting or withholding of female symbolism enacts, what kinds of fantasies it conjures or forecloses. Stepping back, we might ask: how do we make sense of the various elements that went into creating *The Dinner Party*, from the cooperative teamwork that included feminist consciousness raising to the female imagery, from the mythical and historical women to the connections made across time and textiles in the creation of the runners, from its historical antecedents to the utopian feminist fantasies it fosters? There are many ways to answer these questions and many answers to them. I want to propose one, which is that *The Dinner Party* is no less than a work of mythology woven by Chicago and her cooperative team.

Religion around the Table

Chicago experienced a curious epiphany early in the process of making *The Dinner Party*. Though she had not given up on achieving success within the art world, she often found greater support outside of it. In the winter of 1975, she recalled in an interview, the College of St. Catherine (now St. Catherine University) in Minnesota organized an exhibition that included miniature porcelain models of her plates. Chicago described how dismissive the art world had been of such work, discarding it as "nothing but vaginas."[62] "What they really are is metaphysical," she insisted, and concerned with "what it means to be 'feminine,' and with what the word 'feminine' means in the whole history of civilization."[63] If the art world couldn't see these meanings, she continued, the nuns at St. Catherine, a women's college founded by the Sisters of St. Joseph of Carondelet, could.

"The nuns knew," Chicago explained: "they understood that I was struggling with the issue of making the *feminine holy.*" The nuns' understanding lent new authority to Chicago's project, which was no longer merely about making art, but about making a new sacred. "And that was fascinating to me," she continued: "Here I am a Jewish woman, right? And the *nuns* understood."[64] Chicago also found a "gold mine" of books that explored the longer history of matriarchal culture, showing how "all of the early female figures (such as goddesses, priestesses, queens, warriors, and so forth) were transmogrified into Christian figures (saints)." The nuns got it, she suggested, because "Christianity was built right on top of all of those earlier religions—most of which had been matriarchal."[65]

Chicago's account of this visit to the College of St. Catherine gestures to key religious elements that have shaped *The Dinner Party*. Most important, we see Chicago's investment in the feminine divine—something that, to her surprise, the nuns could also see. The surprise comes, perhaps, because the religious culture of the nuns would seem opposed to the sexual symbolism of the plates. Yet, Chicago suggests, they saw beyond the mere sexual to the metaphysical, to the larger project of making the feminine holy. The nuns saw this, we learn, because their very Christianity was built atop this tradition of matriarchal spirituality. This feminist spirituality and Christian history would join Chicago's own Jewish background to shape her greatest work.

The feminist political and artistic impulses behind *The Dinner Party* emerge from these broader religious currents, especially feminist spirituality, postwar Judaism, and Catholicism. Most scholarly and popular accounts of *The Dinner Party* tend to secularize it—even much of Chicago's discussion moves in this direction, as the piece becomes something of a history lesson, a pedagogical exercise meant to symbolize women's history. To the extent that scholarly accounts take note of religion in *The Dinner Party*, they usually highlight its Christian and Goddess movement iconography and, perhaps, mention Chicago's Jewishness. But readers learn quickly that Chicago was no goddess worshiper herself.[66] She was mostly regarded as a secular feminist—and has described herself this way—during the time she was making *The Dinner Party*. Writing in the late 1980s, Chicago explained, "I have never been particularly interested in the goddess rituals that developed in feminist culture. After all, I never believed in a male god or God; why would a change in gender alter my fundamentally anti-religious stance?"[67] Rather, Chicago says, what grabbed her attention was the abundance of goddess imagery found in the historical record.

Nor, in most tellings, is *The Dinner Party* regarded as especially Jewish. In the 1980s and 1990s, Chicago would take up Jewish themes more intentionally and explicitly in works like *Holocaust Project: From Darkness into Light* (1985–93), for which she collaborated with her husband Donald Woodman. In her solo exhibition *Judy Chicago: Cohanim* (2021–22), she playfully explored a shared rabbinic heritage with lyricist Leonard Cohen. "Leonard Cohen's lyrics often seemed to perfectly express my feelings at various points in my life," Chicago explained: "I am so deeply moved by the rhythms that inform his music, perhaps because of our shared lineage. He is the grandson of a Talmudic scholar and I am descended from twenty-three generations of rabbis."[68] These works found Chicago researching her own Jewish heritage alongside the history of the Holocaust, the remembrance of which has become a cornerstone of Jewish American practice since the 1960s.[69]

But Chicago's earlier work is often understood as secular and feminist rather than Jewish. Until recently, Chicago has also underplayed Jewish influences on early work like *The Dinner Party*. In *Through the Flower*, her first autobiography, Chicago nods to her Jewish upbringing, underscoring the Jewish ethics she learned as a young girl. But in her telling, this upbringing had little impact on her art, which was shaped more by feminism than Judaism.[70] Art historian Lisa Bloom makes a stronger point, contending that Chicago's feminist politics grew from her commitment to traditional art historical conventions of "quality" and "the 'artist-genius'" in ways that led to "her public erasure of her Jewish ethnicity."[71] Chicago's choice to rename herself from the Jewish-marked "Gerowitz" to the seemingly ethnically unmarked "Chicago" becomes a case in point.[72] For Bloom, this quest for feminist autonomy simultaneously masked her Jewishness, as the elevation of gender as the primary concern among feminist artists like Chicago obscured the realities of intersectional oppression (a point, she notes, that Chicago herself later acknowledged).[73] Bloom argues that the way *The Dinner Party* draws upon Christian imagery—especially through its invocations of *The Last Supper*—likewise contributes to a larger racialized image.

Visual studies scholar Nancy Ring builds on this point, arguing that Chicago's choices suggest an effort at "claiming whiteness."[74] As *The Dinner Party*'s historical narrative progresses, she writes, "scores of Jewish women lose their Jewish markings."[75] In its effort to capture gender solidarity, in other words, Chicago's work elevates sexism over antisemitism or racism.[76] As Bloom puts it, *The Dinner Party*, "dominated by famous Anglo-American and European women who are mostly Christian, avoids even a 'managed' harmony among ethnic groups," including ethnically Jewish people.[77] Indeed, responses to *The Dinner Party* in the late 1970s and early 1980s, whether positive or negative, used specifically Christian terms. Fans and critics alike, nearly all white, might have been imposing their own Christianizing gaze in such discussions or, following Bloom and Ring, may simply have picked up on the piece's own commitments to Christian symbolism.

During the years I've been researching *The Dinner Party*, I kept thinking there was more to the story than this—that there is a Jewish sensibility to the piece that needs further exploration. Drawing on Jewish history and the tools of religious studies helps us to see how Jewish forms animate *The Dinner Party*. In part, we see these forms in Chicago's very interest in history itself and in the formation of women's culture. Historian David Biale argues that "secular Jews often describe their relationship to their identities in terms of history."[78] What he means by this, for instance, is that many secular Jews read the Hebrew Bible, not for religious or spiritual inspiration, but "as a prescription for social justice or as a document of culture." The sacred text becomes a historical narrative of collective Jewish identity. But, Biale insists, this historical approach is not "merely academic or antiquarian." Rather, "modern Jews have created their own secular versions of collective Jewish memory, often grounded in nontheological readings of the Bible as well as in later history."[79] Of course, one may argue that we should better parse Jewish religion from Jewish culture—and secular from religious forms of Jewish practice. American Jewish studies scholar Rachel Gross has addressed this too-easy separation of religion from culture. "When Jewish communal leaders and sociologists distinguish between Jewish culture and Jewish religion," she writes, "many of the ways that American Jews create individual and communal meaning in their lives are flattened or erased."[80] Biale and Gross help us to see how what appears to be a secular refusal of religion—say, in Chicago's description of her relationship to feminist spirituality or Jewishness—is more layered than it first appears.

In this instance, Chicago's work may well demonstrate less a secular refusal *tout court* than a specifically modern *Jewish* response, one that emphasizes historical narrative as a route to collective memory and creation. In fact, Chicago has recently said as much in a reappraisal of her early work. While writing this chapter I stumbled upon a series of short pieces from 2011, for which *Moment Magazine* asked Jewish writers and artists to consider the "origins of Jewish creativity." According to Chicago, "when I started studying Jewish culture and history, I realized that the way I had formulated *The Dinner Party*—this was at the height of Modernism—was to teach women's history through art, which completely contradicted all the Modernist impulses." And where did this impulse come from? "I'm sure that comes from my rabbinic tradition," she responds: "It seeped into my pores."[81] Chicago's anti-modernist impulse, her artistic focus on history and pedagogy, arises in this reading from her own Jewish upbringing.

There is another Jewish style that shapes *The Dinner Party*—humor. At least one journalist has described Chicago as "a woman of great humor," and that sense of humor often comes through in the ways she plays with biblical stories and religious imagery.[82] Her fusion of humor and religion sits within longer histories of Jewish humor. In *Funny, You Don't Look Funny*, religious studies scholar Jennifer Caplan traces the history and meaning of "Jewish humor" from the Silent Generation to the present generation. Comedians like Woody Allen, Mel Brooks, and Amy Schumer have reworked Jewish texts and traditions through various means, including parody.[83] For Caplan, humor and parody become additional ways that Jewish Americans perform their Judaism. We see this in much of Chicago's work.

The Dinner Party is many things—and one of those things is funny. Early writers and critics often noted the "deliberate irony" of Chicago's work, as one writer put it.[84] In *The Dinner Party*, we see that irony in the use of feminist imagery and crafts to compose a work of high art—and in the combination of feminist sexuality with liturgical seriousness. While not all irony is comedic, too often the comedy of *The Dinner Party* has come from making fun of it, rather than seeing humor in the work itself and having fun with it. This mocking humor comes through in a long history of clever wordplay poking fun at *The Dinner Party*, often rendering it an exercise in overly serious or hysterical feminist schooling.[85] At the risk of stating the obvious, though, it shouldn't be hard to find the humor—Chicago's humor—in recasting *The Last Supper* with a table of vulvar forms. Indeed, comedians Mo Gaffney and Kathy Najimy recognized the humor of this move in their early 1990s show *Parallel Lives*, which included a scene playing on Chicago's work. Two women enter a health food restaurant called Las Hermanas (the Sisters) as part of a women's studies event. They observe the art on the walls. One lauds a "vibrant" watercolor, before her friend quips, "No, it's not a floral water color. It's a vagina on a plate."[86] Deliberately or not, though, so many critics miss *The Dinner Party*'s humor—feminist, Jewish, or otherwise—and in doing so miss another way that American Jewishness animates the work.

One might wonder how serving up vulvar imagery on dinner plates would not strike one as funny, as if it never crossed Chicago's mind. I want to suggest two reasons: gender and religion. First, in her study of comedy and feminist readings of the Bible, Melissa Jackson captures a long-standing stereotype when she writes: "feminists (and by extension, their work) are by nature serious, and comedy is by nature inherently carefree, clearly a dichotomous construct that would prohibit any collaboration between these two."[87] Christopher Hitchens, one of the four horsemen of New Atheism, leaned into this stereotype in the pages of *Vanity Fair* when he pronounced, "Women aren't funny."[88] And if women aren't funny, feminists have no chance. Second, we often assume religion itself to be earnest and patently unfunny. Hitchens even drew both together. "In all cultures," he averred, "it is females who are the rank-and-file mainstay of religion, which in turn is the official enemy of all humor."[89]

It's probably fitting that someone who spent so much of his career dicking around couldn't see the impotence of his own thinking. But he was far from alone. The refusal to understand that both feminist art and religion could be funny—often drawing on parody, irony, or camp—has also shaped *The Dinner Party*. But there is a more nuanced point here. The deliberate humor of Chicago's *Dinner Party* competes with an earnest streak. As the piece has become more well known, more institutional, and more didactic, the earnestness risks taking over. Art historian Viki Wylder writes that the elements of pop art and Happenings in Chicago's installation "are all transformed by an earnest rather than a jaded attitude."[90] To be jaded is hip, even masculine, and sometimes funny; to be earnest is to risk humor for sentimentality. *The Dinner Party*—or at least its viewers—cannot quite hold together the work's humorous elements under the pressure to make it speak seriously to the needs of women's history—or to make the feminine holy. This is one of the rich tensions of the piece. It's a tension built into *The Dinner Party* myth.

Chicago, the Mythographer

Chicago is a mythographer, a maker of myths, and *The Dinner Party* remains her greatest story. Let me explain what I mean. When scholars of religion talk about myth, we rarely use the term in its colloquial sense, in which it names a falsehood—like when one dismisses something as "just a myth." Rather, myths are narrative stories that structure people's lives and give meaning to them. Historian of religion Bruce Lincoln defines myth as "a discursive act through which actors evoke the sentiments out of which society is actively constructed."[91] Granted, those meanings or sentiments can be or can feel true or untrue, but that doesn't necessarily make myth less powerful. The thing about myths is that people don't really have to "believe in" them—nor must they be "real," in a modern sense—to matter. They often work on us whether we believe in them or not. In this sense, myths are less descriptive than performative: myths do things.

Like many feminists writing at the time, Chicago knew this well. When asked how Marxist thought influenced her work, for instance, she balked: "Very little. I am not a Marxist. I don't believe that economics predates everything." Rather, she explained, "I believe that *myth* predates everything." For Chicago, humans create myths to express and act on our needs and desires. "I believe that *myth*, at its base," she continued, "has to be challenged before economics or sociology or philosophy will change."[92] To challenge patriarchy, then, would require challenging its foundation in myth. And it would require new myths.

The Dinner Party would become for Chicago not only "a symbol of our heritage" but also a rich visual and material myth—one that upended the sexist myths undergirding Western culture.[93] "What I'm doing is a sort of *Genesis*," she wrote in her journal in 1975, "starting with early Mother Goddess figures and working through the change from matriarchy to patriarchy—then on through the centuries, trying to make a link-up between women and their efforts, aspirations, and situations."[94] It is no accident that Christian, Jewish, and Goddess iconography combine to provide an architecture for *The Dinner Party*. Chicago's work clearly recalls Leonardo's *Last Supper*, which operates as an artistic referent but just as importantly, if not more so, as a religious one. Many artists have reimagined the final supper—often read as a Passover meal—that Jesus shared with his twelve apostles, as recounted in the New Testament gospels. Leonardo's version is only the most famous. This biblical resonance was important for Chicago. "The Last Supper existed within the context of the Bible, which was a history of a people," Chicago explains. "So my *Dinner Party* would also be a people's history—the history of women in Western civilization."[95] By gesturing to the thirteen witches needed for a coven and forming the table as a triangle—"one of the basic forms associated with matriarchal cultures"—Chicago extends the work's symbolic meaning, adding new mythic elements.[96] *The Dinner Party* becomes a feminist play on a Christian play on a Jewish ritual (a Passover seder). It reworks sacred stories by imagining new ones and returning to much older ones, including those of the Goddess.

Chicago's interest in myth, in undoing patriarchal myths and scripting new feminist ones, emerged from the broader world of feminist spirituality in the 1970s and 1980s. Most scholars don't pay enough attention to this history. As art historian Jennie Klein has noted, "feminist spirituality has always remained on the margins of mainstream culture and academic respectability."[97] Reading scholarship on US religion since World War II reveals relatively few references to key feminist theologians and writers like Mary Daly, Rosemary Radford Ruether, and Judith Plaskow, who were grappling with major religious traditions like Christianity and Judaism. Even as scholars chart the rise of New Age spirituality and the language of "spiritual but not religious" since the 1960s, feminist spirituality and the Goddess movement receive far too little consideration.[98] This is a major oversight, as the feminist spirituality movement has shaped women's activism both within major religious traditions like Judaism and Christianity and alongside them, leaving an enormous impact on both postwar US religion and art. Chicago may not have counted herself a key practitioner, but her feminism and art were shaped by feminist spirituality and, in turn, her work proved a major source of inspiration for many feminist theologians and women involved in the Goddess movement.

What is the Goddess movement? In 1978, the feminist magazine *Heresies* hosted a full issue on "The Great Goddess." In one of its essays, theologian Carol Christ explained three key meanings that the Goddess has held for women:

> (1) the Goddess as divine female, as a personification who can be invoked in prayer and ritual; (2) the Goddess as symbol of the life, death and rebirth energy in nature and culture, in personal and communal life; (3) the Goddess as affirmation of the legitimacy and beauty of female power (made possible by the new becoming of women in the women's liberation movement).[99]

Christ's definition illustrates the power of the Goddess—a diffuse female power that could be taken up, conjured, or experienced in any number of ways—but also the power of symbolism itself. Cultural feminists in the 1970s emphasized the ubiquity of male symbols of power, from phallic shapes dotting city skylines and launching wars to the ways that, in some Abrahamic traditions, God became male. If men's language and forms have dominated history, religion, politics, literature, and even architecture, then women needed to find alternatives. Many turned to the arts to imagine new ways of seeing. In doing so, they also looked to a mythical past—to a time when women held power.

Feminist art critic Gloria Feman Orenstein, in that same issue of *Heresies*, heralded "the artist" as "the avatar of the new age, the alchemist whose great Art is the transformation of consciousness and being."[100] She surveyed the range of feminist artists working to conjure the Goddess, from Mary Beth Edelson and Ana Mendieta to Carolee Schneemann and Betye Saar. "By summoning up the powers associated with the Goddess archetype," she writes, these artists "are energizing a new form of Goddess consciousness, which, in its most recent manifestation is exorcising the patriarchal creation myth through a repossession of the female visionary faculties."[101] Orenstein includes Judy Chicago among these avatars, emphasizing how *The Dinner Party* rewrites Western history through a feminist lens. She also gestures to some of the installation's accompanying publications, which were to include, along with a catalogue of feminist myths and legends, an "illuminated manuscript" containing "a rewriting of Genesis as an alternate creation myth in which the Goddess is the supreme Creatrix."[102] Chicago would publish that feminist creation myth, though it did not take the form she and Orenstein had expected.

While creating *The Dinner Party*, Chicago and her collaborators read widely in feminist spirituality, including the work of theologian Mary Daly.[103] Daly's landmark *The Church and the Second Sex* (1968) unmasked the sexism of the Roman Catholic Church, and her follow-up *Beyond God the Father* (1973) worked toward a feminist reinterpretation of God.[104] Inspired by feminist theology, Chicago found herself drawn to the idea of a religion centered on women and began writing a feminist creation story that she hoped to publish alongside *The Dinner Party*. She worked with Diana Press, a feminist publishing house founded in 1972, to create her illustrated creation story, which was to include an opening poem by Adrienne Rich. As Jane Gerhard explains, during revisions between 1976 and 1977, Chicago changed the title of this manuscript to "The Heavenly Banquet."[105] It offers a feminist revision of the Genesis story recounted in the Hebrew Bible and, in doing so, mimics much of the biblical language and form of that creation myth. Chicago's manuscript included four parts: "Revelations of the Goddess," "History Tales," "Silhouettes," and "Visions of the Apocalypse."[106] She drafted a version of the manuscript running over 150 pages but never published it, at least not in full. She began working with a larger publishing house—Doubleday—that had more resources than Diana Press but was less interested in this feminist creation myth than they were in a book on *The Dinner Party* itself, which they published in 1979.[107]

Chicago ended up publishing a version of "Revelations of the Goddess" (the first part of her creation myth) in *The CoEvolution Quarterly*, a journal founded by Stewart Brand, who is most well known for cofounding and editing the countercultural magazine *Whole Earth Catalog*. Chicago's piece came out in the spring of 1979 to celebrate the opening of *The Dinner Party*. Much like the biblical Genesis, "Revelations of the Goddess" begins with darkness and chaos. But from this chaos came first a sigh, then a moan, then a wail, "and the wail became the scream of birth."[108] The screams beget the Universe and the planets on the first day. On the second, the Earth divided into the "Vagina Primera," which birthed the "ovum of life" in the form of the Moon. The next day, the Earth Gaea, "the mother of all living things," would in turn create Woman, who would give birth to the full human race. In this world, run by women, peace and the feminine were sacred. But, as in the biblical Genesis story, the fall would soon come. Men envied women's power and sought to overturn it. While women initially defended themselves and would have won, they sacrificed their lives to the men. "What caused them to cherish life," Chicago writes, "doomed them to defeat." The story ends with men taking charge, but not without a whisper of hope: that one day the wisdom of women would be needed again and they would be restored.[109] In its language and form, Chicago's creation story pulls from Jewish scripture—the object of its retelling—but invests that narrative with female power, translating it through the vocabulary of feminist spirituality into a new myth.

The full version of Chicago's creation story did not make it into *The Dinner Party*, but it still gave shape to the project. Elements appear in the installation's entryway banners. Feminist spirituality informs not only the content of the poetry but also its materiality. "The importance of the Goddess in relationship to the development of textiles cannot be overemphasized," Chicago writes, explaining that, in ancient myths, spinning and weaving were attributed to female deities.[110] So the banners (along with the runners on the table) recreate this historical and mythical connection. The creation myth also appears in the first *Dinner Party* book that Chicago published with Doubleday to accompany the installation, not as its own chapter, but instead in a single cursive line that runs across every page of the book. This is how it starts: "In the beginning, the feminine principle was seen as the fundamental cosmic force. All ancient peoples believed that the world was created by a female Deity."[111] The writing here shifts, as Chicago's earlier creation myth starts to sound more like a historical account. This version tells the reader about a history of myths, feminist stories that are meant to provide a usable past. One might read this as a shift from myth to history, a secularizing move. Such a reading, however, flattens the ways that many modern Jews understand biblical texts as repositories of historical and ethical insight, as Biale argued. What's more, it also misses how historical narratives themselves can be made sacred.

Chicago's narrative conjures what religion scholar Cynthia Eller calls, following Mircea Eliade, the "sacred history" of the feminist spirituality movement. She refers here to what became a widespread narrative among many feminists in this moment that charted the elevation of the feminine in a matriarchal prehistory, its waning, and then its resurgence. "The entire cycle," Eller writes, "from bliss to destruction to rejuvenated hope, is a narrative that functions religiously: a sacred history. It explains who we are, how we came to be, where we are going, and how to get there."[112] Eller underscores that most spiritual feminists take this sacred history as fact, despite mixed interpretations of the evidence for ancient matriarchies.[113] Following Eller, I want to take up this sacred history as a particular kind of story, as myth. I'm less concerned with its truth or falseness (though I don't disagree with Eller on this point)—many religious practitioners have questionable takes on what historians would deem "true" history. In fact, many people, religious or not, also have questionable understandings of secular history—historians among them. Faulty historical knowledge does not stop people from doing what they do, from making meaning from the stories they tell. As people retell stories, reiterating certain narrative templates, they reveal the power of myth. Myth is not necessarily opposed to truth, in a modern or secular sense, but stands beside it.

Chicago also understood something of this different relationship between myth and truth. "There is poetic truth and there is real truth," she explained, "and I am often happy with poetic truth."[114] If *The Dinner Party* is Chicago's ode to poetic truth, to the power of myth, we cannot finally understand it without encountering it *in situ*. After all, Chicago explained, it was "intended as a permanent shrine."[115] How then, we should ask, have visitors experienced *The Dinner Party*?

Exhibiting Symptoms: *The Dinner Party* Debut

Five years in the making, *The Dinner Party* officially opened in March 1979 at the San Francisco Museum of Modern Art. And it was a sensation. Thousands showed for the opening alone, and upward of ninety thousand people visited during its first three months on display, sometimes waiting in line up to five hours to see it.[116] In a letter to Chicago, one fan described viewing *The Dinner Party* on its final day in San Francisco, when she was told there would be a three-hour wait to enter. At first, she balked—"I didn't believe him"—but finally took her place in line. She described soft and beautiful singing among some of the other people waiting that grew as more people joined. As visitors entered the final hallway, they burst into singing of all kinds—"church songs, Hebrew songs, children's rounds, 60s songs, spirituals." In turn, the "walls and the floor and the air were vibrating!" This pilgrim admitted her initial discomfort with the vulvar symbolism of the plates: "At first I disliked symbolizing women by cunts, but as I passed from one plate to another my uncomfortable feeling finally congealed into meaning." In the end, she wrote, "the vaginas made me feel vulnerable. Some were strong, some sensual, qualities of elasticity, creativity, flexibility, mystery and variety came to mind—but always, always vulnerability too."[117]

For opening night, artist Suzanne Lacy, one of Chicago's former students, joined *Dinner Party* studio member Linda Preuss to organize "The International Dinner Party," during which women from around the world—across two hundred cities from Ghana to Scotland to New Zealand—would dine together to celebrate *The Dinner Party* and to honor additional women of their choosing.[118] It was feminist ritual and clever marketing all in one—and another testament to the power of *The Dinner Party*.[119]

Despite this early success, and sometimes even because of this popularity, most major museums would pass on *The Dinner Party*. Size was partly to blame—it's an enormous undertaking to house the installation. But museums also turned down invitations to host *The Dinner Party* out of plain sexism. Many leaders in the art world questioned whether it was true art or mere craft, a worthy aesthetic achievement or feminist propaganda. If the art world tossed its invitation, though, *The Dinner Party* found great appeal among community leaders and women's organizations, who often scrambled to find ways to bring it to their cities. Much of this support came from members of religious organizations, including local synagogues and churches.[120] And *The Dinner Party* would continue to be a success, drawing numbers that easily rivaled modern religious revivals—including around sixty thousand visitors in Houston, forty thousand in Boston, thirty-three thousand in Cleveland, nearly fifty thousand in Chicago, seventy-five thousand in Montreal, fifty thousand in Toronto, and over five hundred thousand during its first tour in Brooklyn.[121]

Henry Hopkins, the director of the San Francisco Museum of Modern Art, captured the galvanizing power of *The Dinner Party* when he responded to questions about whether it was truly art. "The audience found it a real experience," he declared: "That's art."[122] That's also, quite often, religion.

We've seen the many religious elements that went into making *The Dinner Party*. But the installation itself also fostered feelings of religious experience and transformation, and visitors drew upon religious language to describe their experiences seeing it. Often, they wrote in ways that easily blended conventional Jewish or Christian language with elements of feminist spirituality and emphasized the power of *The Dinner Party* to conjure those feelings. In a letter to Chicago, one woman described driving to see *The Dinner Party* twice—once for six hours and another for twelve. Her pilgrimage was shaped by her background in Judaism and in Goddess spirituality. Her letter explained how Chicago had influenced her husband, a rabbi, before detailing how the artist impacted her own life as well. "Your influence has opened passages within me that has affected not only my artwork, but my spiritual inclinations as well," she explained, as she had realized the need to reinterpret Jewish sources alongside the "need for feminist spirituality." She also discussed seeing a retrospective on Chicago's work. "'A Decade of Judy Chicago' spoke to my soul in a language that yearns for femaleness," she explained: "It was deeper than any liturgy. It was sexual, sensual and sacred all at once . . . I thanked the Universal Mother for having sent a goddess in your form to the planet earth at this time in our existence."[123] Here, she refused to separate the sexual and the sacred, as she experienced Chicago's work as more than mere liturgy—it was the real thing.

Another visitor recorded her experience in a guestbook after visiting *The Dinner Party* in Cleveland. "As I entered the first hallway," she wrote, "I knew that I was entering a place of worship." Her comment drew together the need for women's space, the great Goddess, and the importance of having a specific place, a shrine or sacred center. "I want to stay and stay," she explained:

> I want to sit in the middle of the triangle, I long to surround it with women-loving women and let the energy crystallized here flow into all of us and back into *The Dinner Party*. The great goddess is beginning to be known again—we worship her under the trees, at the new moon and the changes of the year. And we worship her here. Specific details are unimportant—but this shrine deserves a permanent home and we, women, all people NEED to have it as a place to return to, to remember and cherish our heritage over these millennia.[124]

And such experiences were not limited to the mostly women visitors of *The Dinner Party*. In a fan letter, one man described having a mystical experience, although Goddess and feminist elements notably did not appear in his account. "I had for an instant a grasp of millenniums—something I have felt only when looking over vast expanses of land or water," he wrote: "as if on the lip of the Grand Canyon or over the Pacific from Big Sur, and seeing a spiritual history as vast as if I were beholding numerous Van Goghs with a single glimpse of my eye."[125] His description captured the experience of collapsing time—and connection across history—that came up for other visitors and even Chicago herself, who sometimes found working on women's plates brought her into contact with the women themselves. For many, *The Dinner Party* became not simply an artwork to behold but a vehicle for religious transformation, even transportation across time and space.

Journalists and art critics likewise drew upon religious language and comparisons in many positive reviews of *The Dinner Party*. Several recounted the religious imagery that went into making *The Dinner Party*, but they also went further, drawing upon their own religious metaphors to make sense of it and to capture the experience of seeing it. Lucy Lippard, Chicago's longtime supporter, penned an essay in 1979 characterizing *The Dinner Party* as "a feminist counterpart of the Sistine Chapel or the Matisse Chapel, consecrated instead to the insurrection of female energy—political and spiritual."[126] In the *Village Voice*, Diane Ketcham lauded *The Dinner Party* as an "awesome undertaking." She quoted an older woman seeing the exhibition with her who explained: "I felt I was in church. It was like visiting the cathedrals in France. She made these women into something holy."[127] Writing for *Woman's Art Journal*, art historian Susan Havens Caldwell likewise perceived the "religious aura" of the installation: "Voices were hushed in the darkened room as viewers proceeded very slowly around the brilliant triangle, visiting each place setting as if it were a chapel." Comparing it to medieval religious art, her specialty, she continued, "I had no difficulty in responding to the religiosity, the appeal to emotion before intellect, the meticulous craft . . . even the prescribed procession about the piece."[128] She concluded with the hope that *The Dinner Party* might inspire future projects that would make art "as meaningful to us today as the cathedral was to medieval society."[129]

In the same issue, literary scholar Carol Snyder also called attention to the religious elements of *The Dinner Party* but offered a more hesitant response. She noted how the "devotional attitude" succeeds in some important ways, in giving women much-needed affirming symbols and even, repeating Chicago, in " 'making the feminine holy.' " But in doing so, Snyder wrote, it also "works against perception of the piece's ironies and its occasional light touches."[130] Snyder was drawn to *The Dinner Party*'s "ironic tensions"—the juxtaposition of intense lighting and darkness that gestures toward "women's radiance and historical obscurity." The table set for guests who never show. The play on serving up women on plates to be consumed—a twist on the Eucharist through a double play on consumption.[131] But for Snyder, this final "bitter, rather Pop pun is subsumed in the Eucharistic metaphor; and the whole, with its hieratic iconography, its gilded ecclesiastic splendor, and its oversize chalice/goblets, nearly transubstantiates the profane (the historical and sociological content) into the sacred."[132] For Snyder, these religious elements impeded *The Dinner Party*'s greater possibilities, as this "devotional" gloss smooths irony in earnestness, crushing the work's biting playfulness under the weight of seriousness.

But note how Snyder drew attention here largely to the Christian elements of *The Dinner Party*. Often, in the ways we think about "religion," it does just this: it lends gravity. Indeed, from the many accounts we see, visitors witnessed this very devotional seriousness. It's not merely some phantasm of "the secular" but part of how a secular approach to "religion" as such begins to take root, forming habits through the expectations of haunting Catholic gothicness and Protestant earnestness. But we can also name it as that—as a specific way we moderns have come to see and to experience the work of "the religious." Haunted by modernist assumptions about the sacred—as something set apart, outmoded, and ossified—"religion" becomes opposed to irony, playfulness, and humor. What remains harder to see, though, is that religious languages (and religious people) do other things, too. They can be ironic, or light, even playful. And, sometimes, religious language lives in this tension between irony and earnestness, even exploiting it. We might ask what it would mean to resist the temptation to presume the sacred aligns with earnestness and against irony—might the "devotional attitude" also elevate some of these ironic tensions?

If Snyder thought religious staging and iconography muffled *The Dinner Party*'s more ironic gestures, other feminist writers and art critics found it damning. They saw in its popular appeal, feminine imagery, and transgressions against modernist aesthetics not signs of the sacred but symptoms of kitsch. Again, religious language animated the responses, as Chicago's work became a shrine not only to "bad art" but also to what scholars sometimes call "bad religion"—religion that is too popular, too experiential, too *feminine*. Some of the very things that made Chicago's piece appealing to its many fans rendered it unacceptable for others. Writing for *Time* magazine, Robert Hughes derided *The Dinner Party* as an "obsessive feminist pantheon" that was "no better than mass devotional art." He continued: "It is simple, didactic, portentous, gaudily evangelical and wholly free of wit or irony."[133] In the Catholic magazine *Commonweal*, Maureen Mullarkey dismissed the "women who file worshipfully past this cunnilingus-as-communion table."[134] Journalist Dorothy Shinn complained that the piece wasn't really art but, "first and foremost, an indoctrination" and even the "religiofication of the feminist cause."[135] In the *Village Voice*, Kay Larson faulted Chicago for "not being more open about the gay theme: sitting down to 'dinner' before plates depicting women's labia." Larson sewed this sapphic sensibility to what she took as Chicago's spirituality: "how do you create a major art event that speaks for all women yet derives mainly from your personal involvement with the goddess cult?"[136]

Some critics took the religious resonances as signs of Chicago's literalism and cultish propaganda. In *Artforum*, Hal Fischer complained, "Chicago's conception originates in her own interpretation of medieval art: just as art taught the Bible to illiterates, so should *The Dinner Party* instruct us. To this end, the presentation is obsessively literal and cloyingly ecclesiastic." It suffered, he continued, from "proselytizing self-righteousness that replaces art with cultism and offers literalism under the guise of education."[137] The cult accusation arose in a decade during which "cults" fascinated and horrified many Americans, and this line was published just months before the events at Jonestown. To attack Chicago and her work in this way tapped into broader disgust with and fear of religion run wild. In *The Boston Globe*, Robert Taylor also contended that *The Dinner Party* was "presented not so much as a work of art as a religious experience." He didn't mind "the mixture of reverence and awe" as much as others but faulted its "literal scheme"—including its distasteful "anatomical tableware," when, he argued, a more abstract approach would work better than a "representational idiom."[138] Here, Fischer and Taylor rendered obviousness or clarity, combined with the impetus to teach, into literalness, an accusation that pinched even more than the one of cultism. In the pages of *Sojourner*, Diane Gelon, the project coordinator for *The Dinner Party*, countered Taylor's assertion of literalism. It was not a literal work, she insisted, but rather "a symbolic history of women in Western civilization."[139]

We might observe how these criticisms conflated the literal and the didactic, particularly in the comparison to medieval art. Though didactic, *The Dinner Party* was also lavishly symbolic. As was much medieval art, to be sure, as historians like Caroline Walker Bynum have long taught us.[140] But to characterize *The Dinner Party* as *merely* didactic, as simply descriptive of a historical narrative about women, is part of a broader history of sexist reading that refuses the almost over-the-top symbolism of the work. If the phallic form has long served as a symbol of erotic energy, power, and even war, the vulvar form could only be taken for what it apparently is—the anatomical index for women. Aesthetic tastes aside, Chicago's historical feminist narrative also resists easy reduction to a school lesson. As the experiences of fans and critics alike suggest, *The Dinner Party* was not just an artistic rendering but also the creation of feminist myth itself. Chicago was not simply describing women's history but creating the occasion for women's spirituality, whether or not she was always successful or intentional in doing so. It is this move that has proved particularly divisive in the history of *The Dinner Party*'s reception.

Popular religion and kitsch, both feminized and devalued, thus came together for many of *The Dinner Party*'s fans and detractors alike. I want to pause to consider in particular how these forms have motivated accusations of literalism, sincerity, and explicitness. As we have seen, some early critics focused on the vulvar imagery in ways that literalized it. In a review for *Women's Art Journal*, Lauren Rabinowitz put it directly: "Chicago literalizes the genital image. Chicago's presentation does not soften or camouflage genitalia with color, materials, or humor."[141] A critic for the *San Francisco Chronicle* called *The Dinner Party* "primarily biological," given what he saw as its focus on women as sites for reproduction and nutrition, while *New York*

Times art critic Hilton Kramer complained that it "remains fixed on the external genital organs of the female body."[142] Chicago's creativity, he wrote, "is the kind of ingenuity we associate with kitsch."[143] In a review for the women's studies journal *Frontiers*, Lolette Kuby criticized the work for reducing individual women to a "common biological denominator" before comparing Chicago's vulvar symbolism to depictions of naked women in *Playboy* and *Penthouse*, which she found "curiously less reprehensible than *The Dinner Party*."[144] While *The Dinner Party* might work "best as a joke," she continued, it fails to rise to the level of satire: "It presumes to be earnest, solemn, elegant; as such, it's a joke at the expense of women."[145] She concluded by mocking the "flow of the faithful" who would nonetheless come to see it, women "hoodwinked" by Chicago like the devotees of a charlatan preacher.

Conservative art critic Maureen Mullarkey took the comparison a step further, casting *The Dinner Party* itself as the hoodwinking evangelist. Writing for *Commonweal*, she described *The Dinner Party* "moving around the country like an itinerant revivalist, abetted by populist resentments and generating its own Awakening," while dismissing the "women who file worshipfully past this cunnilingus-as-communion table."[146] Like Fischer, Mullarkey bemoaned the "didactic nature of the imagery" and the "preachiness" of the exhibition, "outdone only by the prettiness of it." She attacked *The Dinner Party*—and "the feminist art movement as a whole"—for its attempt to challenge conventions of the high and low. This "folkish desire to pit intellect against feeling and its willingness to play on the susceptibilities of its audience," she wrote, was no less than "a continuation of the fundamentalist impulse in American Protestantism." Chicago's iconography, including its "abuse of sincerity," she contended, shared "more in common with Carl McIntire," a well-known fundamentalist pastor, than with the playful work of artists like Marcel Duchamp, most well known for turning a urinal into art. "After the fundamentalism of the cross and the flag," she quipped, "we now have the fundamentalism of the vagina."[147] For Mullarkey, Chicago's *Dinner Party* cosplayed as the worst of evangelical Protestantism—a sentimentalized moralism masquerading as serious work. It was, for her, the pinnacle of feminist kitsch.

From Criticism to Culture Wars

The Dinner Party's debut witnessed a range of responses, from visitors who experienced religious epiphanies and mystical transports to critics who blasted the work's sentimental appeal and supposed reduction of women to their genitals. Across these various assessments, fans and critics alike attributed religious elements to *The Dinner Party*, whether they remarked on its devotional setup and choreography or compared it to medieval didacticism, cult sway, or old-fashioned fundamentalist preaching. But Chicago's shrine underwent a new baptism in 1990 when it entered the sights of culture wars politics. The excess of religious significations it had sparked the previous decade would be largely replaced with one of two narratives: religious and political opponents attacked it as explicit pornography, while Chicago and her supporters defended it as an artistic monument to women's history. The story of this transformation reveals the power of culture wars hermeneutics.

After sitting in storage for two years, *The Dinner Party* seemed to have finally found a permanent home at the University of the District of Columbia (UDC), where it would be housed at the Carnegie Library in downtown DC. It was to become part of a larger multicultural arts initiative that would include a growing collection of work by Black artists, such as Sam Gilliam, Elizabeth Catlett, Alma Thomas, and Lois Mailou Jones, as well other artists from DC and among UDC faculty.[148] The hopes for this project were outlined by Nira Hardon Long, chair of the UDC board of trustees and one of the founding members of the Congressional Black Caucus Foundation, a nonprofit organization that supports the mission of the Congressional Black Caucus through public policy research and educational programming.[149] Like many public universities, especially historically Black ones, UDC was strapped for cash after years of underfunding and looking to the private sector to increase revenue. Chicago's gift of *The Dinner Party*—valued at around $2 million at the time—would be a huge attraction to visitors and potential donors alike. UDC leaders projected a quick and long-lasting windfall, one that would more than make up for the need to reallocate roughly $80 thousand in non-appropriated funds to pay for moving *The Dinner Party* to DC, in addition to expanding the plan for renovations to the Carnegie Library that had already been approved to ensure it could house Chicago's monumental work.[150] The city council approved a $1.2-million bond from UDC's capital budget to cover the costs. Long explained that the board of trustees hosted a public session to discuss the gift in March 1990, where there was no opposition, and the donation received unanimous approval from the trustees—a vote that was reaffirmed, again unanimously, that June.

But when Chicago arrived in DC for the gifting ceremony on July 20, trouble was afoot. The story varies a little based on who is telling it, but those supporting the donation argued that, throughout June, "an underground sabotage campaign" arose among some members of the faculty senate and "shadowy outsiders" lurking in the aftermath of the firing of UDC's president the previous May. According to Lucy Lippard, some argued that, as a predominantly Black institution, UDC shouldn't center work by a white artist. Others "within the rightwing of the faculty senate" opposed members of the board of trustees who had been appointed by Mayor Marion Barry, who was then enmeshed in a trial for drug charges. The leader of this conservative faction, which included "the alleged Moonie contingent," was Dave Chatman, who had been floated as a mayoral candidate by *The Washington Times*, which was founded in 1982 by Sun Myung Moon, the leader of the Unification Church. Others worried about the terms of the deal itself, arguing that it would largely benefit Chicago personally and that it was siphoning funds from more pressing educational programs.[151]

On July 18, journalist Jonetta Rose Barras penned a front-page story in *The Washington Times*—titled "UDC's $1.6 Million 'Dinner': Feminist Artwork Causes UDC Indigestion"—that brought the underground campaign against *The Dinner Party* into the light of DC politics. Two key issues came to the fore in the public debate that followed. The first had to do with the politics of money, race, and power in DC. As a public institution in the nation's capital, UDC's funding was allocated by Congress, which meant that university leaders found themselves at the whims not only of local politicians but of politicians from around the country with little understanding or interest in DC itself. A majority Black city, DC residents had long struggled for political control of their home against the interests of mostly white national politicians.[152] Being in the national spotlight also meant that culture wars concerns, including pressure from the Christian Right, could easily blow up what should be pro forma budgetary approvals, which is what would happen in this case. It led to the second key issue, which brings in religion, sex, and visual culture. Conservative leaders in Congress balked at the idea of allocating public funds to support a feminist work of art, one many would blast as pornographic.

Barras's article twisted the financial matters. It opened with a line that made it seem as though the $1.6 million was being used to buy Chicago's piece rather than to house it and cover renovations that were already in the works. She also tethered *The Dinner Party* to the National Endowment for the Arts—from which Chicago had received a grant in the 1970s—thus fueling the incendiary political battles over public funding for art that some conservatives, often led by Senator Jesse Helms, considered immoral. Barras also claimed that *The Dinner Party* "was banned in several art galleries around the country because it depicts women's genitalia on plates and has been characterized by some critics as obscene."[153] Barras's coverage continued the next day, describing how members of Congress "sharply rebuked" approving funds for "a dramatic piece of sexual sculpture." "Its major feature," she continued, "is a huge triangular dining table with elaborate place settings depicting female sexual organs, specifically vaginas." The genre and language here are important. As a journalist, even for a conservative-leaning publication, Barras's writing was neither meant to be and wasn't read as figurative. By convention, it is descriptive, a mode that entails a different relationship to "truth" than other forms of creative writing. This would prove important, as *The Washington Times* coverage was picked up by others. In Congress, Representative Stanford Parris called *The Dinner Party* "clearly pornographic." And some UDC administrators worried Chicago's piece "may be offensive to the moral values of many of our constituents."[154] *Washington Post* columnist Mary McGrory likewise attacked *The Dinner Party*: "The creation depicts female genitalia; you don't need to be Jesse Helms to regard it as obscene."[155]

Chicago and the UDC board responded to concerns voiced about these two critical issues: money and pornography. They corrected details about the money, how it would be used, and that UDC was not buying *The Dinner Party*—it was a gift. At a press conference, Chicago also addressed a question from a man in the audience that many wanted an answer to. "Exactly what are those shapes on the plates in *The Dinner Party*?" he asked. "That's a fair question," she replied: "If the Washington Monument's thrusting sexual form and aggressive shape can be discussed in terms of aesthetic rather than phallic implications, why can't open organic metaphoric forms be understood in terms of their multi-layered beauty?"[156] Chicago tried to shift the focus from anatomical vaginas to the work of sexual metaphor, but these intractable literalist readings proved contagious.

The following week, members of the House of Representatives debated *The Dinner Party* on the congressional floor. Representative Robert Dornan quipped that calling Chicago a feminist was an insult to feminists. "She's not a feminist," he insisted: "She's a weirdo, wacko, three-dimensional ceramic pornographer."[157] The following day, he bemoaned that it was "getting increasingly frustrating to serve in this House with any kind of honor." "We now have the pornographic art," he complained: "I mean, three-dimensional ceramic art of 39 women's vaginal area, their genitalia, served up on plates that requires a whole room at the University of the District of Columbia to be set aside." He was also frustrated that the UDC board expected Congress to follow their lead "and hope for the best, while everybody concedes it is pornographic," rather than debate the university's fiscal issues themselves.[158] But debate they did.

The House fought over UDC's budget for almost an hour and half. As Jane Gerhard writes, "it was hard to miss the simultaneous racial drama unfolding," in which a cast of all white, male conservatives debated all Black (and male) politicians who supported DC's ability to govern itself without direct congressional oversight.[159] As punishment for supporting pornographic art, Representative Stanford Parris proposed an amendment that would reduce UDC's budget by $1.6 million, the amount requested to house *The Dinner Party*. Democratic Representative Ron Dellums pushed back. "We deal with pornography every day," he insisted: "I think it is pornographic to see nuclear weapons standing erect."[160] But it's hard to defend smut with C-SPAN cameras rolling and reporters listening in. The amendment to withdraw funding from UDC passed by a 297 to 123 vote.[161]

Outside of Congress, leaders of the Christian Right also joined the attack. Televangelist Pat Robertson called Chicago's work obscene on the *700 Club*. Lucy Lippard reports that "the black religious right, which had connections at UDC, also got into the act."[162] According to Chicago, rumors even circulated "that the reason *The Dinner Party* was in storage was that the crates contained the Devil and that I was the Antichrist."[163] While the Christian Right mobilized followers in a letter-writing campaign to lobby politicians to defund immoral art, Chicago likewise enlisted allies from across the country, who defended *The Dinner Party* as a work of historical importance and on the grounds of freedom of expression. People for the American Way, an organization founded by Norman Lear in 1981 to oppose the rising Christian Right, also threw its support behind Chicago. In Congress, at least, these efforts proved successful, as a Senate subcommittee restored the funds cut by the Parris Amendment.[164]

But by then pressure was also mounting from students at UDC. Several hundred staged a protest with a series of demands for university leaders, which included rechanneling the money set aside for *The Dinner Party* into educational programs and more pressing student needs and calling for the resignation of Barry-appointed trustees. By some accounts, the students were riled up by the right-wing misinformation campaign, but no doubt they were also fed up with the long history of underfunding and mismanagement of their university.[165] It's also quite likely that the sexual and racial politics of *The Dinner Party* did not speak to many of these students in the ways it had spoken to its mostly white supporters and fans a decade earlier.

In light of the student protests, Chicago decided to pull her donation. On October 2, she released a statement to the UDC students and trustees and to the media. She insisted that the meaning of *The Dinner Party* was "being distorted; it is a work of art aimed at *promoting* empowerment and a monument to those who have struggled for freedom." The campaign against her donation was creating a "division in values" where there shouldn't be one—between her work and the students at UDC. She affirmed the protesting students' "valid set of demands that will promote their own growth and the needs of the University." "Moreover," she concluded: "as my life's work has been dedicated to the self-determination of all peoples, we withdraw the gift in support of the students' right to determine their own destiny."[166] One could say that the financial matters debated among students and in Congress really mattered most in this debacle, while the sex stuff was simply culture wars rhetoric. In Congress, though, the provision or withholding of money is often tied to the politics of sex, race, and morality and used as a rhetorical tool itself. In this case, the Senate restored UDC's funding, and then Chicago wound up pulling her gift, so it turned out not to be a lasting issue. Meanwhile, the rhetorical production of *The Dinner Party* as obscene, as feminist pornography, not only played into the media sensationalism of culture wars politics but has had lasting political and material effects, including on what kinds of art (if any) receive funding and how people "see" such art.

The Dinner Party, the Culture Wars, and the Politics of Literalism

The Dinner Party's varied receptions reveal its curious religious resonances and dissonances, but they also demonstrate the cultural work of its interpretation in recent US history. I want to emphasize how accusations of literalism, in particular, that have variably construed Chicago's installation as feminine, religious, sacrilegious, didactic, fundamentalist, and pornographic. There is also a significant shift in how these accusations have worked across *The Dinner Party*'s career.

Following its debut in 1979, some feminists worried *The Dinner Party* reduced women to their sexual organs, but most early accusations of literalism, largely from art critics, faulted its didactic apparatus and the obviousness of the feminist message. This "transgression of the prohibition against direct representation," explains art historian Amelia Jones, skirted the orthodoxy of modernist art, which emphasizes abstraction, even elitism.[167] Such accusations pointed to *The Dinner Party*'s early gender trouble, as its religious sensibilities, mass popularity, and kitschiness only confirmed its transgressions against the masculinist (and secular) norms of high art.

By the 1990s, Chicago's work was caught in a different web of gender trouble. Literalism was no longer something ascribed to *The Dinner Party*—part of its feminized, didactic kitschiness—but became instead a political and hermeneutic tool wielded by its opponents to flatten symbolism into mere obscenity. The religious readings of *The Dinner Party* so central to its previous celebration and denunciation alike were largely absent from the culture wars debate, as opponents narrowed their attention to its "explicit"—and presumably secular—sexuality. Of course, this debate featured a different set of actors—more opponents than critics—with different intentions.[168] But the departures are instructive. Conservative politicians and Christian leaders repositioned themselves on the side of religion and *The Dinner Party* against it, rendering it a profane vision threatening American morality. No longer did opponents complain that *The Dinner Party* was part of the "goddess cult" or its fervor overly evangelical. Indeed, few commenters during the 1990 debacle even noted the Christian or Jewish imagery or feminist spirituality animating the piece, as this culture wars script considered the work fully anathema to anything that could be recognized as "religion" (or art).

This culture wars shift in public rhetoric about *The Dinner Party* marks many things, including the intensification of media battles waged by the Right and the increasingly polarized rhetoric of moral values and national citizenship. It also demonstrates the power of a culture wars framework that not only categorizes but constructs conservative religion apart from and against progressive secularism.[169] We should underscore the labor it took to rescript Chicago's *Dinner Party* as secular feminist pornography, including the pedagogy of unseeing that this move required—especially the unseeing of the religious and symbolic elements others had previously observed, experienced, or criticized. How does one learn to see symbolism in literalist ways?

This historical moment of unseeing emerged from broader habits of literalist interpretation elevated during the culture wars of the 1980s and

1990s—what I call an aesthetics of literalism (and describe in greater detail in chapter three). This approach reads feminist and queer visual culture reductively, dismissively, and through appeals to the obviousness of its sacrilege or obscenity. If *The Dinner Party* joined a broader movement in feminist art to foreground content, to blend content with form, this style of culture wars literalism largely stripped that away. For religious and political conservatives, the problem wasn't that *The Dinner Party* was too religious or that its symbolic representation was too obvious, but that it was "literally" or "explicitly" depicting women's genitals in public. The rhetorical shift may be subtle, but note how this revisioning reduced *The Dinner Party* to its plates, decontextualizing them from the larger piece, and rendered the butterfly/vulvar symbolism as "explicit" "female genitalia," "labia," or plated vaginas. The complaint was no longer that the symbolism was too obvious, too essentialist, or too religious, but that *The Dinner Party* publicly displayed women's sexuality by putting vaginas on plates. In this conservative rhetoric, women out of place were a threat to society.

And such literalist readings were not limited to the religious and political Right. The *New York Times* repeated the rhetoric of conservative attacks, which led Chicago to respond with a letter requesting the paper stop referring to the plates as "female genitalia." She balked at the use of such "inappropriate, clinical terminology" to describe "my abstract, organic, aesthetic—not anatomical—forms." Chicago offered a prescient conclusion: "It is shocking to me that the *New York Times* employs authoritatively the language of the rightwing anti-arts faction in America. I could understand the distorting language coming from the Reverend Donald Wildmon of Tupelo, Mississippi. I cannot understand it coming from *The New York Times*."[170]

Conflating Chicago's plates with the whole of *The Dinner Party*—and literalizing the plates as female anatomy—rendered this work little more than a monument to women's sexuality and, for many conservatives, justified its denunciation. These culture wars condemnations went beyond disagreements over aesthetic taste, and Chicago and other feminist and queer artists often placed such right-wing attacks within longer histories of artistic censorship. Chicago captured this feeling in "The Great American Fax Attack," a somewhat silly two-sided drawing she created in September 1990 to "strike a blow against artistic repression." The first side features Jesse Helms as a Nazi soldier, part of the "art police," yelling, "I see porn." The other side depicts a corner of *The Dinner Party* stabbing a man in his Adam's apple, with the accompanying line: "It's enough to give anyone a pain in the neck."[171] Even as her artistic vision was under attack, Chicago's sense of humor remained.

The "Fundamentalism of the Vagina," or, This Party's a Drag

If the habits of interpretation traced here sought to literalize Chicago's symbolism, they also inaugurated other forms of imagination. Gender theorist Judith Butler has examined the curious consequences of censorship, including efforts by conservatives like Jesse Helms to censor artists in the 1980s. Butler understands attempts to limit representations of sexuality deemed immoral—what they call efforts "to censor the phantasmatic"—to lead to even more imaginative fantasies. In other words, attempts to regulate such representations through political censorship often wind up creating new returns, revisitations that operate like "insistent ghosts," Butler explains, "to undermine those very efforts."[172] Butler's discussion focuses on responses to the work of Robert Mapplethorpe, but attacks on *The Dinner Party* have led to some curious births of imagination as well.

I want to close by considering some of the fantasies conjured through culture wars attacks on *The Dinner Party*, which traded Chicago's "abstract, organic, aesthetic" forms for descriptions of vaginas served up on plates. Such readings replaced the symbolic with the anatomical, but they hardly foreclosed the work of fantasy. Indeed, rhetoric that literalized Chicago's feminine symbolism ironically fostered the explicit sexuality found there. In *The Washington Times*, for instance, Wesley Pruden insisted that "Miss Chicago's sculpture actually depicts a table set with dinner plates serving up vaginas— yes, Virginia, vaginas—of famous women of history."[173] If Chicago's art and writing reflected a grounding in women's experience common to the 1970s, culture wars conservatives took the cis-normative equivalency of women with vaginas even further. It's one thing to create a symbolic vulvar form for a goddess, quite another to read feminine symbols as women's genitalia (or as particular historical women's genitalia). Such descriptions summon the explicit sexuality of *The Dinner Party* and even raise the specter of lesbian eroticism. Pruden described how one employee at his local adult bookstore interpreted Chicago's piece as no less than "a dyke's-eye view of some of the tough broads of the past."[174] Of course, such pornographic fantasies are not progressive. They reveal the limited vocabulary available to imagine feminist iconography without collapsing women into their imagined anatomy—or into patriarchal fantasies of lesbian ghosts.

But we can fantasize to different ends, as well. Mullarkey's earlier, acerbic review is oddly generative here. A conservative Catholic, Mullarkey bristled at Chicago's feminist politics and metaphorical imagery; her review repositioned *The Dinner Party* as Protestant, with its folksy commitment to simplicity and sincerity. But Mullarkey's language is so creatively excessive—"a fundamentalism of the vagina"—that one might find it hard not to laugh. It led me to wonder: what if we made more of over-the-top readings of *The Dinner Party*, critiques that it is too kitschy, too sincere, or even exhibits "flamboyant excess," as Amelia Jones has playfully noted?[175] Butler argues that "it is important to risk losing control of the ways in which the categories of women and homosexuality are represented."[176] In *Gender Trouble*, they name the parody often seen in camp, especially in drag performances, as one potential site for new representations to proliferate.[177] What work might such playful readings of *The Dinner Party* do?

I have suggested that *The Dinner Party* rests on a tension between sincerity and humor. Chicago has repeatedly presented it as an earnest lesson in women's history. And *The Dinner Party* has also become its own institution—in 1977, Chicago and her collaborators even created an organization called Through the Flower dedicated to its preservation and continued legacy. This move, alongside the ever-proliferating explanatory texts that accompany *The Dinner Party*, enhance this sense of earnest history—not because bureaucratization necessarily leads to a dampening of the spirit, but because Chicago never fully explored the playful possibilities of what performance historian Patrick McKelvey calls "bureaucratic drag," the transformation of bureaucratic forms themselves into sites of play and resistance.[178]

But at the same time, *The Dinner Party* offers its own drag performances—a Jewish feminist's revisioning of *The Last Supper*, a piece that's already kitsch-adjacent, given its mass paint-by-numbers appeal.[179] *The Dinner Party* presents key women throughout history in symbolic butterfly/vulvar drag—and not only women but also the mythic goddesses who are invited to what many consider a Passover seder. Its feminist history, its pedagogy, works at least in part through the power of these juxtapositions, through this very tension between sincerity and humor.[180] Serving up vulvar drag at *The Last Supper* suggests not only a didactic move but also, at times, a theological one—not an "abuse of sincerity," a critique that Christianizes the piece, but feminist political humor stylized through religious forms. Its future may or may not be religious, but it need not be literal, either.

There is something excessive about *The Dinner Party*, including its exhibition and reception—an excess of imagination, of sensuality, of seriousness, of hushed tones and choreographed devotions, of polarized commentary. This excess works alongside its pedagogical sincerity. I don't underscore this mix of earnest and parodic excess simply to recuperate *The Dinner Party* (or to denigrate it), but to suggest additional ways to see the work it does and the work it may do, the "giddiness" it invokes—perhaps even the possibility for conversions and subversions to come.[181] Indeed, Chicago herself has become a subject for artist Audrey Chan, who playfully created a piece called "Practicing Judyism" that captures some of the humor often missed in feminist art. By donning Judy Chicago drag—Chan has called herself "Judy Chicago's Chinese-American doppelganger"—she forges a connection to a feminist and artistic mentor while also playing with questions about art, identity, and humor.[182] Her Judy drag refuses the reductive temptations of literalism. It participates, instead, in the ongoing creation of feminist myth.

3
Wojnarowicz/Wildmon:
Between Queer Imagination and the
Aesthetics of Literalism

Hell is a place on earth. Heaven is a place in your head.[1]

—David Wojnarowicz

Pornography breeds destruction.[2]

—Donald Wildmon

In the spring of 1990, Donald Wildmon, an ordained United Methodist minister, mailed a two-page pamphlet to every member of US Congress and over 3,000 Christian leaders. He had planned to send additional copies to nearly 1,000 Christian radio stations, 100 Christian television stations, over 1,500 newspapers, and over 178,000 Christian pastors on his mailing lists, but would later claim to have changed his mind.[3] He sent the pamphlet under the auspices of the American Family Association (AFA), a non-profit, right-wing Christian organization that promotes a "Biblical ethic of decency in American society with emphasis on moral issues that impact the family."[4]

Born in 1938, Wildmon had made a name for himself by the 1980s as "the man the networks love to hate" through his work with the National Federation for Decency, the precursor to the AFA, which he founded in 1977.[5] Through this organization, he planned and led economic boycotts and other pressure campaigns to tackle the problems of "promiscuous sex, crude profanity and gratuitous violence" on television. His organization also confronted what he considered to be the overwhelmingly negative portrayal of Christianity in the media, including Christian characters represented as "con men, rip-off artists, adulterers, murderers, rapists, thieves, liars."[6] In

Provoking Religion. Anthony M. Petro, Oxford University Press. © Oxford University Press 2025.
DOI: 10.1093/9780190938468.003.0004

1989, he turned his attention to the world of high art and to the National Endowment for the Arts (NEA) in particular, which he accused of misusing taxpayer money to support pornography and assaults on Christians.

This was the topic of the AFA's 1990 pamphlet, through which Wildmon sought to alert members of Congress and fellow conservative Christians about the NEA's support for exactly such work—gay pornography and sacrilege masquerading as "works of art." To get their attention, he included graphic depictions of queer sex, which appear in the majority of the fourteen images included in the flier (Figures 3.1 and 3.2). But he did so with some trepidation. "What I'm trying to do is put it into the hands of key leaders," Wildmon explained, but "it's not the kind of mailing you can send to the general public." In fact, he told one reporter, "I could be prosecuted by the U.S. Postal Service for that mailing."[7]

Before saying more about the AFA pamphlet, I want to introduce a second piece, David Wojnarowicz's *Spirituality (for Paul Thek)*. Born in 1954, Wojnarowicz (pronounced *Voyna-ROH-vich*) emerged as one of the hottest artists of the 1980s East Village art scene.[8] A noted writer, he also worked across photography, painting, film, and performance art. He grew up in suburban New Jersey in an abusive household with an alcoholic father before moving to New York City to live with his often-absent mother. During his youth, Wojnarowicz was sometimes homeless and hustled to make money. He dropped out of high school and was mostly self-taught. Coming of age in the New York of the 1970s, Wojnarowicz took advantage of the city's bustling queer culture and experimental art scene—both of which drew him to the deteriorating piers lining the Hudson River that were home to artistic creation and cruising alike. Shaped in part by his own experience living on the margins, his writing and visual art often explored historical and ongoing forms of economic exploitation, racism, and homophobia.[9]

By the 1980s, he and his friends would find themselves on the frontlines of the HIV/AIDS crisis. The early association of this disease with homosexuality would stymie medical and political efforts to end the epidemic for years, especially as religious and political conservatives characterized AIDS as a just punishment for queer people. Wojnarowicz directly addressed the politics of the AIDS crisis in his work, before his own death from the disease in 1992. For one piece, he created a photomontage from a series of seven photographs and dedicated it to his friend and fellow artist Paul Thek, who died from AIDS-related complications in 1988 (Figure 3.3).

Your Tax Dollars Helped Pay For These "Works Of Art"

The photographs appearing on this sheet were part of the David Wojnarowicz "Tongues of Flame" exhibit catalog. The University Galleries at Illinois State University recently exhibited "Tongues of Flame". The National Endowment for the Arts, a federal agency funded by tax dollars, awarded the University Galleries $15,000 to help pay for the exhibit.

The exhibit came after Congress passed a law last year prohibiting the NEA from funding "depictions of sadomasochism, homo-eroticism, the sexual exploitation of children, or individuals engaged in sex acts..." and after John Frohnmayer became chairman of the NEA.

At a hearing on the NEA earlier this year, Congressman Pat Williams, D-MT, asked Mr. Frohnmayer if the NEA should permit grants for the creation of such material. Mr. Frohnmayer responded: "I would say yes." Congressman Williams praised the chairman for his attitude: "It shows real determination that the NEA not be used as a censorship agency."

NEA spokesman Josh Dare said, "We have no power to suggest anything to them (artists) or to exercise any control over what they do with the money we've given them." Dare denied that the NEA funded the Wojnarowicz "Tongues of Flame" exhibit, explaining: "Illinois State applied for a grant to support a retrospective of this particular artist's work. We approved the money for them. They are the ones providing money for Wojnarowicz."

For years efforts have been made to stop the NEA from funding such "works of art". But because the NEA has friends in key positions in Congress, Congress has been unwilling to cut off NEA funding. The NEA says that if Congress refuses to provide tax dollars to support artists who produce such material as appears on this sheet, that would be censorship.

This is the year for reauthorization for the NEA. Last year the NEA received $171,000,000. This year the request is for $175,000,000.

Before you vote, find out if your Congressman and Senators voted to reauthorize the NEA for another 5 years and thus continue using tax dollars to fund such "works of art" as those on this sheet. If they do vote for reauthorization, remember that when you vote in the upcoming Congressional and Senatorial races. This sheet has been presented to all members of the House and Senate for their information.

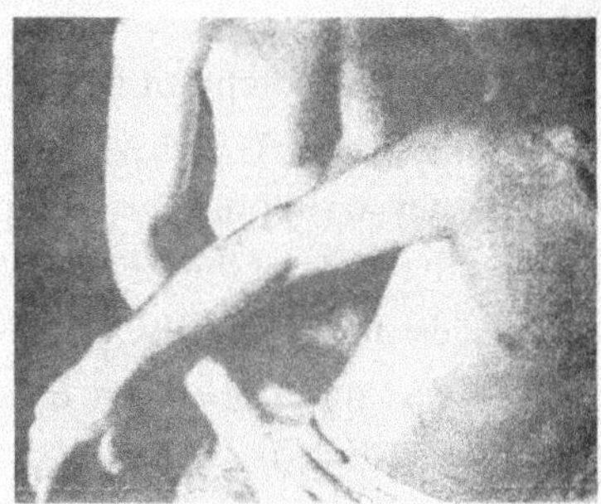

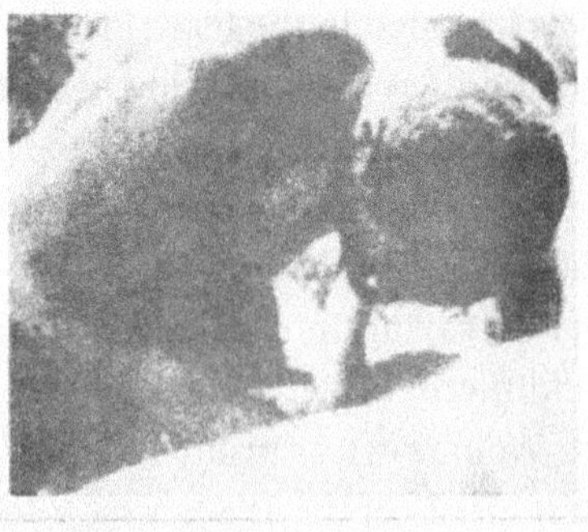

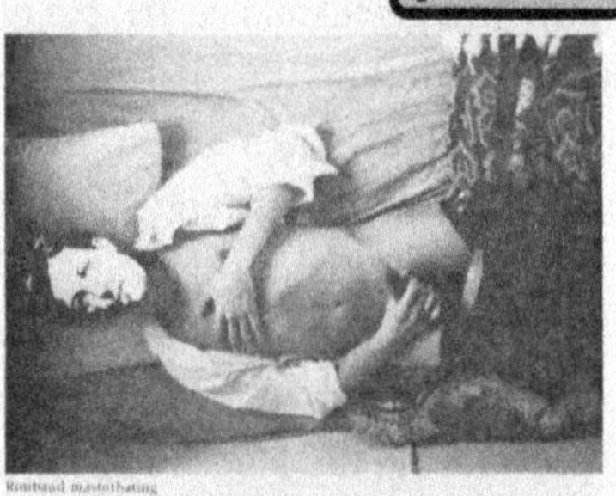

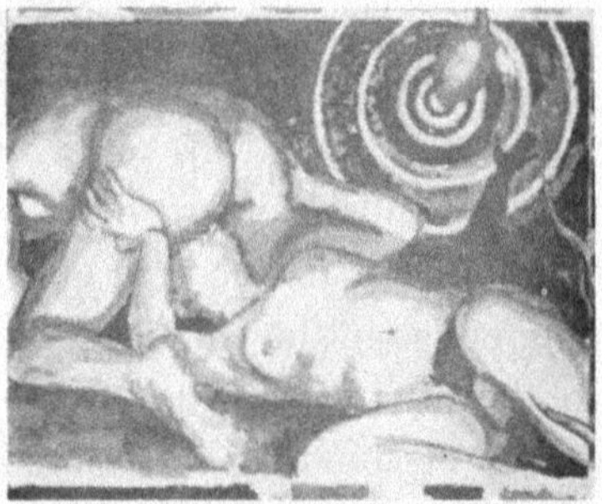

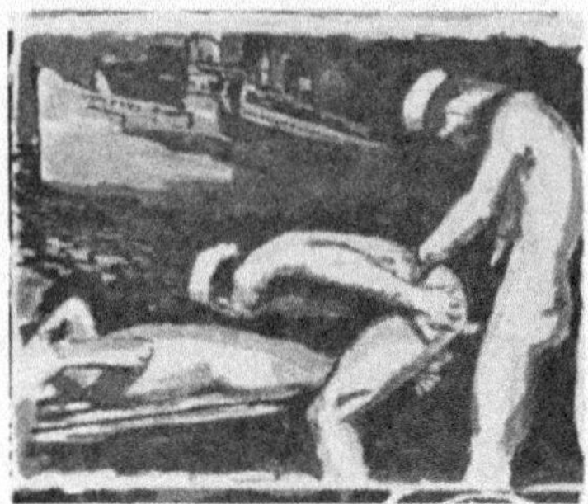

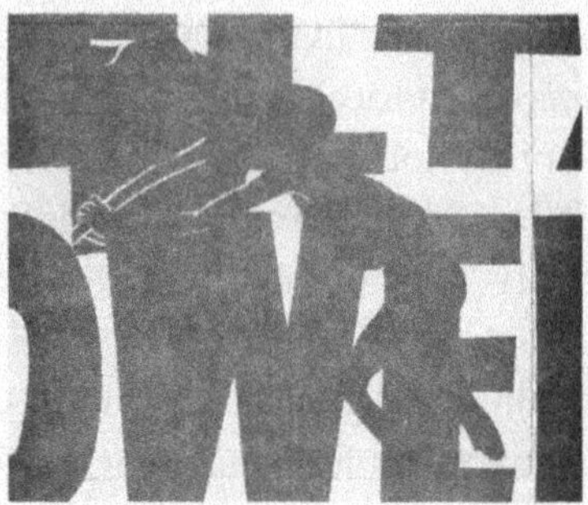

Figure 3.1 First page, Plaintiff's Exhibition #1, *Wojnarowicz v. American Family Association*, AFA Flyer using images taken from works by Wojnarowicz, 1990. David Wojnarowicz Papers, MSS 092, Box 14, Folder 70. Fales Library and Special Collections, New York University Libraries. Copyright Estate of David Wojnarowicz. Courtesy of the Estate of David Wojnarowicz and P·P·O·W, New York.

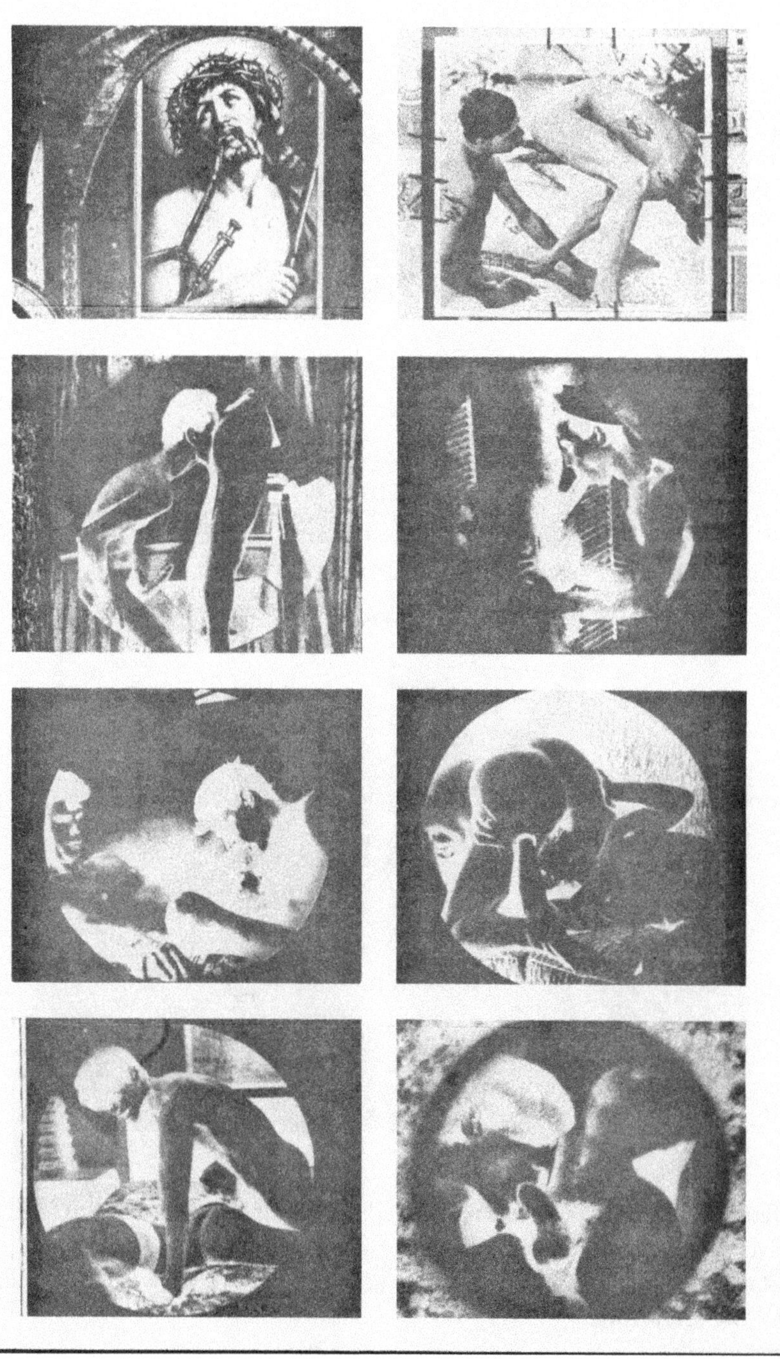

Figure 3.2 Second page, Plaintiff's Exhibition #1, *Wojnarowicz v. American Family Association*, AFA Flyer using images taken from works by Wojnarowicz, 1990. David Wojnarowicz Papers, MSS 092, Box 14, Folder 70. Fales Library and Special Collections, New York University Libraries. Copyright Estate of David Wojnarowicz. Courtesy of the Estate of David Wojnarowicz and P·P·O·W, New York.

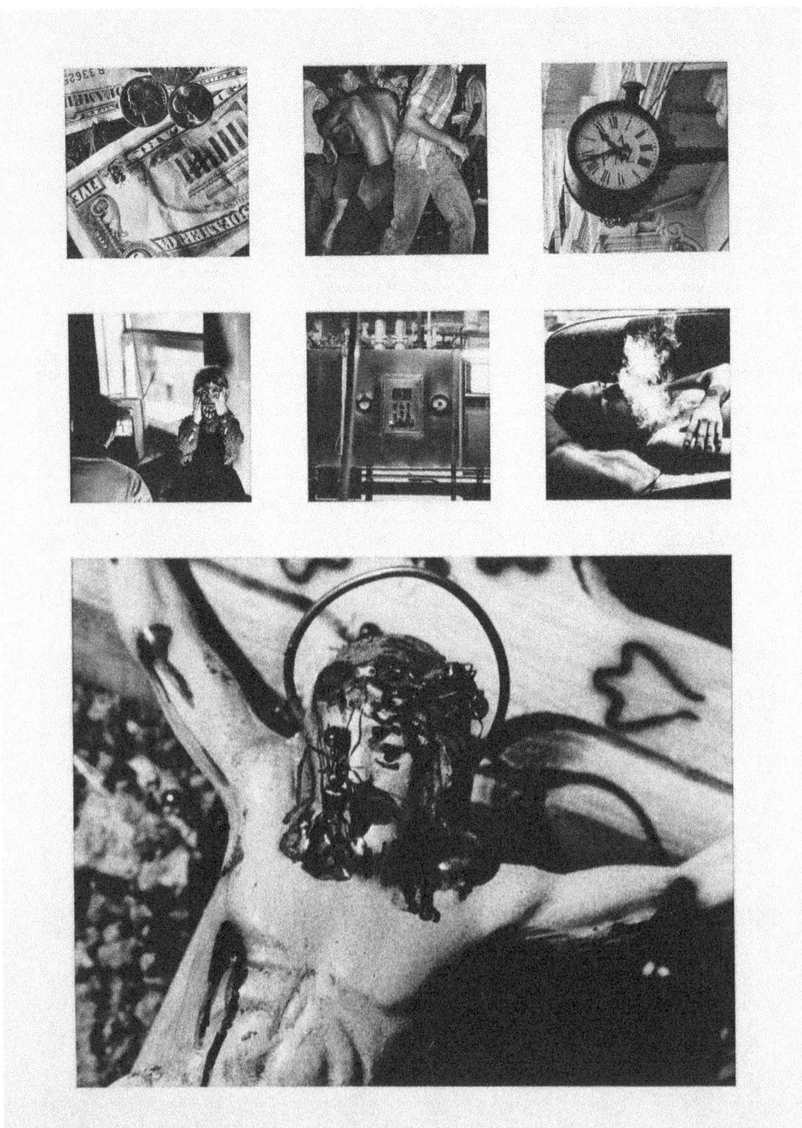

Figure 3.3 David Wojnarowicz, *Spirituality (for Paul Thek)*, 1988–89. Gelatin silver prints on museum board, 41 × 32.5 in. (104.1 × 82.6 cm). Copyright Estate of David Wojnarowicz. Courtesy of the Estate of David Wojnarowicz and P·P·O·W, New York.

Looking at the AFA pamphlet and *Spirituality (for Paul Thek)* side by side reveals some peculiar similarities. Both present photographic images in black and white, squared, and arranged in grid formations. Both feature images of bodies in motion. And both include images of Jesus. In the AFA pamphlet, he appears on the second page, in the top left corner, wearing a crown of thorns and tightening a tourniquet around his arm while shooting up. In *Spirituality (for Paul Thek)*, an image of a crucifix with an ant crawling across Jesus's face takes up the lower half of the piece.

If the formal aspects and content of these pieces seem similar in some ways, that shouldn't come as a surprise—Wildmon rephotographed various selections from Wojnarowicz's work that he found offensive and reassembled them for his pamphlet. He also included written text: "Your Tax Dollars Helped Pay for these 'Works of Art.'" (Note that "Works of Art" here is in quotation marks.) The pamphlet was mailed in an envelope marked *"WARNING! Extremely Offensive Material Enclosed."*[10] For Wildmon and the AFA, these images represented what was going wrong with the United States: not only were queer people living out in the open, but the government was funding art, queer art, that any common citizen would find obscene or sacrilegious—and often both.

Wojnarowicz disagreed. And he was furious about Wildmon's pamphlet, which he thought "mutilated" his work and made him seem like a "banal pornographer."[11] He heard about the AFA pamphlet around April 19, 1990, a week after the first copies were mailed, when he got a call from Barry Blinderman, the director of the University Galleries at Illinois State University in Normal, Illinois.[12] Blinderman had invited Wojnarowicz to put on a retrospective earlier that same year called *Tongues of Flame*. The show was quite popular, drawing around six thousand attendees from the small university town, including over seven hundred on opening night, a record-breaking number for the gallery.[13] A $15,000 grant from the NEA helped fund the publication of the exhibition catalogue, which included reproductions of works exhibited at the show alongside essays and interviews.

This was the catalogue that Wildmon ordered in the mail and used to create his direct-mail testimony to obscenity and sacrilege. Looking at the AFA pamphlet, Wojnarowicz charged, "they're not even my pieces, when they've gotten through with them." Rather, he insisted, Wildmon and the AFA were "creating pieces of their own."[14]

Wojnarowicz was so frustrated by what he saw that he took Wildmon to court. The 1990 case—*David Wojnarowicz v. American Family Association and Donald E. Wildmon*—was heard in the United States District Court in New York.[15] Wojnarowicz and his legal team presented four legal claims against Wildmon and the AFA. They contended that the AFA pamphlet committed copyright infringement; violated the New York Artists' Authorship Rights Act, which protects artists from having their work altered, distorted, or mutilated in reproductions that risk damaging the artist's reputation; violated the Lanham Act, which curbs the appearance of counterfeit merchandise; and constituted an act of libel against the artist.[16] Wojnarowicz got his day in court on June 25, 1990, at a "spirited" bench trial with Judge William C. Connor presiding.[17]

This is a relatively minor court case in the context of legal history, but it provides a critical case study for understanding the culture wars. This showdown between a queer artist and one of the architects of the Christian Right takes us to the center of struggles over interpretation—over where Wildmon and Wojnarowicz saw the obscene or the profane as opposed to the political, the spiritual, or even the sacred. This was not merely a debate over the use or misuse of an artist's work, over good or bad art, over acceptable or obscene art, or over the question of whether the state should fund art deemed offensive. It was all those things. But it was also a culture wars contest over proper expressions of sexuality, religion, and spirituality—over what could even be called "religion" or "spirituality" and what visions of sexuality should enter the public sphere.

This chapter places Wojnarowicz's case against Wildmon in a broader historical context to offer two main arguments. First, this case study helps demonstrate how conservative culture warriors like Wildmon drew upon specific habits of interpretation in debates over feminist and queer art. They tended to read visual culture on the model of language, which is taken to be fundamentally representational and sincere, rather than expressive or performative. This was true even when historical actors have sometimes manipulated language in ways that invoke sincerity as a tool of bad faith. I show how this approach, which we could call an aesthetics of literalism, animated Wildmon's response to queer art, including the creation of his pamphlet.[18] But this is only part of the story. This chapter also explores how Wojnarowicz's writing and visual art—especially his commitment to imagination—were haunted by Catholicism and by his interests in nature and mythology. This eclectic mixing tapped into a longer history of what historian Catherine Albanese calls "metaphysical religion" and helps to reveal the work of "spirituality" in his political and artistic imagination, an imagination that so often worked against the reductive consequences of literalism.

Wojnarowicz, Art, and the Politics of Imagination

On its face, the trial focused on whether Wildmon's pamphlet violated Wojnarowicz's rights as an artist. But the AFA defense team sought to make it as much about the infamous art wars, especially complaints that the federal government funded work many considered sacrilegious or obscene. During Wojnarowicz's deposition, AFA lawyer Joseph Secola asked the artist when he first learned about the "NEA funding controversy," that the federal government was bankrolling art that "could be considered sexually explicit homoerotic or blasphemous to some people."[19] Following various objections and clarifications, Wojnarowicz testified to hearing about the controversies surrounding Serrano and Mapplethorpe the year prior, when they were in the news. Secola asked if he supported the NEA funding "that kind of art."[20] Another round of objections led the AFA lawyer to clarify: he wanted Wojnarowicz to reflect on media comparisons between his work and the controversies which had embroiled previous artists. "I'm not aware of anybody comparing Robert Mapplethorpe's or Andres Serrano's work to mine," Wojnarowicz responded: "I think they do very different work than the work that I do."[21] No doubt well prepared by his own legal team, Wojnarowicz resisted efforts to lump together all manner of creative works based on their presumed offenses to decency. There was not one kind of art, even feminist or queer art, but several. We might add, following Wojnarowicz: there was not one "NEA funding controversy," but several.

At trial, Benjamin Bull, another lawyer for Wildmon and the AFA, returned to the defense's rhetorical framing when he asked Wojnarowicz about his "involvement in the NEA funding controversy."[22] But Bull did not ask about Serrano and Mapplethorpe. Rather, he asked Wojnarowicz about his own first brush with the art wars—a debacle surrounding an art exhibition called *Witnesses: Against Our Vanishing*, which had initially brought him to the attention of Don Wildmon.

AIDS and the Art of *Witnesses*

In November 1989, newly appointed NEA Chair John Frohnmayer revoked a $10,000 grant given to the nonprofit New York–based gallery Artists Space for a show focused on the HIV/AIDS crisis called *Witnesses: Against Our Vanishing*.[23] Photographer Nan Goldin curated the show, which included work by artists such as Kiki Smith, Peter Hujar, Cookie Mueller, Greer Lankton, and of course David Wojnarowicz. In the exhibition's catalogue, Goldin explained that the idea for *Witnesses* emerged from the personal and collective feelings of sorrow and rage so many people were experiencing because of the AIDS crisis. This was nearly a decade into the epidemic, which disproportionately affected members of the queer community and intravenous drug users, including many Black and Latinx New Yorkers, and which had no cure. There wasn't even a good treatment—the earliest versions of the AIDS cocktail, which made the disease into a chronic condition for those who could access and tolerate the medicines, only became widely available in the mid-1990s. Several artists featured at the show lived with AIDS or had died from it. Mueller died from AIDS-related pneumonia less than a week before *Witnesses* opened.[24]

Throughout the 1980s, the Reagan White House avoided discussing the crisis, which was largely associated with homosexuals, sex workers, and drug users. When it did come up, key White House aides like William Bennett and Gary Bauer took a page from their friends in the Christian Right, including the Moral Majority's Jerry Falwell Sr., who declared AIDS to be God's wrath, not only for homosexuals but also for the nation harboring them.[25] They insisted that AIDS education campaigns ought to promote what they considered to be the Christian moral values of heterosexuality and monogamy. Bennett and Bauer even balked at the advice of US Surgeon General C. Everett Koop, an evangelical Christian who argued for reasonable sex education and refused to exclude members of the queer community in his appraisals of the growing pandemic.[26]

They found greater support in North Carolina Senator Jesse Helms. At one point, Helms got wind of a pamphlet created by the Gay Men's Health Crisis (GMHC) that used graphic depictions of queer sex to educate people about the transmission of HIV. Repulsed by what he saw, he proposed an amendment to block federal funding for educational materials that "promote or encourage, directly or indirectly, homosexual activities."[27] Helms's AIDS amendment passed the House and the Senate and was signed into law by Reagan—a blow to Koop's campaign for comprehensive AIDS education, and an even harsher one for the AIDS activists tirelessly fighting for their lives and those of others. For Helms and fellows conservatives, though, homosexuality itself seemed to cause AIDS, and the best path to eliminate the medical disease was to blot out the moral and social one.

Things were not much better in New York City, where Cardinal John C. O'Connor, the archbishop of New York, took a hard stance against any discussion of condoms as part of AIDS prevention efforts. AIDS activists quickly charged the cardinal with moral malfeasance. This was not simply a religious leader sharing his views, they contended; the cardinal oversaw the city's Catholic hospitals and schools, and his policies were disseminated widely throughout a city reeling from the crisis. This was why so many AIDS activists balked when Reagan appointed the conservative Catholic to the President's Commission on the HIV Epidemic in 1987, a group that lacked a single member living with HIV or AIDS. Two years later, when O'Connor was invited to speak about the AIDS crisis at the Vatican, he bemoaned the "dishonesty" of healthcare workers who refused to "confront the moral dimensions of sexual aberrations or drug abuse." "Good morality is good medicine," he insisted—a clear slap in the face of anyone who veered from the strictest versions of Catholic sexual ethics, including, of course, gay and bisexual men.[28]

This was the context for the sorrow and rage that Goldin wanted to amplify at Artists Space. At first, she planned to call the exhibition *Sexuality, Spirituality and Recovery in the Age of AIDS* to "celebrate the indomitable spirit of our community."[29] The final name—*Witnesses: Against Our Vanishing*—dropped the language of spirituality and recovery but maintained the rhetoric of testimony, as Goldin asked participating artists to share work "that represents their personal responses to AIDS."[30] Unsurprisingly, these personal responses often proved quite political, as artists, including Wojnarowicz, openly attacked politicians and religious leaders like Helms and O'Connor because of their AIDS policies. It was this political rhetoric that concerned the NEA's Frohnmayer, who criticized the show for replacing art with politics and, thus, misusing NEA funds.[31]

Frohnmayer's worry over political art stemmed from the recent art wars battles over NEA-funded work by Serrano and Mapplethorpe, which had led Senator Helms once again to propose an amendment to limit the use of public funding for artwork deemed offensive. Even though Helms's amendment would not take effect until 1990, Frohnmayer feared that the political nature of *Witnesses* would run afoul of the NEA's new charge and risk more controversy in DC. He penned a letter to Susan Wyatt, the executive director of Artists Space, requesting that the organization return the $10,000 NEA grant it had received and to include the following disclaimer on appropriate materials: "The National Endowment for the Arts has not supported this exhibition or its catalogue."[32] Wyatt countered: "I am writing to inform you that our Board has met and voted unanimously *not* to relinquish the funds."[33] And so the debate over funding the show continued.

Frohnmayer visited the gallery on November 15—the day before the exhibition's opening—to see the artwork and to meet with artists and activists. Ultimately, he reversed his decision and restored the grant. But he stipulated that none of the NEA funding could go toward the exhibition's catalogue.[34] The reason? A short essay by David Wojnarowicz called "Postcards from America: X-Rays from Hell."[35]

Wojnarowicz's X-Rays from Hell

"Postcards from America" has become Wojnarowicz's most widely read piece of writing. First published in the *Witnesses* catalogue, it was reprinted in the catalogue for *Tongues of Flame* (1990), which Wildmon would later comb through, and in his memoir *Close to the Knives* (1991). In the essay, Wojnarowicz indicted American society for its failure to end the AIDS crisis. "When I was told that I'd contracted this virus," he wrote, "it didn't take long to realize that I'd contracted a diseased society as well."[36] His diagnosis surfaced what he already knew: "Not just the disease but the sense of death in the American landscape."[37]

There is an urgency and intensity to the essay—one shared with much of his painting, photography, and film. The intensity is grounded in grief and rage as much as in erotic and spiritual play, as much in critiques of politics and organized religion as in explorations of mythology. This intensity conveys a deep pessimism but also a glimmer of metaphysical hope. In other writings, Wojnarowicz dazzles the reader with descriptions of vast southwestern landscapes, tales of making art in the ruins of the Christopher Street piers, facts about whales, and records of erotic rendezvous. In such writings, humor (often dark) and sensuality (never innocent) layer his frustrations with American society. If "Postcards from America" offers some of this, too, it conveys even more urgency, more sorrow, more rage. Wojnarowicz's characteristic stream-of-consciousness prose offered no less than a harrowing critique of the United States, a lament on mortality, and a plea for action.

The Preinvented World of American Society

In "Postcards from America," Wojnarowicz described what he often called the "preinvented world" or "preinvented existence" into which people are born.[38] This preinvented world provides a limited set of acceptable scripts for people's lives, often created or sustained by the government or organized religion. The scripts are disseminated through newspapers, radio, and television, through the constant bombardment of messages telling people how to live, what to desire or possess, and who to love and how. In another essay, Wojnarowicz recalled "waking up one morning and realizing that government and god were interchangeable and that most people in the landscape of my birth insisted on having one or both determine the form of their lives."[39] These scripts lead to the illusion of the "ONE-TRIBE NATION," which includes the sense that there is a "general public"—notably singular—in whose name political and religious leaders act. That general public, he reminded his readers, is presumed straight, white, and middle class. It was this "general public" that needed to be defended from AIDS, as it infiltrated from the margins (from queer people, sex workers, drug users, and Black people and other people of color). It was this "general public" (which conservatives also called the "average taxpayer") that would regard artistic work showing queer sex as obviously offensive. But Wojnarowicz also insisted on ways to reveal this homogenous, imagined public to be an illusion—what he called "the possibility of an X-ray of Civilization, an examination of its foundations."[40] Often, for Wojnarowicz, people on the margins were best situated to perform this deep vision. He would know, as he lived his whole life on the edges of society.

Wojnarowicz grew up, mostly in New Jersey, in an often unstable and violent home.[41] His parents—Dolores, who was Australian, and Ed, a Polish-American—had a tumultuous marriage that ended in an ugly divorce in 1956, when Wojnarowicz was around two.[42] At one point, Ed kidnapped Wojnarowicz and his older brother and sister to keep them from his ex-wife. They lived for a while in Michigan, where Ed was from, before returning to New Jersey. The children feared their father, who was an abusive alcoholic. He was also a devout Catholic who sent the children to Catholic school for at least a few years.[43] Wojnarowicz and his siblings eventually reconnected with their mother, who was living alone in New York City, and fled their father's home to live with her. Wojnarowicz was probably around eleven at the time, as he entered the sixth grade at Public School 111 on West 53rd Street.[44]

Dolores wasn't physically abusive, but she was largely absent from her children's lives. Wojnarowicz thought she regretted taking them in.[45] He began spending time on the streets, where he discovered at a young age that he could trade sex with older men for money. At fourteen, Wojnarowicz enrolled in the High School of Music and Art in Manhattan, but he quit before graduating and "lived on the streets full-time."[46] To support himself, Wojnarowicz found work in bookstores and as a busboy (and later security detail) at the nightclub Danceteria, where he labored alongside fellow aspiring artists like Keith Haring and Zoe Leonard.[47] He never made much money, even once he started to become more successful as an artist. But in the 1970s, New York's East Village was cheap, and he managed to get by.

Wojnarowicz's experiences of violence and instability in his childhood homes would shape his artistic pursuits and political critique throughout the late 1970s and 1980s. Indeed, just as the emerging Christian Right sought to make "the family" the foundation of US American morality and national success in these years, Wojnarowicz was spray-painting one of his first iconic symbols around New York, a stencil called "Burning House" (1979) that captures a deeper truth beneath the idealized home. As historian Linda Gordon has shown, the family has long served as a key site for violence, especially against women and children, rather than a safe or sacred space.[48] Wojnarowicz's burning house joined a larger array of visual symbols, as we will soon see, that he used to critique US colonialism and racism, right-wing nationalism, and organized religion. But he also put these criticisms in writing, often in searing prose.

When Wojnarowicz described the "diseased society" he had contracted along with HIV, he pointed directly to Cardinal O'Connor. In "Postcards from America," he recalled seeing a story in the newspaper in which the Archbishop of New York discussed wanting to participate in activities led by Operation Rescue, a right-wing anti-abortion group that staged sit-in demonstrations and used other tactics to block access to women's health clinics.[49] Wojnarowicz responded, "This fat cannibal from that house of walking swastikas up on fifth avenue should lose his church tax-exempt status and pay taxes retroactively for the last couple of centuries." He also criticized O'Connor for opposing comprehensive sex education. "This creep in black skirts," Wojnarowicz continued, "has kept safer sex information off the local television stations and mass transit spaces for the last eight years of the AIDS epidemic thereby helping thousands and thousands to their unnecessary deaths."[50] The anger here is palpable, and Wojnarowicz did not seek to temper it, even in writing, as he grappled with the immediacy of mortality—his friends' and his own.

Confronting Mortality

"Postcards from America" weaves blistering criticisms of the United States, especially of its political and religious leaders, into a larger meditation on death, including "this culture's refusal to deal with mortality."[51] Wojnarowicz described "witnessing the deaths of dozens of friends and a handful of lovers, among them some of the most authentically spiritual people I've ever known." He placed the blame for their deaths "on the shoulders of a bunch of bigoted creeps" in positions of power who do too little.[52] To capture both the political moment and this sense of grief, we should recall how queer people had begun to forge friendships—what anthropologist Kath Weston calls "chosen families"—through the emergence of new communities in places like New York and San Francisco, often after leaving behind their biological families in the face of judgment or exclusion. These chosen families—friends, mentors, lovers, and former lovers—lacked the legal protections and cultural acceptance that most biological or normative families enjoyed, which made the impact of the AIDS crisis even more harrowing.[53]

Among Wojnarowicz's chosen family was the photographer Peter Hujar. They met early in 1981 (or possibly late December 1980) at a bar in the East Village. Hujar was twenty years his senior and already an established photographer. That night, when they retired to Hujar's apartment, the photographer showed Wojnarowicz his book *Portraits in Life and Death* (1974).[54] It includes portraits of various friends—fellow artists and writers like John Waters, Divine, Diana Vreeland, and Fran Lebowitz—as well as photographs of mummies in catacombs shot in Palermo, Italy, in the 1960s. But Wojnarowicz was already familiar with the book. He was moved by Hujar's ability to capture the aesthetic and emotional power of mortality. Although their sexual relationship was short-lived, Hujar recognized a certain intensity and talent in Wojnarowicz's work. The two men shared an enduring artistic and intellectual connection until Hujar's death from AIDS. "I love him and how much he means to me," Wojnarowicz wrote in *Close to the Knives*, "and I tell him everything in my head, all the contradictions all fear and all love and all alone."[55]

Hujar's eventual decline from AIDS likewise shaped Wojnarowicz's thinking about mortality in ways he could hardly have anticipated. He recalled the final moments they spent together, along with their friend, the drag performer Ethyl Eichelberger, who called out, "David ... look at Peter," just as he took his final breaths.[56] It was November 26, 1987.

Once everyone left the room, Wojnarowicz took out his Super 8 camera and took photos of his dead friend—"my brother, my father, my emotional link."[57] He barely cried. A nun entered the room—Hujar had become more serious about his Catholicism in those final days—but Wojnarowicz asked her to leave. He looked at his friend to say some final words, but nothing came. "This is the most important event in my life," Wojnarowicz later wrote, "and my mouth can't form words." Finally, they arrived. "All I want is some sort of grace," he recalled, "And then the water comes from my eyes."[58]

The experience of Hujar's death and Wojnarowicz's own diagnosis with AIDS animate the intense emotional register of "Postcards from America." After these brushes with mortality, Wojnarowicz explained, "I tend to dismantle and to discard any and all kinds of spiritual and psychic and physical words or concepts designed to make sense of the external world or designed to give momentary comfort."[59] This process—"like stripping the body of flesh in order to see the skeleton, the structure"—became a way to cut through the preinvented world to find the raw experience underneath it.[60] Wojnarowicz wanted to confront mortality directly, alongside his mounting sorrow and deepening rage. But he did not simply turn inward. "To turn our private grief for the loss of friends, family, lovers and strangers into something public," he insisted, "would serve as another powerful dismantling tool."[61]

Rituals of Protest and Powers of Imagination

Wojnarowicz wrote in "Postcards from America" that "the ritual of memorials" helped to make personal grief into something public. But it wasn't enough. Like so many of his contemporaries, he attended memorial after memorial as the numbers of people killed by the AIDS crisis multiplied. Yet, he lamented, little was happening outside these memorials and within the immediate communities most impacted by AIDS. He worried that friends would become "professional pallbearers" "perfecting their rituals of death."[62] Instead, Wojnarowicz wanted people screaming in the streets, and he provided a roadmap to express this rage:

I imagine what it would be like if friends had a demonstration each time a lover or a friend or a stranger died of AIDS. I imagine what it would be like if, each time a lover, friend or stranger died of this disease, their friends, lovers or neighbors would take the dead body and drive with it in a car a hundred miles an hour to washington d.c. and blast through the gates of the white house and come to a screeching halt before the entrance and dump their lifeless form on the front steps.[63]

This passage became a mantra for many AIDS activists, including those who had marched alongside Wojnarowicz as part of New York's chapter of the AIDS Coalition to Unleash Power, or ACT UP. Inspired by his fantasy of protest, AIDS activists made it a reality when they organized the "Ashes Action" in October 1992. During this "political funeral," demonstrators launched the cremated remains of loved ones over the gates of the White House onto its immaculately kept lawn.[64] Wojnarowicz had died that July, but this was exactly the type of public ritual of protest he wanted to see, as the Ashes Action brought his imagination new life.

Wojnarowicz thought imagination offered "one of the last frontiers left for radical gesture." "At least in my ungoverned imagination," he wrote, "I can fuck somebody without a rubber, or I can, in the privacy of my own skull, douse Helms with a bucket of gasoline and set his putrid ass on fire or throw congressman William Dannemeyer off the empire state building."[65] Wojnarowicz's imagination may have been ungoverned, but it was exactly this kind of language that worried Frohnmayer and had led him to pull NEA funding for *Witnesses*. And America's key culture warriors took notice.

A week after the show opened, Patrick Buchanan, who had served as White House communications director under Reagan (1985–87) and would seek the 1992 GOP presidential nomination, blasted the exhibition in the pages of the conservative *Washington Times*. He complained that the "gay rights community" and the "art community" both "suffered from an infantile disorder." Buchannan mocked how "the gays yearly die by the thousands of AIDS, crying out in rage for what they cannot have: respect for a lifestyle Americans simply do not respect" and funding for medical research "to save them from the consequences of their own suicidal self indulgence." He reserved a particular frustration for "AIDS victim David Wojnarowicz." The right-wing politico cited passages from "Postcards from America," including those quoted above about O'Connor, Helms, and Dannemeyer, as examples of the government funding "ever-cruder defamations of conservatives and the Catholic Church."[66]

These were the same lines from "Postcards from America" that Wildmon's legal team wanted to get on record while questioning Wojnarowicz during his trial. Wildmon's lawyer asked the artist about his essay in the *Tongues of Flame* catalogue alongside another called "The Seven Deadly Sins," a "fact sheet" Wojnarowicz had written with the help of some friends in ACT UP/NY.[67] Wojnarowicz never thought "Postcards from America" would gain the attention it did. He didn't regret his choice of words but wished his reasons for blaming conservative religious and political leaders for the AIDS crisis were clearer. To fix this, he handed out copies of this fact sheet at the opening of *Witnesses*.[68] The AFA lawyer wanted to bring up this public writing and commentary to build an argument that Wojnarowicz was a public figure regarding the NEA controversy. He suggested a parallel between Wojnarowicz's criticisms of the NEA and various conservative leaders' (including Wildmon's) criticism of the artist's work in the AFA pamphlet.[69]

These were also the key lines that conservatives picked up and reprinted in direct mail and newspaper advertisements denouncing the use of public funding to subsidize what they considered obscene and anti-Christian speech. Wildmon created two such advertisements himself—the first ran in the *Washington Times* in February 1990, and the second ran in *USA Today* the following month. The AFA ads, which Wojnarowicz's attorneys submitted as exhibits in the trial, asked in large, bold print: "Is This How You Want Your Tax Dollars Spent?" They included a fact sheet of their own listing various projects funded by the NEA, from Mapplethorpe's *The Perfect Moment* to the San Francisco Lesbian and Gay Film Festival (considered obscene for featuring lesbian and gay themes). Both ads mention Wojnarowicz's essay. The *Washington Times* ad describes an art exhibition "in which angry homosexuals denounced Catholic clergyman John Cardinal O'Connor" and cites some of Wojnarowicz's words without naming him.[70] The *USA Today* ad repeats this line and adds another mentioning Wojnarowicz by name and retelling his fantasies of dousing Helms with gasoline and chucking Dannemeyer off the Empire State Building.[71] It also includes the image of Jesus shooting up that was extracted from one of Wojnarowicz's collages.

Perhaps it was ironic that the AFA and fellow conservative activist groups recycled tendentious reports of the NEA debacle surrounding *Witnesses*. Indeed, Frohnmayer likely would never have thought to investigate Wojnarowicz's work if not for the previous efforts of Don Wildmon who, "more than anyone else," according to Illinois Congressman Sidney Yates, "initiated the furor that enveloped the NEA."[72] But Wildmon did not start out with his eyes trained on queer art and the NEA. His crusade against obscenity and sacrilege emerged from a longer campaign for decency.

The Decency of Donald Wildmon

Don Wildmon—who cheekily reports being dubbed the "Tupelo Terror" and the "Ayatollah of the Airwaves"—would probably be among the first to say he seemed an unlikely candidate to become one of the Christian Right's key leaders in the fight to restore moral decency in the United States.[73] "He looks more like a pharmacist than a demagogue," wrote one journalist in a mostly positive profile in the evangelical magazine *Christianity Today*, with a "rural Southern accent thick enough to spread on pancakes."[74] Wildmon was born and raised in a humble Methodist family in northeast Mississippi. The youngest of five children, he grew up with no phone, electricity, or indoor plumbing. His father had to sell the family cotton farm after several bad years but eventually found work as, of all things, an STD investigator for the state department of health. His mother worked as a teacher.[75] Wildmon recounted these years with fondness—a simpler time, he explained, when he could leave his car parked with the keys left in the ignition in the busy town square without worrying anyone would steal it.[76] In this nostalgic story, communities were tight-knit and grounded in a shared (if particular) Christian ethic. It was the kind of society to which Wildmon hoped the country might return.

Even as a child, Wildmon was competitive—he probably had to be to fend off his four siblings. He recalled one instance during a Boy Scout training course when his peers voted him down for an award because he was too obnoxious. His mother called him determined. It was this same determination that led Wildmon to apply not once but twice to seminary at Emory University. He was rejected the first time, having earned paltry grades as an undergraduate at Millsaps College. But, as he tells the story, he regrouped and sought out connections through his own social and religious networks to find a way in. This time he succeeded—and he learned the lesson that persistence, even a little pushiness, yielded results. Wildmon even graduated from the three-year seminary program a year early, in 1965, before returning to Mississippi to pastor a new Methodist congregation in Tupelo.

In 1976, he was reassigned to a larger and more affluent church, the First United Methodist Church of Southhaven, Mississippi, located just outside of Memphis.[77]

After working as a pastor for over a decade, Wildmon sensed a new calling. The story of the reverend's shift from leading a congregation to taking on purveyors of violence and pornography through the National Federation for Decency (precursor to the AFA) has become something of an origin myth, one repeated in interviews and in his own publications. Wildmon offers an abbreviated version in his 1985 book *The Home Invaders*, whose cover reveals as much as its title. It shows two young white boys, one with blonde hair and blue eyes. They face the viewer but do not make eye contact. Instead, the boys stare into a television, positioned between them and the viewer, its glow ensnaring their faces. Wildmon offers a more fleshed out account in *Don Wildmon: The Man the Networks Love to Hate* (1989). The cover of this book also tells a story. It features Wildmon, dressed in a white shirt and tie, standing next to a television sitting on a wooden table. His left elbow presses down on the top of the TV, his hands clasped together, united to pressure networks to clean up the airwaves.

Wildmon's journey started one late December night in 1976, when the pastor joined his wife Lynda, their four children, and their Pekinese Charlie Chu sitting around the living room looking for something to watch on television.[78] They tried all three primetime channels—their options at the time were ABC, NBC, and CBS—but found every station airing shows that featured adultery, profanity, or excessive violence. Frustrated, Wildmon asked his kids to turn off the television. The menu of options—"promiscuous sex, crude profanity, and gratuitous violence"—kept Wildmon up that night. It was not simply that cultural norms had shifted in the last decade or two, he explained, but that "the changes in TV's attitudes toward morality were now coming into the sanctity of my own home."[79] He decided to do something about it.

The first thing Wildmon did was to challenge his congregants at the First United Methodist Church to take part in "Turn the TV Off Week."[80] The press took notice, and Wildmon's first public stand against indecency found widespread support. He grappled with what to do next: "I remember lying in bed thinking, 'Is this what the Lord wants me to do?'"[81] After debating his next move for a month, Wildmon committed to his new path. In 1977, he left his church to dedicate his time to founding and running the National Federation for Decency. Wildmon and his family returned to Tupelo,

Mississippi, where his wife Lynda started working as a substitute teacher to supplement their income. The reverend used the $5,000 he had in savings to start his organization, which he set up in the family dining room.[82]

Wildmon first appealed directly to television network executives. "I thought that if you appealed to a person's moral base rationally and reasonably and explained the progressive nature of something that is abhorrent," he recalled in his 1989 memoir, "then that person would respond."[83] But that didn't work. The network executives he met with in the late 1970s mistakenly thought that "they *were* being moral."[84] He had to find another way to convey his message, another common language, which he found in money. The way to get television executives to listen was to go after companies that paid for advertisements to be aired during their programs. Wildmon compiled his own statistics about the frequency of sexual content on television programs, ranked the shows with the most sex, and determined which companies ran the most advertisements during those programs (which he referred to as "sponsors" of "this sexual and profane content").[85] One of the leading offenders, he learned, was Sears, Roebuck and Company, which he criticized for their "frequent sponsorship" of three of the most sexually offensive programs—ABC's *Three's Company* and *Charlie's Angels* and NBC's *James at 15*. When Wildmon met with Sears's senior vice president of public affairs, though, he found himself once again rebuffed.

These initial meetings would establish a narrative precedent for Wildmon, in which elite city executives dismiss the country preacher as a backwoods moralist. He welcomed it. "I'm from Mississippi, which means I don't wear shoes," he joked at one point.[86] He even found these caricatures useful, casting himself as a modern-day David ready to slay his Goliaths. Wildmon relished when opponents underestimated him, casting him as little more than "a Bible totin', Scripture quotin', hell fire and damnation Elmer Gantry type who could perceive 'pornography' in the Sears Roebuck catalog."[87] He wasn't a fundamentalist—though many of his friends were, he explained—but Wildmon was more than happy to play the role if it gave him the upper hand. "The more mistaken they are the better it is for me," he explained.[88]

And, in his telling, Sears did underestimate him. Finding little traction with company spokespeople, Wildmon's National Federation for Decency changed tactics and staged a nationwide consumer boycott in 1978.[89] The protest received national press. The *Washington Post* even declared "victory for the rebels" at the NFD, when Sears announced its decision to withdraw all of its advertisements from *Three's Company* and *Charlie's Angels*.[90] Sears maintained that NFD's protests—which included picketing outside Sears Tower in Chicago and at local stores across the country—played no role in their decision. But Wildmon took it as a win for the underdog, and the threat to boycott became a key tool in his battles for decency.[91]

Wildmon soon began courting support from other conservative Christians in the quickly emerging Christian Right. In 1981, he joined with the Moral Majority's Jerry Falwell Sr. to form the Coalition for Better TV. With the help of Richard Viguerie, the new Right's architect of direct mail marketing and funding campaigns, Wildmon and Falwell claimed millions of followers in their efforts to return morality to television. Their partnership was short-lived, as disagreements about boycotting tactics led the leaders to part ways before even a year had passed.[92] But Wildmon continued to seek broader support.

In the mid-1980s, Wildmon rallied Christian leaders from across ten denominations to draft a statement of concern about the prevalence of violence, sex, profanity, and anti-Christian bias on television. Some 1,600 Christian leaders eventually signed on to this statement. To harness this energy, he helped found CLeaR-TV (Christian Leaders for Responsible Television) in 1986. The group claimed an expansive base of conservative support, including leaders from dozens of Protestant denominations and more than a hundred Catholic bishops. Wildmon was elected to serve as its executive director.[93] Practically speaking, CLeaR-TV operated much like the AFA, and the lines between the two easily blurred. But it gave Wildmon another title and an extended audience for his jeremiads against indecency, which increasingly underscored two themes: anti-Christian bias and pornography.

Anti-Christian Bias and Hollywood's Secular Humanism

Though the NFD initially focused on violence, profanity, and sex, Wildmon quickly noticed what he considered anti-Christian bias on television and in the media more broadly.[94] In the spring of 1980, he brought together a team of more than five hundred trained volunteers to survey over seven hundred hours of television programming. Their goal was to determine what kinds of values came across the airwaves. They had a guide for discerning and scoring "Christian" values, which included "love, respect for God and persons, honesty, marital fidelity, hope, faith, attitude, clean speech, kindness, faithfulness, proper perspective toward possessions, fairness, forgiveness, etc." "Non-Christian values," Wildmon wrote in an NFD media alert, "were the opposite."[95]

For Wildmon and his followers, the results of the survey were clear—television programming favored non-Christian values over Christian values by nearly three to one. They reported 8,877 instances of non-Christian values that were shown favorably, compared to only 3,618 instances of Christian values represented positively.[96] Volunteers also gave programs an overall rating on Christian values, from +5 to –5 (with 0 being neutral). Only NBC scored in the black (at 0.415). Both ABC and CBS scored below zero (–0.4 and –0.413, respectively). Wildmon's team then assessed depictions of Christian characters on television. They found that only 22.4 percent of Christian characters were shown very favorably, 16.8 percent moderately so, and 26.1 percent in average light, while 14.3 percent were unfavorable and 20.02 percent were shown in a very negative light.[97] Wildmon noted three trends. Representations of Christianity appeared more often in programs set further in the past, such as *Little House on the Prairie* (NBC) and *The Waltons* (CBS); Christianity was "conspicuously absent" in shows set in the present; yet, when Christians did appear in such shows, they were cast negatively, often as "closed-minded, ignorant fools," if not worse.[98]

Wildmon attributed this anti-Christian bias to "secular humanism."[99] At first, the Mississippi Methodist was weary of even using the term, which he explained was becoming a catchword for the Christian Right. But he quickly came around. "I believe Jerry [Falwell] wouldn't say that 'secular humanism has become the religion of America,'" he wrote, "unless he knew what he was talking about."[100] Falwell had laid out his case against secular humanism in his 1980 book *Listen America!*, naming it the source of major social ills besetting the country, from the breakdown of the "traditional family" and the rise of the feminist and homosexual revolutions to mounting indecency on television.[101]

Opposition to secular humanism was grounded in the older rhetoric of the Cold War, which pitted Christianity, capitalism, and individual freedom against godless communism. Moral panics around sexuality—especially homosexuality—would also constitute a key part of the crusade against communism in this period.[102] For religious conservatives, secular humanism named the powerful worldview—notably singular—that replaced God with humankind as the arbiter of ethics, values, and truth. Evangelical theologian Francis Schaeffer famously outlined the argument against secular humanism in his 1981 *Christian Manifesto* (his rejoinder to Karl Marx's *Communist Manifesto*). He discerned two competing worldviews in Western civilization—the Christian one (sometimes, in a gesture to ecumenicism, he would say "Judeo-Christian") and the humanist one. Schaeffer was responding not only to Marxism but also to the more recent *Humanist Manifestos I* and *II* (from 1933 and 1973, respectively), which he thought elaborated humanism as no less than a religion in itself, one diametrically opposed to Christianity.[103] Wildmon, too, picked up on these later manifestos— "real eye-openers," he wrote, that seemed at first to bear much in common with the Declaration of Independence. "However," he warned, "these men and women weren't declaring their independence from another nation but from God and the rules of order he gives us through Scripture."[104] Put simply, he explained, "humanism is a religion which teaches that man is his own god."[105] For followers of this humanist religion, he charged, Christianity had become "irrelevant" and "meaningless."[106]

Wildmon argued that the writers and producers—the often-cited "Hollywood elites"—behind the vast majority of television espoused this secular humanist worldview, one that found "adultery, fornicatious promiscuity, homosexuality, bestiality, even incest" to be "all quite acceptable."[107] To back up his charge, he pointed to a 1983 survey of Hollywood executives. He underscored the demographics—"59 percent were Jewish, 5 percent were Protestant, and 12 percent were Catholic"—and the clincher: though most were raised religious, more than 90 percent reported seldom attending any kind of religious services at all.[108] Wildmon made much of these statistics in his claims of anti-Christian bias, which even dipped into antisemitic rhetoric, when he suggested a correlation between the relatively high percentage of Jews among Hollywood writers and executives and the immorality of their programs. Under pressure from the Anti-Defamation League, Wildmon eventually backed off some of these claims and began to emphasize shared "Judeo-Christian" values, a phrasing that has provided cover for many Christian projects—liberal and conservative alike—that have sought to appear pluralistic.[109]

Wildmon's reports on anti-Christian prejudice found traction among his readers and yielded donations to his growing organizations. But he was just as adept at harnessing the rhetorical possibilities of *negative* responses, through which he could figure himself a modern martyr for decency. He recounts an apt example in his memoir. In 1980, he was invited to give a speech for the National Broadcasters Association for Community Affairs in Vail, Colorado. Wildmon recalls how his speech—called "Religious Discrimination on Network Television"—drew hisses and taunts from the audience. One person in the front yelled "G-- D---," while another exclaimed, "That's bull sh--."[110] But Wildmon would not be silenced. Such taunts only fueled the rhetoric of Christian persecution underlining his efforts. As he explained in a separate interview, Christians were too reluctant to take on "the cross," to risk doing what was unpopular if it "means rejection, pain, humiliation, and suffering."[111]

Wildmon soon realized he was engaged in a "spiritual war" against a bigger enemy.[112] "When I first started this in 1977," he explained, "I thought I was dealing with sex and violence on TV. I've discovered we are dealing with a war between the Christian view of man, and a secular, or humanistic or materialistic, view of man."[113] But that day in Vail, at least one supporter was willing to carry the cross with him. "I was especially encouraged by a young black woman representing a large TV station in my home state," he recalled, who said she agreed with him and thanked him "for having the courage to tell it like it is."[114]

Wildmon's Case Against Pornography

For Wildmon, the scourges of secular humanism also included the growing prevalence of pornography. The 1970s had witnessed the "Golden Age of Pornography" or "Porno Chic," as sexually explicit films multiplied, gaining a wider audience alongside popular adult magazines like *Playboy* and *Penthouse*. By the 1980s, pornographic films would take over the VHS market, providing easy, at-home erotic entertainment. Suddenly, explicit sex seemed to be everywhere.[115]

Like many conservative Christians, Wildmon saw in the sexual revolutions of the 1960s and 1970s not the unfurling of new pleasures and freedoms, including those of pornography, but the foreshadowing of the fall of Western civilization itself. "America and Rome," he warned: "We are beginning to have a lot in common."[116] Wildmon was gesturing here to Edward Gibbons's *Decline and Fall of the Roman Empire*, which conservatives read as placing sexual license at the center of the Roman Empire's undoing. The United States could be next. The fight against pornography thus became part of Wildmon's broader "spiritual war." Without the participation of Christians, he claimed, "our society will be so saturated with this secular and humanist mindset that the chances of preventing the secular and humanist view of life from becoming the foundation of our society will be nil."[117]

Wildmon decided to educate fellow conservatives and call them to action with his 1986 book *The Case Against Pornography*. He makes his case on several rhetorical levels. Appealing to the rhetoric of empirical truth, Wildmon offered a "book of facts" that marshalled carefully selected (and selective) evidence from psychologists, political scientists, pediatricians, police detectives, and Christian leaders, alongside stories of "victims" of pornography, to present a damning case. Emotionally, the book appeals to readers' presumed disgust by defining pornography as an anything-goes genre of absolute debasement. "Whatever sexual aberration the mind can conceive is now available," Wildmon wrote, "from adults having sex with babies just a few months old, to humans having sex with animals, to humans eating the feces of other humans and animals, to humans drinking urine, and on to 'snuff' films," in which, he claimed, "a person is actually killed during the filming of a pornographic movie."[118]

This was the moral rot hastening the downfall of Western civilization, Wildmon warned. He borrowed the words of Catholic anti-pornographer Charles Keating Jr.: "If this is allowed to go any further, does anyone doubt that God should destroy us?"[119] It is no mere coincidence that, through Keating, Wildmon invoked the biblical story of Sodom and Gomorrah. Conservative Christians read this story as a warning not only against sodomy and sexual sin generally, but also about the dangers to a society that harbors such sexual sin, for which God's punishment is the destruction of the guilty city, nation, or even whole civilization. The invocation also gestures to the way Wildmon conflated pornography with what he considered other forms of sexual sin, including incest, child abuse, secular sex education, homosexuality, and, by the mid-1980s, the raging AIDS crisis, which, for many conservative evangelicals, emerged from homosexual immorality itself.[120]

Wildmon's case against pornography was also part of a longer history of mobilizations against obscenity and the broader movement within the emergent new Right to use pornography as a political tool. The NFD director found a model in the work of Charles Keating, the Roman Catholic quoted above, who had founded Citizens for Decent Literature (CDL, later renamed Citizens for Decency Through Law) in Cincinnati in the mid-1950s. Keating himself followed a longer history of Catholic censorship groups, such as the Legion of Decency and the National Organization for Decent Literature, whose influence had largely waned by mid-century. As historian Whitney

Strub argues, CDL succeeded in large measure because Keating downplayed its roots in conservative Catholic politics and distanced himself from the rhetoric of censorship in favor of the language of obscenity law, which the Supreme Court upheld in *Roth v. United States* (1975). Keating also reached out to like-minded Protestant and Jewish leaders. In doing so, writes Strub, he "helped shape a template for using sexual politics to forge Catholic-Protestant political alliances."[121] Wildmon picked up this template—literally so, at least in one case, when he included a "model obscenity statute" from CDL in his *Case Against Pornography* for readers to use in their own communities.

Wildmon was happy to work alongside conservative Catholics.[122] In a 1986 interview for the right-wing Catholic magazine *The Wanderer*, he boasted about "the tremendous amount of support from Catholics" he had received for his campaigns against pornography, including his efforts to convince drugstores to stop selling *Penthouse* and *Playboy*. He also underscored the many Catholic leaders involved in CLeaR-TV, including "96 Catholic Bishops, 17 Archbishops, and two Cardinals."[123] Outside the Church hierarchy, Wildmon's many Catholic allies against pornography included the Eagle Forum's Phyllis Schlafly and the president of Morality in Media, Joseph J. Reilly Jr.[124] Schlafly had made a name for herself in the 1970s through her campaign against the Equal Rights Amendment and would continue to lead conservative attacks on abortion rights, gay rights, and pornography in the decades to come. Morality in Media was founded in 1962 by Father Morton A. Hill, S. J., as Operation Yorkville (the name changed in 1968), originally at the bequest of his superiors.[125] Catholic Church leaders worried about shifting sexual mores, from Alfred Kinsey's 1948 publication of *The Sexual Behavior of the Human Male* to Hugh Hefner's founding of *Playboy* in 1953. And they especially wanted to keep sexually explicit material out of the hands of minors. One of their first campaigns sought to ban John Cleland's erotic romp *Fanny Hill*.

In 1967, President Lyndon B. Johnson appointed Morton Hill to his Presidential Commission on Obscenity and Pornography. Keating also lobbied to join the Commission, though he only succeeded in gaining an appointment once Nixon took over in 1969. But when the Commission released its report the following year, it was a major disappointment to conservatives. It argued that pornography, on the whole, did not pose a major social problem, that it did not adversely affect moral values or character, and that adults should not be restricted from accessing it. The report even called for the repeal of prohibitions on the sale or exhibition of sexually explicit materials at federal, state, and local levels.[126] Nixon balked at the findings, and political conservatives readily panned the report. Hill joined another member of the Commission to pen a dissent that characterized the report as "a Magna Carta for the pornographer."[127] Keating blasted the report for espousing a "libertine philosophy" and charged that the commission unthinkingly fell into the hands of an extremist ACLU agenda.[128]

While Keating downplayed the Catholic elements of his anti-porn work, evangelical Protestants within the burgeoning Christian Right—including Wildmon, Falwell, and the Council for National Policy's Tim LaHaye—readily centered the threat of God's wrath in their campaigns against pornography.[129] And they found greater support for their cause in President Ronald Reagan, who ordered another investigation into the effects of pornography in 1985. The Attorney General's Commission on Pornography, known as the Meese Commission (after Attorney General Edwin Meese), was stacked from the start with anti-porn activists, including Focus on the Family's James C. Dobson. The new commission, which was allotted only a fraction of the budget and time of the earlier investigation, sidelined the previous group's social scientific approach in favor of dramatic public hearings about the ill effects of porn. As Strub writes, the Meese Commission "showed the Reagan Administration's preference for superficial gestures designed to placate the Christian Right over substantial policy support," as the public hearings appealed to the desire for "newsworthy, highly emotional flashpoints where porn opponents could voice their arguments."[130]

To no one's surprise, the Meese Commission opposed pornography and detailed its harmful effects in its 1986 report. The report linked pornography directly to aggressive behavior and sexual violence. But to make this case, the Meese Commission mostly eschewed empirical evidence, which its authors admitted was in short supply. Rather, the commission asserted that assumptions about this link "are plainly justified by our own common sense."[131] It also capitalized on a seemingly unlikely alliance between right-wing opponents of obscenity and a vocal subset of the feminist movement, including feminist activists Catharine MacKinnon and Andrea Dworkin, who spoke before the committee. Sometimes called anti-porn feminists amid the infamous "sex wars," activists like MacKinnon and Dworkin opposed pornography and sought to censor it through legal means. They drew a strong and direct connection between pornography and sexual violence, even intentionally collapsing distinctions between the representational world of porn and reality through readings that "literalized" visual pornography. As Susan Brownmiller, a founding member of Women Against Pornography, argued, "pornography *is* violence against women."[132] Wildmon would agree, but without the accompanying commitment to progressive feminist politics.

The Meese Report came out the same year Wildmon published *The Case Against Pornography* and may have offered hope to the reverend and his followers. But pornography remained only one piece of a much larger problem. "Pornography is not the disease but merely a visible symptom," he explained: "It springs from a moral cancer in our society, and it will lead us to destruction if we are unable to stop it."[133] For Wildmon, this "moral cancer" developed from the same secular humanism which had earlier cast Christianity as meaningless. In this spiritual war between Christianity and humanism, he also linked pornography to homosexuality. Following the rhetoric of the Cold War, writes Strub, "if communism embodied the greatest political perversion, homosexuality played its internal, domestic counterpart."[134] Homosexuality, in other words, already figured in the national rhetoric as a sickness coming from within. Through the 1980s, conservative Christians built upon these older conflations of pornography, obscenity, and homosexuality when they saw in the AIDS crisis an even more literal sign of the moral cancer of sexual sin and the secular humanism that fostered it. Indeed, Wildmon and other members of the Christian Right counted any support for homosexuality (or feminism) as itself advocating pornography and spreading anti-Christian bias, as obscenity and sacrilege overlapped in their theo-political imagination.[135]

These rhetorical conflations fueled Christian Right organizing—and funding. By the early 1990s, the American Family Association boasted twenty-three employees. Its budget had grown from the $5,000 in savings Wildmon had started with in 1977 to roughly five to six million dollars a year, largely gleaned from annual donations. The AFA claimed over 450,000 members from 65 chapters across the United States, along with a team of 2,500 volunteers committed to fighting the onslaught of pornography, violence, and anti-Christian rhetoric overtaking the nation.[136] Some of Wildmon's most publicized campaigns focused on removing pornographic magazines from 7-Elevens, opposing Martin Scorsese's 1988 film *The Last Temptation of Christ* (based on Nikos Kazantzakis's 1955 novel), and pressuring Pepsi Co. to drop Madonna from their ad campaigns. In the last case, Madonna's music video "Like a Prayer" had set off a firestorm of controversy. Wildmon characterized her representation of Christianity as "sacrilegious to the core," in part because of her blending of religion and eroticism.[137] The AFA also staged a campaign against the hip-hop group 2 Live Crew, labeling obscene their 1989 album *As Nasty as They Wanna Be*. The leader of an AFA chapter in Florida referred to their music as "mind pollution and body pollution." Opposition to 2 Live Crew eventually led to the arrest of three of the group's members for public obscenity while they were performing at a venue in Hollywood, Florida, in 1990. A jury eventually acquitted the musicians, but the broader debate over obscenity would continue to rage in the public sphere and in the halls of Congress.[138]

It was not until the spring of 1989 that Wildmon would turn his attention to the federal government, helping to ignite the infamous art wars when he alerted Congressional conservatives like Jesse Helms and Alfonse D'Amato that the government was funding work by Andres Serrano and Robert Mapplethorpe. That fall, he tuned into the NEA debacle over *Witnesses: Against Our Vanishing*, which provided fodder for AFA advertisements. But it was not until the following February, when Wildmon learned about Wojnarowicz's exhibition at Illinois State, that he found another smoking gun—one just as provocative as Serrano's *Piss Christ* and Mapplethorpe's homoerotic nudes, if not more so.

Seeing Wildmon Seeing Wojnarowicz

Tongues of Flame was David Wojnarowicz's first major solo exhibition. The show was curated by Barry Blinderman at the University Galleries at Illinois State University and ran from January 23 to March 4, 1990. It featured Wojnarowicz's painting, photography, and sculpture spanning from 1979 to 1989. By most accounts, it was a massive success, even drawing a record number of people for its opening night. More than four thousand shuffled through during its first month, Blinderman noted—and he had not received a single complaint.[139] That would soon change.

On February 20, California Republican Rep. Dana Rohrabacher issued a statement to fellow members of Congress blasting the NEA for funding the exhibition, which he called "an orgy of degenerate depravity."[140] Other right-wing organizations picked up his critique. Wildmon first learned about the *Tongues of Flame* exhibition from a piece in *Human Events*, a conservative weekly (and longtime favorite of Ronald Reagan).[141] On

February 24, 1990, *Human Events* published a one-page attack ad with the headline "Very Important!!! Late Information!!! NEA-Funded Blasphemy." An accompanying black-and-white image of "Christ as a drug addict," according to the ad, was pulled from "*a portion of a collage* by artist David Wojnarowicz." The same image appeared in Rohrabacher's statement and was recirculated through various Christian Right mailers. The *Human Events* page mentions the *Tongues of Flame* exhibition by name, along with the $15,000 NEA grant awarded to the University Galleries at Illinois State.[142] Wildmon included the one-page announcement in various AFA mailings, along with a note that AFA members could receive a discounted subscription to *Human Events*. As these attack ads reached broader and broader audiences—including the large number of Americans on conservative Christian mailing lists—complaints about *Tongues of Flame* started pouring in.

Reading through the many letters saved in Wojnarowicz's archive reveals how often everyday partisans of the culture wars recycled and even amplified the language of right-wing ads, including concerns about the supposed misuse of government funding, about the sinful (homosexual) nature of the artwork, and about direct attacks on Christians through the artist's sacrilegious depiction of Christ. A woman from Danvers, Illinois, for instance, explained in a letter to the president of ISU how she had heard about the show from friends and wanted to see it for herself. She hated it, blasting the show as "anti-Christian, anti-family, anti anything that we as moral and decent Americans hold dear." She especially worried about the possibility of children seeing "so much satanic content, not disguised, but blatantly portrayed along with the perverted sexual scenes."[143] Beverly S. wrote in a letter to Blinderman that the galleries should hire another director: "Someone who has a love for God and Country."[144] Nine members from First Christian Church in Salem, Illinois, also penned a letter to Blinderman to express their outrage that the exhibition featured a photo of "Jesus as a dope addict" and "explicit photos of homosexual acts."[145] Sometimes letter writers mixed accusations of blasphemy with prayers offered for Wojnarowicz. A woman from North Dakota wrote, "What a Blasphemy to our (my) Lord, Jesus Christ." "I'll pray for the artist David Wojnarowicz," she continued, explaining that someone who blasphemes "and denies Christ will burn in eternal flames forever."[146] Jay H. implored Wojnarowicz to accept Jesus: "He's the Winner! Christians are winners because of Him." "Are you going to be a winner," he asked, "or do you want to be a loser?"[147]

These kinds of letters started arriving after right-wing attacks had become common. They suggest the reach and influence of right-wing campaigns against the NEA but also the degree to which culture wars offense-taking could be manufactured and mobilized to foster a sense of moral decline and Christian persecution. To say much of this offense was manufactured is not to say it couldn't have been sincere (for some) or effective (either for raising money or for building conservative Christian networks). This was the age of the flier, and Christian Right organizations were especially adept at using direct-mail campaigns and emotional appeals alike to further their cause.

Even among the various right-wing attacks on *Tongues of Flame*, Wildmon's approach in the AFA pamphlet stands out for the way it describes and visualizes Wojnarowicz's work. It started with the reverend ordering a copy of the *Tongues of Flame* catalogue to look through it himself.[148] The catalogue was filled with high-quality reproductions of Wojnarowicz's visual art both in color and in black and white. "As I looked through it," Wildmon explained during his testimony at the trial, "I kind of got sick at my stomach. I was angry and upset, because tax dollars went to help pay for some of this."[149] Like Wojnarowicz's testimony, Wildmon's was no doubt coached by his lawyers, and it repeated the political point that the real issue here was the use of public funding to support work that most people would consider obscene or sacrilegious. But I want to back up to pose what may seem like obvious questions: how did Wildmon come to see what he saw, and how did he use what he saw to compose his own pamphlet?

Wildmon's campaigns against violence, sex, and anti-Christian sentiment on television and in other media suggest a certain pedagogy of observation. We saw this in his description of the way volunteers searched for and evaluated anti-Christian bias on television; they used a similar approach when looking for sex. Wildmon's son Tim explained in an interview in 1990 how CLeaR-TV drew upon 61 groups of 42 people—2,562 in all—to scan television and film for offensive material. Volunteers used worksheets to tally scores for each program in four key categories: sex, violence, profanity, and anti-Christian bias. For each, screeners were taught what to look for—to distinguish, for instance, between scenes depicting sex within wedlock versus sex outside of marriage. They also instructed volunteers to report "jiggly scenes," in which the camera "places undue and unnecessary emphasis on human anatomy (breast or buttock or legs)."[150] This approach to visual screening, which had become a method for the AFA as well, would shape how Don Wildmon read the catalogue for *Tongues of Flame*.

Flipping through its pages, the AFA director homed in on images that depicted sexual acts or negatively portrayed Christianity. He reproduced fourteen of these images in his pamphlet. What became important in the trial was *how* Wildmon did this. He extracted each image from larger works or series created by Wojnarowicz. Like his volunteers scouring hours of television programming, he selected precisely what he was looking for and compiled those instances into a litany of offenses. This practice recalls biblical proof texting, the de-contextualization and alignment of scriptural passages to form an argument.[151] Only here the evidence was visual—and the proof, Wildmon assumed, spoke for itself. Both Wildmon and Wojnarowicz testified about these images and what they each took them to mean. Three examples begin to demonstrate their diverging interpretations and competing aesthetics.

Seeing Jesus in *Untitled (Genet after Brassaï)*

Take the image of "Christ as a drug addict," which appears on the second page of the AFA pamphlet in the top left corner. It is the same image in the *Human Events* piece that Wildmon circulated and that appeared in several other Christian Right mailings as an example of sacrilege.[152] Wildmon pulled the image from one of Wojnarowicz's earlier works, a 1978 "xerox collage" called *Untitled (Genet after Brassaï)*. In the larger work, Jesus appears in the top right corner of a Catholic cathedral that was "bombed-out" during World War Two.[153] Angels fly in from the top left, while a soldier fires a rifle from below. But the focal point of the collage is a cut-out of Brassaï's 1948 photograph of Jean Genet, the French novelist and poet, around whose head Wojnarowicz added a heavenly nimbus. Like many queer artists, Wojnarowicz was inspired by Genet's account of homosexuality, sex work, and experiences in prison in his largely autobiographical novel *Our Lady of the Flowers* (1943).[154] In notes written for the trial, Wojnarowicz also recalled a book he had read about saints, explaining how "there seems to be patron saints for every kind of activity and job," including "cab drivers and refrigerator repairmen."[155] After reading philosopher Jean-Paul Sartre's *Saint Genet* (1952), Wojnarowicz explained, "I wanted to nominate Jean Genet as a patron saint for people like myself who had had brutal experiences in living on the street and who were also homosexual and felt alienated."[156] (See Figure 3.4.)

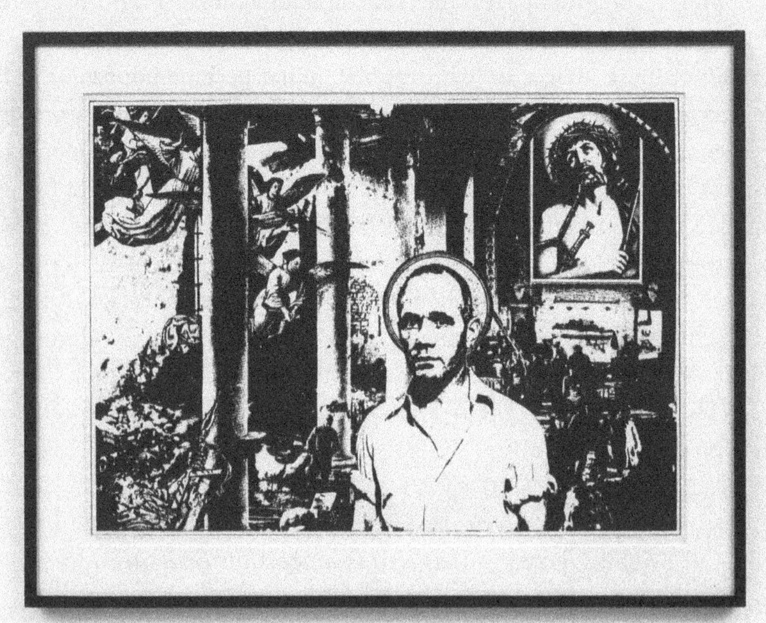

Figure 3.4 David Wojnarowicz, *Untitled (Genet, after Brassaï)*, 1978/1990. Lithograph, 30 × 40 in. (76.2 × 101.6 cm). Copyright Estate of David Wojnarowicz. Courtesy of the Estate of David Wojnarowicz and P·P·O·W, New York.

Wildmon's lawyers were less interested in the artist's canonization of Genet than in the depiction of Jesus with a tourniquet and syringe. AFA lawyer Joseph Secola, who was also a lawyer for Operation Rescue, tried to get Wojnarowicz to explain the meaning of this image during his deposition. The artist resisted, insisting that it be read as part of the whole collage.[157] Wojnarowicz explained how he wanted to "deal with a variety of feelings, about my feelings of spirituality as alienated by organized religion."[158] He created the collage after returning to New York from southern France, where he had spent almost a month in a small village. While in France, he had witnessed an older diabetic man throwing used syringes out of his window that were growing into a notable pile. After returning to New York, Wojnarowicz connected this image of used syringes to the needles used by his friends who had become addicted to drugs. The Jesus image, he offered, reflected "my beliefs and my upraising as a Catholic, and my understanding of who Jesus was." "I assumed that if he were alive in 1979," he continued, "walking through the streets in physical form, that he would also take on the suffering of drug addicts in New York City." In creating this image for his collage, he said, "I tried to depict a modern symbol of human suffering taken on by Christ, if he were present, physically, before me."[159]

Secola then asked Wojnarowicz if he thought someone could see this image and conclude that Christ was represented as a drug addict. Wojnarowicz admitted it was possible. "But," he added, "I think that that's a very simplistic interpretation."[160]

Seeing Pornography in *Sex Series*

Several images in the AFA pamphlet came from Wojnarowicz's set of eight black-and-white photomontages collectively called *Sex Series (for Marion Scemama)*, 1989–90 (See Figure 3.5).[161] Each piece in the series features smaller circular insets, often showing people engaged in sex, set against various larger rectangular backgrounds, including a forest, a train barreling across a mountainside, and an aerial view of New York's East River.[162] Wojnarowicz described the series as his response to anti-sex attitudes he witnessed around him, especially in the midst of the AIDS crisis. In part, he explained during a conversation with art critic Lucy Lippard, the immediate inspiration came from rejection. A different work of his had been turned down for a show in Paris that focused on sexuality. It turned out the show privileged "images of straight white male fantasies," he charged, which included only an "occasional lesbian image" that fit into this erotic imagination.[163]

By contrast, in *Sex Series* Wojnarowicz purposely included a "broad spectrum of the diversity of human sexuality," including gay, lesbian, and straight sexuality, to counter dominant representations of male heterosexual fantasy presented in art.[164] To do so, he used a stack of pornographic photos from the 1950s and 1960s that he got from Peter Hujar, who was cleaning out his apartment toward the end of his life.[165] Wojnarowicz did not merely insert these pornographic images into his photomontages. He deliberately manipulated them, suggesting they were meant not to represent mere sexual titillation but something else. The images he used were cropped from larger photos, which he also rephotographed and developed in an unusual way. "I photographed the black and white images with color slide film," he wrote in his trial notes, "and put them in a black and white darkroom enlarger and

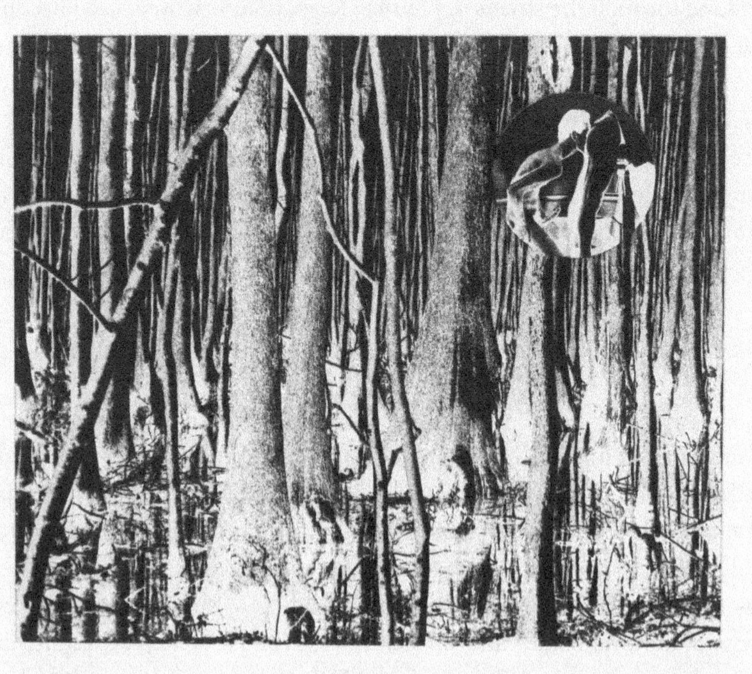

Figure 3.5 David Wojnarowicz, *Untitled*, from *Sex Series (for Marion Scemama)* (detail), 1989–90. 8 silver gelatin prints, 20 × 24 in. (50.8 × 60.96 cm) each. Copyright Estate of David Wojnarowicz. Courtesy of the Estate of David Wojnarowicz and P·P·O·W, New York.

exposed them to black and white paper in order to create an odd negative quality to the images."[166] The images wound up with an "x-ray-like" quality that sits against the larger backgrounds onto which they are placed, which also include a reversed black-and-white tonality. The effect, according to art historian Richard Meyer, is that "rather than conjuring specific scenarios of sexual activity (e.g., an orgy below deck, an afternoon of hotel-room sex), the porn insets signal the space of sexual fantasy itself, a space that punctures the public mappings of the visual field."[167] In other words, the photos recreate not clear windows into queer sex but rather deliberately mediated images— "they function," Meyer writes, "less as explicit scenes of pornography than as generalized emblems of it."[168] Wojnarowicz explained that the circular insets also play on the act of looking into "microscopes, telescopes, and binoculars," thereby suggesting the presence of or even participation in acts of examination and surveillance.[169] The juxtaposition of the varied backgrounds with these highly manipulated sexual images, scenes of magnified surveillance in which it is often hard to distinguish men from women or same-sex sex from straight sex, thus suggests not only the pleasures of diverse sexuality (including queer sex) but also, as Meyer explains, the policing of that very sexuality.[170]

One of Wildmon's lawyers questioned Wojnarowicz specifically about these images. "Are you aware that there are certain people in our society, whether they're right or wrong," he asked, "they are offended by homosexual activity?" "I'm very aware of it," Wojnarowicz answered, adding that he had been a target of homophobic violence. Without missing a beat, the lawyer continued, asking if he thought someone offended by homosexuality "could look at these photographs in the 'Sex Series' and become extremely offended?" After a series of objections from Wojnarowicz's lawyers, the artist answered: "I find it incomprehensible, personally, that somebody could become extremely offended by these images, because of the fact the human body, for me, is not an offensive thing."[171]

Seeing Sex in *Water*

Wojnarowicz's 1987 *Water* combines collage and painting in a way characteristic of much of his work in the mid- to late 1980s. It is difficult to capture the visual and emotional effect of its scale—it measures 72" × 96"—without seeing it in person, which is perhaps why Wojnarowicz's legal team brought a full-size reproduction to the trial.[172] Wojnarowicz created *Water* as part of a series on the elements, joining earth, fire, and wind. Dan Cameron, the senior curator at the New Museum of Contemporary Art, which hosted a retrospective on the artist in 1999, describes *Water* as the most elaborate of the four, since water "is apparently the element to which Wojnarowicz had the strongest spiritual connection."[173] He does not clarify why this is so but likely had in mind common symbolic and ritual associations of water with purification, birth, and even dreams, which often inspired Wojnarowicz's writing and visual art. The large "microbe-shaped" grid, which appears in the center of the painting in black and white, Cameron continues, "creates a surreal black-and-white storyboard that juxtaposes explicit sexual imagery with biological specimens, circular abstractions, landscapes, and other fantasy images."[174] The grid—populated with landscapes, a hand holding a fetus, and an animal skull, among other images—is surrounded by color, mostly shades of blue, gray, yellow, and orange. The left side of the piece features a large frog hovering over a boat sailing into that "amoebic" grid, as Lippard named it.[175] The frog and boat each include inserts—a crashed car in the frog, a squid in the ship—that invert a nature versus culture dichotomy. In addition, a circular inset appears in the grid, again in color, and features a hand reaching through prison bars either grasping or dropping a flower—perhaps another homage to Genet. (See Figure 3.6.)

In *Water*, Wojnarowicz worked through associations, building stream-of-consciousness links between concepts and images.[176] These associations with water led him to imagine desire, bodies, nature, and science. He gestured during the trial, for instance, to the fact that human bodies are made mostly of water and to the reality of sexual fluids involved with sex.[177] Two images in the grid depict queer sex, one with men and the other with women, and the grid itself is surrounded and penetrated by dozens of sperm cells, a scene that conjures associations with the AIDS crisis. But the sperm cells also double as tadpoles, generating an oneiric and even romantic quality. This collapsing of

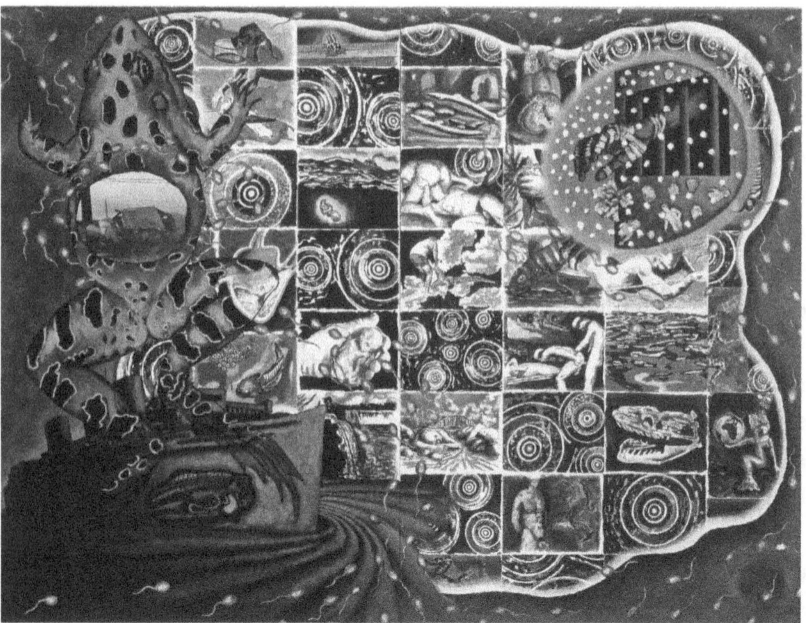

Figure 3.6 David Wojnarowicz, *Water*, 1987. Acrylic, ink, and cut-and-pasted paper on wood; two panels, 72 × 96 in. (182.9 × 243.8 cm) overall. Copyright Estate of David Wojnarowicz. Courtesy of the Estate of David Wojnarowicz and P·P·O·W, New York.

human bodies and animal bodies, along with inversions of nature and culture, animated much of Wojnarowicz's work, as he sought to break through the preinvented sense that humans—including our bodies, our desires, and our technologies—are somehow apart from nature.

There was no debate over whether Wildmon pulled the images used in the AFA pamphlet from these larger works—he admitted as much. But how might he have understood what he was doing and the effects of what he created? What if we take up the AFA pamphlet itself as an aesthetic object and analyze the practices and assumptions through which it was created and disseminated?

Wildmon's Pamphlet and the Aesthetics of Literalism

Wildmon spent three hours creating the AFA pamphlet, which he made from the pages of *Tongues of Flame*.[178] He thumbed through the catalogue with a pair of scissors, cutting out the pages with images he found most offensive—an act of modern iconoclasm much like New York Senator Al D'Amato ripping apart the catalogue containing Serrano's *Piss Christ* on the floor of Congress. Wildmon explained how he selected the pictures "on the basis of the content of each image," as he looked for signs of pornography and sacrilege.[179] He also described his methods of reconstruction: he reshot the images on a photocopier, making them into an "equal size in order to fit on a given sheet of paper," which was the size of a standard legal page.[180] But a certain iconophilic commitment also motivated Wildmon's meticulous work, as he elevated Wojnarowicz's obscene inserts into icons of right-wing rage. Imagine Wildmon carefully cutting, rephotographing, and enlarging these images, which he then evenly laid out across two pages. He took time to square the round inserts of those pulled from *Sex Series*, as he formed the images into a standard grid.[181] What frustrations or stirrings might the reverend have felt, as his hands worked to isolate this sexual imagery, extracting it from larger works to focus and literalize its graphic depictions?

At least twice during this frenzy of editing, Wildmon imagined graphic sex where there was none. "He was so intent on finding what he most feared or desired," Wojnarowicz wrote in his notes on the pamphlet, "that he mistook a video of two guys go-go dancing to be something possibly sexual."[182] Wildmon also reproduced one of two images that Wojnarowicz had found in a German magazine that depicted a boy standing behind a urinating cow.

Wojnarowicz explained how the photos were taken by someone who supposedly witnessed this scene as part of some "african rituals" in a small tribe. But since he could not read German, his understanding was limited. "I was struck by just looking at the images how little I understood of the culture, and the cultural significance of the ritual," he explained at trial. Wojnarowicz imagined the pictures might show a purification ritual, and he reused them in his piece *Delta Towels* (1983).[183] That Wildmon imagined these images, the go-go dancers and the boy with the cow, to be homoerotic pornography speaks to the power of his own assumptions—and to his own fantasies of queer sex, which included bestiality.[184]

Such assumptions and fantasies seemed to run wild among conservative critics of feminist and queer art, as we already saw in Wildmon's case against pornography. Richard Meyer has described a similar instance of right-wing fantasy in the way Senator Jesse Helms had recalled Mapplethorpe's photography during the height of the art wars the previous year. "There's a big difference," argued the North Carolina congressman, "between 'The Merchant of Venice' and a photograph of two males of different races ['in an erotic pose'] on a marble top table."[185] The paraphrase in brackets came from the *New York Times* writer quoting Helms, though, as Meyer writes, one certainly wonders what the senator originally said.[186] The more important point, however, is that no such image actually existed outside of Helms's own imagination. He invented this pornographic image himself, cobbled together from various of Mapplethorpe's works. "But the way in which Helms gets the pictures wrong," writes Meyer, "reveals how the language of censorship summons its own fantasies of erotic transgression and exchange."[187] This interracial queer fantasy is not Mapplethorpe's, in the end, but Helms's own. We could make a similar claim about Wildmon's pamphlet. Meyer has noted, for instance, the ironic effect of including the image of Jesus in this flier. "It is worth noting," he writes, "that Christ has been inserted into a larger field of oral and anal sex *not* by Wojnarowicz but by Reverend Wildmon's ferocious reediting (and reimagining) of Wojnarowicz's work."[188]

Wildmon knew he walked a fine line between demonstrating NEA-funded obscenity through his pamphlet and becoming a purveyor of pornography and sacrilege himself. He understood the danger of these images, especially if they got into the wrong hands. In the lead-up to the trial, for instance, he sent anti-NEA mailers to Christian and Jewish leaders in the home district of Representative Pat Williams in Montana. The NEA was up for reauthorization, and Williams, who headed the subcommittee drafting the legislation, stood firm in his support for the organization and opposed adding content restrictions favored by conservatives. Wildmon planned to show religious leaders in Williams's district evidence of the obscenity that the Montana Democrat ostensibly condoned by sending them a mailer with examples taken from the work of Mapplethorpe and Wojnarowicz. But he ultimately decided against including the pamphlet showing Wojnarowicz's work. "Suppose children in the home opened the mail," he explained: "Those pictures are just too tough, too explicit."[189] If Wildmon needed to protect children from queers like Wojnarowicz, the first step came in the form of withholding his own direct mail attacks.

Parts and Wholes

Wildmon was also busy readying himself for trial, where he would need to defend the AFA pamphlet and its use of images, which became the key point of contention. Wojnarowicz rarely worked with a single image at a time. Rather, he purposely included images in dense, even busy, visual fields, as he saw himself competing with the onslaught of pictures presented on television.[190] He wanted to break up the visual power of preinvented existence by offering alternative juxtapositions and associations. This is why Wojnarowicz became so frustrated when he saw how Wildmon created the AFA pamphlet— by extracting only the images he found offensive within larger works of art.

Wojnarowicz's attorneys repeatedly questioned Wildmon about his process, trying to elicit from him some acknowledgment that he understood the difference between a full work of art versus a small subset taken to represent the whole. Wojnarowicz insisted that such "mutilations" of his art, through this extraction of smaller images from larger works, reduced his richly symbolic creations to mere pornography. Indeed, this difference between parts and wholes was key to the legal case. Recall the *Human Events* ad that Wildmon had mailed out with AFA materials. The accompanying text explained, "reproduced below is *a portion of a collage* by artist David Wojnarowicz."[191] In contrast, the AFA pamphlet described the images themselves as "works of art." Wildmon refused to acknowledge the distinction— how and why he did so become important for understanding the very aesthetics of literalism undergirding his approach.

It started with Wildmon tapping into his old country preacher schtick. His lawyer Benjamin Bull, who had previously worked for Charles Keating's

CDL, played to the reverend's well-practiced "bumpkin defense" that had worked in battles with hotshot Hollywood execs.[192] It helped that a *New York Times* piece on the trial stumbled right into this caricature. It portrayed Wildmon very much like a current-day, bible-toting William Jennings Bryan, who pitched for the fundamentalists in the infamous Scopes Monkey Trial. But this time the country preacher found himself in a battle pitting art against obscenity rather than evolution against creationism.[193] Wildmon's lawyer asked if he knew anything about artwork. The reverend wasn't sure what he meant. "Art or art work?" he asked. "Art," Bull clarified. "Very little," the preacher answered.[194] Bull then asked if Wildmon knew the difference between a collage and a portrait. "No," he replied, sending "chuckles through the artist colony in the audience," according to the *New York Times*.[195] News coverage of sneering New York elites might not have helped Wildmon in the courtroom, but it tapped into his culture wars rhetoric, which figured everyday Americans like him (hardworking, Christian, white) against condescending urban elites (entitled, godless, multiracial, queer). This was the attention he could use to drum up support from fellow conservative Christians.

Wildmon's feigned ignorance about art was part of an interpretive habit and a strategy. When pushed during the trial, Wildmon would not grant that the images he pulled from the catalogue were substantially different from the larger works—he repeated the same words ("photographs" or "images") to equate both, erasing the distinction between the part and the whole.[196] Perhaps he really didn't see any difference or, more likely, it was not a difference that mattered to him or that furthered his cause. So what did matter and how did it come to do so?

Wildmon offered some clues. First, take the "simpleton" defense, which was meant to shield him from knowledge of the acts of misrepresentation—or "mutilation," according to the plaintiff. But it also conveyed a method of reading. He was a simple man, flipping through this catalogue and pulling out images that he thought would offend what he called "the average taxpayer."[197] Wildmon combined this commonsense approach with an emphasis on explicitness. Presenting explicit imagery was an AFA tactic. When Bull asked Wildmon why he even used pictures, rather than just describing the images, he responded, "in some cases you cannot adequately verbally describe" and have to "confront the art."[198] "If you don't show people," Wildmon noted to one journalist, "they would never believe this stuff."[199] In fact, one of the first lessons that members of the AFA were taught when confronting store owners who sold sexually graphic content was to bring a stack of adult magazines with them and dump them directly on that person's desk, forcing them to see it for themselves. Here, visual evidence provides proof for the commonsense reading. This approach wasn't about abstract theorizing or amoral relativism but what the everyday person sees when looking at such images.

It is worth noting, of course, that the everyday person was and remains a rhetorical invention, a work of imagination with its own varied histories and different political uses. What I want to underscore here is how this approach, part of this aesthetics of literalism, takes language—and in this case images—to be sincere, communicative, and representational, even if images also contain some surplus of meaning inherent to their explicitness that exceeds mere description.[200] This tactic, which is also a tension, emerges from longer histories and habits of interpretation.

Literalism, Fundamentalism, Aesthetics

Calling this approach an aesthetics of literalism no doubt invokes the very specific approach to biblical interpretation that became common among Protestant Fundamentalists in Britain and the United States in the early twentieth century. That is not accidental, but it also names something broader. In *Serving the Word*, anthropologist Vincent Crapanzano traces literalism from churches to legal proceedings, observing how it works not only as a method of biblical reading but also as a more generalized theory of language. Literalists, he explains, look "askance at figurative language," whose symbolic richness "can open—promiscuously in the eyes of the strict literalist—the world and its imaginative possibilities."[201] Crapanzano suggests that by the early 1990s it was impossible to overlook "the close relationship between conservative evangelicalism, legal originalism, and the religious right," which he saw spanning from Southern Baptists to the legal philosophy of Robert Bork, the failed nominee to the Supreme Court.[202] But the reach of this literalism extended even further.

Medical anthropologist Byron Good observes similarities between Christian fundamentalist and scientific approaches to language and to the category of belief.[203] He leans on the work of comparative religionist Wilfred Cantwell Smith, who traced shifts in the word "belief" across Christian history.[204] The phrase "I believe in God," he argued, previously meant something like this: "given the existence of God, I devote or pledge myself to Him." This declaration of loyalty gave way during the Reformation and the European Enlightenment to the modern meaning of the phrase: "given the question of whether God exists, I say that God does exist." The earlier version offered a performative—it professed allegiance, binding the speaker to God. The latter makes a propositional claim about the speaker's position relative to the existence of God.[205] Good compares this shift toward propositional claims about God to the emerging dominance of propositional language in the sciences. Advances in scientific methods in the age of Enlightenment, he argues, demanded a new approach to language itself, a demystification of language that would render it conventional and representational, rational and instrumental, more than expressive or performative. Language becomes predominantly a tool to represent and to designate the natural world, one in which correct representations about the world come to constitute correct beliefs.[206] For Good, modern science and Christian fundamentalism share this emphasis on language as representational and instrumental along with the alignment of correct representations with correct beliefs.

What I want to suggest is that this approach, part of what Good calls empiricist or "Enlightenment theories of language and meaning," also informed how twentieth-century conservative political and Christian leaders like Wildmon, Helms, and others understood artistic expression.[207] They read visual culture, like language, as instrumental and representational. This interpretive approach overlaps in many ways with popular forms of biblical literalism, reapplied to new contexts. But, as Crapanzano and Good suggest, it is hardly limited to the Christian Right.[208] Calling this an aesthetics of literalism helps to focus our attention on the ways that literalism works as a style—one applied to the making and reading of visual culture as much as to legal proceedings, scientific research, or biblical exegesis. The aesthetics of literalism, in other words, names this specific application of textual literalism to visual culture—we could define it as the stylized deployment of literalist figurations. My argument here is not that Wildmon and others *are* literalists or fully succeed in their literalism.[209] Indeed, it would be more accurate to say that they *literalize* various objects of attention, as literalism becomes a rhetorical and interpretive tool to advance certain kinds of religious and political projects. This literalist aesthetics has infused culture wars debate, but it stems from a much longer history.

It's Common Sense...

The aesthetics of literalism is in many ways an aesthetics of common sense—that is, it emerged from a long tradition of commonsense thought, inheriting its aversion to mediation and abstraction in favor of clear and direct access to understanding. We can say this another way. When the European Enlightenment came to the United States, it spoke in a Scottish accent.

Religious historian Sydney Ahlstrom captured the importance of Scottish philosophy in North America when he called it "the handmaiden of both Unitarianism and Orthodoxy."[210] The ideals of the Scottish Enlightenment—especially the commonsense realism of Presbyterians like Thomas Reid and Dugald Stewart—flourished in the nineteenth-century United States, as Americans searched for a way to promote scientific and social progress while holding onto "universal moral values."[211] Commonsense philosophy eschewed the skepticism of many Enlightenment philosophers who argued that ideas or concepts interceded between our minds and external reality. Rather, according to historian Henry May, thinkers like Reid and his American acolytes countered that our minds "can know actual objects, and not mere images or ideas of them."[212] For Reid, this meant that intuition itself was rationally justifiable as a way to know truth, an argument that would animate both Romanticist elevations of intuition as well as pragmatic uses, especially among American Calvinists.[213] This approach also fit well within the democratic ethos of the adolescent nation, as many Americans came to eschew elitism and unwarranted complexity.[214] By the 1820s, American thinkers professed a "moral sense" given by God himself that justified moral and ethical truths—moral truths that could be cultivated, along with aesthetic taste, so that people could enjoy both "the good and the beautiful."[215]

Nineteenth-century evangelicals found in commonsense thought a rational and even scientific grounding, not only for their biblical faith but also for their visual culture. Even the Protestant notion of the perspicuity of Scripture—the idea that biblical texts were clear enough for anyone to understand yet contained enough depth for even the shrewdest thinkers—resonated with the commonsense belief in the perspicuity of nature, which has occupied a significant place in American aesthetics.[216] The nineteenth-century English writer and art critic John Ruskin proved especially popular in the United States, as he balanced art with nature and morality.[217] Art needed to be held in check by good moral sense and put into the service of Christianity rather than in competition with it. This alignment of morality with art would stretch into the twentieth century through social gospel leaders like Washington Gladden, who also wrote about the proper combination of Christianity and aesthetics.[218]

Commonsense art, if we might call it that, lent itself to representational depictions—to visual culture that was not merely beautiful for its own sake but also didactic, intended to guide the viewer to greater Christian virtue.[219] But as cultural and artistic tastes changed over time, especially into the twentieth century, even American Protestants started to disagree about the value of commonsense aesthetics.

Competing Christian Aesthetics

By the mid-twentieth century, artistic "taste cultures" increasingly separated liberal Protestants from evangelicals (and from lay Catholics), as historian Sally Promey has shown. Put off by the representational and didactic art of the masses, liberal Protestants, usually well off and white, sought to align themselves with high-modern tastes, as professionals in the worlds of art and religion "promoted a particular theological aesthetic."[220] Alfred Barr, the founding director of the Museum of Modern Art and a practicing Presbyterian, thus brought together "expressionist styles, spirituality, and artistic freedom," while theologian Paul Tillich valued art that directed the viewer toward what he called "ultimate reality."[221] Attracted to "yesterday's avant-garde," as Promey puts it, mid-century liberal Protestants gravitated toward and elevated the expressionist and abstract expressionist art of the previous decades, as they associated such approaches with masculinity, authenticity, freedom of expression, and democracy. They contrasted modernist art to "kitsch," which they aligned with the evangelical and sentimental masses and with totalitarian aesthetics. Kitsch, wrote art critic Clement Greenberg in his well-worn essay on the subject, "keeps a dictator in closer contact with the 'soul' of the people."[222]

Opposed to the avant-garde, kitsch describes art that is popular, mass-produced, and easily accessible—enjoyable "without effort," Greenberg charged.[223] As historian of material culture Colleen McDannell explains, kitsch "provokes immediate emotions that are vividly recognizable."[224] It is both sentimental and earnest—in other words, "totally incompatible with even the mildest forms of questioning; that is, with irony," writes philosopher Tomas Kulka.[225] Tillich considered kitsch not only unseemly but dangerous, "a special kind of beautifying, sentimental naturalism."[226] "In direct response to Adolph Hitler's derision of modernism's 'degeneracy,'" writes Promey, "Tillich characterized this beautifying naturalism or kitsch, which he conflated with all forms of contemporary realism, as the 'really degenerate art.' "[227] Moreover, in contrast to the masculine expressions of abstract art (and its associations with freedom and individual brilliance, nearly always white and male), kitsch was deemed feminine, even sensual. By the 1950s, Catholic leaders, too, worried that the popularity of mass-produced devotional images and objects—what is sometimes called *l'art Saint-Sulpice*—engendered a "feminized church." Even the Vatican took notice, writes McDannell, giving "the green light to Catholic theologians, intellectuals, and artists to attack Catholic kitsch." Modern art thus provided the masculine counterpoint to the association of the church with women, who signified "the realm of the body, the flesh, and the literal."[228]

Such efforts to align abstract art with liberal Protestantism and modern Catholicism never quite took off in the ways people like Barr and Tillich had hoped. By the 1960s and 1970s, the popularity of abstract expressionism had given way to pop art, conceptual art, and body art—not to mention art shaped by racial justice, feminist, and queer movements. Religious elites found these trends less amenable to their theological aesthetics.

What did stick, especially in the context of the emerging culture wars in the 1980s and 1990s, was the association of abstract art with secular humanism and elitism. For many conservatives, abstract art was open to interpretation—*too* open—and that road easily led to relativism or even nihilism. At the same time, they considered abstract art too opaque and thus elitist, since only those versed in the language of art criticism could really follow what was going on.[229] Over these decades, abstract art, previously considered masculine, was also re-gendered. Culture warriors collapsed modern and contemporary art together and deemed this art, and those who made it, "decadent," which was code for effeminate, even homosexual. This art flew in the face of American common sense and moral clarity. Hence, Wildmon would charge in a letter addressed to the members of Congress: "the NEA has become insulated from mainstream American values for so long that it has become captive to a more decadent minority which ridicules and mocks decent, moral taxpayers while demanding taxpayer subsidies."[230] A writer for *Christianity Today* captured this sentiment, too, when he dubbed 1990 "the year when decadence duked it out with decency."[231] Reverend Louis Sheldon of the Traditional Values Coalition put it more bluntly: "Homoerotic avant-garde artists can't depend on hard-earned taxpayer dollars to fund their agenda."[232]

Culture Wars Aesthetics

Given such attacks on art, one might think that culture warriors of the 1980s and 1990s had no aesthetic tastes whatsoever—many a liberal pundit joked as much. But that is too easy. What kind of art, then, did culture wars conservatives like? The short answer is representational art that, once again, fused aesthetics with morality—particularly, in this case, moral visions readily aligned with late twentieth-century white evangelical (and sometimes Catholic) Christianity.

Consider a few examples. In the *Washington Post*, George Will opposed Helms's amendment to put explicit content restrictions on NEA-funded art, but he also blasted abstract art as "baffling to the common viewer." The arts, he averred, should "elevate the public mind by bringing it into contact with beauty and even ameliorate social pathologies."[233] Texas's Republican Representative Dick Armey, who mobilized fellow conservatives to oppose the NEA after learning of Mapplethorpe's work, likewise insisted that "art exists for the purpose of lifting the human spirit with a glorifying reflection of the world in which we live." He preferred artists like Norman Rockwell and American Western sculptor Frederic Remington. "I am not an arts critic," Armey admitted: "If I like it, if it makes me feel good, if it's a joy to me and my family, that's good art."[234]

Jesse Helms, too, expressed his preference for some kinds of art over others. "They say I don't know anything about art," he said, "and I confess that all I know about art is that I know what I like. And I don't like what the NEA has sponsored as art." One of his favorite paintings, hanging in his home in Arlington, Virginia, was by a North Carolina artist. Helms explained that it shows "an old man, sitting at a table, with the Bible open in front of him, with his hands [folded in prayer] like this." "And it is the most inspiring thing to me," he continued. "We have ten or twelve pictures of art, all of which I like," the senator said: "But we don't have any penises stretched out on the table."[235]

Far more palatable for this renewed commonsense aesthetics were the works of artists like the famed illustrator Norman Rockwell and Thomas Kinkade, who would be described as "America's most collected artist" over the course of the 1990s.[236] "My paintings are messengers of God's love," explained Kinkade, who is perhaps most known for his landscapes: "Nature is simply the language which I speak."[237] Kinkade's journey to inspirational art was sealed when, as a student in art school in 1980, he saw the face of Jesus in a vision that led to him being born again.[238] Despite his formal training, he too bristled at the abstractions of modern art. He preferred an art school curriculum, writes historian Randall Balmer, "that avoids the depredations of Modernism and emphasizes the development of traditional skills."[239] Kinkade's preference for representational art infused with moral virtue would resonate in future decades in the work of right-wing artists like Mormon painter Jon McNaughton and the Russian-American Catholic portrait artist Igor Babailov, who in 2019 called for "the resurrection of realism."[240]

The resurgence of this commonsense aesthetics amid the culture wars resisted (if not always successfully) the associations of kitsch with feminine sentimentality. It traded, instead, on the masculine sentimentality of rural America, country music, and John Wayne that helped build the rugged movement for white Christian nationalism over the course of the last half century that many scholars observe today.[241] The resurgence of literalism also contributed to this masculinizing project. Crapanzano discerned the masculinity of modern literalism, which became something of an emblem for the "pragmatic, tough-minded realism that Americans attach to the male persona." Literalism cut through the confusion and the decadence of "ambiguity and figuration"—of the "poetic language, indecision, and confused thinking" so often associated with femininity.[242] It became a way to hold meaning and order in place—including social orders of gender, sexuality, and race.[243]

This masculinist literalism, too, has developed a robust visual culture that joins the representational and devotional art of Kinkade and others. For Protestant Fundamentalists of the early twentieth century, for instance, this visual culture found its form in charts—detailed, seemingly scientific, mass-produced charts matching biblical arguments to depictions of the end times. Surveying this history of fundamentalist chart-making, religious historian Andrew Coates writes, "charts purported to unveil the real meaning of complicated Bible prophecies. Paradoxically, this meaning was considered both obvious and something that needed visual explanation."[244] It is a truism among scholars to observe that Christian Fundamentalists, whether in the 1920s or in the 1980s and 1990s, are at least as modern as they are anti-modern.[245] Protestant charts fused biblical Christianity and Enlightenment rationality with visual culture in a somewhat different way than we see in sentimental depictions of landscapes—or the popular allegorical images of footprints in the sand (based on a popular poem about God walking with us) that I often saw growing up. But they too descended from the marriage of common sense and American Christianity. These cultural forms animated the aesthetic approach of the AFA pamphlet.

Wildmon's Aesthetics of Literalism

Reading through *Tongues of Flame*, Wildmon took photographic images as literal representations of queer sex and sacrilege. Arranged into a grid for the AFA flier, this evidence of obscenity was presented in a way that began to mimic not only the tactics of biblical literalists but also the demystified language of modern science. Let me explain.

Where Wojnarowicz stylized his artistic work by playing with tonality and the association of different images, Wildmon assumed discrete images carried meaning on their own. Of course, Wildmon also stylized images, but he did so within an aesthetics of literalism that unsees that very stylization. He operated as if the meaning of an image was both obvious, through common sense, and fully contained in the image itself, allowing it to be removed from one visual context and applied to another with nothing else changing. The strict literalist, Crapanzano notes, "wants words (or the Word, at any rate) to be as context *independent* as possible."[246] If we take language to be instrumental and rational, as reflective of the world, then it should need little context to be understood. A description of a Levitical code condemning a man from lying with another man is treated as clear in and of itself, just as an image depicting Christ shooting up or submerged in urine is evident in and of itself.

Presumed explicit and unmediated, the visual field amplifies the sense that the meaning of something seen should be automatically clear. In Wildmon's interpretive tradition, when he sees images of queer sex in Wojnarowicz's artwork, he takes them to represent actual queer sex.[247] It doesn't matter that they are part of a larger work or context or that they were stylized to become, as Meyer argued, emblems of sex rather than depictions of sex itself. Wildmon's literalism cuts through this wishy-washy abstraction; it straightens out decadent mediation.

But this literalism required work. Like a scientist, Wildmon labored to build his empirical evidence of obscenity and sacrilege—reading, cutting, enlarging, spacing, and photocopying images for his pamphlet. But images, he understood, have this way of exceeding mere representation. Wildmon wanted to harness their didactic power, even their performative power to elicit disgust, without unleashing their ability to arouse or—worse—to corrupt (if seen by the wrong people, including children and impressionable women).[248] If he could not fully hold the line separating representations of obscenity from obscenity itself—the very distinction he denied in the work of artists like Wojnarowicz—he could try. Wildmon added text to the pamphlet to try to ensure the correct (obvious) reading that detailed what was shown and why it was offensive. He also scripted the very mailing and opening of the pamphlet to tighten this interpretive control.

It began with a kind of liturgy.

Recall the warning that the AFA included on the envelope carrying the pamphlet. "Warning! Extremely Offensive Material Enclosed"—a taunt hailing the reader, daring him to look. This choreography of anticipation builds to the interpretation that Wildmon sought by imitating a basic form: assert a claim and then reveal the evidence. The evidence is all the better when visual rather than textual, as its explicitness speaks for itself. The proof-texted images in the pamphlet, in this way, become "seen" through the liturgy of empirical discovery and the presumed obviousness of the visual field. Disgust foreshadowed and offense confirmed.

Wildmon's Grid

Wildmon often underscored the need to *show* people explicit materials, rather than simply describe them. He did this with Wojnarowicz's work in the AFA pamphlet. But Wildmon did not haphazardly include images of obscenity and sacrilege—he carefully formed them into a grid. In doing so, he created a particular fusion of Christian Right politics, commonsense empiricism, and visual aesthetics. The AFA pamphlet's grid design generates the effect of uniformity and repetition, amplifying its gesture to empirical evidence. But this aesthetic form also exceeds the literalist's touch.

The grid has a particular history in twentieth-century aesthetics, one that augments the power of Wildmon's aesthetics of literalism, including its visual proof-texting. In an essay on grids, art historian Rosalind Krauss argues that this particular form "declares the modernity of modern art" in two ways: spatially and temporally. Spatially, the grid declares the autonomy of the visual field. "Flattened, geometricized, ordered," writes Krauss, "it is antinatural, antimimetic, antireal."[249] The grid, in other words, moves away from nature, and from the real, because its form announces the very work of the artist in creating it. Rather than imitating what exists in the world, it reiterates an "aesthetic decree."[250] Temporally, the grid became so popular as to be wholly unavoidable in twentieth-century art. Yet, Krauss continues, it appeared "nowhere, nowhere at all" in the art from the previous century.[251] This modernism of the grid also bears a notable relationship to religion.

Krauss argues that the grid plays back and forth between the material and the spiritual, the scientific and the symbolic.[252] The grid announces the very materiality of its surface, that is, surface as surface rather than naturalistic representation. Yet most artists do not talk about the grid this way, finding in it instead some access to the spiritual or the universal. Krauss considers this to be the central ambivalence of the grid form, one inherited from its ironic origins in nineteenth-century Symbolism, which allows it to operate both as an emblem of modernity and as a form a myth. But the effort to hold together matter and spirit collapsed in the early twentieth century, she explains, after the Scopes Monkey Trial declared a split between the sacred and the secular, one that would force the artist to choose a path. From this point on, Krauss writes, it would become "embarrassing to mention *art* and *spirit* in the same sentence." The power of the grid, she concludes, thus resides precisely in "its potential to reside over this shame: to mask and to reveal it at the same time."[253] The grid is not a narrative, a story, but rather a structure, Krauss reminds us, one that embeds this tension between science and spirituality in modernism's unconscious, "as something repressed."[254]

The AFA pamphlet enacts this modernist approach, exploiting this ambivalence, even if revealing the work of assembly behind its presentation risks giving up the literalist's sleight of hand. We might even say the grid joins the power of the aesthetics of literalism to erase Wildmon's hand altogether. It marks the pamphlet instead with this "emblem" of "the Modern" while at the same time smuggling in the literalist's myth.[255] Combined with the choreography of discovery, the form itself tricks the viewer into believing the enclosed images speak for themselves. But what do they say? And, taking a cue from Krauss, what might they repress? What lurks behind Wildmon's grid?

Richard Meyer has already noted the irony that it is Wildmon, rather than Wojnarowicz, who placed Jesus within an orgy of queer sex. If the AFA pamphlet sexualizes Christ, might we observe the inverse move as well—that the presence of Christ sacralizes queer lives—by surfacing additional fantasies conjured through the pamphlet's visual forms? Looking closely at the pamphlet, the frequency of oral figurations is striking. Of the fourteen images Wildmon included, eight depict oral sex, cunnilingus, or rimming (nine if you count the image of the young man with the cow). This fixation on orality or eating plays alongside the circular insets taken from Wojnarowicz's *Sex*

Series that Wildmon squared, as the trace of their original form remains. In the pamphlet, they take on a form reminiscent of the communion wafer, now framed and held up on display. What's more, the X-ray-like tonality of the images suggests that, within the divine body of Christ, we might find queer sexuality, or perhaps an emblem of it. On the second page of the pamphlet, Jesus presides vertically over six of these very images, lined up and ready to be taken—these queer hosts that collapse the divine corporeality of Jesus with queer jouissance in a way that even Wojnarowicz may have appreciated. Or perhaps, straying even further from the literal, the traces of these circular insets that Jesus sits among appear more like dinner plates—a nod to Wildmon's own little last supper, a glimmer of the edacious imagination within the culture wars unconscious.

The Queer Art of Metaphysical Imagination

David Wojnarowicz worried his art was too literal.[256] He worked with an expansive but consistent vocabulary of symbols that could seem obvious—a coin representing capitalism or maps symbolizing the politics of nation-states. But he also scoffed at the elitism of the "art world," whose luminaries created work only a select few, in the possession of the right social capital, could understand.

He need not have worried—partly because his art, which is legible on various levels, works through associations. Wojnarowicz's visual style recalls Surrealist and sometimes even Dadaist techniques to spark the imagination, the recesses of the knowable and the yet-to-be-known, as much as the intellect.[257] This commitment to imagination—to challenging society's limited number of acceptable scripts in order to provoke new forms of thinking—proved central to much of his visual and literary work. "My feeling is that the imagination is the key to breaking through pre-invented existence," he recalled in a series of taped journals from 1989: "that in imagination, we can break the images of borders—we can break through the borders of countries, we can break through existing structures of government, or we can break through whatever systems of control are on our shoulders."[258] For Wojnarowicz, imagination carried real power. Not always, but sometimes, he aligned imagination with spirituality. In *Spirituality (for Paul Thek)*, he conjures it through the formation of a series of black-and-white photographs into a grid.

If Donald Wildmon worked through a conservative Christian aesthetics of literalism, a masculinist effort to fix ambiguity and meaning through commonsense and direct-mail appeals, Wojnarowicz worked through semiotics.[259] He played with symbols, remixing and sorting them to conjure new associations and possibilities. Even as Wojnarowicz's visual art ranged across collage, painting, photography, and film, the use and reuse of symbols ran across his career. He arranged these symbols—what anthropologist Claude Lévi-Strauss might call mythemes—into elaborate constructions. Semiotician Roland Barthes may have called his symbols, and their collections, the forms that become filled with new meaning as language (or image) becomes myth.[260]

Wojnarowicz wanted to break down certain normative myths—those of the preinvented existence. But he also wanted to create new ones. "I love mythology, whether it's personal mythology or it's something from a lost civilization," he explained in an interview: "Ever since I was a kid, anything we had no control over—natural events like tornados or floods—signaled other possibilities." "These little myths and pieces of information," he insisted, "signaled other possibilities."[261] Like Judy Chicago, he was something of a mythographer, drawn to "ancient myths," including Mayan, Egyptian, and Native American mythologies, though they sometimes went unspecified.[262] Whereas Chicago was drawn to myths of creation, Wojnarowicz was just as fascinated by mythologies of death and apocalypse.

Wojnarowicz was also a postmodern metaphysical, and this shaped his work with mythology. What I mean is that his mythological imagination emerged from a longer tradition of what historian Catherine Albanese calls metaphysical religion. In *A Republic of Mind and Spirit*, she traces metaphysical religion across the history of North America through its myriad and rarely contained variations, from Spiritualism, Transcendentalism, and New Thought to reinvented (and often orientalizing) New Age adaptations of Native American and Asian spiritualities. Metaphysical religion, she argues, takes its place alongside two other dominant forms of North American "religiosity": the evangelical, which focuses on the emotional conversion experience of the individual, and the liturgical or "mainstream-denominational," which centers on collective ritual (and leans toward Catholicism). The metaphysical form has long been overshadowed by these other two. It focuses on the individual, like the evangelical form, but centers more on the mind than the heart—and on the poetic and intuitive mind more specifically. It also elevates the spiritual possibilities of encounters with nature, with the sublime, espousing a divine more immanent than otherworldly.[263]

If Wojnarowicz was heir to this metaphysical tradition, including its permutations through Transcendentalist thinkers like Ralph Waldo Emerson and Walt Whitman, it came to him refracted through the writings of French Symbolist poet Arthur Rimbaud, novelist Jean Genet, and Beats like William Burroughs.[264] Wojnarowicz identified with the poetry of the outcast and was drawn to their writings on homosexuality, drugs, and mortality. He not only read their works; he also evoked their spectral presences. We have seen his elevation of Genet as a queer saint in *Untitled (Genet after Brassaï)*. For one of his earliest works, a series called *Arthur Rimbaud in New York (1978–9)*, Wojnarowicz photographed friends wearing a mask of the poet's face and posing in various places across the city—the Meat Market, Coney Island, a subway train. If the series testified to his identification with Rimbaud, a fellow outcast, homosexual, and poet, it also summoned this kindred spirit across decades and continents, fostering a spiritual kinship—and a queer one.

Wojnarowicz would incorporate ever more elements of his environment and imagination as his artistic and political visions developed across the 1980s and 1990s. A metaphysical mythmaker, he drew on several highly charged symbols in this work both to shake up the world around him and to provoke alternative possibilities. Many of these symbols recur—clocks, trains, machines, images of sex, maps, newspapers, money or coins, and Jean Genet. I want to focus here on two sources that proved particularly powerful in his work: nature, especially landscapes, frogs, and ants, and Christian symbolism, which he often placed alongside other religious and mythological elements.

The Con of Nature?

Even as a young child, Wojnarowicz was drawn to nature, where he could escape the "tiny version of hell called the suburbs." "Once I discovered the universe of the forests and lakes," he wrote in his memoir, "I went there whenever possible."[265] The woods became a refuge from the violence he experienced at home, but also a source for imagination and for the abundant materials he would use to cathect his mounting frustrations. "In the forests I made human forms out of mud and sticks," he recalled: "When they dried they fell apart or I would throw them against tree trunks."[266]

If his fascination with nature recalled the spiritual possibility that Emerson or Thoreau found there, for Wojnarowicz these possibilities were also erotic—and sometimes apocalyptic. As an adult, then living in New York City, Wojnarowicz delighted in cross-country road trips, especially through the southwestern United States. In *Close to the Knives*, he described the hallucinatory feeling of driving through "dry plains" without a cloud in sight, the way it would alter his senses of perception, as "memory and sight" became indistinguishable from "fantasy and actual vision."[267] He also described passing through these open spaces in erotic terms. "Driving a machine through the days and nights of the empty and pressured landscape," he wrote, "eroticizes the whole world fitting through the twin apertures of the eyes."[268] The erotic vision could become literal. Driving through these vast terrains opened sexual possibilities, encounters with men in cars pulled over on the side of the road, which could also be spiritual ones. Orgasm, like drugs or meditation, Wojnarowicz explained, offers a way to "get outside the physical confines of our body vehicles. It's really about spirituality; we're trying to find this 'presence'—or the location of this presence, and it's really something we contain."[269]

At the same time, nature could disclose apocalyptic terror which, for Wojnarowicz, was no less important or even spiritual. He was unusually attuned to "the sense of death in the American landscape"—the site of colonization and exploitation, violence and death.[270] He recalled looking across the mountains in a New Mexico town, "those postcard perfect slopes and clouds," and thinking: "I didn't trust that fucking mountain's serenity." "I couldn't buy the con of nature's beauty," he insisted, "all I could see was death."[271] Wojnarowicz's vistas, like his dark humor, were quite far from Kinkade's tranquil landscapes. But it helps to understand that Wojnarowicz refused the separation of nature from human life. Indeed, he sought to close the gap opened in human culture through the very naming of "nature" as such—a naming that positioned humans outside nature, distanced from the natural world, "even though we're part of it."[272]

Wojnarowicz played with that tension by drawing upon nature to provide metaphors for human societies and by inviting us to see humans themselves as animals, as part of nature.[273] He used natural life, including landscapes but also animals and insects, as metaphors to build his visual mythologies. "America's nearly spiritually dead," he maintained, "but at least we still deal with a few mythic images—especially in the use of animals." They often come up in cartoons and children's toys, he explained, as he sought to expand their use.[274] He described using such symbols for a series of photographs he took while traveling through northern Mexico in the mid-1980s—images that would appear across several works in the late 1980s, including *Spirituality (for Paul Thek)*. "In the Mexican photographs with the coins and the clock and the gun and the Christ figure and all that," he explained, "I used the ants as a metaphor for society because the social structure of the ant world is parallel to ours. They have queens, they create wars, they keep pets, they keep slaves; there's this whole social structure that isn't that different from our own." "So I just took simple symbols," he said, "things that preoccupy us: money, time, religion, violence."[275]

It was no accident that he found such powerful images while traveling through Mexico (and Argentina). "Once I went south of the border," he wrote, "I discovered there's a vacuum in America and Europe. South of the border that vacuum disappears—maybe it's spirituality, maybe a sense of connection people have to the ground they walk on."[276] Wojnarowicz was drawn to the acknowledgment and even celebration of death in Mexican culture, adding to his visual vocabulary iconography from the Day of the Dead, including José Guadalupe Posada's famous *La Calavera Catrina* (1910).[277] He was especially drawn to Mexican folk Catholicism, including images of the *Anima Sola* (Lonely Soul), which depicted a woman surrounded by flames, and Saint Lucia, the protector of sight. They joined his collection of sacred hearts, Virgins of Guadalupe, and cheap crucifixes, which he photographed covered by fire ants he found amid the Aztec ruins of Teotihuacán.[278] They became part of his *Ant Series* (1988).

Wojnarowicz used many of these elements of Mexican culture—along with images of *tragafuegos* (fire-breathers), lucha libre wrestlers, and a stone sculpture of the Aztec goddess Coatlicue, among others—in his unfinished film *Fire in My Belly* (1986–87). Shot on Super 8 film, it actually includes two reels of footage: a thirteen-minute and a seven-minute version. This footage would be cut and edited into a four-minute version for the 2010 Smithsonian exhibition *Hide/Seek: Difference and Desire in American Portraiture*. This later version stirred controversy when the right-wing Catholic League got wind that it featured a crucifix covered in ants and deemed it anti-Catholic. Amid the brewing debate, the Smithsonian pulled the film, which got a second life on YouTube (which of course did not exist when Wojnarowicz was alive). *Fire in My Belly* unfolds as a series of fragments combining short film clips and still images—the crucifix covered in ants, two halves of a loaf of bread being sewn together with red thread, an image of the *Anima Sola*, an actor playing Jesus looking tired, a cockroach. Toward the end, a blood-shot eyeball spins while engulfed in flames. It recalls Emerson's transparent eye—though, rather than grounded in solitude, this one is overwhelmed, dizzied from the onslaught of images, burning from the imminent death of American spirituality.

Wojnarowicz's Catholicisms

We already see in Wojnarowicz's fascination with Mexican folk Catholicism how Christian iconography likewise haunted his visual imagination. Images of Jesus appear not only in *Untitled (Genet after Brassaï)*, but in paintings like *Excavating the Temple of the New Gods* (1986) and in one of the photomontages in *Sex Series*. His photograph *Untitled Series (Spirituality)* (1988) from the *Ant Series* depicts a crucifix lying on the ground covered in fire ants—much like the one that appears in *Fire in My Belly* and in *Spirituality (for Paul Thek)*. Wojnarowicz also invoked Saint Sebastian, long admired by queer eyes, who appears in *Peter Hujar Dreaming/Yukio Mishima: St. Sebastian* (1982) and *Bad Moon Rising* (1989), one of his most powerful works dealing with the AIDS crisis. Many have read his *Untitled (Bread Sculpture)* (1988–89)—featuring a loaf of bread being sewn back together with red thread that also appears in *Fire in My Belly*—as a commentary on censorship, but its doubling as the body of Christ is too obvious to ignore. This list, far from exhaustive, includes only the most conspicuous manifestations. Sometimes this use of Christian iconography amplified Wojnarowicz's impassioned critiques of organized religion—and of the Roman Catholic Church in particular. But this hardly exhausts the many ways Christian imagery animated his work.[279] Or the ways it populates the artist's ephemera.

I was struck during my archival research by the number of Catholic postcards saved in Wojnarowicz's papers at Fales Library at NYU. His collection of Catholic kitsch ranged from sacred hearts to the Blessed Virgin to an image of *La Cruz del Calvario* in Tandil, Argentina—nearly all of them sent by friends. Nan Goldin mailed Wojnarowicz a postcard showing a boy kneeling during confession circa 1958. "I confess," she wrote on the other side, "I love you."[280] This kitsch was more camp than sentimental, playing in part on the homoeroticism of Roman Catholicism itself, which could foster playful queer temptations as much as it could fuel homophobia.[281] But the cards were only part of his collection.

Wojnarowicz also kept what he called a "Magic Box"—that is the name written on tape over a wooden box with the original label "Indian River Citrus" running across the top. The box (which measures 8" × 17" × 11.5") was found under Wojnarowicz's bed after he died, and its meaning remains largely a mystery—"his final secret," writes Hugh Ryan.[282] When I first learned about the Magic Box, I thought it sounded very Catholic—though Albanese's description of metaphysical religious forms would likewise be well applied. It offered a place to store the relics of loved ones or other trinkets of meaning—little sacred things. Wojnarowicz's Magic Box held fifty-seven items, not counting the wooden box itself. Most are not obviously religious, but many are. They include a prayer card for Peter Hujar, dried flowers (Hujar loved flowers), a bag of seeds, a quartz crystal, two globes, a toy Santa, a bag of plastic bugs, a blue skull, a feather, photos of various Gurus, a Buddha sculpture, a sacred heart, and a crucifix. The Magic Box offered a little archive, one made of the very ephemera from which Wojnarowicz carved out his life and his visionary work—an archive of meaning and materiality saturated as much by Catholic forms as by the eclectic capture of metaphysical religion. Or, perhaps, a metaphysical spirituality haunted by Catholic forms.

These forms helped Wojnarowicz visualize his apocalyptic take on American spirituality but also his somber search for an alternative spirituality. Consider his 1987 painting *The Death of American Spirituality*, which art historian Mysoon Rizk reads as an "enduring critical assessment of contemporary society's predicament." (See Figure 3.7.) It vividly depicts the apocalyptic ravages of Euro-American colonization. "At the same time," Rizk continues, "the painting suggests lingering possibilities for reviving spirituality."[283] What is *this* spirituality? Looking at the painting, the black lines dividing the four sections recall the cross—as Rosalind Krauss reminds us, "there is no painter in the West who can be unaware of the symbolic power of the cruciform shape and the Pandora's box of spiritual reference that is opened once one uses it."[284] Yet Jesus's head, with glazed over zombie eyes, floats alone among the fiery ruins, without much effect, with little power. In contrast, the Hopi kachina doll in the top left sprouts cables, searching for connection. One, as Rizk notes, extends through all four panels, even reaching the lone cowboy riding the bull, whose tail also links up with the snake handler. This depiction produces a tension, as the man on the bull seems to be riding away, straining the attachment to Wojnarowicz's gesture to Native American spirituality, in what art critic John Carlin sees as an

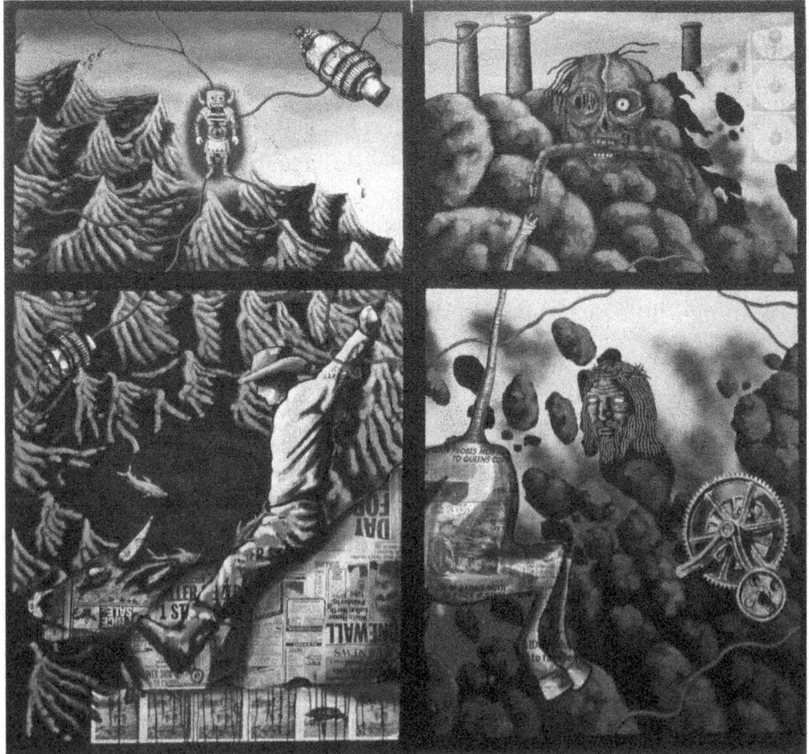

Figure 3.7 David Wojnarowicz, *The Death of American Spirituality*, 1987. Spray paint, acrylic, and collage on plywood; two panels, 81 × 88 in. (205.7 × 223.5 cm) overall. Copyright Estate of David Wojnarowicz. Courtesy of the Estate of David Wojnarowicz and P·P·O·W, New York.

apocalyptic vision of the clash between "man-made mechanical energy" and "the spiritual energy of nature."[285]

Wojnarowicz's Grid

Perhaps some lasting hope to revive spirituality also animates *Spirituality (for Paul Thek)*. I read this piece as both memento mori and another metaphysical myth. Paul Thek was Peter Hujar's lover and friend. A fellow artist haunted by Catholicism, Thek reveled in the corporeal and its ruins. One of his most well-known works, *Meat Pieces*—part of his *Technological Reliquaries* series (1964–67)—featured "gory wax replicas of mutilated flesh that attract and repel in equal measure," writes art historian Paisid Aramphongphan.[286] Wojnarowicz must have appreciated Thek's blend of queer sensuality and dark Catholicism—in *The Tomb* (1967), Thek even created a replica of his own rotting body.

Wojnarowicz's photocollage dedicated to Thek assembles six symbolic images—money, boys dancing at a Louisiana bar, a clock, a young girl wearing a mask, a machine from an old coke factory, and a man named Iola, one of his friends, exhaling smoke. Wojnarowicz explained in a set of notes in his archive that Iola was the first person he knew with AIDS and this image conjured the sense of the man's spirit leaving his body.[287] AIDS underwrites the whole piece. Thek died from AIDS in 1988. Shortly before passing, he created *The Face of God* (1988), which shows a white clock drawn over a greenish-blue background painted over newspaper. Wojnarowicz references *The Face of God* through his own clock, the press of time, which appears alongside the joy of dancing. These six images, arranged in two rows, play against the bottom half of the piece, which is taken up by a painted crucifix with an ant crawling over Jesus's face, a symbol of human corruption of religion. In creating this piece, Wojnarowicz considered "various attempts through history to reach heights in an attempt to touch the sources of mortality and thus possibly immortality," whether that meant creating the Tower of Babel or "spinning [like a whirling dervish] in order to breach distance with speed."[288] He also scribbled at the top of his sketch for this work: "the weight of the earth is about captivity in all that surrounds us."[289] A similar line appears in his taped journals from 1989, as Wojnarowicz was wrestling with his own AIDS diagnosis.[290]

To place this clash of images, of associations, under the sign of "spirituality" was to resist the simplicity of earnest faith, of good religion, for the hope of a future that might be something else. For Wojnarowicz, this wasn't sacrilege but the labor of mythology—the demythologizing of organized religion through his X-ray of civilization combined with the hope for imagination, for creating something different, a better mythology.

Wojnarowicz/Wildmon

Placing Wojnarowicz's *Spirituality (for Paul Thek)* alongside Wildmon's AFA pamphlet might appear to invite an argument about the misrepresentation of art or about censorship—either Wildmon's efforts to censor the work of queer artists like Wojnarowicz or the artist's attempt to silence criticism from conservatives like Wildmon. I want to hold space here to consider something else, to plot two approaches, at times overlapping, at others diverging, to understanding images and how they relate to sexuality, politics, and religion—and to observe the complications that both Wildmon and Wojnarowicz confronted when releasing their visions into the public sphere. I am interested in these two figures—in analyzing their aesthetics and the ways they cause or take offense—because their juxtaposition provides another lens through which to understand modern religion and politics. It pushes us to see the culture wars not only as ongoing fights between religious conservatives and secular progressives but as deeper struggles over interpretation and over the work that images do, including how people read them, what people do with them, and how they do or do not conjure the spiritual, the religious, the sacred, or the obscene.

To write Wildmon off as a simple or stupid Christian misses the quite involved and in many ways modern and even modernist work that he was doing. To write Wojnarowicz off as a sacrilegious pornographer misses how his work visualizes the AIDS crisis as postmodern theodicy. This snapshot of the culture wars shows how much more we have left to see.

* * *

So what happened with Wojnarowicz's lawsuit against Donald Wildmon and the AFA? The judge dismissed three of the four claims but found that Wildmon and the AFA did violate the New York Artists' Authorship Rights Act. Wildmon was ordered to mail out a retraction, notifying everyone who had received the AFA pamphlet that the images represented only *parts* of the artist's original work.[291] The judge also ordered the reverend to pay damages in the amount of one dollar.

Wojnarowicz requested that Wildmon sign the check himself. Asked how he would spend it, the artist responded, "I'll use it to buy either an ice-cream cone or a condom depending how hot I feel."[292] But Wojnarowicz would never cash that check, imagining perhaps that he might use it in a future work—a check whose symbolic value, in the end, no doubt exceeded its literalist worth.

4

Ray Navarro's Jesus Camp, AIDS Activist Video, and the "New Anti-Catholicism"

Camp is the condition of queer critique—and of Christian liturgy. Every serious theology laughs at itself.[1]

—Mark D. Jordan

"This is Jesus Christ! I'm in front of St. Patrick's Cathedral on Sunday," reports a man with long, dark brown hair, a stringy beard, and a crown of thorns. He holds a microphone and speaks directly to the camera. Jesus was out on the streets of New York City that day to cover a major demonstration planned by two activist groups, the AIDS Coalition to Unleash Power (ACT UP) and Women's Health Action and Mobilization (WHAM!). He was played by AIDS activist and artist Ray Navarro, who was also a member of the ACT UP affinity group DIVA TV, a video artist collective that recorded footage at ACT UP/NY's major demonstrations. That day—December 10, 1989—he joined about 4,500 queer and feminist AIDS activists in a demonstration called "Stop the Church." Activists marched along Manhattan's Fifth Avenue to St. Patrick's Cathedral, where they targeted the Catholic bishops, especially Cardinal John O'Connor, the archbishop of New York, who opposed abortion rights, safe sex education, and gay rights in local and national political battles.[2] Inside the cathedral, activists blended with regular Sunday parishioners. When O'Connor started his homily, several protestors began dropping to the floor of the aisles. Their "mass die-in," as it was called, represented the many lives lost because of the Church's positions on abortion and sexuality.

All the while, Jesus remained out on the streets. He was surrounded by demonstrators marching and chanting and carrying signs with phrases like "Keep Your Rosaries Off My Ovaries" and "Keep Your Church Out of My Crotch." Some protestors dressed in clerical drag, mocking the authority

Provoking Religion. Anthony M. Petro, Oxford University Press. © Oxford University Press 2025.
DOI: 10.1093/9780190938468.003.0005

(and sartorial stylings) of the bishops. Others carried racy pictures, like one of a particularly well-muscled Jesus sporting a large erection while promoting the use of condoms. Footage from the demonstration would appear in DIVA TV's 1990 documentary *Like a Prayer* as well as activist and filmmaker Robert Hilferty's 1991 documentary *Stop the Church*. In one scene from *Like a Prayer*, the sounds of protest blend into the daily discord of midtown Manhattan. The jolting and shaking of the handheld camera used to shoot the footage creates a sense of urgency. "Inside," Jesus strains to speak over the noise, "Cardinal O'Connor is busy spreading his lies and rumors about the position of lesbians and gays. We're here to say, we want to go to heaven, too!"[3]

AIDS video activists sought to document the demonstration for the historical record, to help control media narratives of their work, and to further AIDS activist and feminist political causes. They knew this protest would spark controversy—taking on the Catholic Church in New York City was no small matter. They also anticipated that mainstream news coverage would be negative, that it would not fairly portray the reasons activists had assembled that day—and they were correct. Mainstream broadcast and print coverage of the protest—in addition to most Catholic media and even some lesbian and gay press—quickly slotted "Stop the Church" into the binary terms of the culture wars, which pitted ostensibly secular feminist and queer activists against the Catholic Church. New York's daily papers painted an image of "militant homosexuals" who were "Storming St. Pat's" and desecrating the Catholic Church. Broadcast news described how activists turned "holy mass into a holy mess."[4]

This impression would not quickly fade. In 2003, historian Philip Jenkins described the protest at St. Patrick's as one of the "notorious examples" of a "new anti-Catholicism."[5] Since the 1960s, he argues, anti-Catholic sentiment has shifted from older tensions between Protestants and Catholics toward new fights over issues of gender and sexuality. Feminists and gay activists have become the major purveyors of new prejudices against the Catholic Church, faulting its "traditional" stances on contraception, abortion, and gay rights. Even more, Catholic writers like George Weigel suggest that battles for gender and sexual rights have advanced a politics of secularism that seeks to limit the role of religion in the public sphere.[6] In this narrative, "Stop the Church" proved one of the most obvious instances of secular activists pushing not only an agenda for sexual and reproductive rights, but a movement to eliminate religion itself from public sight.[7]

AIDS activist films provided another kind of witness, revealing feminist and AIDS activists to be quite thoughtful about religion, if also playful or even irreverent in their protest tactics. *Stop the Church*, introduced to viewers as a "Robert Hilferty Inquisition," begins with various voices whispering, "What's the Catholic Church? What's the Catholic Church?" Meanwhile, shifting images of mostly Renaissance Catholic art cross the screen. This opening asserts that, whatever the Catholic Church is, it should not be defined by the Roman Catholic hierarchy alone. Hilferty's film follows activists from ACT UP and WHAM! as they debated whether to do the demonstration at all and, if so, how to pull it off without seeming to attack lay parishioners or Catholicism itself. *Stop the Church* also recorded the protest inside the cathedral, including the haunting scene of one activist yelling to the cardinal: "You're murdering us. Stop it. Stop it."[8] In *Like a Prayer*, members of DIVA TV interweave footage from the protest at St. Patrick's, including scenes of Navarro in Jesus drag, with interviews with several Catholic (or formerly Catholic) feminist and AIDS activists. They explain why they were at the protest, offering perspectives that were largely excluded from the mainstream news. By emphasizing the voices of activists connected to the Catholic Church, *Like a Prayer* countered depictions in the mainstream media and Catholic press that reduced "Stop the Church" to a secularist attack upon Catholics or even religion itself.

Staging *Like a Prayer* and the Politics of Camp

In this chapter, I focus on DIVA TV's activist video *Like a Prayer*, emphasizing performances by the gay Chicano AIDS activist and artist Ray Navarro, to reassess two prevailing, but related, narratives in the history of US religion and politics. At its broadest, this chapter challenges the enduring culture wars distinction between secular progressivism and religious conservatism that has animated criticisms of feminist and queer activism and that continues to cast a shadow over debates about same-sex marriage, reproductive rights, transgender rights, and religious freedom into the first quarter of the twenty-first century. This analysis of *Like a Prayer* locates the history of the AIDS crisis and feminist and AIDS activism at the center of culture wars narratives in order to expand the range of subjects who become visible as doing "religion."

Second, reading *Like a Prayer* as part of the archive of US Catholicism exposes common assumptions about the relations between religion and politics, sincerity and performance, and Catholicism and authority that undergird scholarship on the "new" anti-Catholicism. Foregrounding AIDS activist media allows us to consider how feminist and queer activists employed religious (and often explicitly Catholic) imagery in a variety of ways that confound the very division between Catholic and anti-Catholic. This chapter thus expands the archive of the culture wars—and of queer and Catholic history—to include new forms of media, specifically video, as well as another style of political engagement, one that subverts dominant understandings about authenticity and performance, sincerity and parody, and sacred and profane. What is interesting about this historical episode is not simply that it challenges such culture wars distinctions but *how* it does so: through the use of camp.

Camp is a funny thing, not easily defined or contained. The word operates as an adjective or a verb. It usually describes a sensibility or style, one often attributed to gay male culture in the United States since the 1950s. Its scope is broad, potentially endless. Its richest sites have ranged from theater and film, especially classics from the mid-twentieth century or plays on these classics—few could forget Faye Dunaway playing Joan Crawford screaming, "No wire hangers, ever!" in 1981's *Mommie Dearest*—to drag performances staged nightly at queer clubs and on hit TV shows like *RuPaul's Drag Race*. In a classic statement on the subject, critic Susan Sontag explains how camp "sees everything in quotation marks: It's not a lamp but a 'lamp'; not a woman but a 'woman.'"[9] Anthropologist Esther Newton offers three defining characteristics: "Incongruity is the subject matter of camp, theatricality its style, and humor its strategy."[10]

Recent work has emphasized the political dimensions of camp—considering it as both a style of representation and an enactment of resistance. In an essay on Sontag, religion and performance studies scholar Ann Pellegrini reasserts both the political and queer dimensions of camp, alongside its attachments to religion (in this case to Jewish camp).[11] A number of writers describe camp as a tool for marginalized communities—a "strategy for a situation" or "a means of giving gay people a larger space in which to move, loosed from the restraints of dominant society."[12] Performance theorist José Esteban Muñoz broadens discussions of camp, usually attributed to middle-class, white gay men, to include lesbian and Latinx performance. Camp, in his telling, becomes a site for the work of "disidentification," which can be "understood not only as a strategy of representation, but also a mode of enacting self against the pressures of a dominant culture's identity-denying protocols."[13]

Queer activism has long drawn from the aesthetics and politics of camp, but this was especially true with the emergence of the AIDS crisis and the rise of activist organizations like ACT UP in the 1980s and 1990s. AIDS activists joined camp performance to queer politics in several powerful ways, one of which was to take up the Catholic Church itself as an object of camp engagement.[14] Film such as *Like a Prayer* and *Stop the Church* exemplify this politics of camp Catholicism—and both entered the public theater of culture wars attack.[15] Hilferty's *Stop the Church* sparked national attention when the PBS series *POV* planned to air it in 1991. Leaders within the Catholic Church were quick to condemn the documentary as anti-Catholic.[16] After the round of controversy surrounding the plan to show Marlon Riggs's *Tongues Untied* the year before, PBS was reluctant to go to battle again. The screening was ultimately canceled, PBS executives maintained, because of the film's "pervasive tone of ridicule" against the Catholic Church.[17]

When *Like a Prayer* landed in the sights of the Christian Right, Ray Navarro's Jesus drag took the spotlight. In 1991, Don Wildmon sent out a mailer on behalf of the American Family Association attacking the National Endowment for the Arts (NEA) for funding the work of anti-Christian homosexuals—this time the target of attack was the "homosexual film" *Like a Prayer*, which he refers to as "the blasphemous 'Jesus Christ Condom.'" The mailer included a sheet providing examples of how the NEA "spends your tax dollars." The center of the page features an image still from *Like a Prayer* showing Navarro, dressed as Jesus, holding a condom.[18] In an accompanying letter, Wildmon explains that the film "was produced by militant gay activists who call themselves DIVA TV." The mailer also included a series of prewritten postcards that he encouraged readers to mail to President Bush and to the appropriate members of Congress. "Can I count on you to help end government sponsorship of pornography, anti-Christian bigotry and pro-homosexual 'art,'" the text of the card to the president reads: "Please let me know."[19] For Wildmon, at least, Navarro's safe-sex Jesus was more sacrilege than sacred.

DIVA TV footage, including much that went into *Like a Prayer*, has received a broader audience in recent years, as it continues to circulate in mainstream AIDS documentaries. Two such films were released in 2012. David

France's *How to Survive a Plague* was nominated for an Academy Award for Best Documentary Feature.[20] And Jim Hubbard and Sarah Schulman's *United in Anger: A History of ACT UP* remains the best starting point for understanding the history of this AIDS organization; it emerged out of the sustained engagements of ACT UP activists themselves and their long-term project to document the AIDS crisis through oral history.[21] As the early history of the AIDS crisis in the United States gains more attention, this chapter argues for us to take up this episode in queer history as a critical moment of religious politics. Examining the visual and camp history of AIDS activist performance in *Like a Prayer* offers new ways to consider the intersections among media, social protest, and public religion. But first we should understand how this camp work fits within the context of culture wars debate, including efforts to frame feminist and queer politics as the new wellspring of anti-Catholicism.

AIDS, Secularism, and the New Anti-Catholicism

Writing for the magazine *Commentary* in 1992, neoconservative Catholic George Weigel set out an ambitious agenda for cataloging and understanding "new forms of an old bigotry"—what he called instances of the "new anti-Catholicism"—that were "befouling American life."[22] A prolific writer, Weigel had already discerned a "*Kulturkampf*, a culture war" sweeping across the United States in his 1989 *Catholicism and the Renewal of American Democracy*. In his definition, the culture wars were not only fights over national identity, as James Davison Hunter observed, but far more catholic—they were struggles over "fundamental understandings of the human person, human society, and human destiny."[23] Debates over feminism, abortion, and 'gay rights' (which he put in scare quotes) would prove central to these understandings of the human and, indeed, to the formation of the new anti-Catholicism.[24]

Weigel opens his *Commentary* essay—called "The New Anti-Catholicism"—with ten instances that occurred in the years leading up to its publication. The examples start with an art exhibition from 1989 that was partly funded by the NEA. Weigel does not name the show but was referring to *Witnesses: Against Our Vanishing*, which featured New York artists responding to their personal experiences with AIDS.[25] An essay by David Wojnarowicz, included in the exhibition catalogue, attacked conservative politicians like Senator Jesse Helms and Representative William Dannemeyer for opposing AIDS funding and stalling sex education efforts.[26] Wojnarowicz also targeted Cardinal O'Connor. "The catalogue for the show," Weigel writes, "described Cardinal O'Connor of New York as a 'fat cannibal' and 'a creep in black skirts,' and referred to St. Patrick's Cathedral as 'that house of walking swastikas on Fifth Avenue.'"[27] Weigel's list of examples concludes with a demonstration by the activist group Queer Nation during a prayer service featuring Cardinal O'Connor at the National Shrine of the Immaculate Conception in Washington, DC, in 1992. The protest featured a "scantily clad lesbian" who was crucified on a "mock cross," Weigel writes, though one may wonder what made the cross "mock" and whether that lesbian wore any less clothing than the historical savior, who was most likely stripped bare. A sign affixed to the cross explained, "Christ Loves Women and Queers/Why Does O'Connor Hate Us?"[28]

We can start to discern a trend. Among Weigel's ten examples of the new anti-Catholicism, three explicitly mention the AIDS crisis and the work of AIDS activists. Others imply a connection, such as the example of Queer Nation, a group that grew out of AIDS activism.[29] One of his examples included "Stop the Church." Weigel refers to the demonstration as part of a "pattern" among ACT UP actions, which regularly disrupt Catholic services and mock Christians.[30] Taken together, his examples suggest the oversized role that feminist and queer protestors—and ACT UP in particular—have played in casting this new anti-Catholicism.

Claims of anti-Catholicism have a long history—usually in the form of Protestant antipathy toward Catholics, as Weigel also describes in his essay.[31] Such anti-Catholic rhetoric soared in the nineteenth-century United States, when Irish Catholics came under threat from nativist Protestants.[32] Weigel rightly points to the religious and racial dimensions of what he calls the "classic" anti-Catholicism of this period, which built upon centuries of Protestant criticism that Catholics were unfit for democracy.[33] By and large though, as scholars have shown, anti-Catholicism receded over the course of the twentieth century, as Irish and later Italian Catholics were welcomed not only into the religious mainstream, but also into US categories of Christian whiteness.[34] White Americans turned their suspicions in new directions by the 1940s and 50s—to Japanese Americans, to communists, and to homosexuals, all threatening American democracy anew. According to Weigel, however, Protestant anti-Catholicism did not simply disappear: it transformed. And what it became was secularism.

Older proponents of anti-Catholicism, writes Weigel, never "dreamed of advocating a secularist polity in which religion would be ruled out of the public debate."[35] But newer forms of anti-Catholicism, he insists, do precisely this. Weigel looks back to the 1949 publication of Paul Blanshard's *American Freedom and Catholic Power* as first signaling this shift from Protestant against Catholic to secularist against religion.[36] Part of the secular shift Weigel sees would also include "new *Catholic* Catholic-bashing" among Catholic dissidents, like Father Richard McBrien, who compared Pope John Paul II to Mikhail Gorbachev.[37] There are subtler instances. During a campaign speech in Houston, Texas, presidential hopeful John F. Kennedy pledged never to allow his Catholic faith to impinge upon his political beliefs. He envisioned an America "where no religious body seeks to impose its will directly *or indirectly* upon the general populace or the public acts of its officials."[38] In Weigel's estimation, Kennedy adopted "the theory of the *secular* nativists: that moral arguments whose roots were to be found in religious conviction had no business in American public life."[39]

Weigel contends that this new anti-Catholicism, even when it may seem benign, serves "as a crucial component in a more radical and comprehensive campaign to establish secularism—the naked public square—as the official doctrine of the United States."[40] It arises most often in the "prestige press" (especially the *New York Times*), the academy, the entertainment industry, and, perhaps most importantly, among what he calls the "feminist and homosexual lobbies."[41] I want to foreground the moves this argument makes. Weigel joined Philip Jenkins and many religious conservatives in setting the sexual revolution of the 1960s as "the centerpiece of the secularists' agenda (and of the secularists' attack on Catholicism)."[42] In this telling, feminists, gays, and lesbians find themselves at the vanguard of anti-Catholicism— indeed, they attack religion in general, the story goes, when they march in the streets to secure legal access to abortion and antidiscrimination protections. This narrative, in other words, figures progressive movements for gender and sexuality as essentially secularist and anti-Catholic.[43] Feminist and queer activists cannot be thought otherwise in this framework. And, even among this cohort, AIDS activists rank high on the list of Catholicism's offenders. Indeed, Jenkins charges that "gay activists have been among the leading contemporary critics of Catholicism and the Church" and that no voice within the gay movement has been louder than that of ACT UP.[44]

Given this framing, it would seem to follow that ACT UP's "Stop the Church" protest evinced obviously secularist rhetoric, including some of the most obvious attacks on the Catholic Church, if not on religion generally. But to reduce "Stop the Church" to secularist attack requires overlooking much of what was going on in the protest, why activists demonstrated, and how they did so. *Like a Prayer* offers a powerful counterpoint to this charge of blunt, secularist anti-Catholicism. But it does so in ways that are more complicated than merely disproving it. My point here is not that "Stop the Church" was absent of anti-Catholic sentiment. No doubt, many activists loathed the Church, proudly mocked it, and would have been happy to see its doors closed—less because it was Catholic, though, than because it exerted real political power in opposing gay rights, AIDS education, and abortion. But the way that activists criticized the Catholic Church is important: they focused specifically on Catholic political positions and drew from religious—often Catholic—languages, symbols, and practices to stylize their opposition.[45]

The charge of secularist anti-Catholicism runs headfirst, for instance, into the cultural and ritual work of Ray Navarro's Jesus drag and DIVA TV's documentary, which purposely features Catholic and ex-Catholic protestors speaking back against the Church. The documentary shows one of the things that Weigel finds most frustrating about—and most indicative of—the secularist enterprise: the shift from affirming "the classic Jewish and Christian notion of an objective moral order" to denying "on epistemological grounds that there is any such thing as an 'objective moral norm.'"[46] The fear of secularism, in other words, turns on the resistance to what conservatives often call relativism (or sometimes nihilism), but what activists would more likely call diversity and pluralism—or religious and sexual freedom.[47] *Like a Prayer* does not uniformly denounce "religion" or "Catholicism"—nor does it call for a naked public sphere. Much the opposite. It enacts a form of Catholicism, a campy liberation theology, that positions Jesus on the side of feminist and AIDS activists. Before jumping into the analysis of *Like a Prayer*, I offer a brief sketch of ACT UP, the "Stop the Church" demonstration, and the broader history of video activism of which the documentary is a part.

ACT UP/NY, AIDS Activist Video, and *Like a Prayer*

Founded in 1987, ACT UP/NY is a direct-action AIDS activist group that garnered mainstream media attention in the late 1980s and early 1990s for its often-ostentatious protests. ACT UP has employed a variety of methods, from behind-the-scenes conversations with medical professionals and pharmaceutical representatives to agitprop and street theater techniques that have drawn attention to issues that mainstream media outlets neglect. Their targets have included government agencies, pharmaceutical companies, and even the home of conservative Senator Jesse Helms, over which activists draped an enormous fake condom. But the protest at St. Patrick's brought the most mainstream attention to ACT UP—even if the news was largely negative.[48]

"Stop the Church" targeted the public role Roman Catholic bishops played in political debates about abortion, safe sex education, and gay rights. Cardinal O'Connor, the archbishop of New York City, proved one of the most vocal members of the growing conservative wing of the Catholic hierarchy. In 1987, the administrative board of the US bishops released a statement called "The Many Faces of AIDS: A Gospel Response" that allowed for Catholic health workers and hospitals to instruct patients about the use of condoms to prevent the spread of HIV under very specific circumstances.[49] Mainstream media misrepresented the statement as a major shift in the Church's teaching about condoms, and conservative bishops, following the Vatican's lead, quickly sought to clear up any confusion. In 1989, the full board of US bishops released "Called to Compassion and Responsibility: A Response to the HIV/AIDS Crisis." This new statement clarified both the Church's position as an authority on matters of sexuality and its unqualified opposition to any teaching that allowed for the use of contraceptives, including condoms.[50] The following month, O'Connor opened the Vatican's first conference on AIDS, where he declared Catholic morality, rather than clean needles or condoms, was the key to ending the epidemic.[51]

O'Connor's comments and leadership in the Church made him a clear target for feminist and AIDS activists. They were frustrated not simply by O'Connor's position regarding Catholic sexual morality but that he actively promoted this morality in local and national politics well beyond the Church—and he held a lot of sway. In New York City, where he oversaw Catholic schools and hospitals, the cardinal actively opposed gay rights ordinances that protected queer people from discrimination based on sexual orientation, lobbied against rights to abortion, and pressured city leaders to favor abstinence education over sex education that included teaching about condoms. Activists were furious, then, to learn that Reagan appointed O'Connor to the President's Commission on the HIV Epidemic in 1987. For many, this political engagement opened O'Connor and the Catholic Church to political critique—religious freedom, in this sense, does not render religious voices immune from protest. Nor does protest equate to secularist attack.[52]

Not everyone in ACT UP/NY was convinced that organizing against the Catholic Church should be a priority. Some worried that activists would be viewed as infringing on the rights of lay Catholics. To quell these fears, activists emphasized that their protest targeted O'Connor and the Church hierarchy, rather than lay Catholics or religion more generally. They printed their own pamphlets for parishioners of St. Patrick's to explain the reasons for the action, which included the bishops' insistence that Catholics follow traditional teaching with regard to abortion and sexuality—a point, activists asserted, that infringed on the rights of all Catholics. They cited, for instance, recent comments that O'Connor had made denouncing Catholic Governor of New York Mario Cuomo's support for women's legal right to have an abortion, a position on which the Cardinal declared there was no room for interpretation.[53] ACT UP/NY members also attempted to shape media responses to the protest by emphasizing the political authority the Church had gained in New York. Despite these efforts, mainstream coverage proved overwhelmingly negative, characterizing the protest as an attack on religious freedom and on lay Catholics in general. Beyond emphasizing the supposed militancy of activists, most coverage seized upon a single action—the crumbling of a consecrated Host—that came to represent the demonstration as a whole. Catholic leaders like O'Connor and the mainstream press alike narrated this moment as an unwarranted attack by radical activists on innocent Catholics, and even Christ himself, embodied in the wafer.[54]

Members of ACT UP and WHAM! issued press releases and interviews during and after the demonstration to communicate the political reasons for their protest, even as they knew stories in the mainstream news would largely overlook their claims. In fact, AIDS activists had long been critical of news coverage of the epidemic. When the Centers for Disease Control first reported the cases of homosexual men with rare forms of *Pneumocystis carinii* pneumonia and Kaposi's sarcoma in the summer of 1981, medical scientists theorized a common source of infection. It seemed to mostly affect sexually active gay men, though early cases were also reported among intravenous drug users, sex workers, and Haitians. They would call the disease gay-related immune deficiency (GRID) until renaming it acquired immunodeficiency syndrome (AIDS) late in 1982. Because these groups were marginalized, AIDS initially received very little attention in broadcast or print news. The coverage that did exist tended to cast gay men as morally responsible for the illness. Mainstream coverage accelerated rapidly by 1983, when reports began to show that blood transfusions could also transmit the virus that causes AIDS.[55] Media coverage began to vacillate between stories of blameworthy gay men and drug users versus the innocent victims of the disease, especially children with hemophilia.[56]

As AIDS became national news in the mid-1980s, mainstream networks often featured medical and public health experts alongside conservative political and religious ideologues who saw the epidemic as a sign of divine or natural judgment.[57] The Reagan White House was largely silent on AIDS until US Surgeon General C. Everett Koop was finally tapped in 1986 to provide a report and to begin speaking to the broader American public. During these early years, many AIDS activists resisted mainstream representations of the crisis. In 1983, for instance, activists organized a new movement to refer to "people with AIDS" rather than AIDS "victims" as an effort to resist medical stigmatization and to insist that they could continue to live valuable lives even after an AIDS diagnosis.[58] The emphasis in mainstream news on "AIDS experts" also sidelined community-based health workers and lesbian and gay activists who had been combatting the epidemic on the frontlines from the beginning.[59] When activists formed ACT UP in 1987, they were responding in part to years of anger and frustration over mainstream media and government neglect of the AIDS crisis. As part of their movement, they also created new forms of AIDS media. The video activist collective DIVA TV was part of that effort.

DIVA TV and Alternative AIDS Media

DIVA TV, or Damned Interfering Video Activist Television, is the name of the collective that made *Like a Prayer*. It was founded in 1989 by nine members of ACT UP: Ray Navarro, Jean Carlomusto, Gregg Bordowitz, Bob Beck, Costa Pappas, Ellen Spiro, George Plagianos, Rob Kurilla, and Catherine Gund (previously Saalfield). AIDS video activists saw their role as one of providing "countersurveillance" and even witnessing.[60] Film and media studies scholar Roger Hallas describes two senses in which video activists became witnesses. They stood in witness during demonstrations, capturing on video instances of police brutality and documenting the actions of activists that often were overlooked in mainstream news. But, he insists, they also provided witness, or testimony, to activist causes.[61] They recorded events at AIDS demonstrations but also produced their own creative projects that testified to the need for better political interventions into the AIDS crisis—interventions that refused to separate art from politics.[62]

DIVA TV emerged from a longer history of alternative forms of media intervention. In *AIDS TV*, Alexandra Juhasz traces the roots of activist AIDS media back to the decolonization movements of the 1950s and 1960s, when activists engaged in new forms of anti-imperial representation, especially through the production of film; the "New American" and underground cinema movements, which challenged the norm of Hollywood movies by privileging low-budget, community-based work; and radical protest cinema of the civil rights movement and sexual revolution, which gave voice to the political and identity-based movements of the 1960s and 1970s.[63] Advances in film and video technology also shaped later AIDS activist projects. Chief among these changes was the release of the Portapak in the late 1960s, a fairly inexpensive, easy-to-use, and portable device that allowed for instant playback. It was a precursor to the "camcorder revolution" of the 1980s and 1990s, which led to an explosion of consumer video and allowed professional and amateur video artists alike to participate in AIDS video activism.[64]

DIVA TV was founded two years after Testing the Limits, another video collective associated with ACT UP/NY that shared several of the same members and political goals. They differed, however, in their desired audiences. Testing the Limits sought to make documentaries for broader, mainstream audiences, such as those watching PBS programs. In contrast, Catherine Gund explains, DIVA TV "targets ACT UP members as its primary audience and makes videos by, about, and, most importantly, *for* the movement."[65] As Testing the Limits moved in the direction of professionalization, DIVA TV remained a grassroots, collective organization. As a result, Gund writes, their approach emphasized "more process than product," speaking directly to activists' needs and the work of survival in that ethical and political moment.[66] DIVA TV's videos were screened in local bars and nightclubs, at activist meetings, and in members' homes. *Like a Prayer* was DIVA TV's third movie and the last that the collective would make in its first incarnation.[67] The death of two members, Pappas and Navarro, contributed to the growing sense of AIDS fatigue and prompted some members to pursue new directions after 1990.[68]

Witnessing "Stop the Church" in *Like a Prayer*

Like a Prayer is a camp testament to "Stop the Church." The twenty-eight-minute video begins with an extended preface composed of a series of quickly shifting scenes—all initiated by the upbeat chorus of Madonna's hit 1989 song of the same name. The first, short scene features Navarro as Jesus interviewing demonstrators on the street, before the video cuts to a darkened image of the front of St. Patrick's Cathedral. The words "Stop the Church" appear in red letters, as Madonna's chorus strikes up once again: "Just like a prayer, I'll take you there." The video then cuts to a still image of the protest taking place inside St. Patrick's. The sounds of chanting protestors mix with the voice of Cardinal O'Connor reciting the *Gloria Patri*. "Glory to the Father and to the Son and the Holy Spirit," he speaks, "as it was in the beginning." A sequence of white text appears over the image. It reads:

> For centuries the church leadership has tried to govern individual morality and to limit everyone's right to choose for themselves. These men (and they have always been men) must be told that they cannot impose their morality on people who do not share their doctrine. This violates freedom of religion. Church leadership must be recognized for what it is: a powerful, wealthy corporation lobbying to turn morality into medicine, and religion into political policy.[69]

Reading the script draws the viewer's gaze downward, to the bottom of the image, which shows two men kissing amid the chaotic protest inside the cathedral. Madonna's voice crescendos once again: "Let the choir sing!" This opening series of images, including Navarro's scene, playfully positions the protesters from the start on the side of religious freedom—indeed of Christianity itself. Jesus walks among them, and they become the choir that sings.

Like a Prayer then proceeds to "The 7 Deadly Sins of Cardinal O'Connor and Church Politicians," announced in white script over a now lightened image of the front of St. Patrick's. The body of the documentary moves sequentially through seven segments, one for each sin. Stretching back to early Christian writings, the Seven Deadly Sins have informed Christian education and morality—not to mention painting, sculpture, literature, song, and film—for centuries. *Like a Prayer* rewrites these sins, positing them as sins of the Catholic Church, which include Ignorant Denial, Endangering Women's

Lives, No Safe Sex Education, No Condoms, No Clean Needles, Bias, and Assault of Lesbians and Gay Men. The documentary also plays with the Catholic practice of confession, during which the observant admits their sins and seeks absolution. The segments of Deadly Sins include interviews with Catholic and ex-Catholic protestors describing their views on the Catholic Church and the ACT UP/WHAM! protest. Here, *Like a Prayer* turns confession into a vehicle for public testimony: activists speak outward about the Church, by way of documentary video, rather than inward to a priest about their own sins, through the private box of the confessional.[70] In doing so, they also directly challenge the authority of the Church itself.

Footage from the "Stop the Church" protest accompanies several of the sin segments and functions as documentary witness. Under the sin of "Endangering Women's Lives," for instance, an activist explains how a priest told his mom she was sinning because she used birth control—he was shocked that his mother was put in this position. *Like a Prayer* then cuts to several activists dressing up as clowns, and Smokey Robinson's "The Tears of a Clown" raises the energy and playfulness of the scene. They are part of "Operation Ridiculous," a troupe tasked to "boldly go where no clown has gone before." Operation Ridiculous is a camp send-up of the militant pro-life group Operation Rescue, which was founded by Randall Terry, an evangelical Protestant who would eventually convert to Roman Catholicism.[71] In the weeks leading up to "Stop the Church," Cardinal O'Connor was quoted in several newspapers expressing his desire to join a mission with Operation Rescue.[72] The members of Operation Ridiculous explain their commitment to fighting things they considered absurd, including the notion that fetuses have more rights than women, that the pro-life movement ignores the need for broader healthcare, that conversations about reproductive rights have been limited to abortion, and that the Church opposes condoms. The scene ends with protesters chanting, "Safe sex is good morality/Cardinal O'Connor face reality"—a play on the cardinal's claim that "Good morality is good medicine."

Other narrative devices organize and interrupt the serial progression of the Seven Deadly Sins and, in doing so, invite readings of the documentary and the "Stop the Church" demonstration that reveal far more than secular or anti-Catholic protest. I highlight three: storytelling, media commentary, and Jesus vignettes featuring Navarro. In addition to these three, the use of popular music also punctuates many of the documentary's messages and gives form to the camp aesthetic through which it speaks.[73] The appeal to storytelling comes at the end of the first segment on sin. After an activist explains her frustrations with the Church's positions on sex and abortion, the documentary introduces the telling of a parable.[74] A third-person narrator begins to speak; she mimics the drawn-out and dramatic voice of a parent reading a fairytale to a child. She describes an "evil sorcerer" who wanted everyone in his land to be unhappy. He spoke to his people, "filling them with ignorance and blinding them with lies." He wanted women to become slaves to their bodies and refused to speak about a cure for an awful plague, even though the cure itself was readily available. But if the sorcerer would not speak out, she continues, a brave few would, and "they laid their bodies at the feet of the evil sorcerer." The narration unfolds against scenes of Cardinal O'Connor and St. Patrick's, images of protestors (both conservative ones and members of ACT UP and WHAM!), and footage of the demonstration inside. The activists are the heroes of the story, finally entering the lair of the evil sorcerer and speaking the cure.

The story is a parable about good and evil and about overcoming silence— a ubiquitous theme in AIDS activism in this period, emblemized by the famous Silence=Death motto created by the artist group Gran Fury. It is also a story of epiphany, a come-to-Jesus moment, so to speak, when activists discover the power of their voices, after which, "they were never silent again." The use of the parable offers a stylized frame for understanding the "Stop the Church" protest. It mimics the binary terms of good and evil common to fairytales and places AIDS activism into this fictional narrative. But, like all parables, the truth is found not in the content of the story but in the moral lesson that it teaches through an appeal to analogy. It is a simple narrative form that indicates a larger ethical truth. This parable of the activists and the evil sorcerer suggests a camp reading. Its exaggerations—the forces of good and evil, the play of silence and speech, even the rising and falling voice of the narrator—puts the entire "Stop the Church" demonstration in quotation marks, as Sontag might say, and asks that viewers decode what precisely stopping the Church might mean. It subverts the supposed protagonists and antagonists, casting AIDS activists as their own legendary heroes, seeking their happy ending.

A second narrative device in *Like a Prayer* recasts the authority of broadcast news journalism. Hallas describes common techniques that broadcast news employs to script the authority of the journalist, such as the use of the "talking head."[75] Popular news shows in this period often featured a news anchor (usually a white man in a suit—think Ted Koppel or Dan Rather) seated behind a desk in a quiet studio. He speaks from a position of reason, separated from the actual news by the authority of distance. Hallas explains how direct-action AIDS video toyed with this form in order to undermine and expose broadcast news techniques *as* techniques. This form of address functioned as a "structure of power" that positioned viewers in intimate relation to the talking head, while separating both from AIDS activists, who were scripted as "out there," on the streets, and unable to speak from the position of reasoned authority available to the news anchor.[76]

Members of DIVA TV played with this form of media authority in several ways. One approach positioned activists themselves as journalists and put them on the streets talking with other activists. We saw this device in Ray Navarro's opening scene. In additional DIVA TV footage from the protest, Navarro-as-Jesus introduces himself to an activist carrying a large balloon inflated to look like a condom. Their brief conversation unfolds:

NAVARRO: "JC here with the fire and brimstone network with members of Wave 3 Affinity group and we'd like to ask you a little bit about this large [pause] vision you've visited upon us."

ACTIVIST: "Well we decided to rename the Cardinal, he's now Cardinal O'Condom. This is our message to him that condoms are safe. It's no sin."

NAVARRO: "Isn't this a little bit late for the Macy's parade?"

ACTIVIST: "Well we thought of that but we'll get a jump on next year. We'll start a new tradition."[77]

Such vignettes reposition the role of the AIDS activist. In this case, we see a double drag. Navarro plays both Jesus and journalist, taking these roles directly to the people.

In addition to dragging the role of the reporter, *Like a Prayer* documents and counters misrepresentations of AIDS activism that circulated in mainstream news media. In one scene, an activist describes how Channel 11 News asked for some of her footage of the demonstration from inside the cathedral, which she shared. But then the news station used the footage simply to demonstrate acts of "sacrilege" and to turn the protest into the butt of a joke, announcing how activists "turned the holy mass into a holy mess."[78] Mainstream coverage also emphasized scenes where protestors clashed with police in order to represent activists as law-breakers.

Like a Prayer stages these (mis)representations by including its own montage of negative coverage. As one activist explains, mainstream media reduced the protest to questions of "right or wrong" and focused on the activists' tactics rather than the political reasons for the demonstration. In one segment, the video includes footage of a young Matt Lauer hosting a show for the television station 9BP. Turning to a panel of AIDS activists, he says, "Now there are a lot of people who sympathize and agree with the protestors, but other people have been left asking the question, 'Is nothing sacred anymore?' Some are going to say: 'Those homosexuals, here they go again.'" The documentary captures Lauer's resistance to covering why activists protested to begin with. "I think it's important here to refrain from a particular discussion of safe sex or AIDS or abortion," Lauer continues: "and discuss *more* the church's role or responsibility or right to discuss these issues and your right to protest these issues." By staging mainstream news coverage, *Like a Prayer* reveals its positionality and refuses to let such coverage pretend to speak with a neutral voice. As one activist interviewed for the documentary explains, "It's as if they can't imagine an audience that includes lesbians or gay men or more specifically women seeking reproductive rights or people with AIDS." *Like a Prayer* suggests that activists, armed with their own cameras and editing tools, can create their own forms of representation. Indeed, it insists that they should: the media segment ends with the hip-hop trio Salt-N-Pepa imploring activists (and viewers) to "Express yourself!"

Short vignettes featuring Ray Navarro dressed as Jesus constitute a third narrative device that punctuates the list of sins. We see Navarro in footage on the day of the protest standing in the street, but *Like a Prayer* also includes short clips of Navarro that were used in public television ads leading up to the demonstration—this is the footage Don Wildmon blasted in his mailer to members of the American Family Association. These vignettes interrupt the sense of urgency seen in interviews with (ex)Catholic protestors, the frenzy of the live footage from the protest, and the playful energy of the pop songs that intervene throughout the documentary. By contrast, the scenes with Navarro are quiet, calm even, evoking reverence. The sonic shift that sets these scenes apart complements their emphasis on a singular figure: Jesus, seated against a plain wall.

One of the vignettes begins with a close-up on Navarro's face. As the camera pans to a wider frame, Jesus says, "Make sure your second coming is a safe one. Use condoms." Navarro reaches for an opened condom and a Bible, holding them up for the viewer to see. Another vignette, shot in a similar style, starts again with a close-up on Navarro's face. Jesus turns to address the viewer. "You may have been wondering where I've been the last couple thousand years," he says: "Me and my friends at the AIDS Coalition to Unleash Power have been busy opposing the Church's bastardization of my teachings." The camera pulls back to reveal Navarro's body. He wears a white robe draped over one shoulder, leaving the other exposed along with part of his chest. He holds up a Bible and a bookmark-sized ad for the "Stop the Church" protest. "Have you seen a lot of these around town late lately?" he asks, in an earnest voice: "Have you wondered how they could have gone up in such a short space of time? Kind of a miracle, hmm? My hand's been in it." The shot homes in on the ad, before panning back to Jesus's face. "Personally, I oppose the Church's position on abortion," he insists: "and I'm busy fighting its murderous AIDS policy."

What should we make of Ray Navarro's Jesus vignettes? Is this performance merely an instance of mocking the Catholic Church or of parody? *Like a Prayer*, especially through Navarro's performances of Jesus, challenges how we frame queer politics and religion, troubling any clear line between the secular and the religious, between habitation and refusal. It does so by adopting a strategy of camp. Camping Catholicism makes fun of the Catholic Church while, at the same time, revealing a variety of engagements with Catholic symbols and practice, indeed with Catholic imagination, that contest conventional oppositions between Catholic and anti-Catholic.

Ray Navarro's Jesus Camp

One does not have to look too hard to see camp performance in the work of DIVA TV. The very name recalls a longer history of gay sensibility. As Mark Jordan reminds us, "'Diva' entered gay slang with the opera queens, who knew that it meant divine."[79] We see the flair for camp—that is, for exaggeration, for style, especially when it secures the joys of playing effeminate—in the colorful wigs and bright red noses of the clowns in Operation Ridiculous. We see it in juxtapositions of the serious and the humorous—the litany of Deadly Sins cut by the baptizing of "Cardinal O'Condom" or his recasting as an evil sorcerer.

We see it in the repurposing of things that are already camp. The most obvious example is the use of Madonna's "Like a Prayer." Already a gay icon and, for many, an anti-Catholic idolater, Madonna reached new heights with this music video, which became an anthem for queer celebration. Madonna Louise Ciccone already took on Catholic drag when she dropped her middle and last names to become the singular "Madonna." Her status as a queer icon layered camp over camp. Like much feminist and queer activism, Madonna's "Like a Prayer" drew accusations of blasphemy. The Queen of Pop was accused of making fun of Christianity, at best, if not actually denigrating religious tradition by sexualizing a man whom some viewers of her music video saw as a Black Jesus figure—as though there is not a *long* history of Christians eroticizing or racializing Jesus.[80] Using her song was hardly coincidental. It paid homage to the pop diva and foreshadowed that, whatever this video was doing with Catholicism, it would be controversial—and fabulous.

There are different registers of camp. Much of *Like a Prayer* plays with the more ostentatious forms: the ridiculousness of dressing up as a clown, the thrilling sexual innuendo of Madonna's song and music video, the translation of St. Patrick's into the castle of an evil sorcerer. But camp can also emerge from subtlety, from intimacy, and from a seriousness that borders on solemnity. As a character in Christopher Isherwood's *The World in the Evening* famously puts it, "You can't camp about something you don't take seriously."[81] This camp can sometimes take a little more work to decode, but it is often more biting, precisely because of how close one must get to figure it out. In these respects, Ray Navarro may be the camp superstar of *Like a Prayer*.

Born in 1964, Navarro grew up in Simi Valley, California, and graduated from the California Institute of the Arts (after first attending the Otis Art Institute of Parsons School of Design). He moved to New York City in 1988 to join the Whitney Museum's Independent Study Program. The artist, filmmaker, and writer would soon become an activist as well, when he joined ACT UP/NY. Navarro was one of the founders of DIVA TV and also a leader in ACT UP's outreach to racial and ethnic minorities. He identified as Mexican American and as a Chicano activist, championing political commitments to which his mother Patricia Navarro introduced him when he was growing up.[82] Navarro's boyfriend, Anthony Ledesma, became sick during the summer of 1988 or 1989 and was diagnosed with AIDS.[83] Navarro was not tested for HIV until sometime later but knew he likely carried the virus as well. He was diagnosed with AIDS in January 1990, a month after the "Stop the Church" demonstration. Navarro would lose most of his vision and hearing from AIDS complications before he passed away in November 1990. In his final months, he collaborated with fellow artist and activist Zoe Leonard on a triptych of photographs called *Equipped* which, Debra Levine writes, "tantalizingly engages issues of sexual fetishism and desirability in disability."[84]

I never met Navarro in person but first encountered him while doing research many years ago on the history of AIDS and ACT UP/NY at the New York Public Library's AIDS Activist Video Collection. I came across a VHS cassette marked "Ray's Tape," an eleven-minute memorial reel that DIVA TV members made after Navarro's death. I didn't expect the rush of presence and emotion that watching the tape—in a public library—would create. Jih-Fei Cheng, a media studies scholar, has written about the making and recirculation of AIDS activist videos, including this footage of Navarro. Through their collection and circulation, he writes, such videos demonstrate communities of feminist and queer love; they also serve as sources of "AIDS afterlives," especially for activists of color, that "transgress linear history" to make possible alternative futures and social attachments.[85] In other words, they allow the possibility of communion with the dead who remain among us. They bring Ray back to life.

* * *

I introduce Navarro's biography here to gesture to the range of readings that become available for understanding what Gund has called "his favorite role of Jesus with a crown of thorns, toga, and jimmy hat."[86] This is how fellow DIVA TV member Jean Carlomusto described Navarro's role in the "Stop the Church" demonstration:

> Let me just say, it was also really powerful because Ray, whose own illness was progressing very quickly, dressed as Jesus Christ that day outside was sort of leading chants outside of St. Pat's. And in his own way, as someone who had grown up Catholic, too, was sort of reclaiming this Christ figure as a revolutionary—use of Christ as someone saying, "Use condoms."[87]

Carlomusto characterizes Navarro's Jesus drag as a political performance and as a source of spiritual empowerment. She continues:

> As he grew closer to death, he became more and more religious. So for him, that action was a very empowering action for getting him closer to his own spirituality. And for me, it was powerful for that reason, too, to just get in the face of the Catholic Church and go up against this monolithic behemoth that has grown beyond all proportions from its original inception.[88]

It might seem odd, especially from the perspective of conservative writers like Weigel or Jenkins, for a gay Chicano man with AIDS to dress as Jesus, to call for safe sex education, and to criticize the Catholic Church hierarchy—and to do so in a way that was both parodic and deadly serious. But read against centuries of Christian history, it is not so unusual. There is quite a long and diverse tradition of Jesus drag within Christianity. Jesus has been in turns Middle Eastern, white, Black, Native American, Asian, Hindu, Jewish, Christian, male, female, transgender, a gash, a vagina, a vine, a lamb, a carpenter, a businessman, a boxer, a boyfriend, the bread of life, and a wafer.[89] Of course, not all drag is equal. But this is where Navarro's Jesus camp shines.

Performing Jesus, Inhabiting the Sacred

Navarro's performance builds not only upon a longer history of Jesus drag but also upon particular histories of lay Christian engagements with images and with the figure of Jesus himself. Navarro taps into what Jesuit sociologist Andrew Greeley has called the "Catholic imagination," by which he means a tendency for Catholics to see hints of the divine in "objects, events, and persons of ordinary existence."[90] He contrasts this "sensibility" with a Protestant tendency toward a strict separation between a sign or a symbol of the divine and its referent. While Greeley risks overgeneralizing this distinction, it resonates with more recent historical and anthropological writing on religion, secularism, and affect.

Anthropologist Saba Mahmood draws a similar distinction in her discussion of the controversy that erupted over Danish cartoon drawings of Muhammad. They proved controversial because of their depiction of the Prophet and because, within most Islamic traditions, it is considered offensive to visually portray Muhammad or Allah. She seeks to understand why some devout Muslims became upset about the drawings, when so many others (Muslims and non-Muslims alike) readily upheld the rights of the cartoonists on the grounds of free speech. Mahmood's important challenge to dominant readings of this example is to move beyond what she calls the juridical languages of free speech versus blasphemy. She instead asks what it meant for some Muslims to describe the cartoons as a kind of "moral injury." Central to this, she argues, are different ways of relating to images like those of Muhammad in the cartoons. She builds upon the work of anthropologist Webb Keane to suggest alternative "semiotic forms" for interpreting images and for understanding religious practices that do not conform to dominant Western models. Keane traces the genealogy of Western models back to a "Protestant semiotic ideology" that sharply distinguishes between "object and subject, between substance and meaning, signifiers and signified, form and essence."[91] This approach to representation has proved crucial not only to the development of "Western" modernity but also to prevailing ways that we define religion (that is, as adherence to or belief in a series of propositional claims).[92]

Mahmood, in turn, wants to suggest alternative ways that a person can come to relate to a sign or symbol (or image), ways not reducible to this premium on belief. Recent work in affect studies and on material and visual culture resonates with this approach, as scholars have for some time insisted that images and objects may themselves be understood as animated, as helping to exert a kind of force or attachment that blurs the boundaries between an object and its representation or even between a spectator and an image.[93] In this sense, Mahmood is interested in understanding relationships with images (like those of Muhammad) not on the model of representation but on what she calls "attachment and cohabitation."[94] In this reading, the religious imaginary must be understood in relationship both to a history of practice within a particular religious tradition and to the potential power of images and objects themselves. Mahmood focused on a Muslim imaginary, not a Catholic one, but her analysis is helpful for thinking about visual and material culture in the United States and about Navarro's Jesus camp.

Historians of religion in the United States have keenly documented the power of material objects and images, especially among lay Catholics. Colleen McDannell describes how the theology of Incarnation (God made into flesh) opened the doors for Christians to see the divine operating through everyday objects and people. Under the guidance of an ordained priest, Catholics can partake in major sacraments, or rituals, through which the divine becomes present. Perhaps the best known of the sacraments is the Eucharist—a rite during which the Communion wafer becomes the blood and body of Christ, according to the doctrine of transubstantiation, before it is taken into one's own body. Catholics also have a long, related tradition of smaller rituals, or sacramentals, "something that is more than a sign or a symbol but less than a sacrament."[95] Praying with the rosary is one of the most common examples of a sacramental. This power to imbue objects or images with greater meaning, even with divine presence, has not been limited to Catholics. Protestants too become attached to objects and images, often imbuing them with a sense of the divine (and often doing so against the orthodox beliefs of their traditions). Images of Jesus, in particular, have often been welcomed with a reverence that belies any strict acknowledgment that a picture is "merely" a representation—and none more so than Warner Sallman's savior.

Performing Sallman's *Head of Christ*

Warner Sallman's 1940 painting *Head of Christ* is likely the most famous image of Jesus of Nazareth in US history, especially among Protestants, though Catholics have also adopted Sallman's savior as their own. Some evangelicals have even complained that too many Christians make it into an icon.[96] I bring it up here because it helps us to understand the potential power of Navarro's Jesus, which echoed Sallman's *Head of Christ*. While I had hoped to reproduce Sallman's portrait here for closer comparison, the copyright holder curiously declined to give permission after seeing the topic of this chapter. (The image is nonetheless widely available online.) Sallman painted Jesus, in profile, as a white man with glowing brown hair and a nicely kempt beard. One of Navarro's vignettes mirrors this image, as it begins with a shot of Jesus staring off to the right side of the frame, his eyes gazing upwards, much like Sallman's Christ. His face, too, is bathed in light. Navarro holds this pose for several seconds, almost like the shot is meant to mimic a painting, before turning toward the camera (see Figure 4.1).

The resonance extends beyond posture and lighting. As Sallman's painting soared in popularity in the 1960s, critics began to comment on the effeminacy of his Jesus, with his long, flowing hair and soft face. Members of the liberal Protestant elite mocked the painting, hanging in millions of households across the country, as little more than kitsch. They were shocked that anyone, let alone biblically focused Protestants, could imbue it with such presence.[97] Catholics, too, worried over the effeminacy of kitschy depictions of Christ. In 1984, one writer for the Catholic magazine *Commonweal* complained about images of Christ that made him seem like "seated women with short skirts" who called out to their onlookers, "Life is so boring. Come violate me" or "Come, be violated with me." We should note the evident misogyny of this fantasy—and also its homophobic anxiety. The same author then describes his preference for Hans Holbein the Younger's *The Body of the Dead Christ in the Tomb* (1520–1522) over depictions that make Christ look like "a

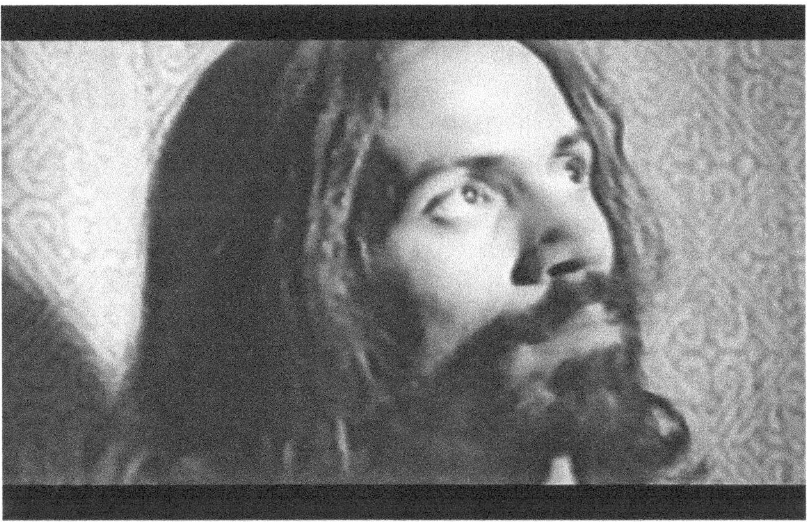

Figure 4.1 Ray Navarro as Jesus in the film *Like a Prayer* (created by DIVA TV, 1990). AIDS Activist Videotape Collection, New York Public Library.

jaded 'gay' athlete posing for a Palestinian center-fold."[98] For such critics, as McDannell notes, "the kitsch Christ is female"—or a homosexual man—a difference that does not quite matter in this fragile masculine imaginary.[99] It is amid these anxious Christian fears of a too-sensuous savior that Navarro's Jesus comes down from heaven.

Navarro's Jesus should be read as a kind of Warner Sallman drag. Like Sallman's Christ, Navarro's is too effeminate, glimpsed not only through his visual depiction but also when he turns to the camera and speaks to his flock. His voice is calm, soft, and slow. Navarro's body is thin and graceful in its movements, as he holds up a condom or a Bible. Of course, the differences between these representations of Jesus, these inhabitations, by Navarro, by Sallman, also matter. The audience for *Like a Prayer* (mostly fellow feminist and AIDS activists and queer people) would have known or suspected that Navarro was a gay man and that he was likely seropositive, factors that would have shaped their reading of his performance. Navarro's Jesus also moves away from Sallman's through its racial significations. US Christians gazing at Sallman's Jesus have almost uniformly seen a Caucasian son of God. Navarro's ethnic markers are less obvious. Certainly, those who knew him were familiar with his Mexican American background. But even without this knowledge, his darker hair, even soaked in light, does not carry the golden highlights of Sallman's blue-eyed and fair-haired Jesus. These shots of Navarro in *Like a Prayer* thus play on the most popular devotional image of Jesus in the United States, while also recasting Christianity's central figure as a gay Chicano man with AIDS. For certain conservative Christians, this is the kitsch gay Jesus of their nightmares. For people with AIDS, this vision could be divine.

Navarro's Jesus also resonates in several ways with what theologian Roberto Goizueta calls "Mexican American popular Catholicism."[100] I do not want to overstate the connection here between popular Catholicism and Navarro's Chicano political identification and AIDS work, as his relationship to Catholicism may appear more "cultural" than devout.[101] But Catholicism surely was not foreign to Navarro, whose mother Patricia attended Catholic schools and whose political identifications with Mexican Americans would have brought him close to many practicing Catholics. And Chicano political movements have long drawn from Catholic imagery and tradition.[102] Navarro's Jesus drag blurs any simple line one might draw between merely cultural Catholicism and devout or practicing forms, which we can see in part through its similarity to popular forms of Catholicism. Goizueta, for instance, describes the powerful role that death plays in the symbolic world of Mexican American Catholicism, a tradition forged in the context of colonization, racism, violence, and poverty. But he suggests that, although death may seem central, this form of popular Catholicism actually "undermines the modern Western dichotomous worldview in which life and death are perceived as contradictory or mutually exclusive realities." "Popular Catholicism," he continues, "also challenges the church to discover among the poor and marginalized the prophetic love of God."[103] This commitment became clear in Navarro's Jesus drag, which joins other manifestations of the divine.

We see one of the most powerful illustrations of this popular piety in reenactments of the Via Crucis (Living Way of the Cross) on Good Friday. Consider how Chicano studies scholar Karen Mary Davalos describes the annual Via Crucis performance that has taken place in Chicago's predominantly Mexican Pilsen neighborhood since the late 1970s. Women and men dress as biblical characters—Jesus, Mary, the Roman soldiers—and march through the neighborhood, performing the stations of the cross. "From the beginning," she writes, "the event conveyed Mexican Catholic sensibilities, social commentary on local injustices, dramatic reversals of power and authority, the sacralization of space, and acts of cultural recovery." It has grown into a "community-wide ritual" that draws people from throughout the region. Media coverage estimates over ten thousand people in attendance each year since the early 1990s. This event collapses conventional binaries that separate the divine from this world, the spiritual from the material, and even acting from reality. One participant explains to Davalos his role as a Roman soldier whipping Jesus. "This is my sin," he insists. In performing the Via Crucis, he continues, "We say forgive us for what we did then—in the past when Jesus was actually put to death—and for what we are doing now, as I whip him." The man explains that what they are doing is not a play: it is "a reenactment of a historical event, but it is not a play."[104] It is not a play because the reenactment, the repetition, partakes in the same economy of sin and grace as the original event. It collapses historical time into sacred time.

It is this combination of a sacramental reenactment of Jesus with the very social and political concerns so characteristic of Mexican American popular Catholicism that Navarro's performance of Jesus shares. What is different is that Navarro and the other members of DIVA TV also queer this performance through their aesthetics of camp.

Camp Performance as Public Catholicism

I have probably already put too much faith in camp, a term that is nearly impossible to define, in part because it resists the serious tone of analysis—and of most theology. Camp is about making fun, subverting meaning, mocking authority—not things most modern readers or scholars align with religion. "The bitter irony of camp juxtaposes the ludicrous and the earnest," writes theologian Mark Jordan: "It is the genius of camp to balance the two, to resist the dreary triumph of earnestness."[105] It can also emerge from deep attachment, even devotion, to the thing that becomes the object of camp, which risks intimacy without sincerity—or perhaps without earnest sincerity.

Catholicism, queerness, and camp share a long history—an obsession with liturgy, with the oscillation between decadence and denial, with the play between sensuality and transcendence. The homosocial spaces of Catholic tradition, from the all-male hierarchy to women's convents, have long served as sites of sexual suspicion and aesthetic possibility. "Catholicism in particular," writes queer theorist Eve Kosofsky Sedgwick, "is famous for giving countless gay and proto-gay children the shock of the possibility of adults who don't marry, or men in dresses, of passionate theatre, of introspective investment."[106] Outside the formal Roman Catholic Church, drag activists like the Sisters of Perpetual Indulgence have, since the late 1970s, donned habits as they parade around gay ghettos blessing their patrons and teaching safe sex. Like Roman Catholic nuns, the parodic Sisters undergo a period of training and take vows, in this case, "to promulgate universal joy and expiate stigmatic guilt."[107] They have also been accused of anti-Catholicism. Like the work of the Sisters, Ray Navarro's Jesus drag is threatening not simply because it is camp, but because it takes place outside the authority of the Church. It brings something of the sacramental to the people—and not just any people: to queer and trans people, to feminists, and to people with AIDS.

The AIDS activism of *Like a Prayer*, including Navarro's performance, unsettles claims about anti-Catholicism and the place of religion in the public sphere. Navarro's Jesus drag was far more than merely secular protest or anti-Catholic parody, in part because such characterizations mistake habitation for representation. Navarro's Jesus moves beyond the type of communicative or representational model that Mahmood and others have aligned with modern Protestant and secular sensibilities—sensibilities that conservatives writing about the new anti-Catholicism impose upon AIDS and feminist activists, sometimes rightly, sometimes not. Navarro's Jesus drag, like drag generally, does not merely represent some "real" referent (in this case the historical Jesus). As gender theorist Judith Butler argues, drag does not simply imitate an original. Its critical and social power comes from foregrounding the work of representation itself. "Gender parody," they write, "reveals that the original identity after which gender fashions itself is an imitation without an origin."[108] Drag, in this account, reveals the original, the object of drag, to be something that is itself constituted through the work of cultural representation and imitation. Drag thus opens a space for queer politics. "Parodic proliferation," Butler continues, "deprives hegemonic culture and its critics of the claim to naturalized or essentialist gender identities."[109]

Navarro's performance layers religious drag over the gender drag that Butler describes. His camp performance exposes the very social conventions that allow for normative representations of Jesus to reign—or, put differently, for some representations to become dominant or "true," such as those authorized by the Catholic Church or dominant styles of Christianity. Navarro's drag not only challenges representations of the "real" Jesus: it challenges the need to appeal to an original Jesus to begin with (and especially one presumed to be a white heterosexual). As we learn in *Like a Prayer*'s fairy tale–telling, moral truth can be far more important than reality, and moral truth can be disclosed through even the most exaggerated stories. Navarro's drag reanimates Jesus, the truth in Jesus, in at least two ways. He reclaims Jesus *from* Christian conservatives, but he also resurrects Jesus *for* secular and Catholic (or formerly Catholic) AIDS and feminist activists. To say this another way, Navarro's camp does not solely—or perhaps even most importantly—expose the contingency of conservative Christian claims upon Jesus. As Eve Sedgwick reminds us, focusing only on the work of exposure that camp performs makes it harder to see how "camping is motivated by love"—including its "passionate, often hilarious antiquarianism," its over-attachment to things debased, and its playful collocations of past and present, high and low, sacred and profane.[110] In Navarro's performance, Jesus becomes a figure to play with, to laugh with, as well as one to aspire toward, even to inhabit. This Chicano AIDS activist Jesus thus not only represents the Son of God, but also brings him to the people—*his* people.

Let me close with two points. First, at the risk of stating the obvious: the "Stop the Church" demonstration—including Ray Navarro's Jesus and the documentary *Like a Prayer*—is not what conservative Christians have had in mind when arguing that religion should have a greater place in the public sphere. Second, "Stop the Church" included some quite spectacular images of religion in public—not least Jesus marching down Fifth Avenue to confront his oppressors. If we were to grant both points, then we might ask: Why do conservative Christians (along with many secular historians and scholars of religion) not see *Like a Prayer* or Navarro's Jesus as examples of religion in the public sphere? How do they come to signify merely secular anti-Catholicism?

Like many other works of feminist and queer art that draw upon religious themes, *Like a Prayer* raises questions about what we mean, and what our historical subjects mean, when we talk about the presence or absence of religion in the public or political sphere. What assumptions about religion do we have in mind? Do we privilege conservative forms of organized religion in such conversations as our default models? How does camp performance challenge prevailing assumptions about what religion is and does? *Like a Prayer* suggests forms of religion that are not propositional, sincere, obvious, conservative, formal, authoritarian, or traditional—asking viewers to see religion where we might least expect it, and then to ask why we assumed it would not be there to begin with. Navarro's Jesus counters the authority of the Catholic Church, and of conservative Catholics, to define Christ. His critics, meanwhile, struggle to imagine an alternative Catholicism, much less the spiritual dimensions of queer life. This failure of imagination—which is a refusal of imagination, a fear of imagination—represents a turning away from the long history of Christianity itself, within which lay Catholics have been inhabiting, altering, mocking, and dragging Catholicism for as long as it has existed.[111]

The debate over anti-Catholicism, in this reading, in the obsession with queer AIDS activists and with "Stop the Church," in particular, reveals itself to be less a battle between secularism and religion than a battle over definitions of Catholicism, over the legacy of Jesus, over the power of religious imagination, and over the fear that imaginative possibilities raise for those most invested in control. This point does not discount that some activists (and scholars) may also push for secularism, even for a naked public sphere—they are many and diverse. But we can already hear the voices of secular activists and their critics asking why religion continues *still* to haunt queer politics. That is a question they will be trying to answer for a long time.

5

Renée Cox's Catholicism, Family Values, and the Politics of Offense

The inner voice is your ancestors whispering in your ear.[1]
—Renée Cox, invoking Queen Nanny of the Maroons

On Tuesday, February 20, 2001, photographer Renée Cox joined the stage to debate William "Bill" Donohue, the president of the Catholic League for Religious and Civil Rights, an organization founded in 1973 to defend the rights of Roman Catholics. The event was called "Exploring the 'Yo Mama' Controversy: Art, Outrage, and the First Amendment," and it was organized by the First Amendment Center and held in midtown Manhattan.[2] The occasion was the recent uproar over *Yo Mama's Last Supper*, Cox's photographic take on Leonardo da Vinci's classic painting. In her version, Cox, a self-described "born and raised Catholic, Jamaican-American Princess," stood in for Jesus, fully nude and surrounded by a cast of mostly Black disciples.[3] The work appeared in the Brooklyn Museum's exhibition *Committed to the Image: Contemporary Black Photographers*, which had opened the previous Friday, February 16 (see Figure 5.1).

Controversy erupted before the show even launched. Two days prior, a reporter from New York's *Daily News* brought Cox's photomontage to the attention of the Catholic League, assuming it was exactly the kind of thing that would set Donohue off. And it did. The Irish American Catholic, who earned his doctorate in sociology from New York University, had made a name for himself as the leading watchdog for negative portrayals of Roman Catholicism. Donohue, who quickly purchased a copy of the exhibition catalogue, was struck by the blatant "anti-Catholicism" displayed in the work and in the museum's decision to feature it.[4] Cox's piece also caught the eye of New York's Mayor Rudy Giuliani, who likewise condemned it as offensive. "If it were done against another group there would be outcry in this city that

Provoking Religion. Anthony M. Petro, Oxford University Press. © Oxford University Press 2025.
DOI: 10.1093/9780190938468.003.0006

would demand that they take the photograph down," he told reporters, "but anti-Catholicism is just accepted prejudice."[5]

Giuliani was experiencing a bout of déjà vu. Only a little more than a year before, artist Chris Ofili's mixed media painting *Holy Virgin Mary* had ignited similar controversy and accusations of sacrilege when it appeared in the Brooklyn Museum's 1999 exhibition *Sensation*. Ofili depicted an Africanized version of Mary adorned with elephant dung. Giuliani and Donohue quickly took offense, and they appeared repeatedly in televised news and in print, from CNN to the *New York Times*, blasting the pervasive and ongoing anti-Catholicism that had seemed to become par for the course among New York's art community and intelligentsia. Indeed, concerns about a "new" anti-Catholicism seemed to be coming to a head in these years. Catholic neoconservative George Weigel had named this threat in the early 1990s, when he listed feminist and queer activists among the leaders of a renewed antipathy toward Catholic religion and values. Now, it seemed, mainstream arts institutions happily condoned explicit attacks on Catholics. And not just in New York.

As debate raged over Cox's *Yo Mama's Last Supper*, Catholics in Chicago protested Dick Detzner's painting *The Last Pancake Supper*, which featured a bottle of Mrs. Butterworth's syrup in the role of Jesus flanked by disciples like breakfast cereal icons Tony the Tiger, Cap'n Crunch, and Toucan Sam. It was part of Detzner's *Corporate Sacrilege* series, which included send-ups of the Adoration, the Ten Commandments, and the crucifixion—the latter, titled *Yee Hee Hee*, features the Pillsbury Doughboy on a cross getting poked by the hand of god.[6] Just weeks after Cox's work was in the headlines, Chicana lesbian artist Alma Lopez would come under fire for *Our Lady*, a digital photograph of the Virgin of Guadalupe wearing a bikini of roses, which was shown at the Museum of International Folk Art in Santa Fe, New Mexico. *Our Lady* ignited a firestorm of controversy fueled by the local archdiocese.[7]

By 2002, mounting concerns about anti-Catholic prejudice would lead Fordham University's Center for American Catholic Studies and *Commonweal* magazine to co-organize a conference called "Anti-Catholicism: The Last Acceptable Prejudice?" Two book-length treatments followed—Philip Jenkins's *The New Anti-Catholicism* (2004) and Mark Massa's *Anti-Catholicism in America* (2005), both carrying the same subtitle as the conference: "The Last Acceptable Prejudice." It was a curious claim given the concurrent rise of anti-Muslim violence in post-9/11 America. But this rhetoric of a new anti-Catholicism was several decades in the making;

it dovetailed seamlessly with the sense among many white and straight US Americans, especially conservative Christians, that they were the ones increasingly victimized.

And Mayor Giuliani was glad to defend them. Taking a cue from congressional leaders like Senator Jesse Helms, the mayor threatened to set up a "decency commission" that would create commonsense standards to guide the distribution of public funds to arts institutions. His announcement sparked outrage over the censorship of the arts and worries about City Hall infringing on artists' right to free speech.

This clash between accusations of anti-Catholic sacrilege and threats to free speech provided the occasion for Cox and Donohue to take center stage that Tuesday afternoon. Advertisements for the debate captured this heated culture wars rhetoric, proposing questions about the mayor's "decency" panel and whether the public should fund "offensive" art. One even asked: "Can offensive art cause hate speech?"[8] The temperature was turned up, and the "fiery exchange" between Donohue and Cox did not disappoint.[9]

Donohue blasted Cox's work as "anti-Catholic propaganda" and argued that such offensive art would not be allowed had it targeted minorities.[10] "Our society tolerates anti-Catholicism to a degree it does not tolerate racism, antisemitism, gay-bashing," he maintained.[11] Proposing a hypothetical, he asked if Cox would object to an image of a white man urinating into the mouth of Martin Luther King Jr. According to *Catalyst*, the Catholic League's journal, Cox became "indignant but never answered him on whether she would simply regard this as art."[12] A few days later, Cox brought up Donohue's what-if scenario in an interview for *Salon*. "I don't think of those things," she said, "I don't go there. There is no art that can offend me." What did offend her, she explained, was that it took City Hall days to respond when police officers gunned down Amadou Diallo, an unarmed Black man, "but they can comment on my art in two or three hours. That offends me."[13]

During the debate, Cox countered that the issue with *Yo Mama's Last Supper* had less to do with anti-Catholicism than with the politics of racial and gender representation. "I feel like perhaps, as an African American woman," she explained, "that somehow maybe that is the biggest affront to people." Donohue responded that representing Jesus as a Black man or woman wasn't the problem. It was the nudity that crossed the line. "Had you managed to keep your clothes on," he quipped, "you wouldn't have gotten any criticism."[14]

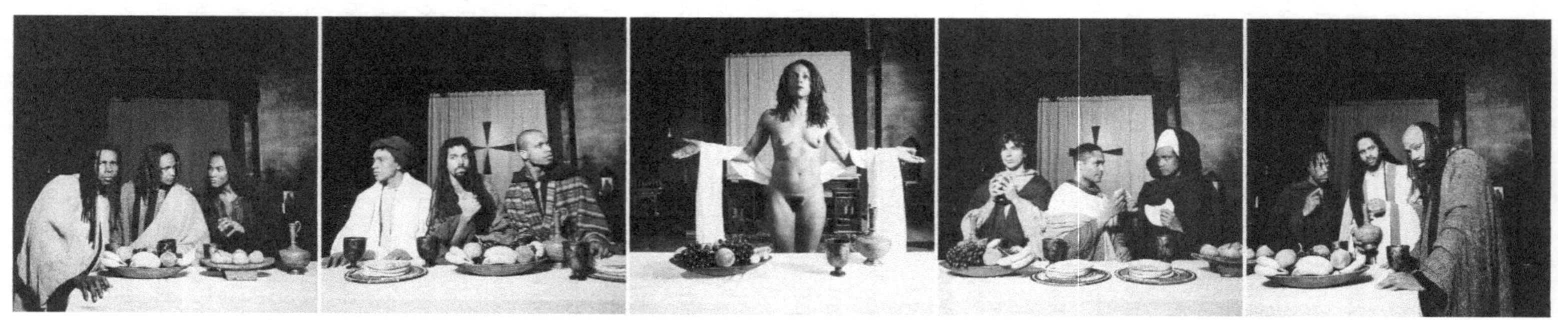

Figure 5.1 Renée Cox, *Yo Mama's Last Supper*, 1996. C-prints, five panels, each 31 ½ × 31 ½ in. (80 × 80 cm). Used with the permission of Renée Cox.

It would be easy to dismiss this debate over *Yo Mama's Last Supper* as little more than another episode of culture wars sensationalism—one that brought Cox international notice and added to Donohue's growing archive of anti-Catholicism. One *New York Post* writer even panned the event for seeming "more like a road show starring two hucksters" than a real debate.[15] But sensationalism is rarely only just that. And the heightened public debate accompanying a sensationalized culture wars outburst such as this one provides an opportunity to take stock of a cultural moment.

This chapter delves into the public outcry over Cox's *Yo Mama's Last Supper* to surface two themes in the history of art and religion amid the recent culture wars. First, it examines how broader debate over Cox's work reveals older and newer entanglements of religion, race, and gender with the rhetoric of "offense" that increasingly animated culture wars politics in the early aughts. Speaking to the *Chicago Tribune*, Ken Paulson, executive director of Vanderbilt's First Amendment Center and the moderator of the panel with Cox and Donohue, described the increasing concern among Americans over offensive material. "The land of the free," he said, "has become the land of the easily offended."[16] In later decades, a slew of popular complaints will target the "snowflake generation," chiding easily "triggered" liberal millennials who need to toughen up.[17] But amid the culture wars of the early 2000s, the dynamics of offense looked different. It was often religious and political conservatives who took offense from culture makers on the left. Accusations of anti-Catholicism become a key part of this rhetoric, much like they did in responses to AIDS activists like Ray Navarro discussed in the previous chapter. But this episode also helps to reveal key racial and gender politics to this rhetoric of offense. This chapter asks what accusations of offense *do*: How does offense not merely enter culture wars debates but shape their formation? How are claims to taking offense or accusations that a work offends refracted through particular histories of gender, sexuality, and race?

These questions lead to a second theme, which turns to the cultural and religious politics of representation and visibility. This chapter explores how Cox challenged dominant forms of racial and religious representation by crafting counter iconographies—by imagining bodies, families, and the sacred beyond the parameters of a culture wars framework that too easily pits religious conservatives against secular progressives. If opponents found her work anti-Catholic or even pornographic, supporters often defended her work on the grounds of free expression. But appeals to free expression, while important and necessary, too often flatten such work, sidestepping exegesis for a defense that cares very little about content.[18] This evacuation of meaning is just as much part of the hermeneutics of the culture wars that I seek to trace as are the disfiguring aesthetics of literalism and the distractions of rhetorical offense. This chapter thus underscores how Cox plays with Christian iconography across various historical, aesthetic, and critical registers and through the lenses of racialized and gendered forms of representation, including the figure of the mother and pervasive representations of Black women as either Jezebels or Mammies. It explores how Cox uses herself, including her own (often nude) body in such pieces, and how it is that such representations of a nude Black woman, standing at the center of Christian iconography in *Yo Mama's Last Supper*, led to public outcry in 2001.

From Fashion Photography to *Yo Mama's Last Supper*

Renée Cox has described herself not only as "born and raised Catholic" but also as a "Roots Woman, photographer, biographer, visual story-teller."[19] Born in Colgate, Jamaica, in 1960, she grew up in Scarsdale, part of New York's well-to-do Westchester County just north of the city, in one of only five Black families in their neighborhood.[20] Cox was raised as an only child, her mother a social worker and her father an insurance executive. "What can I say?" Cox described her experience growing up, "I was middle class."[21] She stresses this to counter assumptions that Black artists must come from poverty, explaining that people often want to hear how "I'm from the projects and I've had a tough life." Rather, she insists, "I'm coming out of a privileged suburb and I'm black and I'm proud."[22] And her work consistently plays with assumptions about race and class. Religious schooling also shaped her visual vocabulary. Cox attended four years of Catholic school at the Blessed Sacrament in Queens, New York, and has drawn on this Catholic upbringing in her artistic work, especially amid the controversy over her alleged "anti-Catholicism." At one point, she explained, "I have a right to critique Catholicism because I was *baptized* Catholic. I'm not coming from the outside."[23] Cox attended a public high school in Scarsdale, where she played basketball for the boys' team and developed an early interest in photography after being mistakenly enrolled in a more advanced class.[24] She then headed to Syracuse University, where she studied film and photography and learned about art history while abroad in Florence, Italy, before graduating with honors in the early 1980s.

After a short stint modeling, Cox spent the next decade working as a commercial photographer, both in New York and in France, for magazines like *Vogue Hommes*, *Glamour*, and *Essence*. She even designed the poster for Spike Lee's 1988 film *School Daze*. During this time, Cox also traveled throughout West Africa and met her husband, a white Frenchman. But she felt like she was missing something. "I was getting PAID," Cox writes in an artist biography, "but I realized fashion photography was not feeding me completely. It was there financially but spiritually and emotionally, it lacked nourishment."[25] Cox decided to return to school, working toward a Master of Fine Arts in photography at New York's School of Visual Art. After graduating in 1992, she was selected to join the Whitney Museum of American Art's Independent Studies Program, an intensive year-long program directed by Ron Clark (the same program Ray Navarro had joined in 1988–1989).

At the Whitney, Cox joined a small cohort that also included Lyle Ashton Harris, whose photography explored intersections of race and sexuality. The two collaborated on a series of photos reimagining Sarah Baartman, a Black South African woman who became the object of racist and sexual fantasy, especially among white audiences, in the early nineteenth century. Caricatures of Baartman emphasized a large backside that became the object of gawking curiosity. Two images created in 1994—including a collaboration with Harris called *Venus Hottentot 2000* (in color) and Cox's self-portrait *Hott-En-Tot* (in black and white)—depict Cox in profile, standing nude but wearing obvious prosthetic amplifications on her breasts and buttocks, as she looks directly at the viewer. Feminist theorist Jennifer Nash argues that Cox's portrayal emphasizes "the most mythologized portions of Baartman's body" in a way that thematizes representations of "black female sexual excess."[26] The aesthetic exaggerations in the costuming point to the very politics of visual representation itself, especially the logics of visual representation that have dominated representations of Black women.

Race, Religion, and Photography from *Black Male* to *Yo Mama*

This visual politics of Black representation would inform much of Cox's photography—and Harris's. Both artists had work featured in the Whitney's landmark exhibition *Black Male: Representations of Masculinity in*

Contemporary Art. Curated by Thelma Golden, the 1994 exhibition focused on representations of Black men in the post–Civil Rights era, featuring artists such as Adrian Piper, Lorna Simpson, Andres Serrano, Christian Walker, and Jean-Michel Basquiat. While often collapsing masculinity and maleness, the show, as Golden writes, affirmed "there is no one black masculinity, no essential 'subject.' There is no single way to represent the black male as a definitive character in American art."[27] In surveying political and aesthetic approaches to representation, *Black Male* sought to move past the binary of negative versus positive images. For instance, the exhibition invited viewers to compare white gay artist Robert Mapplethorpe's iconic, if controversial, Black nudes—photographs noted for their precise formal composition and striking classic aesthetic—to Harris's *Constructs* (1989). In this series of self-portraits, Harris plays on Mapplethorpe's work by imagining himself in more compromised positions. "With a figure bald and nude, a wig askew, or a penis peeking through tulle," Golden explains, "these images are about prosaic reality which, as the photos attest, is far from ideal."[28]

While Harris played on and against Mapplethorpe's formalist aesthetic, Cox found herself working through the longer history of images within Christianity and Jim Crow America in her contribution to the exhibition, called *It Shall Be Named* (1992/1994). This "black crucifixion piece," as Cox described it, found the artist starting to engage Catholicism—including the checkered history of the Roman Catholic Church's response (or failure to respond) to slavery and anti-Black racism.[29] Almost nine feet high and nearly as wide, *It Shall Be Named* is a collage made from photographic negatives of Black men arranged into the form of a cross (Figure 5.2). The mahogany frame appears, from the front of the collage, to emerge from the conjoining of several distinct framed images, unevenly matched, to build the shape of a more rugged or disjointed cross. The Black male figure looks downward, his arms outstretched. He is nude and castrated, a gesture, Cox explained, to the violent act of removing the genitals of lynching victims during Jim Crow. For her, this work was "very academic, intellectual," as it emerged from her studies at the Schomburg Center for Research in Black Culture.[30] She encountered again and again the pervasiveness of anti-Black violence tied directly to white Christianity. Describing the history of lynching, Cox names "the day that they usually did it on: Sunday." And in archival photos, she finds young white girls "dressed in their Sunday best" for the occasion.[31] Lynching was a white Christian ritual—and a family affair.

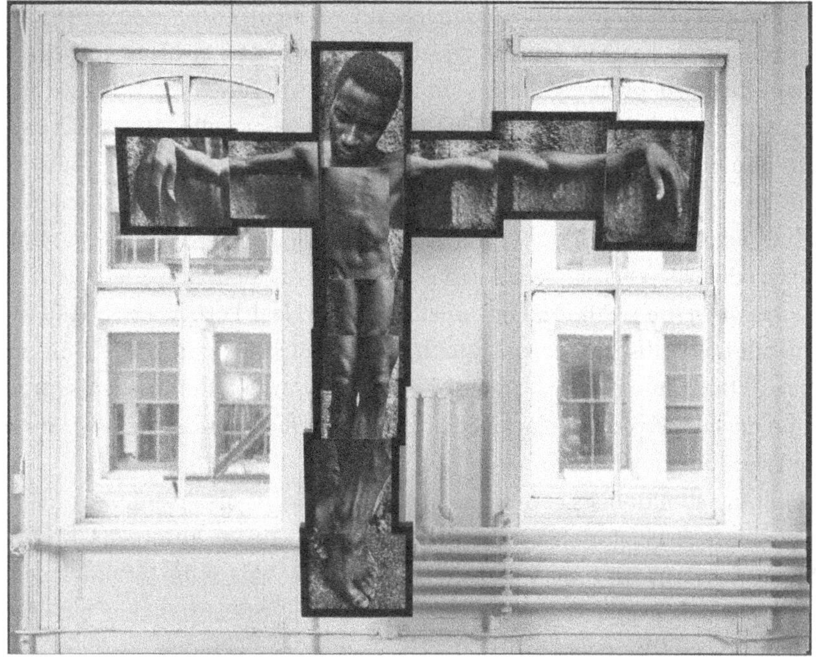

Figure 5.2 Renée Cox, *It Shall Be Named*, 1992/1994. Gelatin silver prints, mahogany, and plexiglass, 105 × 104 ½ × 4 ¾ in. (framed), Peter Norton Collection. Used with the permission of Renée Cox.

This violence wasn't merely historical for Cox. Interspersed with the planning diagrams and mock-ups for *It Shall Be Named* is a newspaper clipping from 1993. It describes three white men in Florida who kidnapped and tortured a thirty-one-year-old Black man visiting from Brooklyn. The man, seriously injured, recounted to police how the white men used racial slurs and kept repeating, "We got one."[32] As a response to this ongoing violent history of white Christianity, Cox created what drafting diagrams for this piece in her archive refer to as "Black Christ."[33]

In *It Shall Be Named*, Cox brought together—both figurately and literally, through the collecting and assorting of images—what Black theologian James Cone has called two of the most potent symbols in African American culture: "the cross and the lynching tree."[34] In doing so, she drew from longer histories of figuring Christ as Black, part of what historian Stephen Prothero calls "the American tradition of reimagining Jesus."[35] Prothero traces "the black Jesus tradition" back to the nineteenth-century history of what historian Albert Raboteau called "the slave religion" of antebellum America.

As Black people converted to evangelical Christianity, they also remade it, fostering new religious rituals and forms. For instance, Black Christians fused the gospel story of Jesus with the Exodus narrative, in which Moses leads his people to freedom. This theological reformation fused Christ's promise of salvation with the promise of a people freed. But the power of this narrative could also hinge on refusing the assumption that Jesus was white, which is just what abolitionist Cassius Clay (namesake of the famous boxer) did when he claimed Christ was not Caucasian in his paper *The True American* in the 1890s. And it is what Henry McNeal Turner, a bishop in the African Methodist Episcopal Church, intended when he asserted "God is a Negro" that same decade.[36] James Cone would develop these insights into a full-fledged theology of Black liberation in the 1960s context of Black Power and freedom movements.

Joining abolitionists and theologians, Black artists also painted Christ in new colors. Art historian Kymberly Pinder has traced the history of Christ in the work of African American painters in the first half of the twentieth century, in which, in many cases, artists made a "one-to-one correlation" between "the crucified Christ and the lynched black man."[37] As Pinder illustrates, artists like William H. Johnson, Romare Bearden, and Henry Ossawa Tanner have imagined Christ in different ways. Tanner, for instance, moved in the direction of historical realism as he researched the historical context of the Middle East and sought to paint "an 'authentic' savior." Johnson and Bearden, in contrast, "explored race in the context of the Afrocentric legacy of the New Negro Movement" in ways that turned away from concerns over historical accuracy in search of other truths.[38]

Moving from painting to photography, Cox fuses these aesthetic approaches. The photographic images in *It Shall Be Named*, though clearly manipulated and arranged into a crucified/lynched figure, retain a documentary effect—one that gestures less to the historical Christ than to the realities of Jim Crow racism. But this nod to historical or archival realism works in brilliant and striking tension with the piece's fragmented wooden frame and exaggerated proportions. The outstretched limbs and enlarged, draped hands of Cox's figure recall Johnson's *Jesus and the Three Marys* (1939; Figure 5.3), in which the hands and arms of his Black Christ reach across nearly the full width of the painting, enveloping the three Black Marys below him (Mary of Bethany, Mary the mother of Jesus, and Mary Magdalene). Composed through fragmentation and exaggeration, Cox's photographic collage combines not only the cross and the lynching tree, but also reality and imagination, realism and myth, history and art.

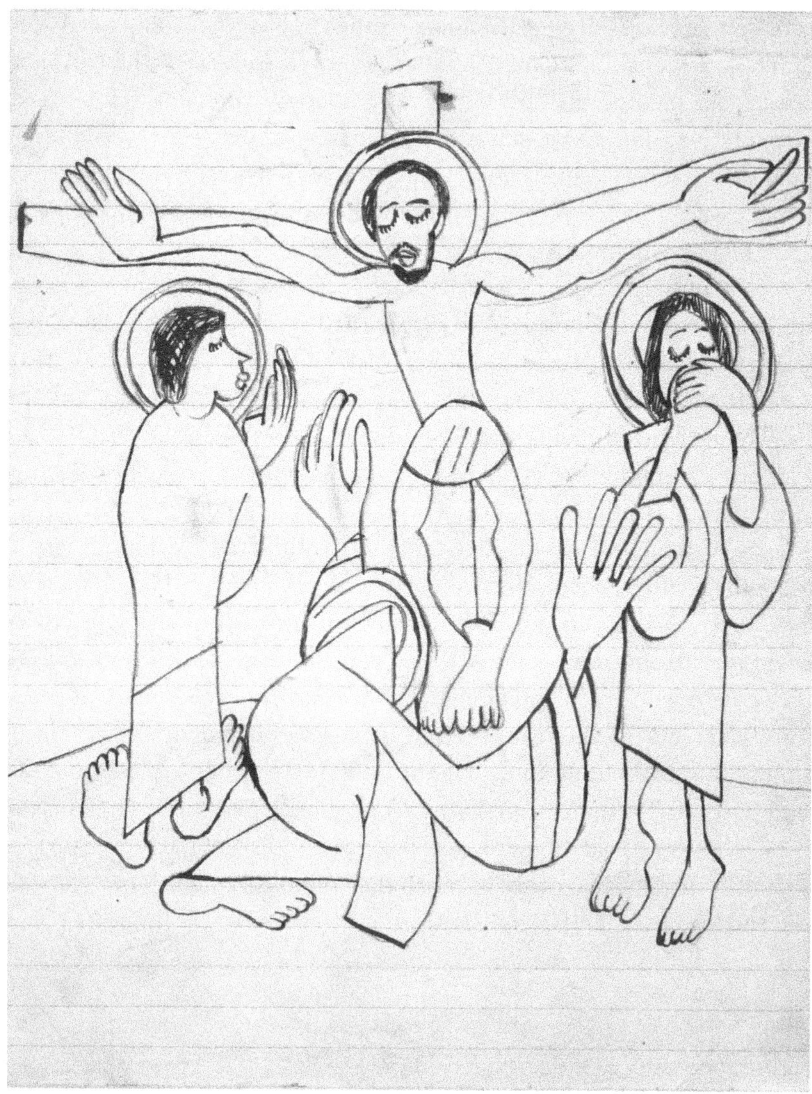

Figure 5.3 William H. Johnson, sketch for *Jesus and the Three Marys*, ca. 1939. Pen and ink and colored pencil on paper, 10 3/8 × 8 in. (26.3 × 20.3 cm), Smithsonian American Art Museum, Gift of the Harmon Foundation, 1967.59.515. Used with permission.

During her year of study at the Whitney, Cox was already grappling with representations of religion, race, and embodiment. She was also carrying her second child, making her "the first woman in twenty-five years to be visibly pregnant in the program."[39] At the time, Cox recalled, "many of my peers felt that I couldn't be both an artist and a mother."[40] But what could have been a limitation became, for Cox, central to a body of work called the *Yo Mama* series.[41] The naming itself plays on the tradition of "yo mama" jokes—as in "Yo mama is so old, she was a waitress at the Last Supper"—a stylized humor featured in Keenen Wayans's popular sketch comedy series *In Living Color* from the early 1990s.[42] Cox plays with this humor while also confronting its sexist treatment of mothers.

In early photographs in this series, Cox poses visibly pregnant and nude; later ones feature her posing with her young sons. In one of the most well known of this series, a seven-foot-high black-and-white image called *The Yo Mama* (1993), the artist stands fully nude, save for a pair of heels, holding her playful eighteen-month-old son horizontally across her waist. Her face is serious, unsmiling, peering down toward the camera. The light reflecting off Cox's skin, contouring her breasts and the muscles of her torso, evokes a classical, statuesque quality, one that plays with hardness and softness. It recalls the aesthetic energy and formal precision of many of Mapplethorpe's nudes, even as Cox's staging of Black maternity, sexuality, and subjectivity moves in different directions. Art historian Andrea Liss describes *The Yo Mama* as "at once bold and contemplative" as it "merg[es] maternity, sexuality, and work."[43] She reads the *Yo Mama* series alongside the history of family photo collections, including the "double meanings" of "mammy and child portraits," to underscore how Cox plays with and subverts this racial and sexual visual field. Cox's photos, Liss writes, "disrupt the serene surface of family portraiture in order to reveal the multiple paradoxes between the seen and the obscene."[44]

"Flippin the Script"

Cox plays with these "multiple paradoxes between the seen and the obscene" to subvert iconographic conventions—not only of family portraiture but also of canonical works of Western art and religious visual culture. In her series *Flippin the Script*, Cox restages a number of iconic images, from famous works of Renaissance art to histories of colonialism, with humor and wit.[45] In *The Colonization of White People* (1997), she photographed the white parents of her French husband in African-styled attire. In the black-and-white photo, her father-in-law appears bare-chested, wearing a beautifully patterned garment around his waist. He stands next to Cox's mother-in-law, who wears a spotted-print dress wrapped around her chest and a layered necklace. Their faces look serious, as their eyes meet the gaze of the viewer.

Several of the images in *Flippin the Script* play with Catholic themes often seen in Renaissance art, and Michelangelo is a favorite among Cox's archive of revisions. Her enhanced *David* (1994) features a svelte Black man with an afro standing fully nude and holding a book in one hand. *Pieta* (1994) centers Cox as Mary; a draped hood falls across her locs and shoulders but leaves her bare chest delicately exposed. In her lap, she embraces a nude, fallen Black Christ. In *Seven Minutes in Heaven And/Or They Have Sinned* (1997), a more ribald piece from the series, Cox faces the viewer while donning a full nun's habit; in front of her, a nude white woman kneels to pray. The use of humor in this piece and others, especially the humor of subverted expectations, propels a broader argument about the racial and gender politics of visual representation.

Cox often restaged canonical images in European (and frequently Christian-themed) art. In *Yo Mamadonna and Child* (1994), she plays on classical representations of Mary and the infant Jesus, including Michelangelo's *Madonna of Bruges* (1501–4). In her restaging, Cox wears a colorful printed ensemble and a feathered headdress while holding her undressed infant son. In *Olympia's Boyz* (2001), she recreates the scandalous pose of Édouard Manet's *Olympia* (1863–65), in which a white woman, pictured as a prostitute, lays nude on a chaise as a Black servant brings her flowers. Cox's revision features her two sons dressed as warriors standing behind her. We could add many other examples. In the press release for her 1995 show *Blackskins*, Cox described the importance of African Americans redefining themselves and the conventional representations of Black people found throughout history. "By placing us in Renaissance paintings," she explained, "I am 'flippin' tha script.' Doing what was done to all Africans of the diaspora: erasing history and recreating a new one. A history that affirms our beautiful blackness."[46]

Cox opened the press release for *Blackskins* with a quotation from bell hooks's 1993 *Sisters of the Yam*. "Clearly," hooks wrote, "if black women want to be about the business of collective self-healing, we have to be about the business of inventing all manner of images and representations that show us the way we want to be and are."[47] Cox was drawn to hooks's work on the importance of image-making and remaking—and on the particular importance of photography for Black Americans. The camera, hooks insisted, offered Black Americans the ability to "participate fully in the production of images," to become image-makers rather than merely objects of representation. Photography offered "the possibility of immediate intervention," allowing for the creation of "counter-hegemonic representations even as it was also an instrument of pleasure."[48] But hooks also worried that the radical potential and pleasure of Black photography had lost its edge after integration. Blackness itself was increasingly commodified, she charged, while questions of representation too often focused on parsing "good" from "bad" rather than confronting the broader "*politics* of representation."[49]

As a photographer, Cox does just this: she creates images that move beyond simply good or bad representations to emphasize the visual field itself as a locus for politics, for contestation, and even for pleasure. Religious—especially Catholic—iconography provided a powerful tool for this work. "Christianity is big in the African-American community, but there are no representations of us," Cox has explained: "I took it upon myself to include people of color in these classic scenarios. That is the most important thing."[50] This is precisely what Cox does in her most famous, or notorious, piece.

Renée Cox's Dinner Party

Shot in a church in Queens, *Yo Mama's Last Supper* (1996) is a grand photomontage with five panels, each measuring 31×31 inches. A nod to Leonardo's *Last Supper*, the center panel features a Jesus figure, who faces the viewer while set slightly apart from the twelve apostles. Leonardo's fair-skinned Jesus, eyes gazing downward, is seated and framed by a window. He's flanked by twelve male apostles in two groups of three on both sides. Some face Jesus; others are caught up in conversation. In Cox's Last Supper, Jesus occupies a single panel in the center, and the role of the savior is played by the artist herself. She stands before her disciples, fully nude save for a white shawl wrapped around her arms and behind her back—a possible reference, writes historian Stephen Prothero, to "the chains of slave Christianity."[51] This Jesus, Black and female, gazes upward to the heavens. She is framed, from the waist up, by a vibrant gold curtain. Her stance—standing with arms outstretched in what art critic Eleanor Heartney calls a "benedictory gesture"—recalls the Jesus of the Last Supper but also invokes Jesus on the cross and the resurrected Christ, as she rises above her apostles.[52]

In *Yo Mama's Last Supper*, Cox mirrors Leonardo's painting of the apostles in groups of three, though she gives each trio their own panel. Her apostles are dressed in colorful robes, often purple, gold, and white, though one wears what looks like a nun's habit. While the Renaissance Italian imagined the apostles as white, Cox pictures them Black—save Judas. "I was saying, 'This is my dinner party,'" Cox explained in an interview, "Why not?" "With Judas," she continued, "I was conscious of this. But I didn't make him that Caucasian, either. I could have done blond, blue eyes and Aryan." She says her version of Judas could be read as American Indian or Latino, insisting, "He's not a super-Caucasian."[53] Cox's remarks remind us that neither representation nor realism should be conflated with reality, that the "real" race of her Judas need not fully determine how he is read in such work.

This racial and ethnic ambiguity also recalls Leonardo's painting, but in a different way. In *The Last Supper*, Judas appears darker than the other apostles. Historically, Judas has often been depicted through antisemitic stereotypes drawn from a long Christian tradition of blaming Jews for the death of Jesus. For many viewers, it appears that Leonardo painted Judas with stereotypically "Semitic" features, including darker skin, to exaggerate his "Jewishness" against the lighter depiction of the other apostles. Other readings attribute the darker complexion to Judas leaning back into a shadow.[54] Either way, Leonardo's rendering employs darker shading to single out the betrayer. Cox inverts this iconographic portrayal of whiteness and darkness, while also pressuring dominant gender and racial representations of Jesus and the apostles.

If *Yo Mama's Last Supper* sits within a longer history of representations of Christ as Black, including *It Shall Be Named*, it also appears alongside the many plays on Leonardo's *Last Supper* as well as representations of Christ as a woman in the history of modern art. Plays on Leonardo's work abound. There are comedic spoofs, like A. J. B. Lane's 2018 political cartoon in the *Boston Globe* lampooning Trump as the Christ figure. The embattled president is surrounded by "disciples" like Steve Bannon and Stormy Daniels. Another—Omarosa Newman—jokes, "Really? Just one of us?" (referencing, of course, the role of the betrayer).[55] And then there is Andy Warhol's *Last Supper* series, created in the mid-1980s. In some of the series' works, which number over a hundred, the gay, Catholic pop artist superimposed commercial brand logos and advertisements over Leonardo's image.[56] Later pieces, such as MADSAKI's painting *Last Supper (The Big C) II (inspired by Andy Warhol)* (2019) and Dick Detzner's painting *Last Pancake Breakfast* (2000), play on Warhol's play on Leonardo. Cox's Last Supper joins these plays on plays, while adding her own embodied take. In fact, this was not even her first dinner party. Cox had created a precursor to *Yo Mama's Last Supper* called *Black Panther Last Supper* in 1993, though it was not shown in a gallery until 2023, as she worried it was too radical.[57]

Just as important for situating Cox's work are feminist reimaginings of *The Last Supper* and of the figure of Christ. Judy Chicago's *The Dinner Party* (1979) no doubt provides one of the most monumental feminist reworkings, as we saw in chapter one. Chicago cast no clear Christ figure in her rendition, but Mary Beth Edelson's earlier poster *Some Living American Women Artists* (1972) placed feminist icon Georgia O'Keeffe in the starring role. Edelson superimposed an image of the artist's face onto that of Jesus in Leonardo's version and surrounded her with women artists, including Faith Ringgold, Yoko Ono, and Alice Neel. Edelson offered a clear feminist statement, if not an explicitly theological one.

Other feminist artists challenged theological and political assumptions about the gender of Jesus more directly. English sculptor Edwina Sandys's *Christa* (1974) was probably the first modern representation of Christ as a woman to make major headlines. Sandys originally made the bronze sculpture depicting a crucified woman Christ for the United Nations Decade (1976–85), a campaign to promote equal rights that followed the first women's meeting at the UN in Mexico City in 1975. But Sandys's *Christa* sparked little controversy until 1984, when it was exhibited during Holy Week in the Episcopal Cathedral of St. John the Divine in New York City. The *New York Times* recorded responses ranging from "joy to dismay."[58] For opponents, the sculpture flew in the face of historical and theological truth. Walter Dennis, suffragan bishop of the Episcopal Diocese of New York, explained that it was okay to "enhanc[e]" symbols of Christ by altering his skin tone or ethnicity, but making Christ a woman was "symbolically reprehensible" because it was "totally changing the symbol."[59] But defenders argued that, even if the historical Jesus was male, *Christa* could symbolize the role of women in the church and the fight for equality. Feminist biblical scholar Phyllis Trible explained that *Christa* alluded to "Christ's mystical body that transcends sex" and did not require "denying the male Jesus of history."[60] In a press release, Episcopal Bishop Paul Moore Jr., a well-known progressive Christian leader, recorded his initial shock: "Years of speaking of God in male terms, years of imagining God primarily as male, did not prepare me for this image." But, he insisted, the work revealed "theological truths" about Christian notions of Incarnation— how "the word became flesh and dwelt among us" (John 1:14)—that meant the suffering of Christ transcended sexual difference.[61]

Like Sandys, many feminist artists in the 1970s and 1980s challenged sexist assumptions in Christian traditions, especially the notion that Christ must be represented as a man. Consider the work of visual and performance artist Cheri Gaulke. Gaulke, who would become a leading lesbian artist, was raised in a Lutheran family—four generations of clergy, she has explained— and attended Lutheran schools.[62] While studying feminist art at the lauded Woman's Building in the 1970s, she became interested in the goddess movement and began to question how Christianity devalued women.[63] In the early 1980s, she cofounded a performance art group called Sisters of Survival (S.O.S.), for which members dressed as colorful nuns to agitate for nuclear disarmament and world peace.[64] In those same years, Gaulke debuted a solo performance called *This Is My Body* (1982). The piece plays with Christian imagery, especially through symbols of the serpent and the tree, which Gaulke contends were celebrated in goddess spirituality but later corrupted in Christian thinking. Western tradition, she explained, separates flesh from the spirit, matter from the divine.[65] In the performance, Gaulke appears as Eve, bare-breasted and unapologetically erotic, in the Garden of Good and Evil. Toward the end, the artist reappears as Jesus, again nude from the waist up, as she climbs onto a cross.

Gaulke's performance piece joins many other examples of women-Christ figures in modern art, including Almuth Lütkenhaus-Lackey's sculpture *Crucified Woman* (1976), James Murphy's sculpture *Christine on the Cross* (1984), and Margaret Argyle's mixed textile panel *Bosnian Christa* (1993). Never one to shy away from controversial imagery, pop icon Madonna even scaled a mirrored cross in her 2006 Confessions Tour.[66] This longer history and range of representations helps us to situate *Yo Mama's Last Supper*—to appreciate how it draws upon and diverges from the ways other works of visual and performance art have reimagined *The Last Supper* and the gender of Christ.[67]

Standing fully nude at the center of her dinner table, Cox plays not only on the history of Christian iconography but also with conventions for representing Black women. If Chicago hesitated to depict Black women's sexuality at her *Dinner Party*—painting Sojourner Truth's plate with three faces—Cox places it front and center, framed by the draped fabric of her white shawl. The use of photography underlines the message, as Cox recalls the explicit performances of white feminist artists like Carolee Schneemann or Cheri Gaulke. But she also signifies "more." Cultural studies scholar Nicole Fleetwood explains how "black women's bodily enactments signify beyond 'explicit,'" figured as "excess" in relation to the norms of "the white female body and femininity."[68] Cox plays with this "excess" and its attendant "hypervisibility," which, Fleetwood writes, "is a performative strategy for black female cultural producers, one that emphasizes the faulty notions of a 'visual truth' of blackness by representing excess and fantasy."[69] Cox portrays this hypervisibility in ways that set her Last Supper apart from most others by gesturing to the visual politics of religion, race, gender, and representation. In the racist and sexist conventions of modern representation, Cox's body cannot signify outside of the burden to represent "excess and fantasy," so she puts all on the table.

But *Yo Mama's Last Supper* also works against an erotic reading—that is, Cox presents the cultural dominance of such a reading only to undermine it. Her apostles hardly notice her. Her face is serious, gazing upward. Her posture conveys strength more than seduction. Cox has addressed her approach. "I chose to play the Christ figure in the nude because it represents a sense of purity," she explains: "I come to the table with nothing to hide."[70] In other interviews, she says that nudity erases markers of class, creating a "pure state."[71]

The overdetermined significance of Black women's bodies thus confronts a competing provocation to read nudity as a symbol of purity. Indeed, there is a long Christian tradition for such a provocation. In the early years of the movement, catechumens would undress before public baptisms. Writing in the fourth century, St. Cyril of Jerusalem explained the reasoning behind this practice: "Having stripped yourselves, ye were naked; in this also imitating Christ, who was stripped naked on the Cross, and by His nakedness put off from Himself the principalities and powers, and openly triumphed over them on the tree."[72] To be naked in this way, in the way Cox reveals herself, is to imitate Christ on the cross, to overlay representations of racial and sexual excess with the visual presence of the divine. "O wondrous thing!" Cyril continued, "ye were naked in the sight of all, and were not ashamed; for truly ye bore the likeness of the first-formed Adam, who was naked in the garden, and was not ashamed."[73]

Yo Mama's Controversy

Yo Mama's Last Supper did not enter the crossfires of the culture wars until 2001. It stirred little controversy when it first debuted in 1996 at the

Aldrich Museum of Contemporary Art in Ridgefield, Connecticut. Three years later, it was shown in Venice in a deconsecrated church dating to the sixteenth century—again without controversy.[74] The cacophony was not sparked until February 2001, when *Yo Mama's Last Supper* was included in the Brooklyn Museum's *Committed to the Image: Contemporary Black Photographers*.

Curated by Barbara Head Millstein, the exhibition ran from February 16 to April 29, 2001, and featured the work of ninety-five contemporary Black photographers. While most of the photographs in the show date from the 1980s and 1990s, the images go back as early as the 1940s. It included work by artists ranging from Carrie Mae Weems and Collette Fournier to Adger Cowans and Albert Chong. In an essay in the exhibition catalogue, poet and critic Deba Patnaik places Black photography in a longer tradition of "jazz and blues," aesthetic styles of improvisation with "modulated tones and forms" that foster "a polyrhythmic structure of interrogation, affirmation, and reconnection with the community's shared history, experience, and destiny."[75] These modulated tones and forms no doubt trouble the exhibition's organization into themes—people, beauty, family, and religion. Looking through the catalogue, it is striking how often religious iconography appears, often in ways not easily partitioned from family, politics, or beauty.[76]

Cultural historian Clyde Taylor captures this "abundance of spirituality" in his essay in the show's catalogue. "The charisma found here," he writes, "conveys a spirituality that is an ethno-spirituality," an intentional fusing of Blackness and religion. Taylor points to these moments of spirituality as "breaks" from dominant trends in modern art history, both in the focus on spirituality generally and in the particular religious styles represented, varieties of spirituality "not easily located in the modern Western tradition."[77] The religious or spiritual iconography that animates these works pulls from many sources, including Christian, Muslim, Buddhist, Africana, and New Age traditions, from Salimah Ali's *Day of Atonement at the UN Plaza, Muslim Women* (1996) and Lonnie Graham's *Living in a Spirit House: Aunt Dora's Room* (1992) to Fern Logan's *Earth Goddess* (1997) and Cheryl Miller's *Tribute to the Ancestors of the Middle Passage—"Juneteenth"* (1995). Some of the works conjure images of Christ or the crucifixion. Anthony Barboza's *Untitled* (1996), for instance, stages the haunting funeral of a murdered Black boy, his face appearing on a television screen laid over a white sheet; a black cross just below it represents his body.

The sheer range and depth of religious imagery in *Committed to the Image* demand greater attention, but only two artists in the show drew intense public scrutiny—Renée Cox and Willie Middlebrook. Culture wars media coverage often paired them in stories of artistic scandal. Middlebrook had two pieces in the exhibition. His digital image *Black Angel No. 20* (1999) centers a nude, pregnant Black woman depicted with angel wings. His other work drew more attention. *The God Suite, Pomp No. 628* (n.d.) is a collage featuring a crucified Black woman, topless with arms outstretched. From below, another pair of arms reach out holding an infant child toward her body. An inscription running along the right side reads: "She who bears fruit, love, life is Earth!"

Cox included work in the show from her Afrofuturistic *Rajé* series, a Cibachrome print called *Chillin' with Liberty* (1998). The *Rajé* series imagines Cox as a superhero—originally called "Rage"—whose mission is to teach children about the history of African Americans, to combat racism, and to "give little girls and women a sense of empowerment."[78] One piece in the series, for instance, pays homage to artist Betye Saar; it shows Rajé liberating Aunt Jemima and Uncle Ben against a backdrop of boxes of their pancake mix and brown rice. The piece included in *Committed to the Image* shows Rajé sitting atop the Statue of Liberty, clad in the red, yellow, and green of the Jamaican flag and ready for her next act of heroism. But, of course, it was *Yo Mama's Last Supper* that sparked outcry.

Offending Catholics

Accusations of anti-Catholicism came quickly. In fact, they started before the show even opened, as New York's sensationalizing daily papers instigated culture wars debates as much as they reported on them. The *Daily News* tipped off Donohue at the Catholic League, leading him to pen a letter to curator Barbara Millstein, which he also published on the Catholic League's website, a day before the exhibition started. Along with the Catholic League's journal *Catalyst*, which operated as a regular online briefing of anything deemed "anti-Catholic," this website fostered a counterpublic of conservative Catholic paranoia, one that perpetuated the sense that Catholics were always under attack, victims of the "last acceptable prejudice."[79]

In his letter, Donohue lauded many of the works in *Committed to the Image* but deemed *Yo Mama's Last Supper* "worthy of condemnation." He argued that Cox had a history of using anti-Catholic images. "To wit," he wrote, "she has portrayed Christ on the cross castrated; she has appeared half naked as Our Blessed Mother holding a Christ-like figure in her work, 'The Pieta'; and she has dressed as a nun with a naked woman kneeling before her in prayer."[80] A follow-up story in *Catalyst* extolled the "new war" ramping up as the Catholic League staged a national protest over Cox's piece. The report boasted about their coverage on *The Today Show*, CNN, the *New York Times*, and Fox News, suggesting the wide and often mainstream reach of right-wing Catholic opposition.[81]

Donohue, whom one *Newsday* writer dubbed "officially offended," commented as a lay Catholic leader of a political organization. But members of New York's Roman Catholic leadership also readily condemned Cox's work.[82] Archbishop of New York Edward Egan used his pulpit at St. Patrick's Cathedral to blast Cox as a "pathetic individual" during his first mass after being elevated to cardinal. The following year, Egan would publicly acknowledge that "mistakes that have been made" in failing to disclose accusations of Catholic sexual abuse during his previous years as bishop in Bridgeport, Connecticut. But on that Sunday, he insisted, "we stand for what is right and decent" and "against the tide" of fine art "sophisticates" and others committed to undermining Christian faith. He and other Christians would do so "without applause and only ridicule."[83] In a letter to Cox, one New Yorker explained, "I have to agree with Cardinal Egan. You are pathetic." He accused Cox—who was "sent of the Devil"—of mocking Jesus and included a tract about hell for her to read.[84] Bishop Thomas Daily of Brooklyn also added to public condemnations of Cox's work. He suggested the Brooklyn Museum showed "no regard for the religious sensibilities of the community." "Why another vulgar display of anti-Christian sentiment?" he asked: "Is publicity more important than respect for religious belief?" Bishop Daily saw no irony in his own efforts to protect the church from bad publicity by hushing accusations lodged against infamous Catholic sex abuser John Geoghan in the 1980s.[85] I underscore these Catholic leaders' ties to sex abuse cover-ups not to force a bad faith comparison, but because their involvement in this history helps to situate accusations of anti-Catholicism and claims to offense—moral outrage was preserved for some sexual offenses over others.

None of Cox's critics got more airtime, though, than New York City's Mayor Giuliani, who blasted *Yo Mama's Last Supper* as "disgusting" and "outrageous." Giuliani also pointed to Cox's "anti-Catholic" agenda. Her work "isn't artistic expression," he insisted: "It's an expression of prejudice, it's an expression of bigotry, and it's an expression of hatred."[86] The mayor vowed to form a "decency" commission to review art displayed at museums that received city funding. This debacle was hardly new. Less than two years earlier, Giuliani had objected to a piece by artist Chris Ofili in the Brooklyn Museum's *Sensation* exhibition. Indeed, most news coverage of the debate over *Yo Mama's Last Supper* recalled this earlier public spat, which first pitted Giuliani against the Brooklyn Museum and made him a key spokesman against the rising tide of anti-Catholicism.

An Earlier Sensation

The Brooklyn Museum hosted *Sensation: Young British Artists from the Saatchi Collection* from October 2, 1999, to January 9, 2000. The intentionally shocking exhibition was first shown at London's Royal Academy of Arts to matching success and dispute. In England, the controversy largely focused on Marcus Harvey's painting *Myra* (1995). Harvey manipulated children's handprints to replicate the mugshot of the infamous Myra Hindley, who was convicted for the serial murder of children in Manchester between 1963 and 1965. In the United States, the outrage would turn instead to Ofili's *The Holy Virgin Mary* (1996).

Ofili's "hip-hop" version of Mary, as he called it, depicts the mother of God as an African woman set against a shimmering orange background. She is surrounded by flying cherubim that closer inspection reveals to be images of women's backsides cut from pornographic magazines. Art historian Moyo Okediji interprets the porn cutouts as gesturing to representations of female deities in Yoruba culture, including Oshun, Yemoja, and Olokun sculptures that commonly portray female sexuality.[87] But the pornographic cutouts barely entered the culture wars spotlight, perhaps because few opponents actually looked closely enough at Ofili's *Holy Virgin Mary* to make them out. As W. J. T. Mitchell reminds us, "it is the imaginary, fantasized image provoked by the words, not the perceived visual image" that most often offends.[88] What was taken up in news headlines as offensive about the image was Ofili's use of elephant dung, balls of which he lacquered and decorated. He used one for Mary's bare breast and two others for the base for the painting. Ofili claimed to have had an epiphany while traveling in Zimbabwe that led him to use elephant dung to ground his artistic works, "giving them the feeling that they've come from the earth rather than simply being hung on a wall."[89]

Several news accounts described the Virgin Mary "splattered" with elephant dung, which led to quick condemnation from Mayor Giuliani, Bill Donohue, and Cardinal John O'Connor, among others, who considered the work not only offensive but to be mocking Catholics specifically. Giuliani tried to cut city funding to the Brooklyn Museum, arguing that public money should not be used to support such offensive art. His motives were mixed. While the Italian American mayor had been a staunch defender of Catholics, this was also an election year, and Giuliani was running against First Lady Hillary Clinton for one of New York's senate seats. He needed to shore up his support among Catholics and conservative voters, and his charge to cut public funding for the museum put his opponent in a difficult spot. Giuliani assumed Clinton would defend the museum and the artist on the grounds of free expression, which would create an opening to paint her as excusing attacks on Catholics specifically and on religion generally.[90] Clinton had to tread carefully. While opposed to Giuliani's censorship, Clinton explained, she nonetheless "shared the feeling many New Yorkers have that there are parts of this exhibition that would be deeply offensive. I would not go to see this exhibition."[91]

It is not clear what other "parts of this exhibition" Clinton found troublesome, but Ofili was not the only artist in *Sensation* who played with Christian themes in ways that could be construed as offensive. He was, however, the only one labeled offensive in this way, suggesting a curious racial politics to offense in this culture wars episode. In *Wrecked* (1996), Sam Taylor-Wood recreated another play on Leonardo's *Last Supper*. In the Cibachrome print, Taylor-Wood stands at the center of the table, a topless white woman with her arms outstretched, surrounded by her friends, both women and men. The title references British slang for getting drunk. But this bawdy take on the Last Supper yielded very little reaction from New York's culture warriors—neither in 1999, when it appeared in *Sensation* at the Brooklyn Museum, nor in 2001, when *Yo Mama's Last Supper* became the occasion for controversy and reignited discussions of Ofili's piece.

New York Times art critic Michael Kimmelman was among the few to note the discrepancy in how opponents targeted Cox and Ofili rather than white artists like Taylor-Wood. Do some works draw more controversy because they "happen to be by black artists showing black women?" "Why the different reactions?" he pondered, "The title? The quantity of skin? The race?"[92] Cox put it more directly. "The hoopla and the fury are because I'm a black female," she explained, as she pointed to the seeming coincidence that she and Ofili "are both of African descent."[93]

Defenses of *The Holy Virgin Mary* often emphasized the importance of free expression over censorship, but they also pointed to Ofili's background as a Black British artist born to Nigerian parents and raised Catholic in Manchester, where he had served as an altar boy. Supporters, including Arnold Lehman, the director of the Brooklyn Museum, characterized his use of elephant dung as a reference to its veneration in some African cultures. But this explanation likely says more about stereotypes of African cultures in white and European imaginations than anything else. Artist and critic Coco Fusco has noted the tendency among art critics to situate Ofili's work within the tradition of white modernists appropriating "traditional" African aesthetic forms. She argues for other ways of reading his work, including how it "expands upon a century-long exploration of African visual culture and style by Black diasporic artists."[94] Fusco places Ofili alongside artists like Kara Walker who play with stereotypes about Black women's presumed hypersexuality. And his use of excrement recalls David Hammons's earlier series of elephant dung sculptures from the 1970s and 1980s, which juxtaposed assumptions about abjection with Black culture. This is the more important context for Ofili's work, rather than gesturing to his use of curious "African" traditions of veneration.[95] "It is Ofili's reliance on the most abject, most historically overdetermined association of Blacks with excrement," Fusco writes, "that gives his work its peculiar power and that even offers him a way of inscribing his own experience as a Black artist into his work."[96] We should note how this play with abjection, race, and religion is not necessarily a secularizing move, either—rather, it pulls his work closer to the incarnational aesthetics in work by artists like Cheri Gaulke, Andres Serrano, and Ron Athey.

Granted, this incarnational aesthetic did not assuage the concerns of culture warriors like Mayor Giuliani or Cardinal O'Connor—it likely only intensified their frustration. Even if there was some "Catholic" sensibility to Ofili's art, it was not an acceptable one. As Donohue complained, the news media "never fails" to name Catholics as "devout" whenever one "trashes his religion." But, he insisted about Ofili, "it would be more accurate to describe him as a 'self-hating Catholic.'"[97] For Donohue and others, only one style of Catholicism was true and legitimate: their own. All others were just bad faith. And bad art, in the cases of Ofili and Cox. If Donohue didn't have the power to quash it, the mayor thought he did.

Giuliani's Great Commission and Its Discontents

After failing to cut city funds to the Brooklyn Museum for showing Ofili's work, Giuliani tried another tactic in the debate over Cox's *Yo Mama's Last Supper*—he called for the formation of a decency commission. And this time he followed through, using his mayoral power to revive the Cultural Affairs Advisory Commission, which was charged "to develop reasonable, common-sense criteria for the investment of public funds along neutral, unbiased grounds."[98] Knowledge of art—or even interest in art—was not a qualification for membership. Giuliani appointed several of his friends to the commission, including his own divorce lawyer. One member, radio host Curtis Sliwa, explained to New York 1's *Inside City Hall* his credentials for joining the commission were that he grew up in New York when "liberals and artists were telling me that graffiti was art." That wasn't art, he insisted: "That was a crime." Asked about his background, Sliwa admitted, "I don't often go to museums."[99] In the end, the mayor's commission was largely for show, as Giuliani was on his way out the door, and Michael Bloomberg, the incoming mayor, assured voters no such committee would be needed to vet art. But just the threat of the "decency" commission had three overlapping effects.

Headlines for God's Side

First, the call for a decency commission not only ensured more headlines for the pugnacious mayor but also positioned him as a key defender of religion and of moral values. During the *Sensation* debacle, Giuliani had a clear political motive in his run against Hillary Clinton. But this time, he was not up for election, mayoral or senate. Fellow politicos and the press wondered why he cared. Could he really be offended on religious terms? Peter Vallone, who worked closely with Giuliani as the speaker of the New York City Council, thought so. Both were repeatedly identified in the news media as Catholics (as were Cox and Ofili). Vallone expressed how he was "personally offended" as a Catholic by Cox's work but publicly opposed Giuliani's commission, which he called "play[ing] culture cop."[100] Nonetheless, he insisted, the mayor's motives were rooted in his religious convictions. "This is the kind of issue that he can get very passionately involved in," Vallone said, explaining that Giuliani "feels he's on God's side."[101]

Cox countered the mayor's supposed alignment with the divine, accusing him of being a hypocrite. "Now that he's been busted with the other woman," she said, referencing a very public affair the married mayor was having, "I wouldn't be talking about moral issues."[102] "There is a commandment," she quipped, "Thou shalt not commit adultery."[103]

Beyond Censorship and Free Speech

Second, Giuliani's call for "decency" standards raised the specter of censorship, which was sure to fire up many liberals. This squaring off carried a specific rhetorical effect: it slotted the fight over Cox's work into the all-too-common culture wars framing of censorship against free speech. Such confrontations reached new heights in the late 1980s and 1990s in debates over the work of artists like Andres Serrano, Robert Mapplethorpe, David Wojnarowicz, and the NEA Four—and more recently in the debate over Ofili's work. This culture wars rhetoric frames the debate as having two specific sides—opponents of immoral or offensive art versus saviors of free expression—as we saw in the thematic focus of the debate between Cox and Donohue organized by the First Amendment Center.

To be sure, arguments about free speech are often necessary, both pragmatically and ideologically. But in the zeal to defend free speech, such arguments frequently sideline the artistic works they seek to defend, including the ways such works challenge dominant forms of representation, competing claims to the sacred, or alternative articulations of ethics. What's more, they often reduce the work of feminist, queer, and Black artists (and art by other people of color) to "identity politics," a buzzword used to attack work presumed to focus merely on cultural positions or social justice, rather than the (ostensibly) pure aesthetic motivations of modernist art. Indeed, several art and culture critics gave short shrift to Cox's work, even dismissing it in these terms. Art historian Nicole Fleetwood explains how even though "Giuliani's response was quite reactionary and in many ways uncomplicated," she was especially frustrated by the *defenders* of Cox's work. Their "ambivalence," she writes, was even "more troubling," as were the terms used to characterize her work, which critics found to be "lacking nuance" or "self-indulgent."[104] Writing for *Salon*, for instance, Laura Miller defended Cox against charges of anti-Catholicism but insisted her photography was "fairly ham-fisted" and "self-aggrandizing."[105]

The culture wars framing, including the buzz created by the threat of censorship, meant that Cox's work was largely dismissed, even by opponents of Giuliani's commission. The issue here was not that some critics did not like Cox's work, but that many of New York's most notable writers failed even to take it seriously, dismissing it in ways that often betrayed their own liberal racism. Consider how Michael Kimmelman, the *New York Times* art critic, covered Cox's work in two separate pieces. His first column bemoaned "our sorry culture wars" that are "fueled by the media" before rehearsing the *Sensation* scandal as pretext. While Kimmelman did question whether there was some racial motive for the hoopla over *Yo Mama's Last Supper*, as we saw earlier, he focused more on the pervasive politics of offense. Cox's work "isn't a masterpiece," he concluded, "but, for better or worse, neither does it exceed the bounds of normal provocation today."[106]

Kimmelman's second piece addressed Cox's work more directly. He placed her art alongside that of other Black artists, like Robert Colescott and Jacob Lawrence, but dubbed it "frankly narcissistic." He continued: "She also seems to aspire to the ranks of young black photographers of identity politics like Lyle Ashton Harris (who photographed her as well) and of feminist stars like Cindy Sherman, a photographer who assumed multiple guises."[107] This framing—"young black photographers of identity politics"—might seem innocent enough, but it was a dismissal. When Lyle Ashton Harris read the review, he penned a letter to the editor taking aim at exactly this line. "The fact remains," Harris wrote, "that the term identity politics is still a code word for non-white visual art cultural production. These words still encode art as less valuable in the annals of the New York art world." He also noted how Kimmelman consistently names the race or ethnicity of artists of color, while white artists go unmarked, a trend that reinforced the "hegemony" of whiteness in the art world.[108]

Katha Pollitt, a regular columnist for *The Nation*, also placed Cox's work in the context of *Sensation* and what she considered unfounded accusations of Catholic bashing. When discussing the art itself, though, Pollitt offered a quite odd assessment. She characterized *Yo Mama's Last Supper* as "negligible," "awkwardly composed," and "rather silly," as she joked, "apparently the first Christians spent a lot of time in the gym and at the hair salon, getting elaborate dreadlocked coiffures." She contrasted Cox's disciples to Leonardo's, whom she lauded as "highly individualized and dramatically connected." Looking at Cox's photomontage, Pollitt continued, "my eye kept going to the limited food on offer: bowls of wax-looking fruit (did they have bananas in Old Jerusalem?), rolls, pita bread. Was the Last Supper a diet seder?"[109] Pollitt's tongue-in-cheek style should not distract us from the rhetorical work of her comparison, which pokes fun at Cox's fussy disciples and anachronistic dinner table. Yet Pollitt's literalist reading gives Leonardo a pass on historical accuracy. Apparently, she had no trouble seeing the original Christians as white Europeans with flowing honey-brown hair, but locs proved too silly. Cox noted the double standards. If Leonardo could paint his friends, she insisted, then so could she. "He wasn't at the Last Supper," Cox said to one interviewer: "This isn't documentary here. But everybody accepts his work as dogma and every other [work] as not worthy."[110]

What I hope to show here is how even opponents of Giuliani's commission often proved dismissive of Cox's work, which was reduced to mere "identity politics" or culture wars art. By contrast, consider Arthur Danto's take in *The Nation*. While *Yo Mama's Last Supper* should be protected by the First Amendment, he insisted, "one loses a great opportunity in thinking of her work—or anyone's work, for that matter—merely in terms of the artist's right to make it or the museum's right to display it." Rather, he wrote, "Cox is a serious artist, with serious things to say in her chosen medium."[111] The hermeneutics of the culture wars too often resists grappling with that seriousness—and sometimes even acknowledging it.

A Democracy of Taxes

Finally, in calling for a decency commission, Giuliani made this debacle seem like a good faith debate over the uses of public funding, as he advocated for an assumed "public" that would abhor Cox's imagery. In the art wars (and beyond), right-wing organizations routinely riled people up through this precise rhetorical maneuver—claiming that their tax money directly supported something they presumably wouldn't like, as we saw in the American Family Association's campaign against David Wojnarowicz in chapter three. The use of tax money becomes a stand-in for the exercise of democratic freedom. That there may be some relationship among taxation, representation, and democracy, though, does not mean that citizens of a democracy have (or ought to have) the ability to itemize their contributions. Appeals to "the public" in such cases frequently arise in bad faith—as the main goal for many conservatives has been to cut *all* public funding for the arts—or construe a largely homogenous "public," one in which everyone agrees on "reasonable, common-sense" standards.[112]

In a pluralistic country like the United States, appeals to common sense and reason more often become tools for leveling difference than for protecting it—much less celebrating it. It seems reasonable to many people, for instance, that students in secondary school or in college might study arguments about the history and persistence of structural racism. Yet in recent years conservative politicians have sought to curtail even the possibility of such discussions in the Right's ongoing war against the bogeyman of "critical race theory." Likewise, it does not stretch credulity to say that a very many Americans oppose the "don't say gay" and anti-trans bills that have multiplied—often in the name of morality, decency, and the common good— just as queer and trans people have gained increased mainstream support, care, and legal protections.[113] Invocations of neutrality and common sense all too often obscure the very motivated and particular moral visions of some people being elevated over those of others. These claims cast the boundaries of what elsewhere I have called "moral citizenship," in which the language of morality (or decency) intensifies the power of rhetoric, positioning disagreement as beyond the pale.[114]

Giuliani's "public good" framing, which was carried across headlines, radio waves, and television screens, also fostered rhetorical confusion and slippage among the various criticisms put forward: Is the problem with *Yo Mama's Last Supper* that it was blasphemous, that it was deemed offensive, or that it was publicly funded? The mayor ensured all three claims circulated simultaneously. Patrick Scully, a spokesperson for the Catholic League, brought these rhetorical threads together when talking to *Newsday*. "The question is why would a publicly funded museum give a forum to a woman who has a history of ridiculing Catholic imagery," he asked: "You have to be brain dead not to be offended by it."[115] And such responses were not limited to the paid foot soldiers of the culture wars. According to Everton McIntyre, a language arts teacher and deacon at his Pentecostal church interviewed for the *New York Times*, "There has to be limits, guidelines on what you can and cannot do." "As liberal as I am," he continued, "this is out there. It's just blasphemous. This is public funds here and I'm the public. Why should I pay for this to be in a museum?"[116]

The Performative Politics of Offense

I want to slow down here to consider such charges that Cox's work was offensive—and that it was offensive for its nudity, blasphemy, or anti-Catholicism, as it was variably put. What work does the charge that something is "offensive" do, and is there a particular politics to offense-taking?

We should keep two points in mind: accusations of "offense" and the taking of offense are culturally and historically situated, and some claims to taking offense matter more than others. In recent years, much public discussion in news and popular media has focused on how certain people are too *easily* offended—especially college students with "coddled minds" seeking "safe spaces" and trigger warnings; certain demographics who cannot take a joke or overreact to "microaggressions"; and the woke warriors seeking to cancel anything with which they disagree.[117] This public discourse points a finger at the "culture of victimhood" supposedly created by members of "generation snowflake."[118] According to Greg Lukianoff and Jonathan Haidt, two authors who have popularized this public complaint, "the current movement is largely about emotional well-being," as fragile students (or liberals) seek protection from psychological harm.[119]

Philosopher Emily McTernan offers a different take: reducing claims of offense to a culture of victimhood or to the psychology of well-being misses how taking offense often indicates an effort to defend one's social standing. In our current moment, she writes, "to take offense is one way to resist the everyday patterning of social hierarchies."[120] For instance, a woman who intervenes in the telling of a sexist joke challenges the inferior standing of women relative to men, resisting the sexist conventions that make women the punchline of men's jokes.[121] Understood this way, many of the claims to offense attributed to thin-skinned snowflakes actually serve as challenges to deeply embedded social hierarchies that disadvantage women, LGBTQ people, and people of color, among others. In contemporary discourse, we rarely see these kinds of arguments pointed toward conservatives or white men, the ones often (but of course not exclusively) accused of doing the offending.

But in the early 2000s, the demographics of offense looked quite different. Amid debate over Cox's work, especially in the mainstream press, it was largely white Catholics and political leaders who took offense at *Yo Mama's Last Supper* (and, earlier, at Ofili's *Holy Virgin Mary*). Unlike the claims of overly sensitive millennials today, their claims to offense found a largely receptive audience in the news media. To be sure, some commentaries pushed back on claims of Catholic bashing and calls for censorship, resisting the dramatic flair of spokespeople like Giuliani and Donohue. As far as I can tell, though, no one accused the mayor or the archbishop of New York of having coddled minds or hiding within a culture of victimhood. Rather, the offended parties enjoyed national and international press coverage, often on their own terms, without pseudo-experts reducing their claims to offense to an epidemic of oversensitivity.

But if there was a "culture of victimhood" during this culture wars episode, it manifested less among liberals, students, or minoritized groups than within the discursive communities of mostly white, conservative Christians. Culture warriors like Giuliani and Donohue—not incidentally an Italian American Catholic and an Irish American Catholic—tapped into much older rhetoric of Christian persecution and American anti-Catholicism. They mobilized the threat of religious (and racial) injury to white Christians in particular, whom they figured as minoritized victims (despite their then and ongoing political and demographic power). We could situate this broader moment among three flashpoints: the election of evangelical conservative George W. Bush in 2000, the start of the War on Terror following the 2001 attack on the Twin Towers, and the lead up to the decriminalization of homosexuality in 2003's *Lawrence v. Texas*. Far more happened in the first decade of the twenty-first century, but these signposts help capture the emergence of what would be called the "war on Christians."[122]

Religious studies scholar Elizabeth Castelli underscores the "rhetorical excess" captured in the bellicose naming. But, she insists, "the 'war on Christians' rhetoric is more than *mere rhetoric*; rather, it is a critical element of a comprehensive theo-political framework that blends the sacred and the secular and that sees the story of America unfolding as a story of God's covenantal promise to a chosen people."[123] This rhetoric posits conservative white Christians as a persecuted majority left behind in the shifting winds of US culture and politics—"a majority relegated (in Bill Donohue's words) to seats on the back of the bus," writes Castelli.[124] Donohue's reference to the language of the civil rights movement is no mere coincidence, as conservative Christians have claimed this legacy for themselves.[125] What's more, this rhetoric of Christian persecution drew inspiration from the languages of identity politics of the 1960s and 1970s (even as white conservatives have often disavowed that legacy) as well as "the politics of moral injury."[126]

This was the context in which whiteness, Christian identity, and moral injury converged in this earlier, if largely unnamed, "culture of victimhood."[127] And the biggest bullies in this right-wing rhetorical fantasy were feminists and homosexuals. How did this logic work? Conservative Christians understood homosexuality to be opposed to Christianity. By extension, Castelli explains, they considered calls for LGBTQ rights, like same-sex marriage or anti-discrimination protections, part of "an aggressive attack on Christianity itself and translat[ed] the movement for civil rights for sexual minorities into a critical front in the war on Christians."[128] This rhetorical framework figures feminist and LGBTQ people—their moral politics, their communities, and their art—not only as outside Christianity but as combatants threatening the rights and livelihoods of the beleaguered moral majority. Disagreement becomes moral and divine opposition.

The precise phrasing of the "war on Christians" would not become popular until a few years after the fight over Cox's work, but the seeds of this rhetoric, planted years before, were already sprouting in 2001, as conservative Catholics and political leaders tapped into the rhetoric of persecution, which coincided with their claims about the "last acceptable prejudice." This is the broader rhetorical context that shaped the curious politics of offense animating the debate over *Yo Mama's Last Supper* and that leads me to ask: Who gets to be offended, how are they offended, and what work does offense do within the culture wars?

Offending Images

Cox's *Yo Mama's Last Supper* offended a lot of people and sparked various responses. Scott LoBaido, a thirty-five-year-old man from Staten Island, expressed his anger by protesting at the Brooklyn Museum. He entered the museum carrying a three-foot pornographic painting that depicted the museum's director, Arnold Lehman, "having sex with a pig."[129] After refusing to leave, LoBaido was eventually arrested for criminal trespassing and disorderly conduct. Reports on the incident do not address the motivations behind his particular artistic rendering, but the portrayal of a Jewish man copulating with swine reprises antisemitic tropes. Indeed, anti-Jewish sentiment already circulated in debates over Cox and Ofili. The year before, social critic Camille Paglia, who would also complain about Lehman allowing the Brooklyn Museum to exhibit "anti-Catholic" work like *Yo Mama's Last Supper*, had penned an article in *Salon* about Ofili's *Holy Virgin Mary*. It was subtitled: "Why are a Jewish collector and a Jewish museum director promoting anti-Catholic art?" That line was eventually removed, though the insinuation of Jews attacking Catholics remained within the body of the article.[130] Paranoid Christian fantasies of Jews attacking Catholic symbols have a long history—and this rhetoric likely motivated LoBaido's protest at the Brooklyn Museum.

But LoBaido's run-in at the Brooklyn Museum was not his first protest. During the *Sensation* exhibition, he was arrested for tossing horse manure at the museum, an act that mirrored Ofili's use of dung. And LoBaido was not alone in such attacks. Manhattan resident Dennis Heiner protested by painting directly over Ofili's *Holy Virgin Mother*. He spread white paint across the face and body of the Madonna—an act, notes visual studies scholar W. J. T. Mitchell, that defaced Ofili's painting but also applied a purifying shield over the offended Mary, defiled by dung.[131] In this sense, not only was Heiner offended, but so was the Holy Virgin herself, whose presence was made real through Ofili's work. For Mitchell, images bear a particular relationship to offense. People who take offense understand the image not only to represent its subject but also to carry "a kind of vital, living character that makes it capable of feeling what is done to it."[132] These senses help us understand longer histories of iconoclasm but also these more recent ones—indeed, Mitchell's key example focuses on the protests against Ofili's work. He explains, "ancient superstitions about images—that they take on 'lives of their own,' that they make people do irrational things, that they are potentially destructive forces that seduce and lead us astray—are not quantitatively less powerful in our time." Rather, he writes, "their deep structure remains the same."[133] This is the power that images can carry.

Approached in this way, we might understand better something about the quality of offense when it comes to images deemed sacrilegious. It is not only one's sensibilities that are offended but also what one holds sacred—a god or holy mother. No doubt, this raises the stakes of offense—and questions about the sincerity of taking offense. It is clear in the case of *Yo Mama's Last Supper*, as with Ofili's work, that some people were sincerely offended, while others may have been merely "officially offended," as one writer described Donohue. Keeping in mind questions about sincerity, and the performance of sincerity, we should also attend to the performative effects of naming something as offensive. Here I focus on three effects that arose in the debate over Cox's work: accusations of offense formed powerful social categories, flattened cultural difference, and fostered curious racial and ethnic fantasies.

Categorizing Offense

Recall the Catholic League spokesperson's line that one would have to be "brain dead" not to be offended by *Yo Mama's Last Supper*. The obvious exaggeration turns on a disability affiliation no one would claim in order to mask the creation of a division that pretends not to be one. The phrasing draws a line in the sand, or erects a barricade, if we hold to the metaphor of raging culture wars. Let me put this another way.

The rhetoric of culture wars offense does not merely describe presumed moral and political differences but further constructs these differences through the work of categorization. Such framing is not a given; it's a tactic. When Mayor Giuliani or Patrick Scully or a language arts teacher pronounces an artistic work "offensive," "pornographic," or "blasphemous," they seem to record a mere observation that any rational (or not "brain dead") person would understand using "commonsense" standards. But in doing so, they forge a division. Religious studies scholar S. B. Rodriguez-Plate points to this very form of category-making in claims of blasphemy. "Blasphemy, and the accusation of blasphemy," Rodriguez-Plate writes, "is a culturally symbolic marker that helps define societies and religious traditions, as well as provide identities for people in terms of gender, race, class, and sexuality."[134] In the context of the modern culture wars, to label something offensive—and offensive for its anti-Catholicism—is to claim an identity and to posit a claim: that this offensive thing is not Catholicism, not even religion (unless maybe within the terms of an antisemitic fantasy of Jews attacking Catholicism, as we've seen).

News media, pundits, and even scholars of religion and of the culture wars too readily accept the terms of these accusations, which fit neatly into a broader culture wars framework that posits conservative religion (nearly always read as Christian) against secular progressivism. Any critique of Christianity must, in this framework, be a critique of religion writ large, a secular gauntlet thrown at the ostensibly oppressed and offended Christian. Feminist, queer, or Black art that takes up Christian themes is always already suspect in this approach, rhetorically opposed to normative conservative religion and thus rendered secular, if not anti-Christian.

Offending Differences

If claims of offense from injured Catholics contributed to category-making, to dividing Christians from non-Christians, efforts to redress the injury of offense tapped into what we might consider the equation or flattening of differences. Mayor Giuliani led the charge here, equating supposed anti-Catholic hate speech with other kinds of discrimination. In doing so, he tapped into the rhetoric of identity politics and claims to the legacy of the civil rights movement to justify attempts to rescue Catholics from abuse.

Take the mayor's plea for fairness. "If we're going to prohibit public funding of an exhibit because it attacks people for being Jewish," Giuliani explained, "then it should also apply to Catholics, Protestants, Hindus and Muslims. If there is an exhibit that defames and demeans African-Americans and we don't allow that, then it shouldn't be allowed for any other race. We are one City, with one standard."[135] This rhetoric aligns Jews, Catholics, Protestants, Hindus, and Muslims, all simply people of different traditions, while also layering in racial rhetoric, contrasting African Americans to "any other race." "There are people who have different views on this," Giuliani adds, "but I do not believe that it is right for public money to be used to desecrate religion, to attack people's ethnicity. We're a multifaceted society."[136] Here, the mayor positioned himself on the side of multiculturalism, as a defender against religious and racial discrimination.

But his rhetoric flattens racial and religious differences, as Giuliani tapped into what sociologist Eduardo Bonilla-Silva calls the ideology of "colorblind racism," an approach that downplays racial differences to undercut discussions of racial discrimination.[137] The mayor also equated racial discrimination with attacks on religion—"to desecrate religion, to attack people's ethnicity"—as he defended a specific understanding of Catholicism. As he charged, "anti-Catholicism is allowed to flourish without people getting outraged by it the way they would a racial attack or possibly attacks against other people's religion."[138] The mayor's rhetorical comparisons reified the sense that Black artists—Cox and Ofili in particular—attack (presumably white) Catholics at the same rate and with the same intensity that Black people, Jews, Muslims, and other minoritized religious and racial groups come under attack. Such comparisons work in part by presuming the equation of differences, the notion that differences are mostly superficial (e.g., white and Black are simply different kinds of races just as Catholic and Muslim are simply different varieties of religion).

The equation of racial differences comes to make sense for Giuliani and others not only within the history of colorblind racism—which teaches people to try to "unsee" race or, more practically, to see it but then to renounce the seeing and its effects—but also within the rhetorical framework of neoliberalism. I use neoliberalism here to name a mode of reasoning in political and cultural life that expands the logic of market rationality to increasing spheres of life (not just economics, but healthcare, transportation, education, incarceration, and even the practice of democracy). Neoliberal thinking has a longer history but intensified in the US political context under Ronald Reagan to become a key language through which most Americans understand their lives, politics, and government.[139] Political theorist Wendy Brown argues that the cultural and political framework of neoliberalism disavows the very notion of society, or "the social," including "its intelligibility, its harboring of stratifying powers, and above all, its appropriateness as a site of justice and the commonweal."[140] This dismantling of the social leads to a kind of leveling, in which the aspiration for equality becomes a script for positing all citizens as the same—all equally customers exercising their rational faculties. This framing jettisons social and historical differences, including disparate histories of social discrimination, in the service of positing all citizens as free consumers to the marketplace of life, in which the very definition of freedom is reduced to freedom of choice (as opposed to access, for instance).

The receding of the social propels both the equation of freedom with choice and the popularity of colorblind racism. It makes claims of unfairness equally open to members of the white majority, rather than simply those who have endured social discrimination. Within this thinking, for instance, it starts to make sense how white people may consider it "unfair" for some (for instance, Black Americans) to use the "N-word" while others (say, whites) should not. If everyone is the same, then why are the rules different—shouldn't they apply equally without concern for race? The logic of unfairness here makes sense only if we erase the history and ongoing realities of racial discrimination that have drawn upon that particular word toward specifically anti-Black, violent ends. Within the rhetorical logic of neoliberalism (and its convergence with colorblind racism), though, there is no room to understand how such power works—or that poking fun at a religious or racial majority may be different from punching down.

This is the history of thought that shaped how Giuliani (and Donohue and others) approached religious and racial difference. Religions become essentially the same kinds of thing—like merely different routes up the same mountain—and are treated, in many ways, as interchangeable. This way of thinking about religion also has a longer history, stretching back at least to nineteenth-century models of "world religions," that merges with neoliberal ways of equating differences.[141] Again, this flattening of differences obscures more than it reveals. In this case, treating religions as more or less the same overlooks their very different histories of visual culture and conventions for condoning or condemning representations of the divine.[142] Catholicism, for instance, has a very long and rich tradition of depicting holy figures such as Jesus and Mary—even representing them in ways that some modern eyes might find shocking, such as Renaissance depictions of Christ lactating or giving birth through his side wound. In other traditions, including Judaism and Islam—and to some degree Protestantism—followers tend to avoid representations of divine figures or even forbid them. It is no accident that Cox (and Ofili) works within Catholicism, rather than Judaism or Islam, and finds within this iconographic tradition resources both to criticize and to re-imagine it. That she works within Catholicism, rather than Islam or Judaism, matters here.

Offending Fantasies of Race and Gender

Giuliani's flattening of demographic differences positioned him on the side of racial and religious equality—a version of "equality" that continues to an-imate much conservative rhetoric. And, indeed, he avoided explicitly racist or sexist language (or Islamophobic language, though this debacle erupted a few months before September 11), even as he slotted Cox's work alongside not only acts of desecration but also racist attacks on "other" races. Lurking behind this claim was not only the suspicion that Cox attacked Christians by picturing Jesus as a naked Black woman, but also that she attacked white people, whether by disrupting dominant Euro-American assumptions that Jesus was white or by racializing Judas as white. Such charges, again, traded on a longer history of Christian persecution rhetoric. But they also provoked newer fantasies of racial, sexual, and religious offense that circulated in the debate over Cox's work.

It's possible Giuliani read one creative pundit's take that *Yo Mama's Last Supper* was not really anti-Catholic so much as "viciously anti-semitic." The author was Maggie Gallagher, a white Catholic convert and conserva-tive activist who would later cofound the anti-gay National Organization for Marriage. She was also a regular columnist for the sensationalist *New York Post*. In her editorial on Cox, Gallagher observed that all the disciples are Black except Judas. He's not just white, she insisted, but "actually a crude caricature of a beak-nosed Jew gazing devotedly at the black Jesus figure—just before he (the Jew) is about to betray Jesus (the black woman) and his movement (of black men). Need I say more?"[143] This already says so much. Looking at *Yo Mama's Last Supper*, it is difficult to see the antisemitic caricature Gallagher names—none of Cox's apostles even come close to mimicking such tropes. It may have fit Gallagher's political purposes had Cox represented Judas this way, but she didn't—except in the writer's own imagination, as Gallagher fomented a fantasy that the Black artist was the real racist here, not only against whites but against (white) Jews.

Gallagher was not alone in projecting peculiar fantasies of religious and racial discrimination, though most others worked through the suggestion of hypotheticals. It is important that such fantasies of discrimination appeared in the subjunctive. In the *New York Times*, Michael Kimmelman asked: "Would the defenders of a work like Ms. Cox's react similarly if a contested image were of Martin Luther King rather than Jesus?"[144] King was a popular stand-in. During their debate, as we saw earlier, Donohue asked Cox if she would be offended by an image of a white man relieving himself into the mouth of Martin Luther King Jr. When she failed to respond, he offered another provocation: what about a picture depicting Hitler with a halo while he stabbed a dagger into a Jewish person?[145]

The specter of high art insulting MLK or promoting antisemitism is meant to name a double standard. It rests on the assumption that Cox and her supporters would find such scenarios unacceptable. But it overlooks both Cox's wide tolerance for free expression and, even more, the long history of anti-Black, antisemitic, and sexist art that public museums have long exhibited—and continue to exhibit—that has not sparked the same moral outrage and culture of offense among political and religious leaders like Giuliani and Donohue. Offense appears selective. American studies scholar Deidre Wheaton pinpoints one of the motivations for that selectivity:

That Giuliani was offended by a Black nude woman as Christ but not upset by Anthony Barboza's photograph—also featured in the *Committed to the Image* exhibit—which depicts a murdered young black boy wrapped in white sheets with a black cross representing his body, exposes the fact that there is perhaps more at issue here than Giuliani's concern over the supposed desecration of religion. Cox's use of Christian symbols to promote self-confidence and affirm Black pride gained Giuliani's ire, but an image in the same exhibit using similar Christian symbols to represent a dead black boy is ignored. *It seems that religious desecration promoting black suffering is allowed while religious desecration affirming black life is not.*[146]

Here, Wheaton gets more directly to the politics of race, and especially anti-Blackness, that informs the culture of offense in debates over *Yo Mama's Last Supper* and underscores the dramatic racism of right-wing projections.

Cox directly addressed accusations that her work was offensive and anti-Catholic. She insisted on her right to criticize Catholicism as someone who was baptized and thus an insider to the tradition. She also repeatedly invoked the racist and sexist legacies of the Roman Catholic Church. "It's a commentary about gender and what's happening in the Catholic Church," she explained: "It's also a commentary about African Americans and how Catholicism has had an impact on them from slavery to the abolition movement."[147] In one interview, she exclaimed, "I got a letter from somebody saying *there were no blacks* at the time of Christ."[148] The author of the letter complained that Cox dared to portray Christ in "the presence of BLACKS" before asserting: "There were no BLACKS at the time of Christ and if there were he would not be surrounded with stupid people."[149] As this piece of hate mail (saved in Cox's archive) suggests, the covert racism (and sexism) displayed in Giuliani's commentary and in culture wars fantasies of offense printed in news media becomes explicit in the mail sent to Cox and the Brooklyn Museum. It also gestures to some of the ways that racist and sexist fantasies, hypotheticals, and suggestions of reverse racism circulated.

The negative letters Cox received as she entered the crosshairs of the culture wars range from earnest frustration to uninhibited racism and sexism. They repeatedly return to Cox's identity as a Black woman. In a handwritten letter, a woman who identifies herself as a wife, mother, and grandmother asserts that "the human masculinity of Christ cannot be denied" and that Cox's nude representation offends all Christians. Echoing the terms of colorblind racism, she also faults Cox for looking backward rather than forward, for stereotyping Black people who are simply trying to move beyond the "horrific" legacies of the past in hopes of a better future.[150]

Most of the negative mail takes a more forceful approach. Kathleen H. called Cox a "sick feminist fanatic" and warned her about God's wrath as she expressed her "outrage" at the artist's "desecration" of Christ.[151] A letter from "A. Aryans" bets that Cox would "never do this to the Jews" and asks why she fails to mock the Reverend Jesse Jackson instead. The writer also implores Cox to return to Africa and to live how she deserves—"like savages [*sic*]"[152] Other mail was more graphic—one piece, a play on the insult "dickhead," includes a drawing of a penis with a cut-out image of Cox on the tip. "Black Cox" is written across the shaft, with an arrow pointing to the image of the artist. Along the top, the author insists: "This is art—post!"[153] Such responses surface not only the deep currents of US racism and sexism but also how they become intensified through accusations of sacrilege, through Cox's effort to reimagine the sacred with a Black woman at the table.[154]

Envisioning a Black Feminist Catholicism?

Not all the mail Cox received was negative. She got many positive letters, thank you notes, and sympathy cards from fans and fellow artists, many of whom dealt directly with the content of her work—something most art critics and pundits largely avoided in their race to defend free expression against Giuliani's decency commission. In fact, even some of the negative letters proved more sophisticated, or at least creative, in their readings of her art, often underscoring the theological implications of *Yo Mama's Last Supper*. Frank L. of East Rutherford, New Jersey, penned a letter complaining that taxpayers were footing the bill to support a particular religion. "They are trying to sneak religion in under the guise of art," he claimed.[155] The editor of *Pro Ecclesia* magazine called Cox's art a "blatant promotion of Nestorianism," the view that Jesus was two distinct persons, one human and one divine, which was deemed a heresy by the Roman Catholic Church in the fifth century. "This makes her painting more than just art," he continued, "it is theology" and thus violates the separation of church and state.[156] Readings of *Yo Mama's Last Supper*, not only as art but as theology, also appear in many of the fan letters Cox received.

Some of these letters defended Cox against her Catholic critics. Joseph B. of Fort Washington, New York, apologized for Cox having to "suffer some of our brothers and sisters," especially those from the Catholic League, who do not speak on behalf of the Catholic Church. The true church, he insisted, "includes all its members," among them those who "look to gifted artists to reveal to us the creation of the Lord, the ultimate Creator and Artist."[157] Theodore P. from Kingston, New York, defended Cox from Cardinal Egan's charge that she was "pathetic." "I hope you're not too deeply affected," he quipped in a short, handwritten note: "It's just that he thinks he's so close to God!!! You are closer to God! Your work is great!"[158] Sally T., writing from Orinda, California, threw her arms up at Giuliani and another critic who said, "Jesus was never nude." She was most likely referring to a quotation from Everton McIntyre, the Pentecostal language arts teacher interviewed at the museum and mentioned earlier.[159] "The Lord's Supper means a lot to me," McIntyre had said, "And her being nude bothers me. Jesus was never nude."[160] Sally jokes that she hopes Cox "learned her lesson"—that it is dangerous to inspire people "to think about the meaning of Christian symbols or to speculate as to why certain peoples have been excluded from church iconography."[161]

A number of letters, often by women, championed the feminist and Black political theologies of Cox's work and supported her battle against Giuliani and other conservative Catholics, especially for "speaking out against the obvious sexism and racism obviously promoted by the Catholic Church."[162] One writer offered a "heartfelt thank you" on behalf of herself and other women "who look at the male dominated religions of the world."[163] Another letter writer, identifying herself as a married white woman, saw Cox's work printed in a newspaper and found it "thought provoking and stunningly beautiful." She noted how members of a patriarchal religion must find it hard to see images that challenge them. "God has given you a great gift and you use it well," she wrote.[164] Janet S. lauded how Cox reimagined the Last Supper. She recalled growing up in Boston and gathering for Sunday dinner in her grandmother's dining room, "where the 'Last Supper' presided from its nook," an older, "pewter icon" with bearded men sitting at the table. But, she explained, she keeps her eyes out for "stories of women who are creative, innovative, daring and pushing for a shift in traditional perceptions within the legacy of the Catholic Church and state." She found that in Cox's *Yo Mama's Last Supper*.[165] A postcard from Ronn E. emphasized the intersections of religion, gender, and race, thanking Cox "for having and practicing the courage of your mystical vision of the divinity of <u>black</u> women."[166]

Gabriella V.-W. penned two letters—one to Cox and a second to Arnold Lehman, the director of the Brooklyn Museum, which she also sent to Barbara Millstein, who curated *Committed to the Image*, and the *National Catholic Reporter*, a progressive newspaper. In the letter to Cox, she described how she "could not take my eyes off" *Yo Mama's Last Supper* and how "revealing" it was for her to see what all the "fear, hatred and oppression of women" was about: "the power of women to name their experience and to be seen as <u>subject</u> and <u>not object</u>."[167]

The second letter is more formal. Gabriella introduces herself as an Italian American woman studying art and theology at a Catholic seminary. "I am offended," she wrote, "not by the exhibit, but by the comments of Mayor Giuliani, and others, calling this image disgusting and implying that it is indecent. This is certainly not 'Catholic' bashing." She rehearsed the longer history of sexist representations of women in Western art, including art with Christian themes, across the work of "male artists like Carracci, Domenichino, Tintoretto, van der Berg, Ricci, Rubens, Rembrandt, and others." Why, she asked, doesn't Giuliani spotlight these works as "disgusting or indecent?" Finally, she turned to representations of the divine and the power of imagining women's bodies as divine. "I find this image profoundly sacred," even "profoundly Eucharistic," she concluded.[168]

Such letters foreground the political and theological work of *Yo Mama's Last Supper* without reducing it to the terms of offensive art versus free speech. Nor do they reduce Cox's commitment to thinking about gender and race to the trite terms of "identity politics," as one critic did when he described her work as "fall[ing] under the heading of cliché—too tired for even pseudo-controversy."[169] Instead, these letters and other commentaries emphasized the power and necessity of Cox's art, often taking it further in theological directions than Cox did herself. Literary scholar Shelly Eversley writes that Cox's "full-frontal nudity democratized religion so much so that God could be a woman, and black." For her, *Yo Mama's Last Supper* "undermines an epistemological image," not merely "a religious belief."[170] To put this another way, Cox's Black Christ challenges not only religion, but the visual foundations of knowledge itself, of how we come to know through images.

In a regular column for Florida's *Palm Beach Post*, Steve Gushee, who was also the former senior associate rector of the Episcopal Church of Bethesda-by-the-Sea in Palm Beach, had only one complaint about *Yo Mama's Last Supper*: "that it may not be offensive enough to renew the Church and change the world."[171] Gushee might have found more to work with in an exhibition of Cox's work that opened later that year.

Catholicism, Culture Wars, and Cox's Family Values

Mere months after the media storm erupted around *Yo Mama's Last Supper*, the Robert Miller Gallery in New York hosted an exhibition focused on Cox's work called *American Family*. It opened on October 10, 2001. No one could have predicted the world events that occurred only a month before, which no doubt shifted the attention of political and religious leaders in other directions. Giuliani, whom Oprah dubbed "America's Mayor," would soon be named *Time's* "Person of the Year" for 2001 for his work following the 9/11 attack. The mayor's days as a culture warrior were far from over, but Cox now appeared a less pressing or media-worthy opponent. Had he looked at or read about *American Family*, though, he might have found much cause to take offense.

American Family brought together several themes, representing "a veritable minefield of taboo topics from the miscegenated family album to the erotic display of her own beautiful body," writes art historian Jo Anna Isaak.[172] Cox said the show emerged in part from a midlife crisis—brought on by social assumptions that deem women in their forties no longer sexual or desirable—and called it "the beginning of my spiritual awakening."[173] The exhibition included plays on canonical art. In *Cousins at Pussy Pond* (2001), for instance, Cox reworks Édouard Manet's *Luncheon on Grass* (1862–63), posing as a nude nymph in a field in the Hamptons alongside two Black men stylized as warrior gods. In *41 Bullets at Green River* (2001), she invokes Andrea Mantegna's *St. Sebastian* (1490s) to memorialize the murder of Amadou Diallo. The show also featured family photos, older pictures of Cox's parents and grandparents and images of Cox as a young girl, in addition to more recent ones. *Family Snaps* (2001) presents a collection of sixty 10.5" × 8" prints ranging from family vacation photos to images from the *Yo Mama* series. In *My Son* (2001), Cox presents a striking black-and-white photo of her older son with an American flag draped around him against a black background. Alongside these pieces, Cox includes highly stylized erotic images often featuring an S/M aesthetic, such as *Black Leather Lace-Up* (2001) and a digital video called *The Kiss* (2001) showing a close-up of two mouths in the act.

If neither Giuliani nor the Catholic League appears to have gotten wind of this show, despite the fact that it was marketed as potentially offensive, it did catch the eye of *New York Times* art critic Roberta Smith. She praised Cox's effort to center the subjectivity and sexuality of Black women in work she calls "aggressive" and "technically well-executed." But the way Cox does so, Smith wrote, proves "rarely more than simplistically self-aggrandizing" or as a form of "spirited narcissism."[174] This language sounds familiar. Indeed, Smith recycled much of the loaded vocabulary others had used to dismiss Cox's work. "The main goal" of the exhibit, Smith explained, "seems to be a sometimes campy, sometimes sentimental celebration of black female sexuality, used uninhibitedly to subvert other art."[175] Cox's show did do that, but a closer look reveals, too, the ways Cox played with religion and

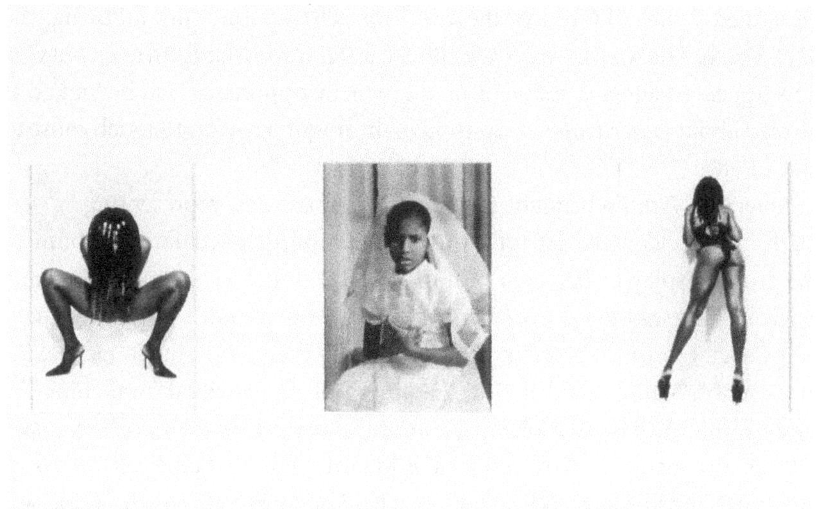

Figure 5.4 Renée Cox, *Holy Communion*, 2001. Gelatin silver prints, 7 × 5 in. (17.8 × 12.7 cm). Used with the permission of Renée Cox.

sexuality—figured through exhibition and constraint—and with that loaded icon of the Christian Right: the family. Let me draw out two of the works that deal most obviously with Catholic themes.

In each of two black-and-white triptychs—*The Good Catholic Girl* (2001) and *Holy Communion* (2001)—Cox places an image of herself as a Catholic schoolgirl between erotic photos of herself as an adult. In *Good Catholic Girl*, she wears a neat school uniform and looks directly at the camera. In *Holy Communion*, the center photo shows a young Cox in a white communion dress and veil, holding a Bible to her chest (Figure 5.4). Again, she looks directly into the camera, lips parted, with a look of concern or frustration. The Catholic girl photos are framed by images in which Cox strikes various erotic poses while wearing stilettos and fishnet stockings or a laced leather corset. All of the adult images obscure her face, which is either outside the frame, covered by long locs, or turned away from the camera to expose her backside.

The triptychs play with the convergence of Catholicism, desire, and the aesthetics of sadomasochism, invoking a long history of tension between repression and arousal in Catholic aesthetics, as it juxtaposes childhood formation with adult display.[176] They play with subject and object. By showing her face and making eye contact, the young Cox becomes subject, even as the image is no doubt posed by an adult, the clothing selected by an adult, the admonishment to be a "good Catholic girl" originating from an adult. The adult poses, meanwhile, play with the history of an objectifying straight male gaze—even a white male gaze at a Black woman's body—while also resisting it. Here, Cox styles herself, poses herself; the images convey strength, not only metaphorically but in the contours of her svelte figure and the energy of her poses. By labeling one triptych *Holy Communion*, Cox again plays with sacramental imagery, staging a Black girl/woman as the Eucharist and with an erotism that simply does not appear in the same way in *Yo Mama's Last Supper.*

If Cox plays here, again, with Catholic iconography—with race, sexuality, childhood, and the sacred—she also plays on the conservative Christian politics of "traditional family values." The rhetoric of family values has animated the rise of the Christian Right and American politics more broadly since the 1970s, as conservatives have sought to hold back the changing tides brought on by civil rights and the sexual revolutions. The family, as Lauren Berlant has argued, becomes part of the national sacred, the cornerstone of American moral citizenship.[177] But the family, in this guise, is imagined in a very specific way, as one headed by an authoritative, working husband and a supportive wife and mother—a callback to an imagined 1950s moral highpoint (the same nostalgic fantasy that animates "Make America Great Again," as in, before the social revolutions of the 1960s, before integration). Read against this politics of the family, Cox's *American Family* refuses the social and religious vision of the Christian Right. It conjures a new iconography of the American family—Black, white, interracial, female, erotic, Catholic.

Afterword

Resurrecting David

David Wojnarowicz died in 1992, but he continued to spark debate in the following decades. In the fall of 2010, the Smithsonian's National Portrait Gallery hosted a landmark exhibition focused on gender and sexual difference in the work of socially marginalized artists, especially queer ones. Curated by Jonathan Katz and David Ward, *Hide/Seek: Difference and Desire in American Portraiture* included a four-minute cut of Wojnarowicz's unfinished film *A Fire in My Belly*. The footage includes a scene with ants crawling over and around a cheap crucifix laying on the ground. Wojnarowicz used various images from this same source material elsewhere, including in his *Spirituality (for Paul Thek)*. Neither the film, nor these images of ants on the crucifix, had previously caused much stir. But in 2010 they caught the attention of the Catholic League's William Donohue, who released a statement calling the images anti-Catholic "hate speech." Congressional leaders, including Speaker of the House John Boehner and Rep. Eric Cantor, quickly joined the chorus of condemnation. Fearing retribution from Congress, the National Portrait Gallery pulled the film from the exhibition. Dropping the film quickly drew criticism from those on the left, who denounced it as caving under pressure at best and as censorship at worst.[1]

This round of culture wars debate featured familiar battle cries, as conservative Christians and politicians squared off against feminist and queer artists and advocates for free expression. And, again, many questions remained just outside of the public spectacle—or struggled to get the same airtime and serious consideration. To mention only the most obvious: Is it immediately apparent what ants crawling on a crucifix would mean or what effect this work might have on viewers, on how they see or understand something about the world?

This episode also saw new lines of comparison and cast additional characters. Speaking to the *New York Times*, Donohue complained about what he considered a double standard: that the artistic community (and

Provoking Religion. Anthony M. Petro, Oxford University Press. © Oxford University Press 2025.
DOI: 10.1093/9780190938468.003.0007

the general US public) would never condone assaulting Islam in the way that it allows attacks on Christianity, such as that allegedly depicted in Wojnarowicz's film. "It would jump out at people if they had ants crawling all over the body of Muhammad," he explained: "except that they wouldn't do it, of course, for obvious reasons."[2]

Such comparisons were not necessarily new—conservatives have imagined similar what-if scenarios by conjuring fantasies of antisemitic art or art attacking Martin Luther King Jr. There have even been earlier comparisons to using Muhammad in such art. But Donohue's reference to the Prophet took on new meaning after 9/11, especially since the start of the War on Terror, during which Islam has so frequently been figured against "Western civilization" (itself often conflated with Christianity). By 2010, conservative culture warriors had slotted Muslims alongside feminists and LGBTQ people as enemies of Christian America and Western values. In these same years, the United States witnessed a rise in blatant cases of Islamophobia.[3] But violence against Muslims was not Donohue's focus. He thought the exhibition of Wojnarowicz's work by the Smithsonian sent a different message. "If an artist offended Jews, African Americans or Muslims," Donohue argued, "the artwork alone would be cause for censorship, never mind investigating any harbored prejudices he may have had."[4] But not so with Christians, he maintained—it was always open season on Christianity.

Conservatives were not alone in casting Muslims—or Islam—against Western notions of freedom, including the freedom of artistic expression. LGBT activist and media pundit Dan Savage, for instance, has argued that the ability to mock Christians should be considered not a sign of ongoing anti-Christian sentiment but instead a mark of secular (even Christian) progress. Consider his comments in 2015, following the shooting at the headquarters of *Charlie Hebdo*, a French satirical magazine that republished controverial cartoons depicting Muhammad. Writing for SLOG, part of the Seattle-based newspaper *The Stranger*, Savage mocked the reticence of US news media to republish the controversial Danish Muhammad cartoons in their coverage of the attack. Even more, he recoiled at news that, in the wake of the attack, the Associated Press went so far as to remove images of Serrano's *Piss Christ* from their website and visual archives as well.[5] Serrano's piece was removed following criticism from the conservative *Washington Examiner* that the Associated Press had readily blurred the Muhammad images but continued to show *Piss Christ*, despite outcries that it too was sacrilegious.[6] Why bow to Muslim demands, the argument went, but not to those of Christians?

Savage wound up chiding both the mainstream press and conservative Christians alike. "The fact that cartoonists, publishers, editors, photographers, artists, comedians, and satirists aren't afraid of 'you'— the fact that they're not afraid to mock Christ, Christians, Christianity," he insisted, "is something that Christians, conservative and otherwise, should be proud of." Even more, he continued, "It is a credit to Judaism and Christianity that both are safe targets of satire in Western societies."[7] Savage's comments implicitly yoked Islam to violence while figuring Judaism and Christianity as both Western and peaceful. For him, the key difference between the Muhammad cartoons and *Piss Christ* had little to do with offense; rather, people in "Western societies" could take a joke (a sign of their progress), whereas Muslims apparently could not. Of course, this rhetorical framing notably figures Muslims outside of Western societies, despite the many Muslims who have lived in the United States and Europe for centuries. Even as the culture wars have shifted from the 1980s to the historical present, such fights over religion, art, and sexuality still so easily become debates over contrasting visions of cultural progress, religion, secularism, and humanity.

Discussing the Danish cartoon controversy, anthropologist Saba Mahmood argues for us to move past "the limited vocabulary of blasphemy and freedom of speech—the two poles that dominated the debate."[8] Framing such battles as blasphemy versus free speech obscures other kinds of questions one might raise. This binary logic has likewise governed culture wars debates over art in the United States, as we have seen in the preceding chapters and in the debate over Wojnarowicz's *A Fire in My Belly*. How does this binary logic work and how might we think beyond it? We can draw upon the lessons of these culture wars encounters with religion, sex, and art to offer three concluding theses.

First Thesis

The conventional culture wars framing is not merely descriptive of deep-seated moral and political differences but also actively constructs these differences through the very work of categorization.

We have seen how the conservative rhetoric of the culture wars reduces feminist and queer artists to a seemingly stable set of offenders against "religion" itself. This categorization makes it very difficult to imagine these artists aside from their presumed opposition to Christianity, to decency, to morality, and to proper citizenship—and, indeed, much scholarship on the modern culture wars and on religion in the United States readily, if unwittingly, reproduces this framing. We need to better understand the logic by which an artist like Andres Serrano is grouped with David Wojnarowicz, or Renée Cox, or Chris Ofili, or Judy Chicago, or Ray Navarro, or Alma López—all targets of political and moral attack—as if their art does the same work. Stepping back from the dominant culture wars framing of these battles allows us to ask how such categorizing works—and in whose interests—and how it continues to shape how and what we see.

Most immediately, this culture wars framing subsumes gender and sexuality into "moral" issues, which in turn become the province of "religion"—and it becomes the job of religion to maintain moral decency. This framing scripts the myriad feminist and queer visions of gender, sexual, and racial justice, and of pleasure, outside the bounds of moral decency and religious life. Even more, this script presumes such activist and artistic endeavors to be secular, at best, if not anti-religious, relativistic, or even nihilistic. This is the right-wing fantasy that feminists and queer people can only exist outside of religious and moral worlds; it is more projection than reality.

Second Thesis

The rhetoric of the culture wars operates with a particular habit of interpretation, an aesthetics of literalism, that reduces visual culture to language—and to a specific theory of language.

Note, for instance, how readily Donohue and Savage reduced visual culture to the model of speech in the example above. Of course, such understandings of "hate speech" or free speech emerge from a particular history of legal discourse in the United States, in which "speech" covers a wide range of speech acts and behaviors.[9] But, as we have seen, this approach also reduces visual and performance art to a specific understanding of language—one that understands language (and now images) to be easily readable, partly because this approach presumes language to be fundamentally representational rather than expressive or performative. This approach also assumes representation is either sincere or insincere. This underlying way of interpreting images has allowed for two things to happen over the history of the US culture wars.

First, it provides the cultural logic by which Islam and Christianity—or Muhammad and Jesus—become interchangeable terms in debates over representation. Arguing that artistic images of Jesus and Muhammad are comparable, if not also substitutable, as Savage and Donohue propose, sidelines the historically and theologically different roles these figures occupy in Christian and Islamic traditions. Granted, this logic works differently for Savage than for Donohue. For Savage, both Jesus and Muhammad are merely religious symbols, tokens of belief (and, for the secularist Savage, incorrect beliefs), that we should have the freedom to mock as we see fit. That one can mock Christian symbols without fear of violence even becomes, for Savage, a sign of civilizational progress. Donohue also understands Jesus and Muhammad as similar kinds of religious symbols. Granting him maximum generosity, the logic of his claim would lead us to think both should be respected, though he presumably finds one to symbolize true religion and the other false. Savage and Donohue both assume a representational model of language and join a longer history of religious comparison.

The presumed substitutability of religious symbols—and Muhammad and Jesus, specifically—stems in part from how we talk about and compare religions as such, a scholarly and popular discourse that emerged from older and often colonialist assumptions about "world religions."[10] This approach has come under considerable criticism, and rightly so. It risks reducing religions to different flavors of the same thing—essentially alike save for minor differences that make for interesting comparison and contrast. But the notion that "religions" are basically alike and comparable is often more of a modern fiction than a reality—and attention to the historical and lived dimensions of religion often reveals the problems with the world religions approach. What we call "Islam" and "Christianity," in this sense, are best understood in their particular historical and local traditions. And, especially important for this discussion, we should note the quite different roles that Muhammad and Jesus occupy within these diverse traditions.

Most Christians in the United States, for instance, consider Jesus to be both human and divine. For Muslims, Muhammad is not Allah but rather his messenger. We should also ask how Christians and Muslims have oriented themselves to these figures, what roles they play, and how they have or have not been represented visually, aurally, materially, and textually. Not without contestation, Christians have long depicted Jesus in painting and other artistic forms; they have conjured Christ in dramatic and filmic productions; and they have understood Jesus as one among us. Different habits of representation have shaped Islamic understandings of the divine and of the Prophet. While written depictions of Muhammad have a long history, many Muslims forbid visual representations of the Prophet, although they are not entirely absent.[11] Christians and Muslims, in other words, have different traditions and habits for approaching representations of Jesus and Muhammad. To consider Muhammad and Jesus not only as mere symbols, but also as comparable symbols, presumes an understanding of discrete religions (or religious symbols) as variable permutations of a common kind; it requires a willful misunderstanding of the roles these figures have occupied within Islamic and Christian histories.

Second, the rhetoric of the culture wars implicitly figures sincere forms of representation against ones that are either sacrilegious (for Donohue) or satirical (for Savage). This approach limits us to a representational model in terms of how people relate to words or images, and it forecloses relations to representation that do not conform to the binary of sincerity versus insincerity. Reflecting on the Danish cartoons, Mahmood calls this approach a "rather impoverished understanding of images, icons, and signs" that "fails to attend to the affective and embodied practices through which a subject comes to relate to a particular sign—a relationship founded not only on representation but also on what I will call attachment and cohabitation."[12] Mahmood sets aside the terms of blasphemy versus free speech in analyzing the Danish cartoon controversy to understand, instead, the sense of "moral injury" that some Muslims felt in seeing these depictions of Muhammad. She looks not to histories of representation—and not to claims that these cartoons broke a prohibition against representing Muhammad—but rather to the ways that some Muslims relate to Muhammad, to the different styles of "attachment and cohabitation" that fall outside the normative ways we understand representation. In other words, Mahmood prompts us to consider the multiple ways that people relate to religious symbols. Consider, for instance, how Ray Navarro's Jesus drag plays with the very boundaries between sincerity and insincerity, or how Renée Cox's manifestation as Christ follows a longer history of gendered and racial reimaginings of the Son of God, which she overlays with the humor of a "yo mama" joke. It takes a great deal of interpretative work to reduce such examples to the binary rhetoric of the culture wars or to the terms of sincerity versus sacrilege.

Third Thesis

In the modern culture wars, we tend to privilege religion as a site of identity and to overlook alternative ways that religious power operates or what it might mean to live under the shadow of something like Christian culture or even Christian secularism.

Today, religion is often understood as a kind of identity. Religious identity may be determined by self-description or ascribed to others through assumptions about how people might have described themselves. Of course, we should not ignore the claims people make about their religious (or secular) identities, but this normative model of religion-as-identity is not the only way we can or should understand the work of religion, including the question of whether one is "inside" or "outside" of religion or of a particular religion—especially when it comes to people living on the margins of society.[13] Let me offer an example.

When I introduce Serrano's *Piss Christ* in the classroom, some of my students immediately worry the image may offend Christians. After looking at the photograph, we read a quotation from Serrano: "I had no idea *Piss Christ* would get the attention it did, since I meant neither blasphemy nor offense by it. I've been a Catholic all my life, so I am a follower of Christ. But I'm an artist, and the role of the artist is to break new ground for himself and for his audience."[14] That Serrano identifies as an insider, as a Christian, is often enough to diffuse anxieties that his work is offensive. It seems far worse for an outsider to appropriate a religious symbol than for an insider to subvert one. And this is fair—it allows us to consider different forms of appropriation or subversion. But I also wonder, as do many of my students, if we can hold space for other ways of thinking about what it means to fall "within" Christianity?

Toward this end, Wojnarowicz provides a more interesting example—a harder one to assimilate to common assumptions about religion and identity. Although he grew up with formal connections to Roman Catholicism, through his father and schooling, Wojnarowicz not only distanced himself from the idea that he was a "believing" Catholic but also actively criticized organized religion, and the Catholic Church specifically. From one perspective, he appears to be a cultural Catholic at best, if not an eventual outsider. If we step away from identity-based approaches to naming the Catholic, though—if we hold space to ask about people who might not name themselves as Catholic, or who do so with ambivalence, and who certainly would not be considered Catholic by many of their opponents—then we might see how Catholicism has nonetheless provided Wojnarowicz a rich visual and ritual vocabulary. This is the Catholic vocabulary I want to know more about.

In this sense, Catholicism is not merely a matter of how one identifies oneself but also a language one speaks, the chill one gets walking into a cathedral, perhaps even the fear one has when his body shakes and tears run down his cheeks as he crumbles a consecrated communion wafer in protest, as one AIDS activist did during the "Stop the Church" demonstration at St. Patrick's. Taking "Catholic" outside the register of identity opens ways to consider and expand the terrain of Catholic (or Christian, or religious) history, but only if we can learn to see it. As a queer man living under the cultural authority of the Archdiocese of New York and within the Christian culture of the United States, Wojnarowicz hardly lived "outside" of Christianity, even though he may not have understood himself as a devout or practicing Catholic. Moreover, it would not make much sense to claim that his appropriation of Christian iconography is that of an outsider—he was most certainly not an outsider to the cultural and political power of Christianity nor to the ways its visual and ritual vocabulary have shaped modern subjectivity, including sexual identity.

Would it be different had Wojnarowicz filmed ants crawling over Muhammad? Absolutely. Not because of a double standard, though, as Donohue claims—not because it is simply okay to criticize Christians but not Muslims. Beyond the different histories of visual culture in Islamic and Christian traditions, it is important that Wojnarowicz lived in a country that was (and remains) culturally Christian, in a moment when the Christian Right had grown vocal and politically powerful, and in a city where leaders in the Catholic Church wielded moral and political sway over AIDS policy, reproductive rights, and sex education. Reducing religion to identity, to insiders versus outsiders, obscures these contexts and safeguards religion from questions of power.

Many of the artists discussed in this book had complicated relationships to Christianity or, in the case of Sheree Rose and Judy Chicago, were not raised Christian to start with. But they were all conversant to various degrees with Christian forms, with particular iconographies and rituals, that animated their creative work just as they have shaped centuries of visual and performance art. They had to be. Sometimes, they blended these forms with others, including Jewish, New Age feminist, Hopi, spiritualist, and Africana religious forms. These artists at times employed their diverse and creative engagements with religious symbols and iconography to critique the conservative Christian politics that shaped their lives. But quite often their diverging visions were haunted by those same forms, reworking them into alternative myths, into new ways of imagining the world.

Forms and their Afterlives

A decade into the AIDS crisis, with the mounting loss of friends, family, and lovers—and no cure or treatment in sight—members of the AIDS Coalition to Unleash Power, or ACT UP, announced a political funeral to take place in Washington, DC. It would be held on Sunday, October 11, 1992 to coincide with a display of the NAMES Project AIDS Memorial Quilt on the National Mall. A flier for ACT UP's event explained the political funeral would augment the representational and more sentimental politics of the quilt, which featured panels for loved ones who died from AIDS. "We will carry the actual ashes of people we love in funeral procession to the White House," it read: "In an act of grief and rage and love, we will deposit their ashes on the White House lawn."[15]

The immediate idea for the action came from David Robinson's intention to send the ashes of his partner Warren to President George H. W. Bush. When fellow activists heard this plan, they decided to honor Robinson's partner with an even grander gesture, one inspired by David Wojnarowicz. His 1991 memoir *Close to the Knives* captured the anger and frustration of those living and dying with AIDS. In those pages, he asked, "what it would be like if, each time a lover, friend or stranger died of this disease, their friends, lovers or neighbors would take the dead body and drive with it in a car a hundred miles an hour to Washington DC and blast through the gates of the White House and come to a screeching halt before the entrance and dump their lifeless form on the front steps."[16] The urgency of this plea from Wojnarowicz gave possibility to the "lifeless form" of the AIDS body.

Leading up to the demonstration, ACT UP released a national call for others to join. Members of DIVA TV followed these activists as they planned the demonstration and then marched down the streets of Washington, DC, to the gates of the White House lawn. Their documentary, called *The Ashes Action*, captures the collective joy and humor characteristic of ACT UP. It also records their intense frustration and sorrow as they launched the remains of lovers, friends, and relatives over the fence. Among their many demands, AIDS activists insisted upon the need to make sorrow, frustration, death, and sex into public events. Through their demonstrations, and through their films, their artistic gestures, they refused the politics of privatization. Their rituals, at least some of the most important ones, were collective and public. Publicity was central to their ritual strategy. Another way to say this is to observe how their publicity was liturgical.

ACT UP activists were known for their use of campy street theater and other modes of performance—from dressing as clowns, as members of the troupe Operation Ridiculous did to parody the militant pro-life group Operation Rescue, to staging a mass die-in at St. Patrick's to protest Cardinal John O'Connor and the Roman Catholic hierarchy. But the Ashes Action was a departure. "We weren't going to do anything symbolic," Robinson explained: "The point was these are the actual ashes. This is the literal physical result of the Bush administration's AIDS policies."[17] Fellow activist Ron Goldberg offered a similar take: "This was again '92, and we went from these symbolic die-ins to actually bringing bodies."[18] "There were many political funerals after that," he continued, "because it went from symbolic to the real thing."[19] How can we better attend to the forms of language, symbolism, and ritual through which presence materializes, from this movement between mere representation to the "real thing"?

Perhaps one way to start would be to observe how the AIDS crisis changed the politics and forms of death in US culture—how the "technologies of the HIV/AIDS corpse," as John Erik Troyer termed it, actually, really, changed the medical and cultural politics of death. AIDS corpses were exceptional. Funeral directors debated how to handle them—even whether to handle them. They possessed special powers of pollution, moral and sexual, that exceeded the logics of biomedicine. They challenged the universality of the dead body. They changed how Americans understood the dead body, including its powers of contagion and resurrection.[20] The AIDS body, once dead, became the site of a haunted irruption of resistance at the horizon of modern power over life and death. How does this "lifeless form" persist?

Resurrections

Consider the vision of an icon, literally. His body is draped over a person holding him from behind. His bare chest arches upward. His head has fallen back, his closed eyes pointed to the heavens. The hand of the one who cares for him wraps under his neck to support its heaviness, like cradling a newborn child or embracing a spent lover. His arms have fallen to the sides. His knees are slightly bent. His body is heavy, worn, expired.

The Pietà is one of the most well-known images in the history of Christian art. It depicts a scene from the Lamentation of Christ, though one that isn't described directly in the gospels. Rather, followers have creatively envisioned it. It is a scene that might have happened. It is theology through imagination. Once Jesus is removed from the cross, his mother Mary cradles his dead body. Soon, in Christian tellings, he will rise again. But at this point no one could know what would come of him, except that this lamb has died and his tomb awaits. And that a loved one mourns.

The Pietà is often rendered in sculpture, as in Michelangelo's Carrara marble masterpiece, but also in painting, as in Giovanni Bellini's 1505 *Pietà*. There are more recent versions—Max Ernst's 1923 *Pietà or Revolution by Night* reimagines the iconic image with the artist held by his father; Renée Cox's 1994 photograph *Pietà* shows the artist dressed as Mary cradling a Black man. I want to draw our attention to an image from an unlikely place— the 2017 French film *120 Battements par minute*—rendered in English as *120 BPM (Beats per Minute)*.

Directed by Robin Campillo, *120 BPM* won the Grand Prix at the 2017 Cannes Film Festival. It is loosely based on the experiences of Campillo and his co-screenwriter Philippe Mangeot, who were activists in ACT UP/Paris in the early 1990s. The film uses a documentary aesthetic to take the audience into the complicated, often contentious, but also powerful meetings of the Paris chapter of ACT UP in the early 1990s. Much of the film revolves around two members, Nathan and Sean. The film hardly countenances religion, though France's Catholic secularism haunts many of its scenes.[21] One scene conjures a queer enactment of the Pietà.

The image flashes quickly across the screen. It's easy to miss, this ephemeral presence. The larger scene in which it appears occurs in a hospital in Paris. Sean, the swishy, energetic activist, is dying from an infection related to AIDS. Nathan, who is HIV negative, joined ACT UP/Paris only months before, where he met Sean. They soon developed a romantic and sexual relationship. They talked about moving in together, and Nathan had been preparing his apartment for Sean's arrival. But now Sean is in the hospital, his health quickly deteriorating. He is in constant pain.

At one point during a visit, Nathan walks over to Sean, who is lying in bed, in pain but also aroused by the sight of his lover. He slips his hand under Sean's loose-fitting hospital-issued pants. He starts pleasuring him, offering

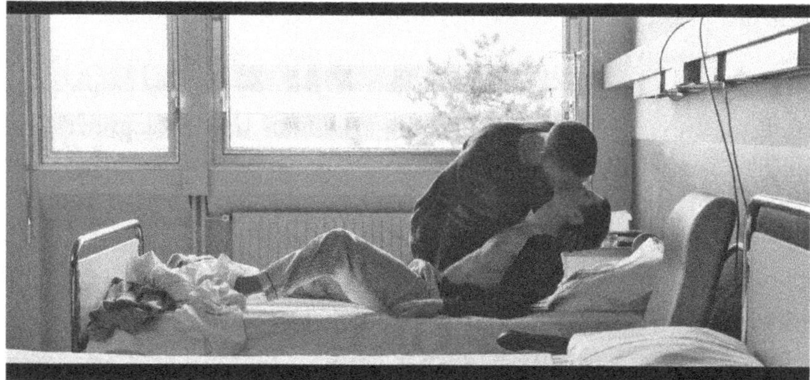

Figure A.1 The film still captures a moment in the film *120 BPM* (2017). Nathan cradles his lover Sean, at a moment of ecstasy, in a shape that evokes the Pietà.

a break from suffering. Sean bends his knees and tilts his head back just as he climaxes, while Nathan cradles his head and kisses him on the mouth. The camera pans out to capture the image—the shape of the Pietà—before moving in for a closer shot of the semen now covering Sean's stomach and chest (Figure A.1).

120 BPM's brief vision of the Pietà may be provocative, but it would not be the first to render the Christ figure so aroused. In *The Sexuality of Christ*, art historian Leo Steinberg argued that portrayals of Christ's unlikely tumescence were common in Renaissance art.[22] Medieval historian Caroline Walker Bynum has noted the difficulty of subsuming such depictions too quickly within a modern understanding of sexuality or eroticism. She finds better visual and textual evidence for thinking about Christ as mother or as food in the many symbolic depictions found in medieval and Renaissance European art. Bynum labels "questionable" Steinberg's argument for images that suggest Christ with an "actual erection under the loincloth."[23] I'm interested in what to make of Bynum's use of the term "actual" to describe a painted erection in Christian art, given her commitment to reading through the multiplicity of Christian symbolism. But I have no doubt that the sexual thrust of *120 BPM*'s imagining differs from that of, say, Willem Key's 1530 *Pietà*. I nonetheless find Steinberg's collection of images helpful for reading the polysemy of queer art and the campy affordances of the risen Christ.

Bynum suggests that the richness of medieval history and theology might "enable modern people to give age-old symbols new meanings that would be in fact medieval." "If we want to turn *from seeing body as sexual to seeing body as generative*, if we want to find symbols that give dignity and meaning to the suffering we cannot eliminate and yet fear so acutely," she writes, beautifully so, "we can find support for doing so in the art and theology of the late Middle Ages."[24] *120 BPM*'s visual materialization of Christ's form—through images of his suffering and joy, the symbolism of his death, and the rituals of care provided by loved ones—offers a way to read the sexual and the generative together, and to do so without subsuming the former (sexuality) to the logic of procreation (generation). It is another queer medievalism, no doubt.

Sean is released from the hospital and goes to Nathan's home, now converted for hospice care, where they are joined by Sean's mother. In the evening, Nathan settles Sean into bed. He prepares his own place to sleep on the floor right next to him. That night, he administers a drug that ends Sean's suffering. The next morning, with the help of some friends (fellow activists in ACT UP/Paris), Sean's mother dresses his lifeless body, and they hold a wake in Nathan's apartment.

120 BPM closes with Sean's friends, fellow AIDS activists, engaged in a political demonstration. They have gathered at a banquet held during a health insurance conference. These uninvited guests quickly transform the occasion into a political funeral, throwing Sean's ashes on the food, decorations, and even various attendees at the dinner party. This was now their dinner party. In the film's final sequence, ashes fly, bureaucrats flee, activists dance, and Nathan makes love to another man. Put differently, politics incites pleasure, history collides with fiction, and forms become myth.

Notes

Introduction

1. Quoted in Fusco, "Sublime Abjection," 174.
2. Quoted in Brustein, "First Amendment and the NEA," 28.
3. Link, *Righteous Warrior*, 363.
4. Of course, an artist could be "secular" and employ religious imagery, though our analytic terms can be more nuanced than this simple division. Here, I'm pointing to a rhetorical framework that is often more normative than descriptive.
5. Buchanan, "Republican National Convention Speech." The spoken version included some minor revisions. Andrew Hartman's indispensable *War for the Soul of America* also begins with Buchanan's speech, which we take in diverging, if complementary, directions.
6. Buchanan, "Republican National Convention Speech."
7. Ibid.
8. These were not the only issues. We could add debates over affirmative action, evolution, multiculturalism, school prayer, the canon wars, sex education, and censorship and the arts. These battles were not the first major skirmishes of their kind, nor did the modern culture wars focus solely on issues of religion, gender, sexuality, and race as opposed to economic or political battles. Although, as I hope this book makes clear, none of these issues exist in isolation. See Dubin, *Arresting Images*; Bolton, *Culture Wars*; Wallis, Weems, and Yenawine, *Art Matters*; Hunter, *Culture Wars*; Hunter and Wolfe, *Is There a Culture War?*; Prothero, *Why Liberals Win*; Griffith, *Moral Combat*; Hartman, *War for the Soul of America*; Rodger, *Age of Fracture*; Du Mez, *Jesus and John Wayne*; Moreton, *To Serve God and Wal-Mart*; Cooper, *Family Values*; Rolsky, *Rise and Fall of the Religious Left*; Self, *All in the Family*; McAlister, *Kingdom of God Has No Borders*; and Zubovich, "U.S. Culture Wars Abroad."
9. I often use "Christian Right," since most of the culture warriors I discuss were Catholic or Protestant. The vast scholarship on the Religious Right includes Harding, *Book of Jerry Falwell*; Williams, *God's Own Party*; Wuthnow, *Restructuring of American Religion*; Young, *We Gather Together*; Dowland, *Family Values*; DeRogatis, *Saving Sex*; Allitt, *Catholic Intellectuals*; Butler, *White Evangelical Racism*; Balmer, *Bad Faith*; Johnson, *This Is Our Message*; and Dochuk, *From Bible Belt to Sunbelt*.
10. Vance, "War on Culture," 230.
11. The diminutive use of "Willie," which Horton seems not to have used himself, only added to the racist politics of these invocations.
12. Major public controversies over art have a longer history in the United States (see Kammen's *Visual Shock*). But public battles that erupted in the late 1980s took on a particular and enduring shape. They were forged out of the racial and sexual revolutions of the 1960s and 1970s, the concomitant rise of the Christian Right, and followed the creation of the NEA itself in 1965. These were not incidental, but indeed essential, to the political fights sparked in the 1980s, which focused disproportionately on art dealing with gender, sexuality, and religion.
13. Wilbur, *Funding Bodies*, 246n16. The NEA received around $170 million from Congress in 1989 and 1990. Once Republicans gained control of Congress in 1994, that number dropped to the high 90s, and eliminating the NEA altogether was a goal in Newt Gingrich and Dick Armey's 1995 *Contract with America*. "NEA Appropriations History."
14. Brustein, "First Amendment and the NEA"; Brensen, *Visionaries and Outcasts*; and O'Neil, "Artists, Rights, and Grants."
15. Pat Buchanan, "Losing the War for America's Culture?," *Washington Times*, May 22, 1989, in Bolton, *Culture Wars*, 32–33.
16. The ad is quoted in Marsha Ginsburg, "Buchanan Ad a Distortion, Filmmaker Says," *San Francisco Examiner*, March 11, 1992 (Marlon Riggs Papers, hereafter MRP, Box 110, Folder 6).
17. Ginsburg, "Buchanan Ad;" K. C. Wildmoon, "Buchanan Commercial Bashes Gays and the NEA," *Southern Voice*, March 4–11, 1992, 1, 4 (MRP, Box 110, Folder 6).

18. Marlon Riggs, "Tongues Re-tied?," *Current*, August 12, 1991, 17 (MRP, Box 107, Folder 4). The film also includes people who are transfeminine and gender queer (to use more contemporary language). See Gossett and Hayward, "Kiyan Williams: An Interview."

19. David Mills, "The Director with Tongues Untied," *Washington Post*, June 15, 1992.

20. Don Kowet, "PBS Turns TV Rooms into Gay-Strip Film Houses," *Washington Times*, July 16, 1991 (MRP, Box 107, Folder 4).

21. American Family Association, "For Immediate Release: Two Hundred PBS Stations Refuse to Air Offensive Film," press release, July 1, 1991 (MRP, Box 106, Folder 2). Wildmon is quoted in Frank J. Prial, "TV Film about Gay Black Men is Under Attack," *New York Times*, June 25, 1991, C13.

22. Christian Coalition, letter to members of the US House of Representatives, September 27, 1991 (MRP, Box 106, Folder 2).

23. Ginsburg, "Buchanan Ad."

24. Marlon Riggs, "Meet the New Willie Horton," *New York Times*, March 6, 1992 (MRP, Box 110, Folder 6).

25. Quoted in Ginsburg, "Buchanan Ad" and Riggs, "Meet the New Willie Horton."

26. Riggs did not miss the irony in Buchanan using the same tactics Bush had used to defeat Michael Dukakis in 1988. Riggs, "Meet the New Willie Horton."

27. Ginsburg, "Buchanan Ad."

28. Signifyin' Works, "Filmmaker Charges Buchanan with Copyright Infringement," press release, March 6, 1992 (MRP, Box 110, Folder 7).

29. Riggs, "Tongues Re-Tied?"

30. Theresa Shea, "Film about Gay Blacks Shown," *Herald-Sun* (Durham, NC), July 17, 1991, C1, C7 (MRP, Box 107, Folder 4).

31. Ibid.

32. On the longer history of art, homosexuality, and decadence, see Hanson, *Decadence and Catholicism*.

33. Hartman calls the period between WWII and the assassination of John F. Kennedy "normative America," an age of compliance when "an unprecedented number of Americans got in line—or aspired to get in line—particularly white, heterosexual, Christian Americans." *War for the Soul of America*, 5.

34. Bailey, *Sex in the Heartland*; Self, *All in the Family*; Dowland, *Family Values*; and Prothero, *Why Liberals Win*.

35. Dailey, "Sex, Segregation, and the Sacred after *Brown*" and Griffith, *Moral Combat*, 83–120. On links between the pro-life movement and busing, see Frank, "Colour of the Unborn."

36. Freedman, *No Turning Back*; Cott, *Grounding of Modern Feminism*; Smith, *Righteous Rhetoric*; and Critchlow, *Phyllis Schlafly and Grassroots Conservatism*. On the longer history of the pro-life movement, see Williams, *Defenders of the Unborn*.

37. Faderman, *Gay Revolution*; Gill-Peterson, *Histories of the Transgender Child*; and Stryker, *Transgender History*.

38. Key changes in religion and law were also taking place. The Supreme Court ruled school prayer unconstitutional in 1962's *Engel v. Vitale*—and again the following year when *Abington School District v. Schempp* outlawed Bible devotionals in public schools. Where conservative Christians saw God being banned from schools, others saw the courts protecting the rights of religious minorities and nonbelievers.

39. Bork, *Slouching Towards Gomorrah*, 140. On culture wars debates about rap, hip-hop, punk rock, and gaming, see Ogbar, "Slouching Toward Bork"; Mattson, *We're Not Here to Entertain*; and Laycock, *Dangerous Games*.

40. Quoted in National Endowment for the Arts v. Finley, 524 US 569 (1998), 574.

41. Selcraig, "Reverend Wildmon's War on the Arts" and Dedman, "Bible Belt Blowhard," 41.

42. Sally Mann also came under fire for photographing nude children—this time, they were her own. No doubt, it is important to debate the ethics of taking photos of children, even with parental consent. The Right consistently and immediately conflated Mann's and Mapplethorpe's photographs with child pornography, which proved an easy way to sensationalize moral panic, even though the images themselves, given their formal qualities and contexts, clearly resist such sexualized readings.

43. Quoted in Maureen Dowd, "Unruffled Helms Basks in Eye of Arts Storm," *New York Times*, July 28, 1989.

44. Quoted in National Endowment for the Arts v. Finley, 524 US 569 (1998), 575.

45. Four artists, called the "NEA Four" (Karen Finley, Tim Miller, Holly Hughes, and John Fleck), filed a lawsuit when NEA Chair John Frohnmayer revoked their funding, which had been approved through a process of peer review, in 1990. They amended their complaint to also challenge the "decency clause" added in Section 954(d)(1).

46. Phyllis Schlafly, "It's Obscene to Call Such Stuff 'Art,'" *Schlafly Report*, May 1990, 1.

47. Dana Rohrabacher, "Shield the Taxpayers from Funding Trash," *USA Today*, March 27, 1990, 10A.

48. The Heritage Foundation, "The National Endowment for the Arts Misusing Taxpayers' Money," *Backgrounder*, January 18, 1991, 21–28, quoted in Dubin, *Arresting Images*, 46–47. Weyrich was raised Roman Catholic but switched to the Melkite Greek Catholic Church after the changes brought by Vatican II. See Patricia Sullivan, "A Father of Modern Conservative Movement," *Washington Post*, December 19, 2008.

49. Bork, *Slouching Towards Gomorrah*, 150.

50. Gaspar de Alba and López, *Our Lady of Controversy*.

51. Later in the 1990s and in the 2000s, the language of "coastal elites" would saturate right-wing attacks.

52. Wallace, "The Culture War within the Culture Wars," 202–14. Of course, race figured into the culture wars in many other ways, too. Sticking with cultural production, the presumed delinquency of rap was a common site of attack in which racist assumptions were often barely veiled. We could add, too, debates over multiculturalism, affirmative action, the war on drugs, the expansion of the carceral state, the surge of Islamophobia after 9/11, and perennial debates over immigration (particularly of people of color).

53. This book joins a rich conversation about religion, art, and visual culture. See Promey, *Religion in Plain View* and "'Return' of Religion in the Scholarship of American Art;" Plate, *Blasphemy*; Morgan and Promey, *Visual Culture of American Religions*; Promey, *Painting Religion in Public*; Morgan, *Protestants and Pictures*; Morgan, *Forge of Vision*; Doss, *Spiritual Moderns*; Heartney, *Postmodern Heretics*; Elkins and Morgan, *Re-Enchantment*; Elkins, *On the Strange Place of Religion in Modern Art*; Gonzalez Rice, *Long Suffering*; Coates, *What Is Protestant Art?*; and Worley, *Memento Mori*.

54. Here, I agree with and build upon Stephen Prothero's claim that the culture wars are "conservative dramas in which liberals are merely props." *Why Liberals Win*, 13. My further question is how and why that drama figures into scholarly assessments.

55. Jakobsen, *Sex Obsession*; Frank, Moreton, and White, *Devotions and Desires*; and Coviello, *Make Yourselves Gods*.

56. See White, *Reforming Sodom*; Wilcox, "Words Kill"; Wilcox, *Queer Religiosities*; Brintnall, *Ecce Homo*; Greene-Hayes, "'Queering' African American Religious History"; Jordan, *Recruiting Young Love*; McGarry, *Ghosts of Futures Past*; Krutzsch, *Dying to Be Normal*; and Petro, "Religion."

57. Hunter, *Culture Wars*, 43–44. Diane Winston offers a fascinating account of the development of the culture wars in mainstream news in "Back to the Future: Religion, Politics, and the Media."

58. Hunter, *Culture Wars*, 248.

59. To be sure, Hunter's "orthodox" impulse also calls for more nuance. But historians and sociologists of religion have been far more attentive to coloring in the many different facets of the Right, including diverging movements of conservative Protestantism and, to a lesser degree, politically conservative movements within Catholicism, Mormonism, and Judaism. Within the history of US religion, though, there remain far fewer studies of radical or progressive voices in the modern culture wars. And we have barely even begun to incorporate (or in many cases even to acknowledge) the moral, spiritual, and political visions of feminist and queer artists and activists into these histories.

60. The bellicose culture wars metaphor and its central binary call for richer psychoanalytic and gender analysis. Note how Hunter's approach rests on a central division between singular and plural. This division mirrors gendered ways of thinking about conservatism, and even literalism (see chapter three), as clear, direct, and masculine while progressive approaches appear uncentered, changeable on the whims of science, or even wishy-washy. This is partly because the two sides—as two—are incommensurate. The better comparison would be between a conservative impulse and any one of the many progressivist approaches.

61. There is another methodological criticism. Hunter's focus on impulses toward moral authority sneaks in a cognitive approach to culture that many scholars of religion, sociology, and anthropology have routinely marked as emerging from normative Protestant assumptions about belief

and that leaves out the ways that habits shape both individual experience and normative culture. See, e.g., Asad, *Geneaologies of Religion.*

62. Hunter, *Culture Wars*, 237, italics mine.
63. Noah, "Armey's Aesthetic," 14. The scene with Pell is described in David Dempsey, "Uncle Sam, the Angel," *New York Times*, March 24, 1974.
64. Hunter, *Culture Wars*, 237.
65. Ibid.
66. Ibid., 238. The notion of "art for art's sake" has a longer history, going back at least to the mid-nineteenth century, but was often associated with fin de siècle Decadents like Oscar Wilde. Hanson, *Decadence and Catholicism*, 14.
67. Quoted in Hunter, *Culture Wars*, 239.
68. Hunter, *Culture Wars*, 248–49.
69. Ibid., 248.
70. Wolfe was highly critical of modernist art and what he took as the elitism of the art world, including critics like Clement Greenberg. I don't need to tell readers from the world of art history, though, that there is a huge gulf between Greenberg and, say, Sheree Rose, Ray Navarro, or David Wojnarowicz. See Wolfe, *Painted Word.*
71. To be fair, many modernist artists also rejected conventional characterizations of modernist art.
72. Steiner, "Introduction: Below Skin-deep," 12.
73. Ibid., 13.
74. Quoted in Fusco, "Sublime Abjection," 174, 176.
75. Andres Serrano's *Piss Christ* and Robert Mapplethorpe's exhibition *The Perfect Moment* have become synonymous with this history of the culture wars. They come up around the edges in this project, but here I want to expand our archive to include a broader set of artists, contexts, and genres.
76. Rodriguez-Plate, *Blasphemy*, 50.
77. This list is hardly exhaustive. My argument is not that all these techniques were conscious or intentional; sometimes they were and sometimes they were not. Nor am I arguing that they were performed earnestly—there is no question that many conservatives acted in bad faith, seeking to score points and gain donations by riling their bases. I'm less interested in mapping conservative volition (or trickery) than I am in surfacing the discursive frameworks and habits of seeing and unseeing that shaped these public debates.
78. We might even gesture toward the emergence of a kind of literalist performativity.
79. Rambuss, "Sacred Subjects"; Rambuss, *Closet Devotions*; Jordan, *Silence of Sodom*; and Heartney, *Postmodern Heretics*. On the longer histories of such engagements, see Bynum, *Jesus as Mother*; Bynum, *Fragmentation and Redemption*; and Steinberg, *Sexuality of Christ in Renaissance Art.*
80. Heartney, *Postmodern Heretics*, 24–25. Of course, Protestants have their own bodily traditions and visual aesthetics, and some artists have drawn upon Protestantism in their artist work, as in the Pentecostal-inflected work of performance artist Ron Athey. See Petro, "Playing Pentecostal"; Gonzalez Rice, *Long Suffering*, 59–88; and Promey, "Pictorial Ambivalence and American Protestantism." On Keith Haring, see Heartney, *Doomsday Dreams* and Montez, *Keith Haring's Line.*
81. Morgan, *Visual Piety.*
82. In the study of US religion, we sometimes struggle to make sense of parodic or ironic gestures, in part because the field emerged from and still largely privileges histories of Protestant Christianity and its accompanying normative earnestness. Notable exceptions include Wilcox, *Queer Nuns*; Caplan, *Funny, You Don't Look Funny*; Booker, " 'Pulpit and Pew' "; Wright, "Comic Belief"; and Brehm, *America's Most Famous Catholic.*
83. McCrary's *Sincerely Held* examines genealogies of sincerity, secularism, and religious freedom in the United States, as does Sullivan's *Impossibility of Religious Freedom.*
84. See Asad, *Genealogies of Religion* and Hall, *Lived Religion in America.*
85. Religion often works as a category of identity, but I hope to show the many other ways it operates, too.
86. See Lofton, "Why Religion Is Hard for Historians." We hear in such accounts older Protestant criticisms of Catholics robotically following rituals rather than forging sincere, ostensibly authentic, religious attachments. Obviously, many of these culture warriors acted in bad faith. They performed outrage not only to foment frustration but also to raise funding and to galvanize voters, even if that meant stretching the truth—or reinventing it to meet their needs. The

ironies abound—a movement that attacks the left for moral relativism plays hard and fast with the truth. I want to insist, though, that for scholars of religion, such actions are not antithetical to "real" religion.

87. Of course, bad faith uses of religion are still uses of religion to which scholars ought attend.

Chapter 1

1. Quoted in Cooper, "Bob's Thing."
2. Quoted in Kardon, "Robert Mapplethorpe Interview," 25.
3. Rose has criticized Dick for not giving her and Flanagan proper credit for their role in the film's creation. Rose, "Why Kirby Dick Is a 'Sick' Prick."
4. McRuer, *Crip Theory*, 187.
5. Quoted in Takemoto, "Love Is Still Possible," 96–97.
6. Bob Flanagan, "13 October 1990 Chelsea Hotel Raymond Foye interviews Bob Flanagan" (Sheree Rose and Bob Flanagan Papers and Photographs Collection (hereafter SRBF), Box 3), 5. This collection was only partly processed when I visited, but I include as much identifying information as possible.
7. McRuer, *Crip Theory*, 194. Gonzalez Rice's *Long Suffering* also offers a useful model for thinking about Flanagan and Rose; see, especially, her chapter on Ron Athey.
8. Garland-Thomson, "Seeing the Disabled," 358.
9. McRuer, *Crip Theory*, especially 171–98. In *Crip Times*, McRuer describes how *crip* was reclaimed by many disabled people themselves (from the derogatory *cripple*) and "has functioned for many as a marker of an in-your-face, or out-and-proud, cultural model of disability," as opposed to the medical model, which reduces disability to pathology in need of treatment, or certain versions of the social model of disability, which focuses not on bodies but on environments that are inaccessible (19). On crip culture and humor, see Clare, *Exile and Pride*, especially 81–85.
10. See Orsi, "'Mildred, Is It Fun to Be a Cripple?'"; Kane, "'She Offered Herself Up'"; Gerber, *Seeking the Straight and Narrow*; Jakobsen and Pellegrini, *Love the Sin*; Griffith, *Born Again Bodies*; and Petro, "Disability Studies and Religion."
11. Not exclusively—he also plays with medical forms, for instance, sometimes combining them with religious ones.
12. Sheree Rose, "In Sickness and in Health: Blurring the Boundaries in Pre-Millennial Relationships," October 11, 1996 (SRBF, Papers Box 1 (notebooks)).
13. Ibid., italics mine.
14. Rose explains that Flanagan converted to Judaism at the end of his life. The two never married and worried his parents might have claimed his body after he died. But after converting, she continued, it would be clear he wanted a Jewish burial service. Rose describes performing Jewish rituals after his death with a female rabbi. Rose, interview with Shira Tarrant, "Ouch! I Love You. Bob Flanagan/Sheree Rose: Life and Art Together," unpublished transcript (SRBF, Papers Box 2, Folder: Sheree Rose Interview (1988)), 14–15.
15. Flanagan, "13 October 1990 Chelsea Hotel Raymond Foye Interviews Bob Flanagan," 6. His mention of the sonnets references his book of poetry called *Slave Sonnets*.
16. The interview, and this conversation, appears in Cooper, "Bob's Thing."
17. Dimock, "Theory of Resonance."
18. Dana Rohrabacher, "Shield the Taxpayers from Funding Trash," *USA Today*, March 27, 1990, 10A; Heritage Foundation, "The National Endowment for the Arts Misusing Taxpayers' Money," *Backgrounder*, January 18, 1991, 24, quoted in Dubin, *Arresting Images*, 46–47.
19. My analysis is necessarily partial. Rose deserves more consideration, including attention to her commitments to Judaism and how they shaped her work with Flanagan. I should also underline the importance of taking up this work *as performance* and considering its place within performance studies—directions that one could push further. As Diana Taylor writes, "performances function as vital acts of transfer, transmitting social knowledge, memory, and a sense of identity" through repeated behavior. *Archive and the Repertoire*, 2. Here, I want to emphasize how performance, like religion, works within the social.
20. To clarify, we need not oppose a sentimental take to a more serious, rigorous one. But a sentimental humanism has become unmarked, indeed *too* effective, in much of our scholarly work. This tender focus on humanist agency is not unique to religion (or lived religion) and likely says more about the political and theoretical trends in scholarship since the 1980s that (importantly and productively) countered the totalizing and reductive analyses of some Marxist and poststructuralist critiques. Feminist anthropologists, though, have convincingly criticized the

"romance of resistance" and presumptions of a volitional, liberal subject at the center of scholarship that celebrates resistance and agency (see Abu-Lughod, "Romance of Resistance" and Mahmood, *Politics of Piety*). Our frustrations with determinant approaches (Marxist ones, for instance) need not lead us to finding and celebrating all manner of subversive creativity or presuming a particular liberal subject without attending as well to issues of power, the limits of individual agency, and ways religion operates outside the immediate, conscious control of human subjects. Many studies of US religion offer excellent models for keeping the power of social forces in view, including Griffith, *Born Again Bodies*; Goldschmidt, *Race and Religion among the Chosen People of Crown Heights*; Mehta, *Beyond Chrismukkah*; Weisenfeld, *New World A-Coming*; Iwamura, *Virtual Orientalism*; McAlister, *Epic Encounters*; and Sullivan, *Impossibility of Religious Freedom*.

21. The phrasing about strategy draws from Newton, "Role Models," 46.

22. Ferraro, "Not-Just-Cultural Catholics," 9.

23. Ibid., italics mine.

24. Ibid.

25. Heartney, *Postmodern Heretics*. Rodriguez-Plate's *Blasphemy*, while not focused specifically on Catholicism or the United States, also discusses much of this history, placing "offensive" art in broader religious and art historical contexts.

26. Greeley, *Catholic Imagination*, 3.

27. Tracy's *Analogical Imagination* offers a powerful argument for the place of theology, and theological truth, not opposed to pluralism but fully in support of it. Art enters his analysis in interesting ways. Describing one's encounter with art and literature, he writes: "somehow the classics endure as provocations awaiting the risk of reading: to challenge our complacency, to break our conventions, to compel and concentrate our attention, to lure us out of a privacy masked as autonomy into a public realm where what is important and essential is no longer denied." Tracy argues that art—this encounter with art, with its truth—is public, and the different interpretations it may yield contribute to our meaningful pluralism. "Whenever we actually experience even one classic work of art, we are," he continues, "liberated from privateness into the genuine publicness of a disclosure of truth." *Analogical Imagination*, 115.

28. Greeley, *Catholic Imagination*, 5.

29. Ibid., 9.

30. Ibid., 184.

31. Ibid., 2.

32. Ibid., 7.

33. Ibid., 57.

34. Ibid., 62, 70.

35. Giles, *American Catholic Arts and Fiction*, 1, 174. He leans more on Tracy than Greeley (whose *Catholic Imagination* was published after Giles's book), though both authors appear (see 16–17 and 27–29). This book could be read in productive tension with Fisher, *Catholic Counterculture* and McDannell, *Catholics in the Movies*.

36. Leighton, *On Form*, 1.

37. Williams, *Marxism and Literature*, 186.

38. See also Levine, *Forms*, 2.

39. Leighton, *On Form*, 2.

40. In addition to Levine, see Best and Marcus, "Surface Reading"; Love, "Close but not Deep"; and Felski, "'Context Stinks!'" On the hermeneutics of suspicion, see Ricœur, *Freud and Philosophy*.

41. See n20. I focus here on the study of religion in the United States because it is my primary field and because scholars of North American religion have made important theoretical and methodological interventions through work on "lived religion" and on ways to rethink religion in volumes such as Tweed's *Retelling U.S. Religious History*—conversations I hope this work will join. But my own disciplinary parochialism should not be mistaken for the parochialism of religious forms, whose circulations and resonances, across history and around the globe, prove quite the opposite. See, e.g., McLaughlin et al., "Why Scholars Must Investigate the Corporate Form."

42. Chan-Malik, *Being Muslim*, 23.

43. Sorett, *Spirit in the Dark*, 9.

44. Kaell, "Seeing the Invisible," 139.

45. Seitz, "Altars of Ammo," 403.

46. Ibid., 404.

47. To clarify, these scholars do not all use form to the same ends or as part of an intentional shift in our analytic vocabulary. But the resonance of form as an analytic category across these examples signals its purchase for future research. Additional examples include Gonzalez Rice's *Long Suffering*, which similarly thinks through religious forms in performance art, and Lofton's *Oprah* and *Consuming Religion*, which reveal how religious forms animate much of American sociality, including popular culture.
48. Levine, *Forms*, 3.
49. Ibid., 4–5.
50. Ibid., 6.
51. Derrida, "Signature, Event, Context" and Hollywood, "Performativity, Citationality, Ritualization."
52. This attention to religious forms thus accents a different current within studies of lived religion, emphasizing how religious practices, even at their most creative or subversive, do not spring sui generis from minds or bodies but instead draw from other practices, from older forms.
53. Quoted in Kardon, "Robert Mapplethorpe Interview," 25. On Mapplethorpe and form, see Brintnall, *Ecce Homo*, 101–34.
54. The robust and growing scholarship on disability, including its intersections with gender, sexuality, religion, race, and performance, includes Kafer, *Feminist, Queer, Crip*; Samuels, *Fantasies of Identification*; Schumm and Stoltzfus, *Disability in Judaism, Christianity, and Islam*; Bell, *Blackness and Disability*; McKelvey, *Disability Works*; Elman, *Chronic Youth*; Imhoff, "Why Disability Studies Needs to Take Religion Seriously"; and Walker-Cornetta, "Without the Lord."
55. Garland-Thomson, "Seeing the Disabled," 335–74.
56. Ibid., 338.
57. Ibid., 339–44.
58. Ibid., 358.
59. Ibid., 372.
60. McRuer, *Crip Theory*, ch. 5.
61. Ibid., 181.
62. Ibid., 183, 188.
63. Ibid., 183.
64. My language here cribs Sedgwick's canonical descriptions of the homo/hetero binary in the modern West in *Epistemology of the Closet* (1). In *Body Art*, Amelia Jones comes closer to what I'm arguing, noting how "Flanagan ritualized his pain through performances that borrow from and transgress the flamboyant fetishization of suffering and martyrdom in the Catholic tradition" (229–30).
65. It is commonplace to observe the overlap between Catholicism and S/M, but nonetheless important to flag how Flanagan's interest in S/M performance emerges from much longer histories of body mortification in Catholicism and in the history of sexuality. See Largier, *In Praise of the Whip*.
66. Orsi, "'Mildred,'" 19–47.
67. Ibid., 36.
68. Ibid., 24–25.
69. Kane, "'She Offered Herself Up,'" 80–119.
70. Juno and Vale, "Introduction," in Juno and Vale, *Bob Flanagan*, 6.
71. Ibid.
72. Flanagan, "Interview One," in Juno and Vale, *Bob Flanagan*, 10–29.
73. See Dick, *Sick*.
74. Flanagan, "Why?," reproduced in Juno and Vale, *Bob Flanagan*, 64–65.
75. Rose, "Why Not?," unpublished (SRBF, Papers Box 3), in Howard, *Rated RX*, 38–41.
76. Quoted in Scarborough, "Coffins and Cameras," 123.
77. Ibid., 124.
78. Rose, "Ouch! I Love You," 30.
79. Rose describes this scene in Scarborough, "Coffins and Cameras," 123.
80. As opposed to the confession of faith, that is. Jordan, *Convulsing Bodies*, 135. See Foucault, *About the Beginning of the Hermeneutics of the Self.*
81. Jordan, *Convulsing Bodies*, 142–51 and Foucault, *About the Beginning*, 59–60.
82. This performance work could usefully be compared to that of Ron Athey. See, e.g., Jones and Campbell, *Queer Communion* and Petro, "Playing Pentecostal."
83. McRuer, *Crip Theory*, 186.

Chapter 2

1. Quoted in Gerhard, *Dinner Party*, 144.
2. Quoted in Vicky Chen Haider, "Chicago's Butterfly," *Chicago Sun-Times*, June 19, 1975, 81.
3. The Brooklyn Museum hosts a wonderful digital display of *The Dinner Party*; see "The Dinner Party," Brooklyn Museum, https://www.brooklynmuseum.org/eascfa/dinner_party/home. Also see Chicago, *The Dinner Party: Restoring Women to History*, a book celebrating the installation of Chicago's work at the Brooklyn Museum.
4. Lippard, "Uninvited Guests."
5. Rep. Dana Rohrabacher, quoted in Jonetta Rose Barras, "D.C. Council's 'Sanity' Question as Hill Learns," *Washington Times*, July 19, 1990, A1. See also Levin, *Becoming Judy Chicago*, 371–73.
6. Simon Romero, "A Museum Honoring Judy Chicago, Star of Feminist Art? Not in This 'Sleepy Little Town,'" *New York Times*, December 15, 2018.
7. Quoted in Romero, "Museum Honoring Judy Chicago."
8. Ruth Lopez, "Proposal for a Judy Chicago Museum Divides New Mexico Town," *Art Newspaper*, November 28, 2018, www.theartnewspaper.com.
9. Butterfield, "Guess Who's Coming to Dinner?," 20.
10. On Chicago's cultural feminism, see Gerhard, *Dinner Party*; Jones, "Sexual Politics: Feminist Strategies, Feminist Conflicts, Feminist Histories"; and Jones, "'Sexual Politics' of *The Dinner Party*."
11. See Jones, "'Sexual Politics' of *The Dinner Party*."
12. Sasha Weiss, "Judy Chicago, the Godmother," *New York Times*, February 7, 2018.
13. Taves, *Religious Experience Reconsidered*, 26–35.
14. Penrose, "Ailey School's Tribute to Judy Chicago's 'The Dinner Party'" and Brooklyn Museum, "Alvin Ailey Tribute to The Dinner Party by Judy Chicago." The video, featured on *Elle* magazine's website, is available from the Brooklyn Museum, accessed July 7, 2023, https://www.youtube.com/watch?v=SDiLIuokOUA.
15. DeFrantz, "Composite Bodies of Dance," 659–78.
16. Croft, *Dancers as Diplomats*, 68–69.
17. Eliade, *The Sacred and the Profane*.
18. Hughes, "An Obsessive Feminist Pantheon," 85.
19. See, e.g., "Dinner Party Curriculum Project" and Johanna Demetrakas's 1980 film *Right Out of History*. There would be many additional *Dinner Party* catalogues and studies over the years, including several mentioned in this chapter.
20. Digital images of the banners with Chicago's poem can be found online at Elizabeth A. Sackler Center for Feminist Art, "Entry Banners," Brooklyn Museum, accessed July 7, 2023, https://www.brooklynmuseum.org/eascfa/dinner_party/entry_banners.
21. One name belongs to a man mistaken as a woman.
22. Chicago, *Dinner Party*, 57. Chicago has a few books with this title. I use *Dinner Party* to refer to the original book, which she published to coincide with the 1979 exhibition, *The Dinner Party: A Symbol of Our Heritage*.
23. Ibid.
24. Ibid., 95–96.
25. Butterfield, "Guess Who's Coming to Dinner?," 22.
26. Meyer, "From Finish Fetish to Feminism," 51.
27. Ibid., 53.
28. Chicago, *Through the Flower*, 38–39. Also see Chicago, *Beyond the Flower*, 18–19.
29. Chicago, *Flowering*, 49.
30. Ibid., 98.
31. Meyer, "The Women's Building," 91.
32. Lippard, "Foreword: Going Around in Circles," 12.
33. Chicago, *Through the Flower*, 179 and Lippard, "Judy Chicago's 'Dinner Party,'" 118.
34. Chicago, *Through the Flower*, especially 175–77.
35. Ibid., 178–79.
36. Jones, "Sexual Politics: Feminist Strategies, Feminist Conflicts, Feminist Histories," 26–28.
37. Over the 1970s and 1980s, feminist theorists increasingly disarticulated sex (marking male or female biological difference) from gender (naming cultural norms of masculinity and femininity). Judith Butler's *Gender Trouble* would unsettle even this distinction, arguing that sex itself is already gendered—and was gender all along.
38. Chicago, *Through the Flower*, 54.

39. Ibid., 54–55.

40. Ibid., 55.

41. Meyer, "The Women's Building," 90.

42. Schapiro and Chicago, "Female Imagery," 14.

43. Ibid.

44. Few feminists in the 1970s named themselves sex essentialists—that naming and consequent critique would come from postmodern feminists in the 1980s and 1990s and often reduced the complexity and variation in essentialist feminist thinking to biological terms. My point here is not to defend Chicago's sex/gender essentialism. It's there and open to the many important criticisms that theorists and activists have made, with which I largely agree. But Chicago and others were also trying to ground their experience in the body in ways that were not, even in their own work, reducible to biology. Amelia Jones writes that Chicago is "not a biological essentialist but is invested in cultural essentialism . . . I like Michèle Barrett's take that she is 'somewhat biologistic.'" Jones, "'Sexual Politics' of *The Dinner Party*," 100. See Garrard, "Feminist Art and the Essentialism Controversy" and Fuss, *Essentially Speaking*.

45. Chicago, *Dinner Party*, 8.

46. Ibid., 23.

47. Ibid., 11–12 and Butterfield, "Guess Who's Coming to Dinner?," 22–23.

48. Quoted in Butterfield, "Guess Who's Coming to Dinner?," 22.

49. Chicago distinguished between a collective and a cooperative effort, noting that this work was not collective, since she remained in creative control. See Butterfield, "Guess Who's Coming to Dinner?," 24. This does not mean Chicago did not recognize the great deal of help she received. Members of her cooperative team were thanked explicitly in the exhibition. "Acknowledgment Panels" display the names of hundreds of individuals and organizations who made major contributions to the project. Much of their work together is captured in Demetrakas's film *Right Out of History*.

50. Jane Gerhard has found little truth to these rumors (*Dinner Party*, 18); on the broader process of collaboration, see Jones, "'Sexual Politics' of *The Dinner Party*," 104–8.

51. Chicago often emphasized this point—her focus on Western civilization emerged from a desire to write women into a history typically dominated by men. The idea of "Western civilization" itself is a discursive and often colonialist construction that emerges from specific cultural and political assumptions about what constitutes "the West" and how its genealogy is traced. See, for instance, Federici, *Enduring Western Civilization*.

52. The first women's studies program in the United States was founded at San Diego State University in 1970. Russell, Loftin, and Shayne, "History of San Diego State University's Women's Studies Program"; see also Corbman, "The Scholars and the Feminists."

53. On textiles and art, see Bryan-Wilson's *Fray*.

54. One could claim that trans politics came later and wasn't available to second-wave feminists like Chicago, but that overlooks the long history of trans experience and activism recovered in work by historians like Susan Stryker and Jules Gill-Peterson.

55. Gerhard, *Dinner Party*, 111.

56. Walker, "'One' Child of One's Own," 383.

57. O'Grady, "The Cave."

58. Walker, "'One' Child," 383.

59. Spillers, "Interstices," 157. Also see Musser, *Sensual Excess*, 21–26.

60. Lippard, "Judy Chicago's 'Dinner Party,'" 122.

61. Chicago has responded to many criticisms of *The Dinner Party* over the years. She has defended her focus on the history of Western civilization, explaining that any attempt to do more would require far more time and resources than she had access to. And she has pushed back at critics for complaining about what she left out rather than what she accomplished. But she has also reflected on the limitations of her work in this period, including the move to locate women in the march of history defined on men's terms in a piece that progresses in a linear way. In her most recent memoir, she also explains how emphasizing gender led her to neglect the writing of people of color, "an unforgivable omission on my part." Chicago, *Flowering*, 85; see also 120, 129–31, 165–66.

62. Quoted in Butterfield, "Guess Who's Coming to Dinner?" 24.

63. Butterfield, "Guess Who's Coming to Dinner?" 24.

64. Ibid.

65. Ibid.

66. See Gerhard's discussion, which draws from an interview with Chicago, in *Dinner Party*, 143 and Wylder, "Judy Chicago's *Dinner Party* and *Birth Project* as Religious Symbol and Visual Theology," 13.
67. Chicago, *Birth Project*, 177.
68. Contemporary Jewish Museum, "*Judy Chicago: Cohanim.*" Chicago was also featured in an exhibition focused on her Jewish identity. See Bloch Rosensaft, *Judy Chicago: Jewish Identity* and Chicago, "Oral History Interview with Judy Chicago," 23, 31, 35.
69. Diner, *Jews of the United States*, 305–58 and Eichler-Levine, *Suffer the Little Children*.
70. Chicago, *Flowering*, 10–12.
71. Bloom, "Ethnic Notions and Feminist Strategies of the 1970s," 138.
72. Bloom doesn't comment on the etymology of "Chicago," which is a French turn on an Algonquin word.
73. Bloom, "Ethnic Notions and Feminist Strategies of the 1970s," 138.
74. Ring, "Identifying with Chicago," 133.
75. Ibid., 137.
76. Ibid.
77. Ibid., 147. According to Paula Hyman, characterizing the emergence of second-wave feminism in the 1960s and 1970s, "Jewish women within the American feminist movement tended initially not to assert a Jewish dimension to their feminism," as "gender trumped all other aspects of identity." "Jewish Feminism Faces the American Women's Movement," 223. This dynamic could be found among key feminist leaders, including Shulamith Firestone, Robin Morgan, and Betty Friedan—and it was true, as well, for Judy Chicago. On Jewish feminism, see Levitt, *Jews and Feminism*.
78. Biale, *Not in the Heavens*, 11.
79. Ibid. On Jewish secularism, see Levitt, "Other Moderns, Other Jews."
80. Gross, *Beyond the Synagogue*, 6. Eichler-Levine's *Painted Pomegranates and Needlepoint Rabbis*, on the Jewish crafting movement, is also relevant here.
81. Chicago, "Origins of Jewish Creativity," 36.
82. Haider, "Chicago's Butterfly," 81.
83. Caplan, *Funny, You Don't Look Funny*, 12, 15.
84. Butterfield, "Guess Who's Coming to Dinner?," 22
85. See Snyder, "Reading the Language of 'The Dinner Party,'" 30 and Butterfield, "Guess Who's Coming to Dinner?," 22.
86. Gaffney and Najimy, *Parallel Lives*, 55.
87. Jackson, *Comedy and Feminist Interpretation of the Hebrew Bible*, 1.
88. Hitchens, "Why Women Aren't Funny."
89. Ibid. Also see Wiltenburg, "Just When in History Did Men Decide Women Weren't Funny?"
90. Wylder, "Judy Chicago: Trials and Tributes," 17.
91. Lincoln, *Discourse and the Construction of Society*, 25.
92. Butterfield, "Guess Who's Coming to Dinner?," 28.
93. Wylder calls Chicago's *Dinner Party*—and her later *Birth Project*—examples of "religious symbol" and "visual theology." "Judy Chicago's *Dinner Party* and *Birth Project.*"
94. Chicago, *Dinner Party*, 24 (entry for February 21, 1975).
95. Ibid., 12.
96. Ibid., 25.
97. Klein, "Goddess: Feminist Art and Spirituality in the 1970s," 578.
98. In my reading, scholarship on US religious history since the 1950s remains dominated by studies of (mostly white) evangelical Protestants, especially since the rise of Trumpism, which has further fueled the scholarly and popular market for such books. There are exceptions, including a smaller but rich body of work on Catholics, Jews, Muslims, Hindus, and African-derived religions; work that thematizes gender, sexuality, or race in ways not driven by denominational approaches to thinking about religion; and scholarship that uses religious studies theory to examine phenomena usually assumed "secular." Even still, the history of the feminist spirituality movement remains largely neglected. Notable exceptions include Cynthia Eller's *Living in the Lap of the Goddess* and *The Myth of Matriarchal Prehistory* and Pamela Klassen's *Blessed Events.* On the intersections of race, racism, colonialism, and the feminist spirituality movement, see Kavita Maya's "Arachne's Voice" and Chris Klassen's "The Colonial Mythology of Feminist Witchcraft."
99. Christ, "Why Women Need the Goddess," 10.

100. Orenstein, "Reemergence of the Archetype," 74.
101. Orenstein draws on the work of Ana Mendieta and Betye Saar to highlight how artists also found sources of the Goddess outside of Eurocentric conceptions of the West and the goddess traditions most common in this writing and artistic work. She says of Saar, for instance: "By delving deeply into the religious practices of Africa and Haiti, Saar resurrects images of the Black Goddess, the Voodoo Priestess and the Queen of the Witches, collecting the amulets and artifacts of these cultures and placing them in her boxes in order to create potent talismanic collections of magically charged objects and icons. For Saar, contemporary black women are all incarnations of the Black Goddess, and in reclaiming black power, women are instinctively venerating an ancient female force still worshipped in other cultures today." "Reemergence of the Archetype," 81–82.
102. Orenstein, "Reemergence of the Archetype," 83.
103. Gerhard, *Dinner Party*, 142, 309n55.
104. Daly would eventually break from the Catholic Church altogether.
105. Gerhard, *Dinner Party*, 144. I first learned about this creation myth in Gerhard's wonderful section "Staging the Goddess at *The Dinner Party*." Several drafts of the manuscript appear in Chicago's archive at the Schlesinger Library, including a version with notes from art critic Lucy Lippard, longtime supporter of Chicago's work and the feminist spirituality and art movement. It is a fully developed manuscript, running over 150 pages. Judy Chicago, "The Dinner Party: A Heavenly Banquet," Xerox with Lucy [Lippard] edit notes, 1976 (Papers of Judy Chicago (hereafter JCP), Carton 15).
106. Chicago, "Dinner Party: A Heavenly Banquet."
107. Gerhard, *Dinner Party*, 145. As this book goes to press, Chicago will release *Revelations*, in which it seems her longer creation story will finally be published.
108. Chicago, "Revelations of the Goddess," 54.
109. Ibid., 54–58.
110. Chicago, *Embroidering Our Heritage*, 26.
111. Chicago, *Dinner Party*, 8–11.
112. Eller, *Living in the Lap of the Goddess*, 151. Eller tracks much of this interest in imagining matriarchal societies back to nineteenth century "armchair anthropologists" and scholars like Friedrich Engels, E. B. Tylor, Margaret Murray, and Lewis Henry Morgan. In *The Origin of the Family, Private Property, and the State*, Engels identifies men usurping women's power as the first instance of class oppression—an act that inaugurated a shift from matriarchy to patriarchy, in which men would seek to control women's reproductive agency and social roles. Before this moment, though, such thinkers imagined a flourishing world of feminine imagery and power, one reflected in the work of myth and religion (152).
113. Indeed, Eller further questions many of the premises upon which the movement understands this history in *Myth of Matriarchal Prehistory*.
114. Butterfield, "Guess Who's Coming to Dinner?," 28.
115. Raven and Rennie, "Interview with Judy Chicago," 93.
116. Gerhard, *Dinner Party*, 163–67 and Levin, *Becoming Judy Chicago*, 305–14.
117. Jean R., letter to Judy Chicago, July 2, 1979 (JCP, Carton 10, File 1).
118. Gerhard, *Dinner Party*, 163–64.
119. I don't mean this snidely. Religion and marketing have long accompanied one another in American history and indeed often merge into one. See Stout, *Divine Dramatist*, Moore, *Selling God*; Schmidt, *Consumer Rites*; Moreton, *To Serve God and Wal-Mart*; Kruse, *One Nation Under God*; Lofton, *Oprah*; and Lofton, *Consuming Religion*.
120. See Gerhard, *Dinner Party*, 180–210 and Levin, *Becoming Judy Chicago*, 250–332.
121. Levin, *Becoming Judy Chicago*, 320–30.
122. Mildred Hamilton, "'The Dinner Party' Left without a Second Sitting," *San Francisco Sunday Examiner and Chronicle*, July 1, 1979, 6, quoted in Levin, *Becoming Judy Chicago*, 314.
123. She also included a feminist religious poem she wrote that explores themes of creation and birth. Shoni L., letter to Judy Chicago, May 22, 1984 (JCP, Carton 10, File 8). For unpublished letters in the archive, I use first name and last initial, except when that information is unavailable.
124. Quoted in Dorothy Shinn, "The Gospel According to Judy Chicago," *Beacon, The Sunday Magazine of the Akron Beacon* (Akron, OH), July 5, 1981, 5–6. Shinn is very critical of this guest, mocking her "unadulterated adulation."
125. James B., letter to Judy Chicago, July 9, 1980 (JCP, Carton 10, File 2).

126. Lippard, "Dinner Party a Four-Star Retreat," 27.

127. Ketcham "Judy Chicago's Dinner Party," *Village Voice*, June 11, 1979, 47–48.

128. Caldwell, "Experiencing 'The Dinner Party,'" 36.

129. Ibid., 37.

130. Snyder, "Reading the Language of 'The Dinner Party,'" 30.

131. Ibid., 31.

132. Ibid.

133. Hughes, "An Obsessive Feminist Pantheon," 85.

134. Mullarkey, "Dishing It Out,'" 211.

135. Shinn, "The Gospel According to Judy Chicago," 4.

136. Kay Larson, "More (or Less) Awful Rowing Toward God," *Village Voice*, December 17, 1979, 113. Lesbian responses were more mixed. Jan Adams, for instance, noted a "lesbian sensibility" in the piece, but remained "conflicted" about its lesbian representation, as few lesbians are identified as such. See Levin, *Becoming Judy Chicago*, 313–14.

137. Fischer, "Judy Chicago: San Francisco Museum of Art," 76–77.

138. Robert Taylor, "'The Dinner Party' Somewhat Unappetizing," *Boston By*, July 3, 1980, 18.

139. Gelon, "Critic's Voice: Who Speaks for Us?"

140. See Bynum, *Holy Fast and Holy Feast* and Bynum, *Fragmentation and Redemption*.

141. Rabinowitz, "Issues of Feminist Aesthetics," 40.

142. Alfred Frankenstein, quoted in Albright, "Primarily Biological," 156, cited in Levin, *Becoming Judy Chicago*, 308; and Hilton Kramer, "Judy Chicago's 'Dinner Party' Comes to Brooklyn Museum," *New York Times*, October 17, 1980, C1, 18.

143. Kramer, "Judy Chicago's 'Dinner Party,'" C1.

144. Kuby, "Hoodwinking of the Women's Movement," 129, 128.

145. Ibid., 128.

146. Mullarkey, "Dishing It Out," 210, 211.

147. Ibid., 210.

148. Lippard, "Uninvited Guests," 39.

149. Nira Hardon Long, "'The Dinner Party': A Matter of Basic Human Liberties," *Washington Post*, August 9, 1990, A23.

150. The terms of the deal vary slightly across some of the documents in the archive. Long wrote that, in their deal, UDC would keep 85 percent of all admissions revenue that would go into its endowment fund, though the Memorandum of Terms for the Gift notes that 20 percent of the admissions revenue would go toward the care and preservation of the work, with 10 percent going to Chicago and 5 percent to her Through the Flower corporation. See "Memorandum of Terms of Gift for The Dinner Party," July 11, 1990 (JCP, Carton 22, File 21).

151. Lippard, "Uninvited Guests," 41 and Robert Mahler, "The Battle of Chicago: Art: Feminist Artist Judy Chicago Fires Back," *Los Angeles Times*, October 12, 1990, F1. The counterargument to Mahler's piece, which included some of the misinformation, can be found in Robert Pedersen, "The Bitter Taste of 'The Dinner Party,'" *Los Angeles Times*, November 5, 1990, SDF3.

152. Long raises this issue in her letter explaining the debacle in "'The Dinner Party:' A Matter of Basic Human Liberties," A23.

153. Jonetta Rose Barras, "UDC's $1.6 Million 'Dinner'—Feminist Artwork," *Washington Times*. July 18, 1990, A1. According to Lucy Lippard, Barras said that initially she had planned to focus on what she considered the inappropriate use of finances, but her editor insisted she deal with the subject matter of Chicago's work as well. See Lippard, "Uninvited Guests," 43.

154. Jonetta Rose Barras, "D.C. Council's 'Sanity' Question as Hill Learns," *Washington Times*, July 19, 1990, A1.

155. Mary McGrory, "Offensive on Campus," *Washington Post*, October 4, 1990, A2. It also ran as "Lessons from College Campuses," *Boston Globe*, October 5, 1990, 15.

156. Quoted in Molly Sinclair, "An Artist's Open-Ended Invitation: Judy Chicago Urges Viewer to Judge Work," *Washington Post*, July 21, 1990, B3.

157. Robert Dornan, Congressional Record-House, July 25, 1990, p19124 (JCP, Carton 22, File 15).

158. Dornan, Congressional Record-House, July 26, 1990, p19745 (JCP, Carton 22, File 15).

159. Gerhard, *Dinner Party*, 252–53. As Gerhard notes, no women testified during the debate.

160. Lippard, "Uninvited Guests," 45.

161. Congressional Record-Daily Digest, July 26, 1990, D506 (JCP, Carton 22, File 15).

162. Lippard, "Uninvited Guests," 45.

163. Chicago, *Dinner Party*, 1996 ed., 221.

164. Through the Flower memo, October 1990 (JCP, Carton 22, File 20); Mahler, "Battle of Chicago," F1; Lippard, "Uninvited Guests," 44–45, and especially 49n23 and Gerhard, *Dinner Party*, 256–57.

165. "Washington Students Criticize Art Decision," *New York Times*, September 27, 1990, C14; Keith Harriston and Gabriel Escobar, "UDC Students Take Over Two Buildings: Administrative Offices Seized; Ouster of Trustees Among Demands," *Washington Post*, September 27, 1990, A1; and Carlos Sanchez and Ruben Castaneda, "Chairman Negotiating Resignation; Gift of 'The Dinner Party' Revoked," *Washington Post*, October 3, 1990, D1.

166. Through the Flower memo, 3.

167. Jones, "'Sexual Politics' of *The Dinner Party*," 92.

168. My switch from critic to opponent follows the helpful distinction made in Julius, *Transgressions*, 8.

169. No doubt, a lot of this heated rhetoric that reduced *The Dinner Party* to pornography was also made in bad faith. But even bad faith bears consequences.

170. Judy Chicago, letter to National Desk, *New York Times*, "Please Advise Your Washington Correspondent, Karen De Witt," 1990 (JCP, Carton 22, File 13). I first learned about this in Gerhard, *Dinner Party*, 257–58. Chicago is criticizing Karen DeWitt's article "Washington Students Gain in Protest" of September 29, 1990: "Some members of Congress have threatened to remove $1.6 million from the university's budget as a protest over the artwork, which depicts female genitalia. Student leaders have said they do not object to the artwork but to the use of so much money to house it." The *New York Times* photo caption from a July 28 story also used this language.

171. Judy Chicago, "The Great American Fax Attack" (JCP, Carton 22, File 19).

172. Butler, "Force of Fantasy," 108.

173. Wesley Pruden, "Big Dinner Bell, But No Groceries," *Washington Times*, July 20, 1990, A4.

174. Ibid.

175. Jones, "Sexual Politics: Feminist Strategies, Feminist Conflicts, Feminist Histories," 24–25.

176. Butler, *Gender Trouble*, 121.

177. Butler qualifies that we ought not consider drag a privileged site of subversion in the 1999 preface to *Gender Trouble*. Here, I'm interested in how camp plays with sincerity in ways that open space to reconsider the political and religious lives of *The Dinner Party*.

178. McKelvey, *Disability Works*, 140–44. See also McKelvey, "Ron White's 'Disemployment.'"

179. Ryan and Rubin, "By the Numbers," 147–62.

180. Such tensions between sincerity and humor may appear to map onto Susan Sontag's partitioning of "Jewish moral seriousness" from gay camp. But, as performance theorist Ann Pellegrini shows, the boundary between the two is hardly as clear as Sontag thought. Exploring Jewish camp, Pellegrini observes how "Christian dominance and heteronormativity" remain "interrelated structures of dominance." Art historian Gail Levin further argues that Jewish feminists often draw on sexual imagery to celebrate "both sexuality and female agency," though such work is frequently "misread as merely erotic." Sontag, "Notes on 'Camp'"; Pellegrini, "After Sontag," 176; and Levin, "Censorship, Politics and Sexual Imagery," 67.

181. Butler, *Gender Trouble*, 187.

182. Battista, "New Critical Positions," 398. Chan is quoted in Hebron, "Putting the Words Back in the F-Word." The video recording of the presentation is available online at Chan, "From Chicago to Chicago."

Chapter 3

1. Wojnarowicz, *Close to the Knives*, 29.

2. Wildmon, *Don Wildmon*, 152.

3. There is some dispute about the actual numbers, which vary across news media accounts and legal records. In a deposition, Wildmon's lawyers claimed only about six thousand pamphlets were mailed and that the reverend had changed his mind about mailing more "because the photographs were too offensive." In his decision, Judge William Connor cites the full amount. See Wojnarowicz v. American Family Association and Donald E. Wildmon, 745 F. Supp. 130 S. D. N. Y. (1990); Wildmon deposition, *Wojnarowicz v. AFA*, 34–36 (David Wojnarowicz Papers (hereafter DWP), Box 15, Folder 77); trial transcript, *Wojnarowicz v. AFA*, 152 (DWP, Box 15, Folder 81); National Endowment for the Arts, "Fact Sheet on American Family Association Fundraising Advertisement," February 13, 1990, in Bolton, *Culture Wars*, 152–53; Allan Parachini, "Edited Photos Fueling NEA Confrontation," *Los Angeles Times*, April 25, 1990, F1 (DWP, Box 14, Folder 74).

4. American Family Association, "Our Purpose"; also noted in Tim Wildmon, "Taking Inventory, Having Impact," *AFA Journal,* February 2003.

5. This phrase is the subtitle for Wildmon, *Don Wildmon.* The name of the AFA changed in 1987.

6. Quoted in Winbush and Wildmon, "Interview with Rev. Donald E. Wildmon."

7. Quoted in Kim Masters, "NEA-Funded Art Exhibit Protested," *Washington Post,* April 21, 1990 (DWP, Box 14, Folder 74).

8. This pronunciation is from biographer Cynthia Carr, *Fire in the Belly,* 1.

9. Carr's *Fire in the Belly* offers the best account of Wojnarowicz's life; Mysoon Rizk's dissertation remains the best account of his artistic work. See Rizk, "Nature, Death, and Spirituality in the Work of David Wojnarowicz."

10. The pamphlet is plaintiff's exhibit #5 in *Wojnarowicz v. AFA* (DWP, Box 99, Folder 4); Parachini, "Edited Photos."

11. This language—"banal pornographer" or "banal pornography"—came up in various interviews and in court. See Allan Parachini, "Artist Sues the Rev. Wildmon Over Mailing," *Los Angeles Times,* May 22, 1990, F4 (DWP, Box 14, Folder 74) and Wojnarowicz, trial transcript, *Wojnarowicz v. AFA,* 31.

12. Wojnarowicz deposition, *Wojnarowicz v. AFA,* 75 (DWP, Box 15, Folder 104).

13. Masters, "NEA-Funded Art Exhibit Protested"; Mark Lebovitz, "Art Exhibit Draws National Attention," *Illinois State University Today* 24, no. 2 (Spring 1990) (DWP, Box 14, Folder 61); Kurt Gottschalk, "Art Exhibit Draws Large Crowd," *Daily Vidette* (Illinois State University), January 26, 1990 (DWP, Box 14, Folder 62).

14. Quoted in Masters, "NEA-Funded Art Exhibit Protested."

15. For excellent takes by art historians, see Rizk, "Regulating Desire and Imagination" and Meyer, *Outlaw Representation,* 255–64; on the legal case, see Inde, *Art in the Courtroom,* 93–148.

16. Connor, ruling, *Wojnarowicz v. AFA.*

17. Karin Lipson, "Judge: Art Excerpt 'Likely' Mutilation," *New York Newsday,* June 26, 1990 (DWP, Box 14, Folder 74).

18. My argument about Wildmon's aesthetics of literalism remains indebted to Richard Meyer's brilliant essay "The Jesse Helms Theory of Art" and Judith Butler's fascinating thinking about Mapplethorpe in "The Force of Fantasy." I am not the first to use the phrasing "aesthetics of literalism," which others have taken in quite different directions. See Alan Fisher's use of this phrase to analyze poetry in his 1973 "The Stretching of Augustan Satire"; Shane Vogel uses it to name strictures on Black representation in "Performing 'Stormy Weather'"; and Leora Maltz-Leca uses it in her 2018 book *William Kentridge.*

19. Quoted in Wojnarowicz deposition, 4–5.

20. Ibid., 6.

21. Wojnarowicz deposition, 7.

22. Bull, trial transcript, 44.

23. Carr, *Fire in the Belly,* 442–61; Dubin, *Arresting Images,* 208–16.

24. Goldin, "In the Valley of the Shadow" and Carr, *Fire in the Belly,* 456.

25. Quoted in Hans Johnson and William Eskridge, "The Legacy of Falwell's Bully Pulpit," *Washington Post,* May 19, 2007, A17.

26. On the Reagan White House's response to AIDS, see Brier, *Infectious Ideas,* 78–121 and Petro, *After the Wrath of God,* 53–90.

27. Jesse Helms, S. Amdt. 963 to H.R. 3058, 100th Congress (1987–1988). On Helms and AIDS, see Crimp, "How to Have Promiscuity in an Epidemic." See also Link, *Righteous Warrior,* 349–50.

28. Quoted in Associated Press, "Vatican AIDS Meeting Hears O'Connor Assail Condom Use," *New York Times,* November 14, 1989, A10. On O'Connor, Catholicism, and AIDS, see Petro, *After the Wrath of God,* 91–136.

29. Goldin, "In the Valley of the Shadow," 4.

30. Ibid., 5.

31. See, e.g., "Statement by John Frohnmayer."

32. John Frohnmayer, letter to Susan Wyatt, November 3, 1989, in Bolton, *Culture Wars,* 125–26.

33. Susan Wyatt, response to John Frohnmayer, November 8, 1989, in Bolton, *Culture Wars,* 126, italics mine.

34. Artists Space, "Press Release."

35. Wojnarowicz, "Postcards from America: X-Rays from Hell," in *Witnesses,* 6–11. The essay was republished in the *Tongues of Flame* catalogue and in Wojnarowicz's *Close to the Knives* (which is the version I cite in this work, labeling it "Postcards" for clarity in this section). Also see Meyer, *Outlaw Representation,* ch. 5.

36. Wojnarowicz, "Postcards from America," in *Close to the Knives*, 114 (the line appears in all capitals).
37. Ibid., 113.
38. Ibid., 117 and Wojnarowicz, *Close to the Knives*, 40.
39. Wojnarowicz, *Close to the Knives*, 40.
40. Wojnarowicz, "Postcards from America," 121.
41. Wojnarowicz and Carr, "Biographical Dateline," in *History Keeps Me Awake at Night*, 285. My account of Wojnarowicz's childhood is drawn largely from Carr's indispensable biography, as well as from his own writings and biographical details from the *Tongues of Flame* catalogue and the updated version of his "Biographical Dateline" with Carr, cited here. As Carr explains, he was not always the most reliable narrator of his own life, sometimes getting dates wrong or even omitting major events.
42. Dolores later changed the spelling of her name to Delores. Carr, *Fire in the Belly*, 592.
43. Carr, *Fire in the Belly*, 10–15 and Wojnarowicz, "Biographical Dateline," in *Tongues of Flame*, 113.
44. Carr, *Fire in the Belly*, 26.
45. Ibid., 25.
46. Ibid., 34.
47. Wojnarowicz, "Biographical Dateline," in *Tongues of Flame*, 116–17 and Carr, *Fire in the Belly*, 159–65.
48. Gordon, *Heroes of Their Own Lives*. Novelist Hanya Yanagihara writes about the stencil in "The Burning House."
49. On O'Connor and Operation Rescue, see Petro, *After the Wrath of God*, 153; "Cardinal Hails Protesters in Operation Rescue," *Buffalo News*, October 12, 1989, A18; and Associated Press, "Cardinal O'Connor Won't Join an Operation Rescue," *Philadelphia Daily News*, October 9, 1989, 12.
50. Wojnarowicz, "Postcards from America," 114.
51. Ibid.
52. Ibid., 115–16.
53. Weston, *Families We Choose*.
54. Carr, *Fire in the Belly*, 170–71.
55. Wojnarowicz, *Close to the Knives*, 102.
56. Ibid.
57. Ibid., 103.
58. Ibid.
59. Wojnarowicz, "Postcards from America," 116.
60. Ibid.
61. Ibid., 121.
62. Ibid., 121, 122.
63. Ibid., 122.
64. Levine, "How to Do Things with Dead Bodies." See DIVA TV's film *The Ashes Action*.
65. Wojnarowicz, "Postcards from America," 120.
66. Pat Buchanan, "Where a Wall Is Needed," *Washington Times*, November 22, 1989, in Bolton, *Culture Wars*, 137–38.
67. "The Seven Deadly Sins Fact Sheet" was included in the *Tongues of Flame* catalogue and in *Close to the Knives*. It includes short profiles on Edward Koch, Cardinal John O'Connor, William Dannemeyer, Stephen Joseph, Jesse Helms, Alfonse D'Amato, and Frank Young. Wojnarowicz's archive includes several drafts of the fact sheet and some of the back-and-forth with fellow AIDS activists who helped him compose it.
68. Wojnarowicz deposition, 61–62.
69. Trial transcript, 48, 50–51.
70. In the end, the catalogue received no funding from the NEA, which was Frohnmayer's stipulation for restoring the funding for the show itself.
71. "Plaintiff's Exhibits (#7 and #8)," *Wojnarowicz v. AFA* (DWP, Box 99, Folder 4).
72. Quoted in Selcraig, "Reverend Wildmon's War on the Arts."
73. Wildmon, *Don Wildmon*, 63, 77. On Wildmon and the Christian Right, see Dubin, *Arresting Images*, 227–32.
74. Tim Stafford, "Taking on TV's Bad Boys," *Christianity Today*, August 19, 1991, 14.
75. Stafford, "Taking on TV's Bad Boys," 14 and Dedman, "Bible Belt Blowhard," 42.
76. Stafford, "Taking on TV's Bad Boys," 16.

77. Ibid.
78. Wildmon keeps the details somewhat vague, but the story remains consistent. See Wildmon, *Don Wildmon*, 26–28; Wildmon, *Home Invaders*, 7; Helle Bering-Jensen, "Don Wildmon's Crusade," *Insight on the News*, July 2, 1990, 11 (DWP, Box 14, Folder 74); and Stafford, "Taking on TV's Bad Boys," 16.
79. Wildmon, *Don Wildmon*, 28, 31.
80. Ibid., 34.
81. Stafford, "Taking on TV's Bad Boys," 16.
82. Ibid.
83. Wildmon, *Don Wildmon*, 40.
84. Ibid.
85. Ibid., 45.
86. Stafford, "Taking on TV's Bad Boys," 14.
87. Wildmon, *Don Wildmon*, 63.
88. Bering-Jensen, "Don Wildmon's Crusade," 11. He also makes this point in Selcraig, "Reverend Wildmon's War on the Arts" and Stafford, "Taking on TV's Bad Boys."
89. Wildmon, *Don Wildmon*, 49, 46.
90. Tom Shales, "The Rebellion of the 'Fed-Ups,'" *Washington Post*, May 15, 1978.
91. Ibid.
92. Selcraig, "Reverend Wildmon's War on the Arts" and Bering-Jensen, "Don Wildmon's Crusade," 11.
93. Bering-Jensen, "Don Wildmon's Crusade," 11; and Wildmon, *Don Wildmon*, 210.
94. Wildmon, *Don Wildmon*, 123.
95. The guide is described and quoted in Don Wildmon, "Christian Values Take a Beating on Prime Time TV," *Conservative Digest*, September 1980, 28 (People for the American Way Collection of Conservative Political Ephemera (hereafter PAWC), Box 91, Folder 17).
96. Wildmon, "Christian Values," 28 (PAWC, Box 91, Folder 17).
97. Ibid.
98. Wildmon, *Don Wildmon*, 122–23 and Winbush and Wildmon, "Interview with Rev. Donald E. Wildmon." I am not suggesting these statistics and their findings were accurate or sound. If nothing else, one could pressure both the assumptions governing how Wildmon defined Christian values and how volunteers were guided to score programs using rather subjective criteria. And Wildmon was known to dismiss results that did not support his goals. Dedman's exposé in *Mother Jones* (though also politically motivated) certainly provides enough evidence to warrant suspicions about Wildmon's statistics (see "Bible Belt Blowhard," 41–43, 74–76).
99. Warner, "Ruse of 'Secular Humanism.'"
100. Wildmon, *Don Wildmon*, 134.
101. Falwell, *Listen America!*
102. Johnson, *Lavender Scare* and Herman, *Antigay Agenda*.
103. He lists Marx's *Communist Manifesto* alongside the two *Humanist Manifestos* at the start of his book (13). They receive fuller consideration in chapter 4, "The Humanist Religion." Schaeffer, *Christian Manifesto*.
104. Wildmon, *Don Wildmon*, 135. Wildmon also explained key tenets of secular humanism in an editorial for Mississippi's *Meridian Star*. See Wildmon, "Humanism: What Does It Mean?," *Meridian Star*, March 21, 1987 (PAWC, Box 91, Folder 17) and *Home Invaders*, 11–12.
105. Wildmon, *Home Invaders*, 12.
106. Wildmon, *Don Wildmon*, 136.
107. Ibid., 137.
108. Ibid., 139. The survey he drew on is Lichter, Lichter, and Rothman, "Hollywood and America."
109. Bering-Jensen, "Don Wildmon's Crusade," 13. On longer history of "Judeo-Christian," see Gaston, *Imagining Judeo-Christian America* and White, "How Heterosexuality Became Religious."
110. Wildmon, *Don Wildmon*, 124. I retained his punctuation. The year is likely around 1980, based on his narration of other events.
111. Quoted in Paul A. Fisher, "The Wanderer Asks … Rev. Donald Wildmon," *The Wanderer*, June 5, 1986, n.p. (second page in file) (PAWC, Box 91, Folder 17).
112. Dedman, "Bible Belt Blowhard," 41.
113. Stafford, "Taking on TV's Bad Boys," 16. Wildmon returns to this language about waging a spiritual war against secular humanism in *Case Against Pornography*, 7.

114. Wildmon, *Don Wildmon*, 127. Like many conservative white evangelical leaders at the time, Wildmon rarely talked about race or racial discrimination, especially not the history and ongoing realities of structural racism. But he would selectively draw on the rhetorical power of Black voices to bolster his message. Two Black supporters are named in his book on battling network television—this unnamed woman at his speech and Steve Gooden, "a handsome young black singer" who attended a rally against *The Last Temptation of Christ* during which he tore up his MCA Records agreement. *Don Wildmon*, 188–90.

115. This account is greatly indebted to Strub, *Perversion for Profit*; Strub, *Obscenity Rules*; Bronstein and Strub, *Porno Chic and the Sex Wars*; and Burke, *Pornography Wars*.

116. Wildmon, *Case Against Pornography*, 29. This analogy between the United States and Rome was common among Christian conservatives in the 1970s and 1980s.

117. Ibid., 7.

118. Ibid., 8. The literalist reading of snuff films—that the actor is "actually killed"—of course takes representation for reality. All of Wildmon's "evidence" should be greeted with a healthy dose of critical suspicion.

119. Quoted in Wildmon, *Case Against Pornography*, 29.

120. On conflations of sexual sin, homosexuality, and AIDS, especially in relation to readings of Sodom, see Petro, *After the Wrath of God*, 25–34.

121. Strub, "Modernizing Decency," 134–35. Also see Strub's *Perversion for Profit*, especially 80–115. On older histories of Catholic censorship, see Black, *Catholic Crusade against the Movies* and Walsh, *Sin and Censorship*.

122. We should understand this history of Catholic anti-obscenity campaigns as part of what Goodwin brilliantly calls "the catholicization of public morality." *Abusing Religion*, 18.

123. Quoted in Fisher, "The Wanderer Asks . . . Rev. Donald Wildmon." On the place of *The Wanderer* in the history of Catholic conservatism, see Hitchcock, "Catholic Activist Conservatism in the United States," 122–25.

124. Bering-Jensen, "Don Wildmon's Crusade," 9.

125. The organization is now called the National Center on Sexual Exploitation and offers a history of its founding at https://endsexualexploitation.org/about/ncose-history/. On Christian responses to Kinsey, see Griffith, *Moral Combat*, 121–54.

126. Commission on Obscenity and Pornography, *The Report*.

127. Quoted in Strub, *Perversion for Profit*, 133.

128. Strub, *Perversion for Profit*, 133.

129. On the history of the Christian Right's anti-porn activism, see Strub, *Perversion for Profit*, 179–212.

130. Strub, *Perversion for Profit*, 199.

131. Commission on Obscenity and Pornography, *The Report*, 325.

132. Quoted in Strub, *Perversion for Profit*, 235, italics mine. Strub, *Perversion for Profit*, 213–55, offers an excellent guide to this history. For feminist arguments against porn, see Dworkin, *Pornography* and MacKinnon, *Only Words*. Gayle Rubin counters the anti-porn feminist position in "Thinking Sex." On "literalism" and anti-porn feminism, see Steiner, *Scandal of Pleasure*, 60–93 and Butler, *Excitable Speech*, 65–69, 71–102.

133. Wildmon, *Case Against Pornography*, 8.

134. Strub, *Perversion for Profit*, 14.

135. Ibid., 194, 211. On the longer history of right-wing conflations of queerness and obscenity (here focused on lesbianism), see Strub, "Lavender, Menaced"; Petro, *After the Wrath of God*; Dowland, *Family Values and the Rise of the Christian Right*; and Cooper, *Family Values*.

136. Stafford, "Taking on TV's Bad Boys," 17 and Dedman, "Bible Belt Blowhard," 42. Dedman's investigative profile of Wildmon disputed the AFA's numbers. Over half the members on the AFA mailing list were inactive, meaning they had not sent in a donation in over two years, for instance. And though Wildmon claimed 65 chapters across the country, setting up a chapter was quite easy—it merely required signing up with a $25 donation, which anyone could do (and which the journalist did for his story). Wildmon testified for the trial that the AFA made $5.2 million in 1989 and that they had 23 employees (some reporters put that number over 30). Wildmon deposition, 21, 12.

137. This was also true of Scorsese's film, to which Wildmon devotes a chapter, alongside the protests he organized against MCM/Universal Studios in *Don Wildmon*, 188–215. See Winbush and Wildmon, "Interview with Rev. Donald E. Wildmon."

138. Quoted in Bering-Jensen, "Don Wildmon's Crusade," 15 and Sara Rimer, "Rap Band Members Found Not Guilty in Obscenity Trial," *New York Times*, October 21, 1990, 1, 30.

139. Associated Press, "Art Display at ISU Draws No Ire from Viewers," *Champaign-Urbana News Gazette*, February 25, 1990 (DWP, Box 14, Folder 62).

140. Dana Rohrabacher, letter to colleagues, February 20, 1990 (DWP, Box 14, Folder 62). Pat Robertson described this image in mailings for the Christian Coalition, and Jerry Falwell mentioned it in mailings for his Moral Majority. See, for instance, the Christian Coalition's flier "To the Congress of the United States" and Pat Robertson's "Important Message to Concerned Christian Citizens," June 20, 1990 (PWAC, Box 16, Folder 25); also see Heritage Foundation, "National Endowment for the Arts: Misusing Taxpayers Money," *Backgrounder*, January 18, 1991, 2 (DWP, Box 14, Folder 62).

141. Reeves, *President Reagan*, 24; and Wildmon, trial transcript, 154.

142. AFA copy of "Very Important!!! Late Information!!!" *Human Events,* February 24, 1990, included as exhibit #6, "Plaintiff's Exhibits," *Wojnarowicz v. AFA* (DWP, Box 99, Folder 4).

143. Sara C., letter to President Wallace, April 20, 1990 (DWP, Box 14, Folder 63).

144. Beverly S., letter to Blinderman, March 15, 1990 (DWP, Box 14, Folder 63).

145. Members of Lifebuilders Class, letter to Blinderman, April 1, 1990 (DWP, Box 14, Folder 63).

146. Emma S., letter, March 15, 1990 (DWP, Box 14, Folder 63).

147. Jay H., letter to Wojnarowicz (no name), August 7, 1990 (DWP, Box 14, Folder 62).

148. Wildmon deposition, 25.

149. Wildmon, trial transcript, 162.

150. Quoted in Bering-Jensen, "Don Wildmon's Crusade," 13.

151. Biblical proof-texting has a long history and has been, no doubt, the matter of much debate. See, e.g., Downing, "Art and Practice of Biblical Proof-Texting."

152. See n140.

153. Wojnarowicz deposition, 16.

154. He described his interest in Genet's work in a draft of an affidavit for the trial, May 16, 1990, 12 (DWP, Box 15, Folder 104). See Amin, *Disturbing Attachments.*

155. Wojnarowicz, trial notes on the Rev. Wildmon mailing, n.d. (likely ca. May 1990), 4 (DWP, Box 15, Folder 91).

156. Wojnarowicz, trial transcript, 19. This explanation came when his own lawyers were asking him to contextualize many of his works.

157. Carr, *Fire in the Belly*, 490 and Wojnarowicz deposition, 16.

158. Wojnarowicz deposition, 16–17.

159. Ibid., 18–19.

160. Ibid., 21–22.

161. A French photographer and filmmaker, Scemama was a close friend of Wojnarowicz.

162. Meyer offers an indispensable analysis of *Sex Series* in *Outlaw Representation*, 247–55.

163. Quoted in Lippard, "Out of the Safety Zone."

164. Wojnarowicz deposition, 36.

165. Wojnarowicz, trial notes on the Rev. Wildmon mailing, 2.

166. Ibid. Also see Meyer, *Outlaw Representation*, 252.

167. Meyer, *Outlaw Representation*, 252.

168. Ibid., 254.

169. Wojnarowicz, trial notes on the Rev. Wildmon mailing, 2.

170. Meyer, *Outlaw Representation*, 254.

171. Wojnarowicz deposition, 38–39.

172. Lippard, "Out of the Safety Zone."

173. Cameron, *Fever*, 27. On Wojnarowicz and spirituality, also see Taylor, "Some Sort of Grace."

174. Cameron, *Fever*, 27.

175. Lippard, "Out of the Safety Zone."

176. He describes this process with other paintings in the series on the elements in Matthew Rose, "David Wojnarowicz: An Interview," *Arts Magazine*, May 1988, 61 (DWP, Box 4, Folder 36).

177. He explained these very associations during the trial. Wojnarowicz, trial transcript, 28.

178. Wildmon deposition, 62.

179. Ibid., 41.

180. Ibid., 74.

181. Ibid., 74–75.

182. Wojnarowicz, trial notes on the Rev. Wildmon mailing, 1.

183. Wojnarowicz, trial transcript, 24–25 and Wojnarowicz, trial notes on the Rev. Wildmon mailing, 1.

184. His mistaken identifications also spoke to the very ways the images became hard to read after Wojnarowicz purposely manipulated them.

185. Quoted in Maureen Dowd, "Unruffled Helms Basks in Eye of Arts Storm," *New York Times*, July 28, 1989.

186. Meyer, "The Jesse Helms Theory of Art," 131n2.

187. Ibid., 133.

188. Meyer, *Outlaw Representation*, 257.

189. Quoted in Joyce Price, "Ministers to Receive 'Smut' Art Mailings," *Washington Times*, May 30, 1990, A3. It is unclear why Wildmon thought Mapplethorpe's work less tough or explicit, since those images depicted not only queer sexuality but also "partially nude children," but perhaps the reverend was more cautious about mailing out the pamphlet targeting Wojnarowicz with his trial on the horizon.

190. The point is clear looking at his art, but he also stated it at trial. Trial transcript, 29–30.

191. Italics mine.

192. Quoted in Selcraig, "Reverend Wildmon's War on the Arts" and Carr, *Fire in the Belly*, 491–92.

193. Of course, this widespread caricature of William Jennings Bryan was also misleading, saying more about representations of Christian evangelicals as rural, white, and uneducated than anything else. See Larson, *Summer for the Gods*.

194. Bull and Wildmon, trial transcript, 160–61.

195. Bull and Wildmon, trial transcript, 160–61 and Selcraig, "Reverend Wildmon's War on the Arts."

196. See, for instance, Wildmon, trial transcript, 142–43.

197. Wildmon deposition, 38.

198. Wildmon, trial transcript, 165.

199. Bering-Jensen, "Don Wildmon's Crusade," 16.

200. Sincerity and literalism differ, but literalist readings often presume (or seek to produce the feeling of) sincerity and, like sincerity, shun irony and sarcasm. McCrary's *Sincerely Held* offers a brilliant reading of sincerity across US law and culture. On what we might call the lived hermeneutics of Protestant literalism, see Bartkowski, "Beyond Biblical Literacy and Inerrancy."

201. Crapanzano, *Serving the Word*, xvi.

202. Ibid., xxi.

203. Good, "Medical Anthropology and the Category of Belief," 7.

204. Smith, *Faith and Belief*, 105–27; Smith, *Belief and History*, 36–69; and Good, "Medical Anthropology and the Category of Belief," 15–16.

205. Smith, *Belief and History*, 44; on performatives, see 42–43.

206. Good, "Medical Anthropology and the Problem of Belief," 9. This does not mean there is no use for figurative language. But within the sciences—and certain biblical traditions—the figurative and performative properties of language ostensibly took a back seat. Ostensibly because, as science studies scholars have shown, scientific writing cannot escape figuration, as cultural metaphors abound. See, e.g., Martin, "The Egg and the Sperm."

207. Good, "Medical Anthropology and the Category of Belief," 9; he draws on Taylor, *Human Agency and Language*.

208. I say popular versions of biblical literalism because academically trained Protestant theologians and biblical studies scholars working in this tradition are often far more careful in how they understand and apply biblical literalism. For a classic study, see Ramm's *Protestant Biblical Interpretation*. Ramm sometimes distinguishes between "wooden literalism" or "letterism" in ways that are far more careful than the popular and political uses of literalistic rhetoric (121–22). Moreover, Ramm explains, while the literalist method begins with literal or plain meaning as the privileged starting point for interpreting texts, this method need not reduce all text to a literal reading. When certain biblical passages call for a figurative reading, the literalist should follow.

209. Nor is my goal simply to criticize the aesthetics of literalism or claim it for conservative Christians alone. Good and Crapanzano are highly critical—and, I think, rightly so—of the ways that literalism (or empiricism, in Good's terminology) has become dominant in certain fields (e.g., religion, law, medicine). But this does not mean literalism itself is "bad" in some objective sense, or that the aesthetics of literalism is only conservative.

210. Ahlstrom, "Scottish Philosophy and American Theology," 257.

211. May, *Enlightenment in America*, 342.

212. Ibid., 344.

213. Ibid., 345.

214. Ibid., 345.

215. Ibid., 356.

216. On these parallels of perspicuity, see Marsden, *Fundamentalism and American Culture*, 16. On the perspicuity of scripture, see Ramm, *Protestant Biblical Interpretation*, 97–98.

217. Stein, *John Ruskin and Aesthetic Thought in America*, x.

218. Ibid., 230; and Gladden, "Christianity and Aestheticism." This section and the next condense an enormously rich history of US Christian visual culture and is greatly indebted to the scholarship of Morgan, Promey, Doss, and McDannell.

219. Morgan examines didactic (and devotional) approaches to visual culture in *Protestants and Pictures*, 9–10 and part 3, "Visual Pedagogy."

220. Promey, "Visible Liberalism," 88.

221. Promey, "Taste Cultures," 256, 260.

222. Greenberg, "Avant-Garde and Kitsch," 19.

223. Ibid., 18.

224. McDannell, *Material Christianity*, 163.

225. Kulka, *Kitsch and Art*, 97.

226. Tillich, *On Art and Architecture*, 132–33; also see Promey, "Taste Cultures," 258–9.

227. Promey, "Taste Cultures," 259.

228. McDannell, *Material Christianity*, 169–71, 174, 178.

229. See Promey, "Visible Liberalism," 91. George Will refers to the relativism of abstract art as nihilistic in "The Helms Bludgeon," *Washington Post*, August 3, 1989.

230. Wildmon, "Letter to Senators and Congressmen," April 12, 1990 (DWP, Box 99, Folder 4). The language of "decadence" also appears in Jesse Helms, "It's the Job of Congress to Define What's Art," *USA Today*, September 8, 1989; and Patrick Buchanan, "Why Subsidize Defamation?" *New York Post*, November 22, 1989.

231. Jones, "Put Up Yer Dukes," 14.

232. Quoted in Diane Haithman, "Frohnmayer Ending Stormy Tenure at NEA," *Los Angeles Times*, February 22, 1992.

233. Will, "Helms Bludgeon."

234. Noah, "On the Hill: Armey's Aesthetic," 14, 16.

235. Quoted in Babington, "Jesse Riles Again," 59. Meyer notes how Helms confuses realism and reality: penises represented versus corporeally present. "The Jesse Helms Theory of Art," 133.

236. Balmer, "Kinkade Crusade," 51.

237. Ibid., 50.

238. Ibid., 49 and Morgan, "Thomas Kinkade," 44.

239. Balmer, "Kinkade Crusade," 53.

240. See Morgan, "Art of Jon McNaughton"; Shrum, "Mormon American Nationalism and the Religiopolitical Art of Jon McNaughton"; and Babailov, "Resurrection of Realism."

241. Du Mez, *Jesus and John Wayne*; Butler, *White Evangelical Racism*; Whitehead and Perry, *Taking America Back for God*; Martin, *Gospel of J. Edgar Hoover*.

242. Crapanzano, *To Serve the Word*, 24; and Bendroth, *Fundamentalism and Gender*.

243. Twenty-first-century literalist arguments about sex and gender common in public discourse offer one of the most obvious examples of this masculinist hermeneutic. Arguments against trans people and rights often conflate "biological sex" with "real sex," which is then figured against the potential flexibility of gender. Pointing out that even "biological sex" might be less fixed than one assumes often leads to additional appeals to nature or to common sense in a significatory dance that circles around itself with seemingly no outside.

244. Coates, *What Is Protestant Art?*, 109–10.

245. Marsden, *Fundamentalism and American Culture* and Harding, *Book of Jerry Falwell*.

246. Crapanzano, *Serving the Word*, 15, italics mine.

247. And perhaps, in some ways, even to *be* queer sex, echoing Helms's confusion of representations of penises with penises themselves.

248. This fear of what images might do is not an exception to or even a contradiction within Wildmon's aesthetics of literalism. It is the very reason why images need to be safeguarded in this way, confined to this significatory prison, kept from the eyes of women and children, lest they run free in the imagination. Literalism, here, operates both as a descriptive account and as

a normative ideal. That is, when its description fails, when representation exceeds its rational constraints, it does not disqualify the description as inaccurate but doubles down with a normative claim about how representation ought to work.

249. Krauss, "Grids," 50.
250. Ibid.
251. Ibid., 52. Krauss finds earlier formations in Renaissance art.
252. Ibid., 63.
253. Ibid., 54.
254. Ibid., 55.
255. See Ibid., 54n1.
256. See Lippard, "Out of the Safety Zone."
257. Ibid. Lippard notes how "the harsh and iconoclastic exuberance of Dada" came through in Wojnarowicz's montages.
258. Wojnarowicz, *Weight of the Earth*, 119–20.
259. Carlin, "David Wojnarowicz: As the World Turns," 22. Jennifer Tyburczy calls him a "professional semiotician" in "Queer Acts of Recovery and Uncovering," 21.
260. See Lévi-Strauss, *Structural Anthropology*, 208; and Barthes, *Mythologies* (especially "Myth Today").
261. Quoted in Blinderman, "Compression of Time," 58.
262. Matthew Rose, "David Wojnarowicz: An Interview," *Arts Magazine*, May 1988, 65 (DWP, Box 4, Folder 36).
263. Albanese, *Republic of Mind and Spirit*, 5–15.
264. Carlin situates Wojnarowicz alongside Emerson and Whitman in "David Wojnarowicz: As the World Turns," 21, 29.
265. Wojnarowicz, *Close to the Knives*, 152.
266. Ibid.
267. Ibid., 26.
268. Ibid.
269. Quoted in Blinderman, "Compression of Time," 63.
270. Wojnarowicz, *Close to the Knives*, 113.
271. Ibid.
272. Ibid., 88; and Blinderman, "Compression of Time," 58.
273. Rizk offers fabulous analysis in "Looking at 'Animals in Pants.'"
274. Quoted in Blinderman, "Compression of Time," 59.
275. Ibid., 58.
276. Ibid., 59.
277. Tyburczy, "Queer Acts of Recovery and Uncovering," 17.
278. Carr, *Fire in the Belly*, 2.
279. Catholic iconography was not the only religious iconography in his work—I raise others in this short section, drawn from nature religion and from Native American spirituality, for instance. But it would require another book to satisfy a worthy analysis.
280. Postcard from Nan Goldin, July 16, 1990 (DWP, Box 3, Folder 22). The postcards appear across his correspondence and his personal papers.
281. See Jordan, *Silence of Sodom*.
282. Ryan, "Final Secret of David Wojnarowicz."
283. Rizk, "Nature, Death, and Spirituality," 148.
284. Krauss, "Grids," 52.
285. Carlin, "David Wojnarowicz: As the World Turns," 25. The reading in this paragraph draws greatly from Cameron and Rizk. Rizk, "Nature, Death, and Spirituality," 148–50.
286. Aramphongphan, "An Artist in the Secular World," 41.
287. Wojnarowicz, "Spirituality for Paul Thek," notes, n.d. (DWP, Box 4, Folder 103).
288. Ibid.
289. Wojnarowicz, sketch of *Spirituality (for Paul Thek)*, n.d. (DWP, Box 4, Folder 103).
290. Wojnarowicz, *Weight of the Earth*.
291. The Wojnarowicz archive includes a copy of the mailed correction, sent on October 25, 1990 (DWP, Box 14, Folder 68).
292. Quoted in Phillips, "Wojnarowicz Bags Buck," 240, cited in Meyer, *Outlaw Representation*, 342n70.

Chapter 4

1. Jordan, *Blessing Same-Sex Unions*, 207.
2. Quoted in DIVA TV, *Like a Prayer*. On the "Stop the Church" protest, see Petro, *After the Wrath of God*, 137–85, which describes in greater detail media responses to the protest that emphasized debates between sexual and religious freedom. This chapter focuses on ACT UP's participation, since DIVA TV was one of its affinity groups. On WHAM!, see Morgan, "From WHAM! to ACT UP." On ACT UP, also see Gould, *Moving Politics*; Brier, *Infectious Ideas*; Crimp and Rolston, *AIDS Demo Graphics*; and Schulman, *Let the Record Show*.
3. Quoted in DIVA TV, *Like a Prayer*.
4. Ray Kerrison, "Opinion Column," *New York Post*, December 11, 1989; Ray Kerrison, "Sacrilege in St. Pat's [Editorial]," *New York Post*, December 12, 1989; Ray Kerrison, "Unjoyful Noise: Worshippers Rights Violated [Editorial]," *New York Newsday*, December 12, 1989; and Ray Kerrison, "The Storming of St. Pat's [Editorial]," *New York Times*, December 12, 1989.
5. Jenkins, *New Anti-Catholicism*, 3, 101–4.
6. Weigel, "New Anti-Catholicism"; Jenkins, *New Anti-Catholicism*; and Massa, *Anti-Catholicism in America*. In 2002, *Commonweal* magazine joined with Fordham University to host a conference called "Anti-Catholicism: The Last Acceptable Prejudice?" that included remarks from several leading scholars of Roman Catholicism coming from a variety of methodological and political perspectives. See Steinfels, *American Catholics, American Culture*, 149–90.
7. These arguments about the secularist elimination of religion from the public sphere draw from Lutheran-turned-Catholic Richard John Neuhaus, *Naked Public Square*. See Griffith and McAlister, "Introduction: Is the Public Square Still Naked?" On histories of public Catholicism and abortion, see Casanova, *Public Religions in the Modern World*, ch. 7.
8. This footage appears in Hilferty, *Stop the Church*.
9. Sontag, "Notes on 'Camp,'" 280.
10. Newton, "Role Models," 46. Also see two important edited volumes: Cleto's *Camp* and Meyer's *Politics and Poetics of Camp*.
11. Pellegrini, "After Sontag."
12. Newton, "Role Models," 46 and Bergman, "Strategic Camp," 92.
13. Muñoz, *Disidentifications*, 120.
14. Not that this was new in itself—Catholicism has long served as a rich site for camp.
15. There are many other films from the period we could add. And not all focus on Catholicism. Gregg Bordowitz's *Fast Trip, Long Drop* (1993), for instance, combines an aesthetics of queer camp, Jewish humor, and reflections on disease, depression, and loss in important and moving ways that call for much greater scholarly attention.
16. Bullert, "Stop the Church" and Robert Hilferty, "Why 'Stop the Church' Was Televised," *New York Times*, October 4, 1991.
17. Quoted in "Robert Hilferty, Writer and AIDS Activist, Is Dead at 49," *New York Times*, August 19, 2009. On *Stop the Church*, see Petro, *After the Wrath of God*, 137–85 and Hallas, *Reframing Bodies*, 77–113. Hilferty's film still calls for greater scholarly attention.
18. Navarro is not named in the mailer or image caption, which refers to "Jesus as depicted in the video." Wildmon's letter confuses some details, such as claiming the film shows activists crumbling communion wafers and stepping on them. There was media coverage of such actions in the aftermath of the "Stop the Church" protest, but such footage does not appear directly in *Like a Prayer* or *Stop the Church*.
19. Wildmon and the American Family Association mailer, "Letter to AFA Supporter," ca. 1991 (People for the American Way Collection of Conservative Political Ephemera, Box 5, Folder 19).
20. For an important criticism of this film, see Cheng, "How to Survive," 73–92.
21. Schulman and Hubbard, ACT UP Oral History Project.
22. Weigel, "New Anti-Catholicism," 25. While Massa and Jenkins make similar arguments, I focus on Weigel here because his article was one of the earliest and in my estimation one of the most compelling presentations of the "new anti-Catholicism" thesis. Massa offers a longer and more measured history of anti-Catholicism, one that attends to the different ways that Protestants and Catholics have come to see the world and that also deepens Weigel's argument about secularism. Jenkins' more polemical account traces the "new" anti-Catholic rhetoric across feminist and gay political movements, mainstream media, popular cultural representation, and the academy.
23. Weigel, *Catholicism*, 5.
24. McKeown, "Drawing Lines" (especially 54–57) offers a helpful guide to histories of anti-Catholicism, including Andrew Greeley's claim in the 1970s that Jewish elites were often

anti-Catholic, which provided another important background for the shift to issues of gender and sexuality by the 1980s.

25. See John Russell, "Images of Grief and Rage in Exhibitions on AIDS," *New York Times*, November 16, 1989 and Artists Space, *Witnesses*.

26. See Carr, *Fire in the Belly*, 442–61.

27. Weigel, "New Anti-Catholicism," 25 and Massa, *Anti-Catholicism in America*, 43–44.

28. Weigel, "New Anti-Catholicism," 26.

29. See Berlant and Freeman, "Queer Nationality."

30. Weigel, "New Anti-Catholicism," 25.

31. Scholars have thoroughly documented the history of anti-Catholic sentiment in colonial North America and the United States. See, e.g., Franchot, *Roads to Rome*; Curran, *Papist Devils*; McGreevy, *Catholicism and American Freedom*.

32. Later waves of Catholic immigrants, including Latinx Catholics, likewise find themselves confronting racial and religious barriers.

33. Weigel, "New Anti-Catholicism," 28.

34. Herberg's *Protestant, Catholic, Jew* represents a classic account of how Catholics were folded into the US mainstream. For a robust discussion of US Catholicism and racial politics, see Cressler, "Race, White Supremacy, and the Making of American Catholicism," which is his introduction for a 2016 forum on this topic in *American Catholic Studies*.

35. Weigel, "New Anti-Catholicism," 28.

36. Blanchard, *American Freedom and Catholic Power*.

37. Weigel, "New Anti-Catholicism," 30.

38. Kennedy, "Address," quoted in Weigel, "New Anti-Catholicism," 29, italics mine.

39. Weigel, "New Anti-Catholicism," 30.

40. Ibid., 30.

41. For similar points, see Massa, *Anti-Catholicism in America* and Jenkins, *New Anti-Catholicism*.

42. Weigel, "New Anti-Catholicism," 30. See John Leo, "The Gay Tide of Catholic-Bashing," *U.S. News and World Report*, April 1, 1991.

43. To be fair, many feminist and queer historians also presume these movements to be essentially secular and opposed to religion. In this case, too, the presumption hides more than it reveals.

44. Jenkins, *New Anti-Catholicism*, 93, 100–102.

45. My claim is not that such activists were not "secular," if we understand "secular" in the ways that scholars of secularism have come to see religion and the secular not as opposites but as overlapping modes of discourse. In this sense, these activists' aims, and the way they approach religion, are shaped by normative secularism in the ways scholars like Pellegrini, Jakobsen, Asad, or Mahmood would understand the secular; but then, so are the Catholics and members of the Church hierarchy whom Weigel would laud (and not see as "secular" in his terms). Let me say this differently. From the perspective of secularism studies, none of the players in Weigel's discussion, including the Catholic hierarchy itself, operate outside of the influence of the secular—many of the ways they think about religion, and especially about the relation of religion to identity, gender, and sexuality, have been shaped by the project of Protestant secularism. Meanwhile, a "secularist" position, if I understand Weigel, would argue that religion should have no role in the public sphere. I would agree with him that secularist positions, in that sense, are faulty and untenable in a democracy. I disagree that movements for gender and sexual rights are wholly secularist in this way. In fact, many such activists have been incredibly devout or have worked with and through religious ritual and practice in their own lives. Scholars are still only beginning to address this. The problem is that many activists have encountered opposition within their religious traditions and thus have had to contest those traditions or forge new religious and ethical communities. That can sometimes look like anti-Catholicism or secularist attack, especially within a discursive framework that already figures religion in opposition to gender and sexual freedom. Jakobsen's *Sex Obsession* is very helpful on these points.

46. Weigel, "New Anti-Catholicism," 31; see also Schaeffer, *Christian Manifesto*.

47. See Jakobsen and Pellegrini, *Love the Sin*.

48. Petro, *After the Wrath of God*, 140–46. The action at Helms's house is documented in Hilferty and Huff, *Deadlier than a Virus*. On the history of ACT UP/NY, see Schulman, *Let the Record Show*.

49. United States Catholic Conference Administrative Board, "Many Faces of AIDS."

50. National Conference of Catholic Bishops, "Called to Compassion and Responsibility."

51. Associated Press, "Cardinal O'Connor Won't Join an Operation Rescue," *Philadelphia Daily News*, October 9, 1989.

52. See Petro, *After the Wrath of God*, ch. 3 and 4.
53. Wayne Barrett, "Holier Than Thou," *Village Voice*, December 25, 1984, 12; Cuomo, "Religious Belief and Public Morality"; and Kenneth A. Briggs, "Cuomo vs. Bishops," *New York Times*, September 14, 1984.
54. Petro, *After the Wrath of God*, 155–71.
55. Kinsella, *Covering the Plague*.
56. Treichler, *How to Have Theory in an Epidemic*; Winston, "News Coverage of Religion, Sexuality, and AIDS"; and Juhasz, *AIDS TV*, 31–74.
57. Winston, "News Coverage of Religion, Sexuality, and AIDS," 377–84.
58. Advisory Committee for People with AIDS, "Denver Principles."
59. See Epstein, *Impure Science* and Patton, *Inventing AIDS*.
60. Saalfield (now Gund), "On the Make."
61. Hallas, *Reframing Bodies*.
62. See, for example, Juhasz, *AIDS TV* and Saalfield and Navarro, "Shocking Pink Praxis." Also see Juhasz and Kerr, *We Are Having This Conversation Now*.
63. Juhasz, *AIDS TV*, 34–44.
64. Ibid., 42 and Hallas, *Reframing Bodies*, 86–87.
65. Saalfield, "On the Make," 26, italics original.
66. Ibid., 31.
67. The other two films were *Target City Hall*, which covered ACT UP's protest against the Koch administration on March 28, 1989, and *Pride*, which covered the twentieth anniversary Pride March in New York City.
68. James Wentzy revitalized DIVA TV after joining ACT UP in 1990. In 1993, he began airing a thirty-minute weekly public access show called "AIDS Community Television." For more information about Wentzy, see Juhasz, "So Many Alternatives," parts 1 and 2 and Juhasz, *AIDS TV*.
69. The writing is in all caps, broken into three separate segments that appear sequentially. DIVA TV, *Like a Prayer*.
70. Early Christian practices of confession were public and served as rituals of moral pedagogy for the broader community. Here, the activists subverted this practice to produce a counter-discourse. See Foucault, "Pastoral Power and Political Reason."
71. The clowns of Operation Ridiculous recalled a major development in queer theater in the 1960s and 1970s, Charles Ludlam's Theatre of the Ridiculous. See Marranca and Dasgupta, *Theatre of the Ridiculous*; Edgecomb, "History of the Ridiculous"; and Bordowitz, *The AIDS Crisis Is Ridiculous*.
72. "Cardinal Hails Protesters in Operation Rescue," *Buffalo News*, October 12, 1989, A18 and Associated Press, "Vatican AIDS Meeting Hears O'Connor Assail Condom Use," *New York Times*, November 14, 1989, A10.
73. My discussion of these narrative devices does not move chronologically, since the devices themselves appear at various moments through the documentary, sometimes repeating. I want to highlight how they work to disrupt any simple chronology in the video that might be suggested by the timeline of the protest or the presentation of the Seven Deadly Sins.
74. One DIVA TV member calls it a fable. Saalfield, "On the Make," 32.
75. Hallas, *Reframing Bodies*, 35–76, 78, 84.
76. Ibid., 81. Bordowitz's *Fast Trip, Long Drop* also plays with news media and authority in fascinating ways.
77. This footage is included in "Ray's Tape" in the AIDS Activist Videotape Collection, New York Public Library. Though this scene did not make it into *Like a Prayer*, I include it here as another example of the journalistic drag that Navarro and DIVA TV brought to *Stop the Church*.
78. Saalfield, "On the Make," 34–35.
79. Jordan, *Blessing Same-Sex Unions*, 155.
80. See, for example, Steinberg, *Sexuality of Christ in Renaissance Art* and Rambuss, *Closet Devotions*. On Madonna's "Like a Prayer" as liberation theology, see Hulsether, "Like a Sermon." Jesuit priest Andrew Greeley offers a positive reading of Madonna in *God in Popular Culture*.
81. Isherwood, *The World in the Evening*, 110. There are other designations of camp, notably the partitioning of high from low camp, but I find them less helpful here.
82. His cohort in the Whitney's studio program included AIDS activists and filmmakers Ellen Spiro and Catherine Saalfield (now Gund). P. Navarro, Interview by Sarah Schulman, July 20, 2007. Also see R. Navarro, "Eso, me esta pasando."
83. P. Navarro, Interview by Sarah Schulman and Levine, "Another Kind of Love."

84. Levine, "Another Kind of Love," 4.
85. Cheng, "How to Survive," 88–89. In this essay, Cheng is also rightly critical of the dramatic employment of Navarro as the sacrificial non-white character of *How to Survive a Plague*.
86. Saalfield, "On the Make," 33.
87. Carlomusto, Interview by Sarah Schulman, December 19, 2002, 34.
88. Ibid., 34.
89. See, e.g., Prothero, *American Jesus*; Pelikan, *Jesus through the Centuries*; Bynum, *Fragmentation and Redemption*; Bynum, *Christian Materiality*; and Blum and Harvey, *The Color of Christ*.
90. Greeley, *Catholic Imagination*, 6.
91. Mahmood, "Religious Reason and Secular Affect," 843 and Keane, *Christian Moderns*.
92. Sullivan, *Impossibility of Religious Freedom* and Smith, *Meaning and End of Religion*.
93. Mitchell, *What Do Pictures Want?*; Bernstein, "Scriptive Things"; Bennett, *Vibrant Matter*; and Chen, *Animacies*.
94. Mahmood, "Religious Reason and Secular Affect," 842.
95. McDannell, *Material Christianity*, 189. Also see Morgan, *Visual Piety* and Promey, *Sensational Religion*.
96. On Sallman's image and its reception, Morgan's edited volume *Icons of American Protestantism* is indispensable.
97. Morgan, "Introduction," 21 and Morgan, " 'Would Jesus Have Sat for a Portrait?,' " 196–203. This discussion is indebted to David Morgan's fascinating analysis of the reception of Sallman's Jesus, including criticisms that it was "effeminate" and even "homoerotic." " 'Would Jesus Have Sat for a Portrait?,' " 197.
98. Lyon, "Of Plaster Statues and Romantic Heresy," 172.
99. McDannell, *Material Christianity*, 182.
100. Goizueta, "Symbolic World of Mexican American Religion." On Mexican American religions, see Espinosa and García, *Mexican American Religions* and Matovina, *Latino Catholicism*.
101. Carlomusto, Interview by Sarah Schulman.
102. See, e.g., Steidl, "Chicano Movement in the U.S. Catholic Church" and García, *Católicos*. On uses of political ritual and spirituality in Chicano activism, see León, *Political Spirituality of Cesar Chavez*.
103. Goizueta, "Symbolic World of Mexican American Religion," 120.
104. Davalos, " 'Real Way of Praying,' " 41.
105. Jordan, *Blessing Same-Sex Unions*, 89. See also Jordan, "Notes on Camp Theology."
106. Sedgwick, *Epistemology of the Closet*, 140. On queer attachments in Catholic aesthetics, see, e.g., Jordan, *Silence of Sodom*; Hanson, *Decadence and Catholicism*; and Giles, *American Catholic Arts and Fictions*, 273–95.
107. Sisters of Perpetual Indulgence, "Sistory" and Wilcox, *Queer Nuns*.
108. Butler, *Gender Trouble*, 175.
109. Ibid., 176.
110. Sedgwick, "Paranoid Reading and Reparative Reading," 149–50.
111. For an indispensable account of "other" Catholics in US history, see Byrne, *The Other Catholics*.

Chapter 5

1. Cox, "Feminist Artist Statement."
2. First Amendment Center, flier for "Exploring the 'Yo Mama' Controversy: Art, Outrage, and the First Amendment," (Renée Cox Papers (hereafter RCP), Box 2, Folder 65) and First Amendment Center, "Exploring 'Yo Mama': Art, Outrage, and the First Amendment," press release and event announcement, February 16, 2001 (RCP, Box 3, Folder 33).
3. Renée Cox, "Artist Statement," ca. 1990s–2008 (RCP, Box 1, Folder 34).
4. Elisabeth Bumiller, "Affronted by Nude 'Last Supper,' Giuliani Calls for Decency Panel," *New York Times*, February 16, 2001, A1, B4 (RCP, Box 2, Folder 65).
5. Stevenson Swanson, "Nude 'Last Supper' Infuriates NYC Mayor," *Chicago Tribune*, February 16, 2001 (RCP, Box 2, Folder 65).
6. Leonard Greene, " 'Critic' Nabbed in B'klyn Museum," *New York Post*, February 23, 2001 (RCP, Box 3, Folder 33). On "Corporate Sacrilege," see Detzner, "Corporate Sacrilege."
7. Bill Hoffman, "Oh, Mama! Mary's a Bikini Babe Now," *New York Post*, April 5, 2001 (RCP, Box 3, Folder 33).
8. First Amendment Center, "Exploring the 'Yo Mama' Controversy."

9. Monte Williams, "'Yo Mama' Artist Takes on Catholic Critic," *New York Times*, February 21, 2001 (RCP, Box 2, Folder 65).

10. "Art Debate Ensues," *Catalyst*, April 23, 2001, https://www.catholicleague.org/art-debate-ensues/.

11. Quoted in Andrea Peyser, "2 Photo Debaters Are Big Negatives," *New York Post*, February 21, 2001, 18 (RCP, Box 2, Folder 65).

12. "Art Debate Ensues."

13. Quoted in Karen Croft, "Using Her Body," *Salon*, February 22, 2001 (RCP, Box 2, Folder 65).

14. Both quoted in Joshua Robin, "'Mama' Artist Faces a Critic," *Newsday*, February 21, 2001, A6 (RCP Box 2, Folder 65) and Williams, "'Yo Mama' Artist Takes on Catholic Critic."

15. Peyser, "2 Photo Debaters Are Big Negatives."

16. Swanson, "Nude 'Last Supper' Infuriates NYC Mayor."

17. See, e.g., Lukianoff and Haidt, "Coddling of the American Mind."

18. Arthur Danto made the same claim about art experts called to testify in Minnesota about Robert Mapplethorpe. Danto, *Playing with the Edge*, 85–89.

19. Renée Cox, "Biography," c. 1990s–2008 (RCP, Box 1, Folder 34). In other statements, she describes herself as "born and raised Catholic."

20. Cox, "Artist Statement."

21. Robert Ingrassia, "Maverick with a Middle Class Start," *Daily News*, February 16, 2001, 5 (RCP, Box 3, Folder 33).

22. Croft, "Using Her Body."

23. Quoted in Robert Morales, "Renée Cox: Shutterbug Saint," *Vibe*, n.d., 67 (RCP, Box 2, Folder 65).

24. Ingrassia, "Maverick with a Middle Class Start."

25. Cox, "Artist Statement."

26. Nash, *Black Body in Ecstasy*, 27–29. On race, sexuality, and excess, see Musser, *Sensual Excess*.

27. Golden, "My Brother," 25.

28. Ibid., 33.

29. "Interview with Renée Cox" (no information) (RCP, Box 1, Folder 34). The text matches an interview in an Italian magazine (Parravicini, "Renée Cox"). Histories of slavery, racism, or civil rights and Roman Catholicism in the United States include Swarns, *The 272*; McGreevy, *Parish Boundaries*; Endres, *Slavery and the Catholic Church in the United States*; Williams, *Subversive Habits*; Cressler, *Authentically Black and Truly Catholic*; and Mickens, *In the Shadow of Ebenezer*.

30. Quoted in White, "Fragmented Souls," 48.

31. Ibid.

32. Clipping in RCP, Box 2, Folder 35. The story appears in the *New York Times* in "3 Whites Charged in Burning of a Black," January 8, 1993, A13.

33. See Cox's drawing and notes for this piece in "Project: Frame for Black Christ" (RCP, Box 2, Folder 35).

34. Cone, *The Cross and the Lynching Tree.*

35. Prothero, *American Jesus*, 206.

36. Raboteau, *Slave Religion* and Prothero, *American Jesus*, 208–14.

37. Pinder, "'Our Father, God,'" 231–32. Prothero and Pinder both note the history of literary renderings as well, as in Countee Cullen's 1929 poem "The Black Christ" and Langston Hughes's "Christ in Alabama" and "Goodbye Christ." On Langston Hughes and religion, see Best, *Langston's Salvation.*

38. Pinder, "'Our Father, God,'" 230.

39. Quoted in White, "Fragmented Souls," 52.

40. Cox, "Artist Statement."

41. Cox, "Feminist Artist Statement."

42. This connection and the Last Supper joke are from Prothero, *American Jesus*, 224. See, for instance, *In Living Color*, season 5, episode 13, "Wheel of Dozens," 1993.

43. Liss, *Feminist Art and the Maternal*, 96, 98.

44. Ibid., 105.

45. Some pieces in this collection overlap with the *Yo Mama* series and other collections.

46. Press release for Blackskins by Renée Cox, April 27–May 20, 1995, at Pulse Art (RCP, Box 1, Folder 34).

47. Quoted in the press release for Blackskins, from hooks, *Sisters of the Yam*, 95–96.

48. hooks, *Art on My Mind*, 57, 60.

49. Ibid., 58.

50. Quoted in Croft, "Using Her Body."

51. Prothero, *American Jesus*, 224.

52. Heartney, "Thinking Through the Body," 12.

53. Croft, "Using Her Body."

54. On its history and reception, see Steinberg, *Leonardo's Incessant Last Supper*.

55. A. J. B. Lane, "The Last Supper of Donald Trump," *Boston Globe*, September 26, 2018, bostonglobe.com.

56. Beck, "Andy Warhol: Sixty Last Suppers."

57. Klaudia Ofwona Draber, "The Ten Commandments of Renée Cox," Princeton Art Museum, accessed May 21, 2024, https://artmuseum.princeton.edu/story/ten-commandme nts-ren%C3%A9e-cox.

58. Clague, "The Christa," 84–87 and Kenneth A. Briggs, "Cathedral Removing Statue of Crucified Woman," *New York Times*, April 28, 1984, 27.

59. Briggs, "Cathedral Removing Statue," 27.

60. Ibid.

61. Mitchel J. Farrell, "Christa: Woman Climbs on the Cross to Challenge Christianity's Male Dominance," *National Catholic Reporter*, April 5, 1985, 11–12.

62. Gaulke, "Cheri Gaulke: An Oral History" and Gaulke, "Interview with Cheri Gaulke."

63. Gaulke, "Cheri Gaulke: An Oral History."

64. Allyn et al., *Sisters of Survival*.

65. Gaulke, "Interview with Cheri Gaulke."

66. Clague, "Divine Transgressions" and Korte, "Blasphemous Feminist Art."

67. One could also read Cox's *Yo Mama's Last Supper* as a play on Mary, as the imagery references back to *The Yo Mama* and *Yomamadonna and Child*, as does the textual naming in "Yo Mama."

68. Fleetwood, *Troubling Vision*, 110–11. Also see Rebecca Schneider's *Explicit Body in Performance*.

69. Fleetwood, *Troubling Vision*, 29.

70. Quoted in Vinita Srivastava, "The Woman Behind the Storm," *Savoy*, May 2001, 39–40 (RCP, Box 2, Folder 65).

71. Cox, "Artist Talk."

72. Cyril of Jerusalem, Lecture XX (Of Baptism), 2:3.

73. Ibid., 2:6–7.

74. Bumiller, "Affronted by Nude 'Last Supper'" and Cox "Artist Talk."

75. Patnaik, "Diasporic Double Vision," 32.

76. Holland Cotter, "Nihilists Beware: A Swatch of Black Life, 'Family of Man' Style," *New York Times*, February 16, 2001, E36 (RCP, Box 2, Folder 65) and Vince Aletti, "Substance Not Sensation in Brooklyn: Body and Soul," *Village Voice*, March 13, 2001, 71.

77. Taylor, "Empowering the Eye," 22, 24. His notion of "ethno-spirituality" resonates with Judith Weisenfeld's theorization of "religio-racial" identity and helps in thinking across aesthetics and identity, not only in the work in this collection but also in that of many artists discussed in this book for whom religious and ethnic identities (Jewish, Irish-American, Chicano) and aesthetics come together in important ways. See Weisenfeld, *New World A-Coming*.

78. Cox, "Feminist Artist Statement"; Cox, "Artist Statement"; and White, "Fragmented Souls," 53–54.

79. Donohue, "Brooklyn Museum of Art Offends Again."

80. Ibid.

81. "Brooklyn Museum of Art Ignites New War," *Catalyst*, March 23, 2001, https://www.catholiclea gue.org/brooklyn-museum-of-art-ignites-new-war/.

82. Joseph Dolman, "There *Are* Other Photos in that Exhibit," *Newsday*, February 21, 2001, A32.

83. David Schwartz and Lauren Rubin, "Cardinal Draws Art Line," *New York Daily News*, March 5, 2001, 3 (RCP, Box 3, Folder 33) and Dean E. Murphy, "Scandal in the Church: The New York Cardinal; Egan Says He May Have Mishandled Sex Abuse Cases," *New York Times*, April 21, 2002, 31.

84. A. Vasquez, letter to Renée Cox, March 5, 2001 (RPC, Box 2, Folder 65).

85. Michael R. Blood, "Rudy and 'Yo Mama' Duke It Out Over Pic: Mayor Wants Museum 'Decency' Panel," *Daily News*, February 16, 2001, 5 (RCP, Box 2, Folder 65) and Sam Roberts, "Thomas V. Daily, Bishop With Legacy Tarnished by Response to Abuse, Dies at 89," *New York Times*, May 15, 2017.

86. Bumiller, "Affronted by Nude 'Last Supper'" and Dan Janison and Ray Sánchez, "Giuliani Blasts Artist: Say Photographer Has Anti-Catholic Agenda," *Newsday*, February 17, 2001, A2.
87. James H. Miller, "Controversial 'Hip-Hop' Version of the Virgin Mary Given to MoMA," Art Newspaper, April 18, 2018, https://www.theartnewspaper.com. Okediji's interpretation is described in Cosentino, "Hip-Hop Assemblage," 44.
88. Mitchell, *What Do Pictures Want?*, 141.
89. Quoted in Cosentino, "Hip-Hop Assemblage," 43.
90. Halle, "Controversy Over the Show *Sensation*," 150.
91. Cosentino, "Hip-Hop Assemblage," 40–43.
92. Michael Kimmelman, "Making and Taking Office, Elevated to Art Form," *New York Times*, February 16, 2001, B4 (RCP, Box 2, Folder 65).
93. Quoted in Croft, "Using Her Body."
94. Fusco, "Captain Shit," 45, 43.
95. Both Fusco and Cosentino make similar points on this front. Fusco, "Captain Shit," 43–45 and Cosentino, "Hip-Hop Assemblage," 47.
96. Fusco, "Captain Shit," 45.
97. William Donohue, "Myths Color 'Sensation' Exhibit," *Catalyst*, November 26, 1999, https://www.catholicleague.org/myths-color-sensation-exhibit/.
98. Giuliani, "Rights and Responsibilities of Public-Funded Cultural Institutions" and Giuliani, "Mayor Giuliani Announces Appointments to Cultural Affairs Advisory Commission." When Michael Bloomberg took over as mayor following Giuliani, he kept the commission but nixed its role in screening for "decency." Jennifer Steinhauer, "Metro Briefing/New York: Manhattan: Mayo Names Cultural Advisors," *New York Times*, February 25, 2003, B4.
99. Quoted in broadcast transcript by Video Monitoring Service of America, Inc., for *Inside City Hall*, NY1-TV, April 3, 2001 (RCP, Box 3, Folder 33).
100. Fred Kaplan, "Religious Renditions Pit Mayor Against Museum Again," *Boston Globe*, February 16, 2001 (RCP, Box 2, Folder 65).
101. Quoted in Bumiller, "Affronted by Nude 'Last Supper.'"
102. Blood, "Rudy and 'Yo Mama' Duke It Out Over Pic."
103. Amy Reiter, "New York's Bully in Chief Meets His Match," *Salon*, February 16, 2001 (RCP, Box 2, Folder 65).
104. Fleetwood, *Troubling Visions*, 108.
105. Laura Miller, "The New Victimology," *Salon*, February 17, 2001 (RCP, Box 2, Folder 65).
106. Kimmelman, "Making and Taking Office."
107. Michael Kimmelman, "Critic's Notebook; 'Yo Mama' Artist's Past as Superhero," *New York Times*, February 17, 2001, B3 (RCP, Box 2, Folder 65).
108. Lyle Ashton Harris, draft of "Letter to the Editor" (RCP, Box 2, Folder 65).
109. Pollitt, "Anti-Catholic? Round Two," 10.
110. Srivastava, "Woman Behind the Storm."
111. Danto, "In the Bosom of Jesus."
112. See n98.
113. Ray and Gibbons, "Why Are States Banning Critical Race Theory" and Wamsley, "What's in the So-Called 'Don't Say Gay' Bill that Could Impact the Whole Country."
114. Petro, *After the Wrath of God*. Of course, progressives also employ moral rhetoric, but conservatives tend to claim it more insistently in public debate and often do so to limit the rights and privileges of citizenship, whereas as liberal and leftist moral rhetoric more often seeks to expand citizenship in various ways. One could argue that "cancel culture" is one way that progressives moralize in the ways I discuss here. But most claims of cancellation are vastly exaggerated, even dramatic—it is not clear, for instance, on what grounds cultural elites with access to major venues like the *New York Times* are "canceled" or what it means for them to be "canceled." If we think of "canceling" as the use of non-state power to shape the grounds of acceptable speech regarding race, sexuality, and gender, we might come closer to what is happening. That would be an example of forging a type of moral community that liberals and leftists might want to see (granted, they often disagree). But shy of liberals earnestly calling en masse for a ban on heterosexuality, cisgender people, or education about the history of the Right, the "both-sides-ism" claim hardly holds.
115. Quoted in Ray Sánchez, "Artist Says Work Critiques Catholic Church's Treatment of Blacks, Women," *Newsday*, February 16, 2001 (RCP, Box 2, Folder 65).

116. Quoted in Nichole M. Christian, "Amid Strong Debate, Mild Curiosity at the Exhibition," *New York Times*, February 17, 2001.

117. See Lukianoff and Haidt, "Coddling of the American Mind"; Lukianoff and Schlott, *Canceling of the American Mind*; Campbell and Manning, "New Millennial 'Morality.'"

118. McTernan, "Taking Offense," 179–80. the "culture of victimhood" comes from sociologists Campbell and Manning, "Microaggression and Moral Cultures."

119. Lukianoff and Haidt, "Coddling of the American Mind," cited in McTernan, "Taking Offense," 180.

120. McTernan, "Taking Offense," 208. See also McTernan, *On Taking Offence*.

121. McTernan, "Taking Offense," 208.

122. Castelli sees in this naming a metaphorical slippage from the "War on Terror." "Persecution Complexes," 175n5.

123. Ibid., 160.

124. Ibid., 159.

125. Ibid., 161.

126. Ibid.

127. The growing body of scholarship on whiteness and conservative Christianity includes Butler, *White Evangelical Racism*; Du Mez, *Jesus and John Wayne*; and Whitehead and Perry, *Taking God Back for America*. Most studies foreground evangelicals, but histories of Catholicism and whiteness (including Irish- and Italian American forms) call for greater examination. See, e.g., Roediger, *Working Toward Whiteness*.

128. Castelli, "Persecution Complexes," 160.

129. Melanie Lefkowitz, "Protestor Arrested at B'klyn Museum," *Newsday*, February 23, 2001 (RCP, Box 3, Folder 33) and Greene, "'Critic' Nabbed in B'klyn Museum."

130. Paglia, "'Sensation' and the Lack of Sensation." On Paglia's Jewish comment and response to "anti-Catholicism," see Blume, "Oops, She Did It Again" and Pollitt, "Catholic Bashing?"

131. Mitchell, *What Images Want*, 136 and Robert D. McFadden, "Painting in Disputed Exhibit Attacked by Man at Museum," *New York Times*, December 17, 1999.

132. Mitchell, *What Images Want*, 127.

133. Ibid., 19.

134. Rodriguez-Plate, *Blasphemy*, 27.

135. Giuliani, "Rights and Responsibilities of Public-Funded Cultural Institutions."

136. Mark Hilan, WNYC-AM Radio, Morning Edition, broadcast transcript, Video Monitoring Services of America, February 16, 2001, (RCP, Box 2, Folder 65).

137. Bonilla-Silva, *Racism without Racists*.

138. NY1-TV, News All Day, broadcast transcript, Video Monitoring Services of America, February 16, 2001 (RCP, Box 2, Folder 65).

139. There are competing definitions and much debate over neoliberalism. Wendy Brown's *Undoing the Demos* guides my thinking here, as it addresses the larger cultural norms of neoliberalism. She draws from Foucault's *Society Must Be Defended*. Also see Harvey, *Brief History of Neoliberalism*.

140. Brown, *In the Ruins of Neoliberalism*, 28.

141. Masuzawa, *Invention of World Religions*.

142. Of course, differences inhere not only across religious traditions but also within them. Even the idea of coherent "religions" and of "religion" as a set of beliefs requires scrutiny. See Asad, *Genealogies of Religion*. On neoliberalism and religion, see Lofton, *Consuming Religion*.

143. Maggie Gallagher, "Art-Crit Tips for Mayors and Moguls," *New York Post*, February 24, 2001, 15 (RCP, Box 3, Folder 33).

144. Kimmelman, "Making and Taking Office."

145. "Art Debate Ensues."

146. Wheaton, "Seeking Salvation," 98 (italics mine).

147. Hilan, WNYC-AM Radio, Morning Edition Broadcast transcript.

148. Morales, "Renée Cox: Shutterbug Saint," 67.

149. The letter includes no author or date (RCP, Box 2, Folder 65).

150. Rose Mary C., letter to Renée Cox, February 17, 2001 (RCP, Box 2, Folder 65).

151. Kathleen H., letter to Renée Cox, March 20, 2001 (RCP, Box 2, Folder 65). It is not obvious from the letter, but one wonders if this author read the repeated naming of Cox as an "overt feminist" in the news.

152. A. Aryans, letter to Renée Cox, October 21, 2001 (RCP, Box 2, Folder 65).

153. The anonymous drawing is in RCP, Box 2, Folder 65.

154. It probably goes without saying but should nonetheless be said that women and people of color in particular often receive excessively hostile, even violent, forms of hate mail.

155. Letter to the editor, "On Artist as Self-Publicist," *The Record* (Bergen County, NJ), February 25, 2001, O3 (RCP, Box 2, Folder 65).

156. Timothy M., letter to New York One, on *Pro Ecclesia* letterhead, n.d. (RCP, Box 2, Folder 65).

157. Joseph B., letter to Renée Cox, March 26, 2001 (RCP, Box 2, Folder 65).

158. Theodore P., letter to Renée Cox, n.d. (RCP, Box 2, Folder 65).

159. Sally T., letter to Renée Cox, February 22, 2001 (RCP, Box 2, Folder 65).

160. Verena Dobnik and Associated Press, "Work Decried, Lauded," *Dallas Morning News*, February 17, 2001, 43A. We might grant that McIntyre meant Jesus was never nude at the Last Supper or in public. The former we cannot know, but it is likely the historical Jesus would have been stripped of his clothing while on the cross, as was the common practice at the time.

161. Sally T., letter to Renée Cox.

162. Cheryl M., letter to Renée Cox, February 19, 2001 (RCP, Box 2, Folder 65).

163. Nancy N-C., letter to Renée Cox, n.d. (RCP, Box 2, Folder 65).

164. L. T., letter to Renée Cox, March 6, 2001 (RCP, Box 2, Folder 65).

165. Janet S., letter to Renée Cox, April 7, 2001 (RCP, Box 2, Folder 65).

166. I believe the name is Ronn E., postcard to Renée Cox, n.d. (RCP, Box 2, Folder 65).

167. Gabriella V-W, letter to Renée Cox, April 6, 2001 (RCP, Box 2, Folder 65).

168. Gabriella V-W, letter to Arnold Lehman, March 31, 2001 (RCP, Box 1, Folder 25).

169. Howard Kissel, "B'klyn Show Merits Far Better 'Image,'" *Daily News*, February 16, 2001, 57 (RCP, Box 2, Folder 65).

170. Eversley, "Renée Cox: The Big Picture," 74.

171. Steve Gushee, "Art Rocks Boat—And So Did Jesus," *Palm Beach Post*, February 23, 2001, 3E.

172. Isaak, "American Family."

173. Cox, "Artist Talk."

174. Roberta Smith, "Art in Review: Renée Cox," *New York Times*, November 2, 2001, E40.

175. Ibid.

176. On the pairing of repression and arousal, see Largier, *In Praise of the Whip*.

177. Berlant, *Queen of America Goes to Washington City* and Dowland, *Family Values and the Rise of the Christian Right*.

Afterword

1. "Smithsonian Pulls Video, Wild Uproar Ensues," *Catalyst*, January 26, 2011, https://www.catholicleague.org/smithsonian-pulls-video-wild-uproar-ensues-4/; "Smithsonian Still Doesn't Get It," *Catalyst*, March 14, 2011, https://www.catholicleague.org/smithsonian-still-doesnt-get-it-2/; Editorial Board, "Bullying and Censorship," *New York Times*, December 6, 2010; Holland Cotter, "As Ants Crawl Over Crucifix, Dead Artist Is Assailed Again," *New York Times*, December 6, 2010; Devin Dwyer, "Art or Hate Speech? Video of Ants Crawling on Crucifix Pulled from Smithsonian," *ABC News*, December 3, 2010, https://abcnews.go.com/US/smithsonian-removes-ants-crucifix-video-exhibit-sparking-debate/story?id=12305404. On Wojnarowicz and moral panics, see Petro, "Sex, Art, and Moral Panic."

2. Quoted in David Itzkoff, "Video Deemed Offensive Pulled by Portrait Gallery," *New York Times*, December 1, 2010. Also see Dwyer, "Art or Hate Speech?"

3. See Jakobsen, "Is Secularism Less Violent than Religion?" and Ernst, *Islamophobia in America*.

4. Quoted in "Smithsonian Still Doesn't Get It."

5. Savage, "*Charlie Hebdo* and *Piss Christ*." We might consider Savage in the broader context of "homonationalism," which figures Islam (and Muslim-majority countries) as necessarily homophobic, in contrast to the culturally Christian countries of "the West." See Puar, *Terrorist Assemblages*.

6. Timothy P. Carney, "Associated Press Censored Muhammad Cartoons While Selling 'Piss Christ,'" *Washington Examiner*, January 7, 2015.

7. Savage, "*Charlie Hebdo* and *Piss Christ*."

8. Mahmood, "Religious Reason and Secular Affect," 841. Also see Mahmood, *Religious Difference in a Secular Age*.

9. See Butler, *Excitable Speech*.

10. Asad, *Genealogies of Religion* and Masuzawa, *Invention of World Religions*.

11. Gruber, *Praiseworthy One*.

12. Mahmood, "Religious Reason and Secular Affect," 841–42.
13. This modern knotting of religion and identity has a longer history. The common ways we understand modern identity are not the only ways to define identity or the work of identification. Foucault, especially in *History of Sexuality*, is helpful in situating particularly modern forms of identity, especially sexual and gender identity. The history of religious identity is not precisely the same as that of sexual identity, but the comparison is instructive. On the modern (and secular) privatization of religion, sexuality and gender, see Mahmood, "Sexuality and Secularism."
14. Quoted in Nunes, "Creator of 'Piss Christ' Photographs Trump, Torture, and a Killer Clown."
15. Flier for Political Funeral, ACT UP/NY, "DIVA TV: The Ashes Action."
16. Wojnarowicz, *Close to the Knives*, 122.
17. Quoted in Silverstein, "Why the Ashes of People with AIDS on the White House Lawn Matter."
18. Halford, "Interview with Ron Goldberg."
19. Ibid.
20. Troyer, "Technologies of the HIV/AIDS Corpse."
21. On French secularism, Catholicism, and art, see Oliphant, *The Privilege of Being Banal*.
22. Steinberg, *Sexuality of Christ*, especially 84, 310–25.
23. Bynum, *Fragmentation and Redemption*, 79–118.
24. Ibid., 117, italics mine.

Selected Bibliography

Archival Collections

AIDS Activist Video Collection (AAVC), 1985–2000. New York Public Library Archive and Manuscripts, New York, NY.

David Wojnarowicz Papers (DWP), ca. 1954–1992. Fales Library and Special Collections. New York University, New York, NY.

Marlon Riggs Papers (MRP), 1957–1994. Manuscripts Division, Special Collections. Stanford University Library, Stanford, CA.

Papers of Judy Chicago (JCP), 1947–2004. Schlesinger Library. Radcliffe Institute, Cambridge, MA.

People for the American Way Collection of Conservative Political Ephemera (PAWC), 1980–2004. Bancroft Library. University of California, Berkeley, CA.

Renée V. Cox Papers (RCP), 1945–2016. Archives of American Art. Smithsonian Institution, Washington, DC.

Sheree Rose and Bob Flanagan Papers and Photographs Collection (SRBF). ONE Archives. University of Southern California, Los Angeles, CA.

Additional Sources

Abu-Lughod, Lila. "The Romance of Resistance: Tracing Transformation of Power through Bedouin Women." *American Ethnologist* 17, no. 1 (February 1990): 41–55.

ACT UP/NY. "DIVA TV." Accessed March 7, 2017. http://www.actupny.org/divatv/.

ACT UP/NY. "DIVA TV: The Ashes Action (1992)." Accessed March 7, 2017. http://www.actupny.org/diva/synAshes.html.

Advisory Committee for People with AIDS. "The Denver Principles." June 1983. Accessed March 7, 2017. http://www.actupny.org/documents/Denver.html.

Ahlstrom, Sydney. "The Scottish Philosophy and American Theology." *Church History* 24, no. 3: 257–72.

Albanese, Catherine. *A Republic of Mind and Spirit: A Cultural History of American Metaphysical Religion* (New Haven, CT: Yale University Press, 2008).

Albright, Thomas. "Primarily Biological." *Artnews* 78, no. 6 (Summer 1979): 156–58.

Allitt, Patrick. *Catholic Intellectuals and Conservative Politics in America, 1950–1985* (New York: Cornell University Press, 1993).

Allyn, Jerri, Anne Gauldin, Cheri Gaulke, and Sue Mayberry. *Sisters of Survival* (Los Angeles: Otis College of Art and Design, 2011).

American Family Association. "About AFA." AFA Media. Accessed November 4, 2023. https://web.archive.org/web/20060206163315/http://media.afa.net/newdesign/about.asp.

Amin, Kadji. *Disturbing Attachments: Genet, Modern Pederasty, and Queer History* (Durham, NC: Duke University Press, 2017).

Aramphongphan, Paisid. "An Artist in the Secular World: Paul Thek's Relics." *American Art* 31, no. 1 (Spring 2021): 41–61.

Artists Space. "Press Release." November 16, 1989. https://texts.artistsspace.org/9ekljhsr.

Artists Space. *Witnesses: Against Our Vanishing* (New York: Artists Space Exhibitions, 1989).

Asad, Talal. *Genealogies of Religion: Discipline and Reasons of Power in Christianity and Islam* (Baltimore, MD: Johns Hopkins University Press, 1993).

Babailov, Igor V. "The Resurrection of Realism: Beauty Will Save the World." *Faith and Culture: The Journal of the Augustine Institute*, March 19, 2019. https://www.faithandcult ure.com.

Babington, Charles. "Jesse Riles Again." *Museum and Arts Washington*, November/December 1989, 58–9, 138.

Bailey, Beth. *Sex in the Heartland* (Cambridge, MA: Harvard University Press, 2002).

Balmer, Randall. *Bad Faith: Race and the Rise of the Religious Right* (Grand Rapids, MI: William B. Eerdmans Publishing, 2021).

Balmer, Randall. "The Kinkade Crusade." *Christianity Today*, December 4, 2000, 48–55.

Barthes, Roland. *Mythologies*, translated by Richard Howard and Annette Lavers (1957; New York: Hill and Wang, 2012).

Bartkowski, John. "Beyond Biblical Literacy and Inerrancy: Conservative Protestants and the Hermeneutic Interpretation of Scripture." *Sociology of Religion* 57, no. 3 (Autumn 1996): 259–72.

Battista, Kathy. "New Critical Positions: Disrupting a White Feminist Canon." *Third Text* 29, no. 4-5 (2015): 397–412.

Beck, Jessica. "Andy Warhol: Sixty Last Suppers." *Gagosian Quarterly*, Summer 2017. https://gagosian.com/quarterly/2017/05/01/andy-warhol-sixty-last-suppers/.

Bell, Christopher M., ed. *Blackness and Disability: Critical Examinations and Cultural Interventions* (Berlin, Germany: LIT Verlag, 2011).

Bendroth, Margaret Lamberts. *Fundamentalism and Gender, 1875 to the Present* (New Haven, CT: Yale University Press, 1993)

Bennett, Jane. *Vibrant Matter: A Political Ecology of Things* (Durham, NC: Duke University Press, 2010).

Bergman, David. "Strategic Camp: The Art of Gay Rhetoric." In *Camp Ground: Style and Homosexuality*, edited by David Bergman (Amherst: University of Massachusetts Press, 1993), 92–109.

Berlant, Lauren. *The Queen of America Goes to Washington City: Essays on Sex and Citizenship* (Durham, NC: Duke University Press, 1997).

Berlant, Lauren, and Elizabeth Freeman. "Queer Nationality." In *Fear of a Queer Planet: Queer Politics and Social Theory*, edited by Michael Warner (Minneapolis: University of Minnesota Press, 1993), 193–229.

Bernstein, Robin. "Scriptive Things." In *Racial Innocence: Performing American Childhood from Slavery to Civil Rights* (New York: NYU Press, 2011), ch. 2.

Best, Stephen, and Sharon Marcus. "Surface Reading: An Introduction." *Representations* 108, no. 1 (Fall 2009): 1–21.

Best, Wallace D. *Langston's Salvation: American Religion and the Bard of Harlem* (New York: NYU Press, 2017).

Biale, David. *Not in the Heavens: The Tradition of Jewish Secular Thought* (Princeton, NJ: Princeton University Press, 2011).

Black, Gregory D. *The Catholic Crusade against the Movies, 1940–1975* (Cambridge: Cambridge University Press, 1998).

Blanshard, Paul. *American Freedom and Catholic Power* (New York: Beacon Press, 1949).

Blinderman, Barry. "The Compression of Time: Interview with David Wojnarowicz." In *David Wojnarowicz: Tongues of Flame*, 2nd ed. (Normal, IL: University Galleries of Illinois State University, 1992), 49–63.

Bloch Rosensaft, Jean, ed. *Judy Chicago: Jewish Identity* (New York: Hebrew Union College-Jewish Institute of Religion Museum, 2007).

Bloom, Lisa. "Ethnic Notions and Feminist Strategies of the 1970s: Some Work by Judy Chicago and Eleanor Antin." In *Jewish Identity in Modern Art History*, edited by Catherine M. Soussloff (Berkeley: University of California Press, 1999), 135–66.

Blum, Edward J., and Paul Harvey. *The Color of Christ: The Son of God and the Saga of Race in America* (Chapel Hill: University of North Carolina Press, 2014).

Blume, Harvey. "Oops, She Did It Again." *American Prospect*, December 3, 2001. https://prospect.org/features/oops/.

Bolton, Richard, ed. *Culture Wars: Documents from the Recent Controversies in the Arts* (New York: New Press, 1992).

Bonilla-Silva, Eduardo. *Racism without Racists: Color-Blind Racism and the Persistence of Racial Inequality in America*, 5th ed. (New York: Rowman and Littlefield, 2017).

Booker, Vaughn A. "'Pulpit and Pew': African American Humor on Irreverent Religious Participation in John H. Johnson's *Negro Digest*, 1943–1950." *Journal of Africana Religions* 8, no. 1 (January 2020): 1–36.

Bordowitz, Gregg. *The AIDS Crisis Is Ridiculous and Other Writings, 1986–2003* (Cambridge, MA: MIT Press, 2004).

Bordowitz, Gregg, dir. *Fast Trip, Long Drop*. 1993. Video, 53:58 min. Museum of Modern Art, New York.

Bork, Robert H. *Slouching Towards Gomorrah: Modern Liberalism and American Decline* (New York: Harper Perennial, 2003).

Brehm, Stephanie M. *America's Most Famous Catholic According to Himself: Stephen Colbert and American Religion in the Twenty-first Century* (New York: Fordham University Press, 2021).

Brensen, Michael. *Visionaries and Outcasts: The NEA, Congress, and the Place of the Visual Artist in America* (New York: New Press, 2001).

Brier, Jennifer. *Infectious Ideas: Political Responses to the AIDS Crisis* (Chapel Hill: University of North Carolina Press, 2009).

Brintnall, Kent L. *Ecce Homo: The Male-Body-in-Pain as Redemptive Figure* (Chicago: University of Chicago Press, 2012).

Bronstein, Carolyn, and Whitney Strub, eds. *Porno Chic and the Sex Wars: American Sexual Representation in the 1970s* (Amherst: University of Massachusetts Press, 2016).

Brooklyn Museum. "Alvin Ailey Tribute to The Dinner Party by Judy Chicago." March 10, 2020. YouTube video, 1:27 min. https://www.youtube.com/watch?v=SDiLIuokOUA.

Brown, Wendy. *In the Ruins of Neoliberalism: The Rise of Antidemocratic Politics in the West* (New York: Columbia University Press, 2019).

Brown, Wendy. *Undoing the Demos: Neoliberalism's Stealth Revolution* (New York: Zone Books, 2017).

Brustein, Robert. "The First Amendment and the NEA." *New Republic*, September 11, 1989, 27–29.

Bryan-Wilson, Julia. *Fray: Art and Textile Politics* (Chicago: University of Chicago Press, 2017).

Buchanan, Patrick. "Republican National Convention Speech." August 17, 1992. https://buchanan.org/blog/1992-republican-national-convention-speech-148.

Bullert, B. J. "Stop the Church." In *Public Television: Politics and the Battle over Documentary Film* (New Brunswick, NJ: Rutgers University Press, 1997), 123–45.

Burke, Kelsy. *The Pornography Wars: The Past, Present, and Future of America's Obscene Obsession* (New York: Bloomsbury, 2023).

Butler, Anthea. *White Evangelical Racism: The Politics of Morality in America* (Chapel Hill: University of North Carolina Press, 2021).

Butler, Judith. *Excitable Speech: A Politics of the Performative* (New York: Routledge, 1997).

Butler, Judith. "The Force of Fantasy: Feminism, Mapplethorpe, and Discursive Excess." *differences: A Journal of Feminist Cultural Studies* 2, no. 2 (1990): 105–25.

Butler, Judith. *Gender Trouble: Feminism and the Subversion of Identity* (New York: Routledge, 1990).

Butterfield, Jan. "Guess Who's Coming to Dinner? An Interview with Judy Chicago." *Mother Jones*, January 1979.

Bynum, Caroline Walker. *Christian Materiality: An Essay on Religion in Late Medieval Europe* (New York: Zone Books, 2011).

Bynum, Caroline Walker. *Fragmentation and Redemption: Essays on Gender and the Human Body in Medieval Religion* (New York: Zone Books, 1990).

Bynum, Caroline Walker. *Holy Feast and Holy Fast: The Religious Significance of Food to Medieval Women* (Berkeley: University of California Press, 1988).

Bynum, Caroline Walker. *Jesus as Mother: Studies in the Spirituality of the High Middle Ages* (Berkeley: University of California Press, 1984).

Byrne, Julie. *The Other Catholics: Remaking America's Largest Religion* (New York: Columbia University Press, 2016).

Caldwell, Susan Haven. "Experiencing 'The Dinner Party.'" *Woman's Art Journal* 1, no. 2 (Autumn 1980–Winter 1981): 35–37.

Cameron, Dan. *Fever: The Art of David Wojnarowicz* (New York: Rizzoli, 1998).

Campbell, Bradley, and Jason Manning. "Microaggression and Moral Cultures." *Comparative Sociology* 13, no. 6 (2014): 692–726.

Campbell, Bradley, and Jason Manning. "The New Millennial 'Morality': Highly Sensitive and Easily Offended." *Time*, November 17, 2015.

Caplan, Jennifer. *Funny, You Don't Look Funny: Judaism and Humor from the Silent Generation to Millennials* (Detroit, MI: Wayne State University Press, 2003).

Carlin, John. "David Wojnarowicz: As the World Turns." In *David Wojnarowicz: Tongues of Flame*, 2nd ed. (Normal, IL: University Galleries of Illinois State University, 1992), 21–48.

Carlomusto, Jean. Interview by Sarah Schulman. ACT UP Oral History Project. December 19, 2002. https://www.actuporalhistory.org/numerical-interviews/005-jean-carlomusto.

Carr, Cynthia. *Fire in the Belly: The Life and Times of David Wojnarowicz* (New York: Bloomsbury, 2012).

Casanova, José. *Public Religions in the Modern World* (Chicago: University of Chicago Press, 1994).

Castelli, Elizabeth. "Persecution Complexes: Identity Politics and the 'War on Christians.'" *differences: A Journal of Feminist Cultural Studies* 18, no. 3 (2007): 152–80.

Chan, Audrey. "From Chicago to Chicago: How I Became a Feminist Artist Despite Never Having Witnessed the 1970s." Video, 26:16. https://vimeo.com/30780054.

Chan-Malik, Sylvia. *Being Muslim: A Cultural History of Women of Color in American Islam* (New York: NYU Press, 2018).

Chen, Mel. *Animacies: Biopolitics, Racial Matter, and Queer Affect* (Durham, NC: Duke University Press, 2012).

Cheng, Jih-Fei. "How to Survive: AIDS and Its Afterlives in Popular Media." *Women's Studies Quarterly* 44, no. 1/2 (Spring/Summer 2016): 73–92.

Chicago, Judy. *Beyond the Flower: The Autobiography of a Feminist Artist* (New York: Viking, 1996).

Chicago, Judy. *The Birth Project* (New York: Doubleday, 1988).

Chicago, Judy. *The Dinner Party* (New York: Viking, 1996).

Chicago, Judy. *The Dinner Party: A Symbol of Our Heritage* (New York: Doubleday, 1979).

Chicago, Judy. *The Dinner Party: Restoring Women to History* (New York: Monacelli, 2014).

Chicago, Judy. *Embroidering Our Heritage: The Dinner Party Needlework* (New York: Doubleday, 1980).

Chicago, Judy. *The Flowering: The Autobiography of Judy Chicago* (London: Thames and Hudson, 2021).

Chicago, Judy. "Oral History Interview with Judy Chicago, 2009, August 7–8." Archives of American Art, Smithsonian Institution. https://www.aaa.si.edu/collections/interviews/oral-history-interview-judy-chicago-15708.

Chicago, Judy. "The Origins of Jewish Creativity." *Moment Magazine*, November/December 2011, 36.

Chicago, Judy. "Revelations of the Goddess." *CoEvolution Quarterly*, Spring 1979, 54–58.

Chicago, Judy. *Through the Flower: My Struggle as a Woman Artist* (New York: Doubleday, 1975).

Christ, Carol P. "Why Women Need the Goddess." *Heresies*, 1978, p. 8–13. In *Womanspirit Rising: A Feminist Reader in Religion*, edited by Carol P. Christ and Judith Plaskow (New York: HarperOne, 1979), 273–87.

Clague, Julie. "The Christa: Symbolizing My Humanity and My Pain." *Feminist Theology* 14, no. 1 (2005): 83–108.

Clague, Julie. "Divine Transgressions: The Female Christ-Form in Art." *Critical Quarterly* 47, no. 3 (October 2005): 47–62.

Clare, Eli. *Exile and Pride: Disability, Queerness, and Liberation* (Durham, NC: Duke University Press, 2015).

Cleto, Fabio, ed. *Camp: Queer Aesthetics and the Performing Subject* (Ann Arbor: University of Michigan Press, 1999).

Coates, Andrew. *What is Protestant Art?* (Leiden and Boston: Brill, 2018).

Commission on Obscenity and Pornography. *The Report* (Washington, DC: US Government Printing Office, 1970).

Cone, James. *The Cross and the Lynching Tree* (Maryknoll, NY: Orbis Books, 2011).

Contemporary Jewish Museum. "*Judy Chicago: Cohanim.*" Accessed July 7, 2023. https://www.thecjm.org/exhibitions/154.

Cooper, Dennis. "Bob's Thing." *Artforum*, April 1, 1996, 74–78. https://www.artforum.com/features/flanagans-wake-202133/.

Cooper, Melinda. *Family Values: Between Neoliberalism and the New Social Conservatism* (New York: Zone Books, 2019).

Corbman, Rachel. "The Scholars and the Feminists: The Barnard Sex Conference and the History of the Institutionalization of Feminism." *Feminist Formations* 27, no. 3 (Winter 2015): 49–80.

Cosentino, Donald J. "Hip-Hop Assemblage: The Chris Ofili Affair." *African Arts* 33, no. 1 (2000): 40–96.

Cott, Nancy F. *The Grounding of Modern Feminism* (New Haven, CT: Yale University Press, 1989).

Coviello, Peter. *Make Yourselves Gods: Mormons and the Unfinished Business of American Secularism* (Chicago: University of Chicago Press, 2019).

Cox, Renée. "Artist Talk." Princeton University Art Museum. April 15, 2021. https://artmuseum.princeton.edu/false/video/artist-talk-l-photographer-renee-cox.

Cox, Renée. "Feminist Artist Statement." Brooklyn Museum. Accessed October 5, 2023. https://www.brooklynmuseum.org/eascfa/about/feminist_art_base/renee-cox.

Crapanzano, Vincent. *Serving the Word: Literalism in America from the Pulpit to the Bench* (New York: New Press, 2001).

Cressler, Matthew J. *Authentically Black and Truly Catholic: The Rise of Black Catholicism in the Great Migration* (New York: NYU Press, 2017).

Cressler, Matthew J. "Forum: Race, White Supremacy, and the Making of American Catholicism: Introduction." *American Catholic Studies* 127, no. 3 (2016): 1–5.

Crimp, Douglas. "How to Have Promiscuity in an Epidemic." *October* 43 (Winter 1987): 237–71.

Crimp, Douglas, and Adam Rolston. *AIDS Demo Graphics* (Seattle: Bay Press, 1990).

Critchlow, Donald T. *Phyllis Schlafly and Grassroots Conservatism: A Woman's Crusade* (Princeton, NJ: Princeton University Press, 2008).

Croft, Clare. *Dancers as Diplomats: American Choreography in Cultural Exchange* (New York: Oxford University Press, 2015).

Cuomo, Mario. "Religious Belief and Public Morality: A Catholic Governor's Perspective." In *Abortion and Catholicism: The American Debate*, edited by Patricia Beattie Jung and Thomas A. Shannon (1984; New York: Crossroad, 1988), 202–16.

Curran, Robert Emmett. *Papist Devils: Catholics in British America, 1574–1783* (Washington, DC: Catholic University of America Press, 2014).

Cyril of Jerusalem. The Catechetical Lectures: Lecture XX (Of Baptism). https://catholiclibr ary.org/library/view?docId=Synchronized-EN/CyrilOfJerusalem.CatecheticalLectures. en.html&chunk.id=00000039.

Dailey, Jane. "Sex, Segregation, and the Sacred after *Brown*." *Journal of American History* 91, no. 1 (June 2004): 119–44.

Danto, Arthur. "In the Bosom of Jesus." *The Nation*, May 10, 2001. https://www.thenation. com/article/archive/bosom-jesus/.

Danto, Arthur. *Playing with the Edge: The Photographic Achievement of Robert Mapplethorpe* (Berkeley: University of California Press, 1995).

Davalos, Karen Mary. "'The Real Way of Praying': The Via Crucis, *Mexicano* Sacred Space, and the Architecture of Domination." In *Horizons of the Sacred: Mexican Traditions in U.S. Catholicism*, edited by Timothy Matovina and Gary Riebe-Estrella (Ithaca, NY: Cornell University Press, 2002), 41–68.

Dedman, Bill. "Bible Belt Blowhard." *Mother Jones*, November/December 1992, 41–43, 74–76.

DeFrantz, Thomas F. "Composite Bodies of Dance: The Repertory of the Alvin Ailey American Dance Theater." *Theatre Journal* 57, no. 4 (December 2005): 659–78.

Demetrakas, Johanna, dir. *Right Out of History: Judy Chicago's "Dinner Party."* 1980. 16 mm film, 1:15:00.

DeRogatis, Amy. *Saving Sex: Sexuality and Salvation in American Evangelicalism* (New York: Oxford University Press, 2014).

Detzner, Dick. "Corporate Sacrilege." Dick Detzner. Accessed October 5, 2023. https://detzner. com/corporate-sacrilege.

Derrida, Jacques. "Signature, Event, Context." In *Limited, Inc.*, translated by Samuel Weber and Jeffrey Mehlman (Evanston: Northwestern Press, 1988), 1–24.

Dick, Kirby, dir. *Sick: The Life and Death of Bob Flanagan, Supermasochist.* Cinepix Film, 1997. DVD.

Dimock, Wai Chee. "A Theory of Resonance." *PMLA* 112, no. 5 (October 1997): 1060–71.

Diner, Hasia R. *The Jews of the United States, 1654–2000* (Berkeley: University of California Press, 2006).

"Dinner Party Curriculum Project." Judy Chicago Art Education Collection. Accessed July 12, 2023. https://judychicago.arted.psu.edu/dpcp/.

DIVA TV. *The Ashes Action.* Produced and edited by James Wentzy, with Jerry Lakatos. September 16, 1996. Video, 29:00. https://vimeo.com/158801570.

DIVA TV. *Like a Prayer: Stop the Church.* 1990. Videocassette (VHS), 28 min. AIDS Activist Videotape Collection, New York Public Library.

DIVA TV. *Pride 69–89.* Videocassette (VHS), 26:30 min. AIDS Activist Videotape Collection, New York Public Library.

DIVA TV. *Target City Hall.* 1989. Videocassette (VHS), 27 min. AIDS Activist Videotape Collection, New York Public Library.

Dochuk, Darren. *From Bible Bet to Sunbelt: Plain-Folk Religion, Grassroots Politics, and the Rise of Evangelical Conservatism* (New York: W. W. Norton, 2011).

Donohue, William A. "Brooklyn Museum of Art Offends Again." News release, Catholic League. February 15, 2001. https://www.catholicleague.org/brooklyn-museum-of-art-offe nds-again/.

Doss, Erika. *Spiritual Moderns: Twentieth-Century American Artists and Religion* (Chicago: University of Chicago Press, 2023).

Dowland, Seth. *Family Values and the Rise of the Christian Right* (Philadelphia: University of Pennsylvania Press, 2015).

Downing, Larry. "The Art and Practice of Biblical Proof-Texting." Adventist Today. January 22, 2017. https://atoday.org/the-art-and-practice-of-biblical-proof-texting/.

Dworkin, Andrea. *Pornography: Men Possessing Women* (London: Women's Press, 1981).

Du Mez, Kristin Kobes. *Jesus and John Wayne: How White Evangelicals Corrupted a Faith and Fractured a Nation* (New York: Liveright, 2020).

Dubin, Steven C. *Arresting Images: Impolitic Art and Uncivil Actions* (New York: Routledge, 1992).

Edgecomb, Sean F. "History of the Ridiculous, 1960–1987." *The Gay and Lesbian Review Worldwide* 14, no. 3 (2007): 21–23.

Eichler-Levine, Jodi. *Painted Pomegranates and Needlepoint Rabbis: How Jews Craft Resilience and Create Community* (Chapel Hill: University of North Carolina Press, 2020).

Eichler-Levine, Jodi. *Suffer the Little Children: Uses of the Past in Jewish and African American Children's Literature* (New York: NYU Press, 2013).

Eliade, Mircea. *The Sacred and the Profane: The Nature of Religion* (New York: HarperOne, 1968).

Elkins, James. *On the Strange Place of Religion in Modern Art* (New York: Routledge, 2004).

Elkins, James, and David Morgan, eds. *Re-Enchantment* (New York: Routledge, 2009).

Eller, Cynthia. *Living in the Lap of the Goddess: The Feminist Spirituality Movement in America* (Boston, MA: Beacon Press, 1995).

Eller, Cynthia. *The Myth of Matriarchal Prehistory: Why an Invented Past Will Not Give Women a Future* (Boston, MA: Beacon Press, 2000).

Elman, Julie Passanante. *Chronic Youth: Disability, Sexuality, and U.S. Media Cultures of Rehabilitation* (New York: NYU Press, 2014).

Endres, David J., ed. *Slavery and the Catholic Church in the United States* (Washington, DC: Catholic University of America Press, 2023).

Epstein, Steven. *Impure Science: AIDS, Activism, and the Politics of Knowledge* (Berkeley: University of California Press, 1996).

Ernst, Carl W., ed. *Islamophobia in America: The Anatomy of Intolerance* (New York: Palgrave Macmillan, 2013).

Espinosa, Gastón, and Mario T. García, eds. *Mexican American Religions: Spirituality, Activism, and Culture* (Durham, NC: Duke University Press, 2008).

Eversley, Shelly. "Renée Cox: The Big Picture." *Nka: Journal of Contemporary African Art*, no. 18 (2003): 72–75.

Faderman, Lillian. *The Gay Revolution: The Story of the Struggle* (New York: Simon and Schuster, 2016).

Falwell, Jerry. *Listen America!* (New York: Doubleday, 1980).

Federici, Silvia, ed. *Enduring Western Civilization: The Construction of the Concept of Western Civilization and Its Others* (Westport, CT: Praeger Publishers, 1995).

Felski, Rita. "'Context Stinks!'" *New Literary History* 42, no. 4 (Autumn 2011): 573–91.

Ferraro, Thomas J. "Not-Just-Cultural Catholics." In *Catholic Lives, Contemporary Lives*, edited by Thomas J. Ferraro (Durham, NC: Duke University Press, 1997), 1–18.

Fischer, Hal. "Judy Chicago: San Francisco Museum of Art." *Artforum*, Summer 1979, 77. https://www.artforum.com/events/judy-chicago-6-229916/.

Fisher, Alan S. "The Stretching of Augustan Satire: Charles Churchill's 'Dedication' to Warburton." *Journal of English and German Philology* 72, no. 3 (July 1973): 360–77.

Fisher, James Terence. *The Catholic Counterculture in America, 1933–1962* (Chapel Hill: University of North Carolina Press, 1991).

Fleetwood, Nicole. *Troubling Vision: Performance, Visuality, and Blackness* (Chicago: University of Chicago Press, 2010).

Foucault, Michel. *About the Beginning of the Hermeneutics of the Self: Lectures at Dartmouth College, 1980*. Translated by Graham Burchell (Chicago: University of Chicago Press, 2016).

Foucault, Michel. "Pastoral Power and Political Reason." In *Religion and Culture*, selected and edited by Jeremy Carrette (1979; New York: Routledge, 1999), 135–53.

Foucault, Michel. *Society Must Be Defended: Lectures at the Collège de France, 1975–1976*. Translated by David Macey, edited by Mauro Bertani and Alessandro Fontana (New York: Picador, 2003).

France, David, dir. *How to Survive a Plague*. 2012. Film, 1:49.

Franchot, Jenny. *Roads to Rome: The Antebellum Protestant Encounter with Catholicism* (Berkeley: University of California Press, 1994).

Frank, Gillian. "The Colour of the Unborn: Anti-Abortion and Anti-Bussing Politics in Michigan, United States, 1967–1973." *Gender & History* 26, no. 2 (2014): 351–78.

Frank, Gillian, Bethany Moreton, and Heather White, eds. *Devotions and Desires: Histories of Sexuality and Religion in the Twentieth-Century United States* (Chapel Hill: University of North Carolina Press, 2018).

Freedman, Estelle B. *No Turning Back: The History of Feminism and the Future of Women* (New York: Ballantine, 2003).

Fusco, Coco. "Captain Shit and Other Allegories of Black Stardom: The Work of Chris Ofili." *Nka: Journal of Contemporary African Art*, no. 10 (1999): 40–45.

Fusco, Coco. "Sublime Abjection: An Interview with Andres Serrano." *Third Text* 5 (1991): 16–17.

Fuss, Diana. *Essentially Speaking: Feminism, Nature and Difference* (London: Routledge: 1989).

Gaffney, Mo, and Kathy Najimy. *Parallel Lives* (1992; New York: Dramatists Play Service, 2006).

García, Mario T. *Católicos: Resistance and Affirmation in Chicano Catholic History* (Austin: University of Texas Press, 2010).

Garland-Thomson, Rosemarie. "Seeing the Disabled: Visual Rhetorics of Disability in Popular Photography." In *The New Disability History: American Perspectives*, edited by Paul K. Longmore and Lauri Umansky (New York: NYU Press, 2001), 335–74.

Garrard, Mary D. "Feminist Art and the Essentialism Controversy." *Centennial Review* 39, no. 3 (Fall 1995): 468–92.

Gaspar de Alba, Alicia, and Alma López, eds. *Our Lady of Controversy: Alma López's "Irreverent Apparition"* (Austin: University of Texas Press, 2011).

Gaston, K. Healan. *Imagining Judeo-Christian America: Religion, Secularism, and the Redefinition of Democracy* (Chicago: University of Chicago Press, 2019).

Gaulke, Cheri. "Cheri Gaulke: An Oral History." Conducted by Jane Collings. UCLA Center for Oral History Research, August 20–21, 2003. https://oralhistory.library.ucla.edu/catalog/21198-zz00097r3c.

Gaulke, Cheri. "Interview with Cheri Gaulke." Conducted by Starr Goode. *Goddess in Art TV Series*, ca. 1986–1991. Video, 28:28. https://www.youtube.com/watch?v=H9b_nMlkGfM&t=1s.

Gelon, Diane. "The Critic's Voice: Who Speaks for Us?" *Sojourner*, October 1980, 5.

Gerber, Lynne. *Seeking the Straight and Narrow: Weight Loss and Sexual Reorientation in Evangelical America* (Chicago: University of Chicago Press, 2012).

Gerhard, Jane F. *The Dinner Party: Judy Chicago and the Power of Popular Feminism, 1970–2007* (Athens: University of Georgia Press, 2013).

Giles, Paul. *American Catholic Arts and Fictions: Culture, Ideology, Aesthetics* (New York: Cambridge University Press, 1992).

Gill-Peterson, Jules. *Histories of the Transgender Child* (Minneapolis: University of Minnesota Press, 2018).

Giuliani, Rudolph. "The Rights and Responsibilities of Public-Funded Cultural Institutions." Archives of Mayor's Weekly Column, 2001. Accessed November 2023. https://www.nyc.gov/html/rwg/html/2001a/weekly/wkly0409.html.

Gladden, Washington. "Christianity and Aestheticism." *Andover Review* 1 (1884): 13–24.

Goizueta, Roberto. "The Symbolic World of Mexican American Religion." In *Horizons of the Sacred: Mexican Traditions in U.S. Catholicism*, edited by Timothy Matovina and Gary Riebe-Estrella (Ithaca, NY: Cornell University Press, 2002), 119–38.

Golden, Thelma. "My Brother." In *Black Male: Representations of Masculinity in Contemporary American Art* (New York: Whitney Museum of American Art, 1994), 18–43.

Goldin, Nan. "In the Valley of the Shadow." In *Witnesses: Against Our Vanishing* by Artists Space (New York: Artists Space Exhibitions, 1989), 4–5.

Goldschmidt, Henry. *Race and Religion among the Chosen People of Crown Heights* (New York: Rutgers University Press, 2006).

Gonzalez Rice, Karen. *Long Suffering: American Endurance Art as Prophetic Witness* (Ann Arbor: University of Michigan Press, 2016).

Good, Byron. "Medical Anthropology and the Category of Belief." In *Medicine, Rationality, and Experience* (Cambridge: Cambridge University Press, 1994), 1–24.

Goodwin, Megan. *Abusing Religion: Literary Persecution, Sex Scandals, and American Minority Religions* (New Brunswick, NJ: Rutgers University Press, 2020).

Gordon, Linda. *Heroes of Their Own Lives: The Politics and History of Family Violence* (Champaign: University of Illinois Press, 2002).

Gossett, Che, and Eva Hayward. "Kiyan Williams: An Interview." *TSQ* 7, no. 4 (2020): 605–10.

Gould, Deborah B. *Moving Politics: Emotion and ACT UP's Fight Against AIDS* (Chicago: University of Chicago Press, 2009).

Greeley, Andrew M. *The Catholic Imagination* (Berkeley: University of California Press, 2001).

Greeley, Andrew M. *God in Popular Culture* (Chicago: Thomas More Press, 1989).

Greenberg, Clement. "Avant-Garde and Kitsch." In *Art and Culture: Critical Essays* (Boston: Beacon Press, 1965), 3–31.

Greene-Hayes, Ahmad. "'Queering' African American Religious History." *Religion Compass* 13, no. 7 (July 2019): e12319.

Griffith, R. Marie. *Born Again Bodies: Flesh and Spirit in American Christianity* (Berkeley: University of California Press, 2004).

Griffith, R. Marie. *Moral Combat: How Sex Divided American Christians and Fractured American Politics* (New York: Basic Books, 2017).

Griffith, R. Marie, and Melani McAlister. "Introduction: Is the Public Square Still Naked?" *American Quarterly* 59, no. 3 (September 2007): 527–63.

Gross, Rachel. *Beyond the Synagogue: Jewish Nostalgia as Religious Practice* (New York: NYU Press, 2021).

Gruber, Christiane. *The Praiseworthy One: The Prophet Muhammad in Islamic Texts and Images* (Bloomington: Indiana University Press, 2019).

Halford, Sarah J. "Interview with Ron Goldberg." Center for Artistic Activism. April 24, 2016. https://artisticactivism.org/2016/04/ron-goldberg/.

Hall, David D. *Lived Religion in America: Toward a History of Practice* (Princeton, NJ: Princeton University Press, 1997).

Hallas, Roger. *Reframing Bodies: AIDS, Bearing Witness, and the Queer Moving Image* (Durham, NC: Duke University Press, 2009).

Halle, David. "The Controversy Over the Show *Sensation* at the Brooklyn Museum, 1999–2000." In *Crossroads: Religion and Art in American Life*, edited by Alberta Arthurs and Glenn Wallach (New York: New Press, 2001), 139–87.

Hanson, Ellis. *Decadence and Catholicism* (Cambridge, MA: Harvard University Press, 1998).

Harding, Susan. *The Book of Jerry Falwell: Fundamentalist Language and Politics* (Princeton, NJ: Princeton University Press, 2011).

Hartman, Andrew. *A War for the Soul of America: A History of the Culture Wars* (Chicago: University of Chicago Press, 2015).

Harvey, David. *A Brief History of Neoliberalism* (Oxford: Oxford University Press, 2005).

Heartney, Eleanor. *Doomsday Dreams: The Apocalyptic Imagination in Contemporary Art* (Silver Hollow Press, 2019).

Heartney, Eleanor. *Postmodern Heretics: Catholic Imagination in Contemporary Art* (New York: Midmarch Arts Press, 2004).

Heartney, Eleanor. "Thinking Through the Body: Women's Artists and the Catholic Imagination." *Hypatia* 18, no. 4 (Fall/Winter 2003): 3–22.

Hebron, Micol. "Putting the Words Back into the F-Word. An Interview with Audrey Chan and Elana Mann." *Artpulse Magazine*, Summer 2012. http://artpulsemagazine.com.

Herberg, Will. *Protestant, Catholic, Jew: An Essay in American Religious Sociology* (Chicago: University of Chicago Press, 1955).

Herman, Didi. *The Antigay Agenda: Orthodox Vision and the Christian Right* (Chicago: University of Chicago Press, 1997).

Hilferty, Robert. *Stop the Church.* 1990. Videocassette (VHS), 24 min. AIDS Activist Videotape Collection, New York Public Library.

Hilferty, Robert, and Robert Huff. *Deadlier than a Virus.* 1991. Videocassette (VHS), 5:30 min. AIDS Activist Videotape Collection, New York Public Library.

Hitchcock, James. "Catholic Activist Conservatism in the United States." In *Fundamentalisms Observed*, vol. 1, edited by Martin E. Marty and R. Scott Appleby (Chicago: University of Chicago Press, 1994), 101–40.

Hitchens, Christopher. "Why Women Aren't Funny." *Vanity Fair*, January 1, 2007. https://www.vanityfair.com/culture/2007/01/hitchens200701.

Hollywood, Amy. "Performativity, Citationality, Ritualization." *History of Religions* 42, no. 2 (November 2002): 93–115.

hooks, bell. *Art on My Mind: Visual Politics* (New York: New Press, 1995).

hooks, bell. *Sisters of the Yam: Black Women and Self Recovery*, 2nd ed. (New York: Routledge, 2015).

Howard, Yetta, ed. *Rated RX: Sheree Rose with and after Bob Flanagan* (Columbus: Ohio State University Press, 2020).

Hubbard, Jim, Sarah Schulman, Ali Cotterill, and James Wentzy. *United in Anger: A History of ACT UP.* United in Anger, Inc., 2012. Video, 93 min.

Hughes, Robert. "An Obsessive Feminist Pantheon: Judy Chicago's *Dinner Party* Turns History into Agitprop." *Time,* December 15, 1980, 85–86.

Hulsether, Mark D. "Like a Sermon: Popular Religion in Madonna Videos." In *Religion and Popular Culture in America*, edited by Bruce David Forbes and Jeffrey H. Mahan (Berkeley: University of California Press, 2005), 75–98.

Hunter, James Davison. *Culture Wars: The Struggle to Define America* (New York: Basic Books, 1991).

Hunter, James Davison, and Alan Wolfe. *Is There a Culture War? A Dialogue on Values and American Public Life* (Washington, DC: Brookings Institution Press, 2006).

Hyman, Paula E. "Jewish Feminism Faces the American Women's Movement: Convergence and Divergence." In *American Jewish Identity Politics*, edited by Deborah Dash Moore (Ann Arbor: University of Michigan Press, 2008), 221–42.

Imhoff, Sarah. "Why Disability Studies Needs to Take Religion Seriously." *Religions* 8, no. 9 (2017): 186.

Inde, Vilis R. *Art in the Courtroom* (Westport, CT: Greenwood, 1998).

Isaak, Jo Anna. "American Family." In *Renee Cox: American Family* (New York: Robert Miller Gallery, 2001).

Isherwood, Christopher. *The World in the Evening* (1954; Minneapolis: University of Minnesota Press, 1999).

Iwamura, Jane Naomi. *Virtual Orientalism: Asian Religions and American Popular Culture* (New York: Oxford University Press, 2011).

Jackson, Melissa. *Comedy and Feminist Interpretation of the Hebrew Bible: A Subversive Collaboration* (Oxford University Press, 2012).

Jakobsen, Janet R. "Is Secularism Less Violent than Religion?" In *Interventions: Activists and Academics Respond to Violence*, edited by Elizabeth A. Castelli and Janet R. Jakobsen (New York: Palgrave Macmillan, 2004), 53–67.

Jakobsen, Janet R. *The Sex Obsession: Perversity and Possibility in American Politics* (New York: NYU Press, 2020).

Jakobsen, Janet R., and Ann Pellegrini. *Love the Sin: Sexual Regulation and the Limits of Religious Tolerance* (New York: NYU Press, 2003).

Jenkins, Philip. *The New Anti-Catholicism: The Last Acceptable Prejudice* (New York: Oxford University Press, 2003).

Johnson, David K. *The Lavender Scare: The Cold War Persecution of Gays and Lesbians in the Federal Government* (Chicago: University of Chicago Press, 2004).

Johnson, Emily S. *This is Our Message: Women's Leadership in the New Christian Right* (New York: Oxford University Press, 2019).

Jones, Amelia. *Body Art/Performing the Subject* (Minneapolis: University of Minnesota Press, 1998).

Jones, Amelia. "The 'Sexual Politics' of *The Dinner Party*: A Critical Context." In *Sexual Politics: Judy Chicago's* Dinner Party *in Feminist Art History*, edited by Amelia Jones (Berkeley: University of California Press, 1996), 82–125.

Jones, Amelia. "Sexual Politics: Feminist Strategies, Feminist Conflicts, Feminist Histories." In *Sexual Politics: Judy Chicago's* Dinner Party *in Feminist Art History*, edited by Amelia Jones (Berkeley: University of California Press, 1996), 20–45.

Jones, Amelia, and Andy Campbell, eds. *Queer Communion: Ron Athey* (New York: Intellect, 2020).

Jones, Timothy K. "Put Up Yer Dukes." *Christianity Today*, December 17, 1990, 14.

Jordan, Mark D. *Blessing Same-Sex Unions: The Perils of Queer Romance and the Confusions of Christian Marriage* (Chicago: University of Chicago Press, 2005).

Jordan, Mark D. *Convulsing Bodies: Religion and Resistance in Foucault* (Palo Alto, CA: Stanford University Press, 2014).

Jordan, Mark D. "Notes on Camp Theology." In *Dancing Theology in Fetish Boots*, edited by Lisa Isherwood and Mark D. Jordan (London: SCM Press, 2010), 181–90.

Jordan, Mark D. *Recruiting Young Love: How Christians Talk about Homosexuality* (Chicago: University of Chicago Press, 2011).

Jordan, Mark D. *The Silence of Sodom: Homosexuality in Modern Catholicism* (Chicago: University of Chicago Press, 2000).

Juhasz, Alexandra. *AIDS TV: Identity, Community, and Alternative Video* (Durham, NC: Duke University Press, 1995).

Juhasz, Alexandra. "So Many Alternatives: The Alternative AIDS Video Movement." *Cineaste* 20, no. 4 (1994): 32–35.

Juhasz, Alexandra. "So Many Alternatives: The Alternative AIDS Video Movement [Part 2]." *Cineaste* 21, no. 1–2 (1995): 37–39.

Juhasz, Alexandra, and Theodore Kerr. *We Are Having This Conversation Now: The Times of AIDS Cultural Production* (Durham, NC: Duke University Press, 2022).

Julius, Anthony. *Transgression: The Offences of Art* (Chicago: University of Chicago Press, 2003).

Juno, Andrea, and V. Vale, eds. *Bob Flanagan: Supermasochist* (San Francisco: Re/Search, 1993).

Kaell, Hillary. "Seeing the Invisible: Ambient Catholicism on the Side of the Road." *Journal of the American Academy of Religion* 85, no. 1 (March 2017), 136–67.

Kafer, Alison. *Feminist, Queer, Crip* (Bloomington: Indiana University Press, 2013).

Kammen, Michael. *Visual Shock: A History of Art Controversies in American Culture* (New York: Knopf, 2006).

Kane, Paula. "'She Offered Herself Up': The Victim Soul and Victim Spirituality in Catholicism." *Church History* 71, no. 1 (March 2002): 80–119.

Kardon, Janet. "Robert Mapplethorpe Interview." In *Robert Mapplethorpe: The Perfect Moment*, edited by Janet Kardon (Philadelphia: Institute of Contemporary Art, University of Pennsylvania, 1988), 23–29.

Keane, Webb. *Christian Moderns: Freedom and Fetish in the Mission Encounter* (Berkeley: University of California, 2007).

Kennedy, John F. "Address of Senator John F. Kennedy to the Greater Houston Ministerial Association." Speech at the Rice Hotel, Houston, Texas, September 12, 1960. www.jfklibrary.org.

Kinsella, James. *Covering the Plague: AIDS and the American Media* (New Brunswick, NJ: Rutgers University Press, 1992).

Klassen, Chris. "The Colonial Mythology of Feminist Witchcraft." *Pomegranate: The International Journal of Pagan Studies* 6, no. 1 (May 2004): 70–85.

Klassen, Pamela E. *Blessed Events: Religion and Home Birth in America* (Princeton, NJ: Princeton University Press, 2002).

Klein, Jennie. "Goddess: Feminist Art and Spirituality in the 1970s." *Feminist Studies* 35, no. 3 (Fall 2009): 575–602.

Korte, Anne-Marie. "Blasphemous Feminist Art: Incarnate Politics of Identity in Post-Secular Perspective." In *Transformations of Religion and the Public Sphere: Postsecular Publics*, edited by Rosi Braidotti, Bolette Blaagaard, Tobijn de Graauw, and Eva Midden (Basingstoke: Palgrave Macmillan, 2014), 228–48.

Krauss, Rosalind E. "Grids." In *The Originality of the Avant-Garde and Other Modernist Myths* (Cambridge, MA: MIT Press, 1986), 8–22.

Kruse, Kevin M. *One Nation Under God: How Corporate America Invented Christian America* (New York: Basic Books, 2015).

Krutzsch, Brett. *Dying to Be Normal: Gay Martyrs and the Transformation of American Sexual Politics* (New York: Oxford University Press, 2019).

Kuby, Lolette. "The Hoodwinking of the Women's Movement: Judy Chicago's *Dinner Party*." *Frontiers: A Journal of Women's Studies* 6, no. 3 (Autumn 1981): 127–29.

Kulka, Tomas. *Kitsch and Art* (University Park, PA: Penn State University Press, 1996).

Largier, Niklaus. *In Praise of the Whip: A Cultural History of Arousal*, translated by Graham Harman (New York: Zone Books, 2007).

Larson, Edward J. *Summer for the Gods: The Scopes Trial and America's Continuing Debate Over Science and Religion* (New York: Basic Books, 1997).

Laycock, Joseph. *Dangerous Games: What the Moral Panic over Role-Playing Games Says about Play, Religion, and Imagined Worlds* (Berkeley: University of California Press, 2015).

Leighton, Angela. *On Form: Poetry, Aestheticism, and the Legacy of a Word* (New York: Oxford University Press, 2007).

León, Luis D. *The Political Spirituality of Cesar Chavez: Crossing Religious Borders* (Berkeley: University of California Press, 2015).

Lévi-Strauss, Claude. *Structural Anthropology*. Translated by Claire Jacobson and Brooke Grundfest Schoepf (Boston: Basic Books, 1963).

Levin, Gail. *Becoming Judy Chicago: A Biography of the Artist* (Berkeley: University of California Press, 2018).

Levin, Gail. "Censorship, Politics and Sexual Imagery in the Work of Jewish-American Feminist Artists." *Nashim: A Journal of Women's Studies and Gender Issues*, no. 14 (2007): 63–96.

Levine, Caroline. *Forms: Whole, Rhythm, Hierarchy, Network* (Princeton, NJ: Princeton University Press, 2017).

Levine, Debra. "Another Kind of Love: A Performance of Prosthetic Politics." *e-misferica* 2, no. 2 (2002). https://hemisphericinstitute.org/en/emisferica-2-2/2-2-essays/a-performance-of-prosthetic-politics.html.

Levine, Debra. "How to Do Things with Dead Bodies." *e-misférica* 6, no. 1 (2009). https://hemisphericinstitute.org/en/emisferica-61/6-1-essays/how-to-do-things-with-dead-bodies.html.

Levitt, Laura. *Jews and Feminism: The Ambivalent Search for Home* (New York: Routledge, 1997).

Levitt, Laura. "Other Moderns, Other Jews: Revisiting Jewish Secularism in America." In *Secularisms*, edited by Janet R. Jakobsen and Ann Pellegrini (Durham, NC: Duke University Press, 2008), 108–38.

Lichter, Linda S., S. Robert Lichter, and Stanley Rothman. "Hollywood and America: The Odd Couple." *Public Opinion*, December/January 1983, 54–56.

Lincoln, Bruce. *Discourse and the Construction of Society: Comparative Studies of Myth, Ritual, and Classification* (Oxford: Oxford University Press, 2014).

Link, William A. *Righteous Warrior: Jesse Helms and the Rise of Modern Conservatism* (New York: St. Martin's Press, 2008).

Lippard, Lucy. "Dinner Party a Four-Star Retreat: A Feminist Counterpart of the Sistine Chapel." *Seven Days*, April 27, 1979.

Lippard, Lucy. "Foreword: Going Around in Circles." In *From Site to Vision: The Woman's Building in Contemporary Culture*, edited by Sondra Hale and Terry Wolverton (Los Angeles: Otis College of Art and Design, 2011), 11–15.

Lippard, Lucy. "Judy Chicago's 'Dinner Party.'" *Art in America*, April 1980, 114–26.

Lippard, Lucy. "Out of the Safety Zone." *Art in America*, December 1990, 131–39, 182, 186.

Lippard, Lucy. "Uninvited Guests: How Washington Lost 'The Dinner Party.'" *Art in America*, December 1991, 39–49.

Liss, Andrea. *Feminist Art and the Maternal* (Minneapolis: University of Minnesota Press, 2009).

Lofton, Kathryn. *Consuming Religion* (Chicago: University of Chicago Press, 2017).

Lofton, Kathryn. *Oprah: The Gospel of an Icon* (Berkeley: University of California Press, 2011).

Lofton, Kathryn. "Queering Fundamentalism: John Balcom Shaw and the Sexuality of a Protestant Orthodoxy." *Journal of the History of Sexuality* 17, no. 3 (2008): 439–68.

Lofton, Kathryn. "Why Religion Is Hard For Historians (and How It Can Be Easier)." *Modern American History* 3, no. 1 (2020): 69–86.

Love, Heather. "Close but not Deep: Literary Ethics and the Descriptive Turn." *New Literary History* 41, no. 2 (Spring 2010): 371–91.

Lukianoff, Greg, and Jonathan Haidt. "The Coddling of the American Mind." *The Atlantic*, September 2015. theatlantic.com.

Lukianoff, Greg, and Rikki Schlott. *The Canceling of the American Mind: Cancel Culture Undermines Trust and Threatens Us All—But There Is a Solution* (New York: Simon & Schuster, 2023).

Lyon, John. "Of Plaster Statues and Romantic Heresy." *Commonweal*, March 25, 1983, 170–5.

MacKinnon, Catharine A. *Only Words* (Cambridge, MA: Harvard University Press, 1996).

Mahmood, Saba. *Politics of Piety: The Islamic Revival and the Feminist Subject*, reis. ed. (2005; Princeton, NJ: Princeton University Press, 2012).

Mahmood, Saba. *Religious Difference in a Secular Age: A Minority Report* (Princeton, NJ: Princeton University Press, 2016).

Mahmood, Saba. "Religious Reason and Secular Affect: An Incommensurable Divide?" *Critical Inquiry* 35, no. 4 (2009): 836–62.

Mahmood, Saba. "Secularism, Hermeneutics, and Empire: The Politics of Islamic Reformation." *Public Culture* 18, no. 2 (Spring 2006): 323–47.

Mahmood, Saba. "Sexuality and Secularism." In *Religion, the Secular, and the Politics of Sexual Difference*, edited by Linell Cady and Tracy Fessenden (New York: Columbia University Press, 2013), 47–58.

Maltz-Leca, Leora. *William Kentridge: Process As Metaphor and Other Doubtful Enterprises* (Berkeley: University of California Press, 2018).

Marranca, Bonnie, and Gautam Dasgupta, eds. *Theatre of the Ridiculous*, revised ed. (Baltimore, MD: Johns Hopkins University Press, 1997).

Marsden, George M. *Fundamentalism and American Culture* (New York: Oxford University Press, 1980).

Martin, Emily. "The Egg and the Sperm: How Science Has Constructed a Romance Based on Stereotypical Male-Female Roles." *Signs* 16, no. 3 (1991): 485–501.

Martin, Lerone A. *The Gospel of J. Edgar Hoover: How the FBI Aided and Abetted the Rise of White Christian Nationalism* (Princeton, NJ: Princeton University Press, 2023).

Massa, Mark S. *Anti-Catholicism in America: The Last Acceptable Prejudice*, 2nd ed. (New York: Crossroad, 2005).

Masuzawa, Tomoko. *The Invention of World Religions: Or, How European Universalism Was Preserved in the Language of Pluralism* (Chicago: University of Chicago Press, 2005).

Matovina, Timothy. *Latino Catholicism: Transformation in America's Largest Church* (Princeton, NJ: Princeton University Press, 2014).

Mattson, Kevin. *We're Not Here to Entertain: Punk Rock, Ronald Reagan, and the Real Culture War of 1980s America* (New York: Oxford University Press, 2020).

May, Henry F. *The Enlightenment in America* (Oxford: Oxford University Press, 1978).

Maya, Kavita. "Arachne's Voice: Race, Gender, and the Goddess." *Feminist Theology* 28, no. 1 (2019): 52–65.

"Mayor Giuliani Announces Appointments to Cultural Affairs Advisory Commission." Press release, April 3, 2001. Archives of the Mayor's Press Office. https://www.nyc.gov/html/om/html/2001a/pr105-01.html.

McAlister, Melani. *Epic Encounters: Culture, Media, and US Interests in the Middle East since 1945* (Berkeley: University of California Press, 2005).

McAlister, Melani. *The Kingdom of God Has No Borders: A Global History of American Evangelicals* (New York: Oxford University Press, 2018).

McCrary, Charles. *Sincerely Held: American Secularism and Its Believers* (Chicago: University of Chicago Press, 2002).

McDannell, Colleen, ed. *Catholics in the Movies* (New York: Oxford University Press, 2008).

McDannell, Colleen. *Material Christianity: Religion and Popular Culture in America* (New Haven, CT: Yale University Press, 1995).

McGarry, Molly. *Ghosts of Futures Past: Spiritualism and the Cultural Politics of Nineteenth-Century America* (Berkeley: University of California Press, 2012).

McGreevy, John T. *Catholicism and American Freedom: A History* (New York: W. W. Norton, 2003).

McGreevy, John T. *Parish Boundaries: The Catholic Encounter with Race in the Twentieth-Century Urban North* (Chicago: University of Chicago Press, 1998).

McKelvey, Patrick. *Disability Works: Performance after Rehabilitation* (New York: NYU Press, 2024).

McKelvey, Patrick. "Ron Whyte's 'Disemployment': Prosthetic Performance and Theatrical Labor." *Theatre Survey* 57, no. 3 (2016): 314–35.

McKeown, Elizabeth. "Drawing Lines." *U.S. Catholic Historian* 21, no. 4 (Fall 2003): 45–61.

McLaughlin, Levi, Aike P. Rots, Jolyon Baraka Thomas, and Chika Watanabe. "Why Scholars Must Investigate the Corporate Form." *Journal of the American Academy of Religion* 88, no. 3 (September 2020): 693–725.

McRuer, Robert. *Crip Theory: Cultural Signs of Queerness and Disability* (New York: NYU Press., 2006).

McRuer, Robert. *Crip Times: Disability, Globalization, and Resistance* (New York: NYU Press, 2018).

McTernan, Emily. *On Taking Offence* (Oxford: Oxford University Press, 2023).

McTernan, Emily. "Taking Offense: An Emotion Reconsidered." *Philosophy & Public Affairs* 49, no. 2 (March 2021): 179–208.

Mehta, Samira K. *Beyond Chrismukkah: The Christian-Jewish Interfaith Family in the United States* (Chapel Hill: University of North Carolina Press, 2018).

Meyer, Laura. "From Finish Fetish to Feminism." In *Sexual Politics: Judy Chicago's* Dinner Party *in Feminist Art History*, edited by Amelia Jones (Los Angeles: University of California Press, 1996), 46–81.

Meyer, Laura. "The Women's Building and Los Angeles' Leading Role in the Feminist Art Movement." In *From Site to Vision: The Woman's Building in Contemporary Culture*, edited by Sondra Hale and Terry Wolverton (Los Angeles: Otis School of Art and Design, 2011), 85–114.

Meyer, Moe, ed. *The Politics and Poetics of Camp* (London: Routledge, 1994).

Meyer, Richard. "The Jesse Helms Theory of Art." *October* 104 (Spring 2003): 131–48.

Meyer, Richard. *Outlaw Representation: Censorship and Homosexuality in Twentieth-Century American Art* (New York: Oxford University Press, 2002).

Mickens, Leah. *In the Shadow of Ebenezer: A Black Catholic Parish in the Age of Civil Rights and Vatican II* (New York: NYU Press, 2022).

Mitchell, W. J. T. *What Do Pictures Want? The Lives and Loves of Images* (Chicago: University of Chicago Press, 2006).

Montez, Ricardo. *Keith Haring's Line: Race and the Performance of Desire* (Durham, NC: Duke University Press, 2020).

Moore, R. Laurence. *Selling God: American Religion in the Marketplace of Culture* (New York: Oxford University Press, 1995).

Moreton, Bethany. *To Serve God and Wal-Mart: The Making of Christian Free Enterprise* (Cambridge, MA: Harvard University Press, 2010).

Morgan, David. "The Art of Jon McNaughton, the Tea Party's Painter." *Religion and Politics* (now *ARC*). July 25, 2012. https://arcmag.org/the-tea-partys-painter-the-art-of-jon-mcn aughton/.

Morgan, David. *The Forge of Vision: A Visual History of Modern Christianity* (Berkeley: University of California Press, 2015).

Morgan, David, ed. *Icons of American Protestantism: The Art of Warner Sallman* (New Haven, CT: Yale University Press, 1996).

Morgan, David. "Introduction." In *Icons of American Protestantism: The Art of Warner Sallman*, edited by David Morgan (New Haven, CT: Yale University Press, 1996), 1–24.

Morgan, David. *Protestants and Pictures: Religion, Visual Culture, and the Age of American Mass Production* (New York: Oxford University Press, 1999).

Morgan, David. "Thomas Kinkade and the History of Protestant Visual Culture in America." In *Thomas Kinkade: The Artist in the Mall*, edited by Alexis L. Boylan (Durham, NC: Duke University Press, 2011), 29–53.

Morgan, David. *Visual Piety: A History and Theory of Popular Religious Images* (Berkeley: University of California, 1999).

Morgan, David. "'Would Jesus Have Sat for a Portrait?' The Likeness of Christ in the Popular Reception of Sallman's Art." In *Icons of American Protestantism: The Art of Warner Sallman*, edited by David Morgan (New Haven, CT: Yale University Press, 1996), 181–206.

Morgan, Tracy. "From WHAM! to ACT UP." In *From ACT UP to the WTO: Urban Protest and Community Building in the Era of Globalization*, edited by Benjamin Shepard and Ronald Hayduk (New York: Verso, 2002), 141–49.

Mullarkey, Maureen. "Dishing It Out: Judy Chicago's 'Dinner Party.'" *Commonweal*, April 10, 1981, 210–11.

Muñoz, José Esteban. *Disidentifications: Queers of Color and the Performance of Politics* (Minneapolis: University of Minnesota Press, 1999).

Musser, Amber Jamilla. *Sensual Excess: Queer Femininity and Brown Jouissance* (New York: NYU Press, 2018).

Nash, Jennifer. *Black Body in Ecstasy: Reading Race, Reading Pornography* (Durham, NC: Duke University Press, 2014).

National Conference of Catholic Bishops. "Called to Compassion and Responsibility: A Response to the HIV/AIDS Crisis." *Origins* 19, no. 26 (1989): 421–36.

Navarro, Patricia. Interview by Sarah Schulman. ACT UP Oral History Project. July 20, 2007. https://www.actuporalhistory.org/numerical-interviews/084-patricia-navarro.

Navarro, Ray. "Eso, me esta pasando." In *Queer Looks: Perspectives on Lesbian and Gay Film and Video*, edited by Martha Gever, Pratibha Parmar, and John Greyson (New York: Routledge, 1993), 38–40.

"NEA Appropriations History." National Endowment for the Arts. Accessed August 5, 2023. http://arts.gov/about/appropriations-history.

Neuhaus, Richard John. *The Naked Public Square: Religion and Democracy in America* (Grand Rapids, MI: Eerdmans, 1984).

Newton, Esther. "Role Models." In *Camp Grounds: Style and Homosexuality*, edited by David Bergman (Amherst: University of Massachusetts Press, 1993), 39–53.

Noah, Timothy. "On the Hill: Armey's Aesthetic." *New Republic*, September 11, 1989, 14–15.

Nunes, Andrew. "The Creator of 'Piss Christ' Photographs Trump, Torture, and a Killer Clown." *Vice*. February 12, 2017. https://www.vice.com.

Ogbar, Jeffrey O. G. "Slouching Toward Bork: The Culture Wars and Self-Criticism in Hip-Hop Music." *Journal of Black Studies* 30, no. 2 (1999): 164–83.

O'Grady, Lorraine. "The Cave: Black Women Directors." *Artforum*, January 1992, 22–24. https://www.artforum.com/print/199201/black-women-directors-33639.

Oliphant, Elayne. *The Privilege of Being Banal: Art, Secularism, and Catholicism in Paris* (Chicago: University of Chicago Press, 2021).

O'Neil, Robert M. "Artists, Rights, and Grants: The NEA Controversy Revisited." *NYLA Journal of Human Rights* 9, no. 1 (1991): 85–109.

Orenstein, Gloria Feman. "The Reemergence of the Archetype of the Great Goddess in Art by Contemporary Women." *Heresies* 2, no. 1 (Spring 1978): 74–84.

Orsi, Robert. "'Mildred: Is It Fun to Be a Cripple?': The Culture of Suffering in Mid-Twentieth Century American Catholicism." In *Between Heaven and Earth: The Religious Worlds People Make and the Scholars Who Study Them* (Princeton, NJ: Princeton University Press, 2006), 19–47.

Paglia, Camille. "'Sensation' and Lack of Sensation." *Salon*, October 6, 1999. https://www.salon.com/1999/10/06/sensate/.

Parravicini, Cristinerose. "Renée Cox: Interview by Cristinerose Parravicini." *virus mutations*, November 14, 1998. https://1995-2015.undo.net/it/magazines/933692078.

Patnaik, Deba P. "Diasporic Double Vision." In *Committed to the Image: Contemporary Black Photographers*, edited by Barbara Head Millstein (New York: Merrell, 2001), 29–39.

Patton, Cindy. *Inventing AIDS* (New York: Routledge, 1990).

Pelikan, Jaroslav. *Jesus through the Centuries: His Place in the History of Culture* (New Haven, CT: Yale University Press, 1999).

Pellegrini, Ann. "After Sontag: Future Notes on Camp." In *A Companion to Lesbian, Gay, Bisexual, Transgender, and Queer Studies*, edited by George E. Haggerty and Molly McGarry (Malden, MA: Wiley-Blackwell, 2007), 168–93.

Penrose, Nerisha. "The Ailey School's Tribute to Judy Chicago's 'The Dinner Party' Will Move You Into the Weekend." *Elle*, March 6, 2020. https://www.elle.com/culture/art-design/a31262362/alvin-ailey-judy-chicago-the-dinner-party-video/.

Petro, Anthony M. *After the Wrath of God: AIDS, Sexuality, and American Religion* (New York: Oxford University Press, 2015).

Petro, Anthony M. "Bob Flanagan's Crip Catholicism, Transgression, and Form in Lived Religion." *American Religion* 1, no. 2 (Spring 2020): 1–26.

Petro, Anthony M. "Disability Studies and Religion." In *Religion: Embodied*, edited by Kent Brintnall (Farmington Hills, MI: Macmillan Reference Group, 2016), 359–76.

Petro, Anthony M. "Playing Pentecostal." *Religious Studies Reviews* 48, no. 1 (March 2022): 35–39.

Petro, Anthony M. "Ray Navarro's Jesus Camp, AIDS Activist Video, and the 'New Anti-Catholicism.'" *Journal of the American Academy of Religion* 85, no. 4 (2017): 920–56.

Petro, Anthony M. "Religion." In *The Routledge History of American Sexuality*, edited by Kevin Murphy, Jason Ruiz, and David Serlin (New York: Routledge, 2020), 290–300.

Petro, Anthony M. "Sex, Art, and Moral Panic." *Modern American History* 1, no. 2 (2018): 237–41.

Petro, Anthony M. "US Religious History, the Culture Wars, and the Arts of Secularity." *Journal of the American Academy of Religion* 87, no. 4 (December 2019): 968–81.

Phillips, Christopher. "Wojnarowicz Bags Buck." *Art in America*, October 1990, 240.

Pinder, Kymberly N. "'Our Father, God; Our Brother, Christ; or Are We Bastard Kin?': Images of Christ in African American Painting." *African American Review* 31, no. 2 (1997): 223–33.

Pollitt, Katha. "Anti-Catholic? Round Two." *The Nation*, March 19, 2001. https://www.thenation.com/article/archive/anti-catholic-round-two/.

Pollitt, Katha. "Catholic Bashing?" *The Nation*, October 14, 1999. https://www.thenation.com/article/archive/catholic-bashing/.

Promey, Sally M. *Religion in Plain View: Public Aesthetics of American Display* (Chicago: University of Chicago Press, 2024).

Promey, Sally M. *Painting Religion in Public: John Singer Sargent's "Triumph of Religion" at the Boston Public Library* (Princeton, NJ: Princeton University Press, 1999).

Promey, Sally M. "Pictorial Ambivalence and American Protestantism." In *Crossroads: Religion and Art in American Life*, edited by Alberta Arthurs and Glenn Wallach (New York: New Press, 2001), 189–231.

Promey, Sally M. "The 'Return' of Religion in the Scholarship of American Art." *Art Bulletin* 85, no. 3 (2003): 581–603.

Promey, Sally M. *Sensational Religion: Sensory Cultures in Material Practice* (New Haven, CT: Yale University Press, 2014).

Promey, Sally M. "Taste Cultures: The Visual Practice of Liberal Protestantism, 1940-1965." In *Practicing Protestants: Histories of Christian Life in America, 1630–1965*, edited by Laurie F. Maffly-Kipp, Leigh E. Schmidt, and Mark Valeri (Baltimore, MD: Johns Hopkins University Press, 2006), 250–93.

Promey, Sally M. "Visible Liberalism: Liberal Protestant Taste Evangelism." In *American Religious Liberalism*, edited by Leigh E. Schmidt and Salley M. Promey (Bloomington: Indiana University Press, 2012), 76–96.

Promey, Sally M., and David Morgan, eds. *The Visual Culture of American Religions* (New Haven, CT: Yale University Press, 2001).

Prothero, Stephen. *American Jesus: How the Son of God Became a National Icon* (New York: Farrar, Straus and Giroux, 2003).

Prothero, Stephen. *Why Liberals Win the Culture Wars (Even When They Lose Elections): The Battles That Define America from Jefferson's Heresies to Gay Marriage* (New York: HarperOne, 2016).

Puar, Jasbir K. *Terrorist Assemblages: Homonationalism in Queer Times* (Durham, NC: Duke University Press, 2007).

Rabinowitz, Lauren. "Issues of Feminist Aesthetics: Judy Chicago and Joyce Wieland." *Women's Art Journal* 1, no. 2 (Autumn-Winter 1980–1981): 38–41.

Raboteau, Albert J. *Slave Religion: The Invisible Institution in the Antebellum South* (New York: Oxford University Press, 1978).

Rambuss, Richard. *Closet Devotions* (Durham, NC: Duke University Press, 1998).

Rambuss, Richard. "Sacred Subjects and the Aversive Metaphysical Conceit: Crashaw, Serrano, Ofili." *ELH* 71, no. 2 (Summer 2004): 497–530.

Ramm, Bernard. *Protestant Biblical Interpretation: A Textbook of Hermeneutics*, 3rd ed. (Grand Rapids, MI: Baker Books, 1970).

Raven, Arlene, and Susan Rennie. "Interview with Judy Chicago." *Chrysalis*, no. 4 (1977): 89–101.

Ray, Rashawn, and Alexandra Gibbons. "Why Are States Banning Critical Race Theory." Brookings Institution, November 2021. https://www.brookings.edu/articles/why-are-states-banning-critical-race-theory/.

"Ray's Tape." 1990. Videocassette (VHS), 11:20 min. AIDS Activist Videotape Collection, New York Public Library.

Reeves, Richard. *President Reagan: The Triumph of Imagination* (New York: Simon and Schuster, 2006).

Ricœur, Paul. *Freud and Philosophy: An Essay on Interpretation*. Translated by Denis Savage (New Haven, CT: Yale University Press, 1977).

Ring, Nancy. "Identifying with Chicago." In *Sexual Politics: Judy Chicago's* Dinner Party *in Feminist Art History*, edited by Amelia Jones (Los Angeles: University of California Press, 1996), 126–47.

Rizk, Mysoon. "Looking at 'Animals in Pants': The Case of David Wojnarowicz." *Topia* 21 (Spring 2009): 137–59.

Rizk, Mysoon. "Nature, Death, and Spirituality in the Works of David Wojnarowicz" (Dissertation, University of Illinois, Urbana-Champaign, 1997).

Rizk, Mysoon. "Regulating Desire and Imagination: The Art and Times of David Wojnarowicz." In *Crime and Punishment*, edited by Austin Sarat (Boston: Elsevier, 2005), 3–32.

Rodgers, Daniel T. *Age of Fracture* (Cambridge, MA: Belknap Press, 2011).

Rodriguez-Plate, S. B. *Blasphemy: Art that Offends* (London: Black Dog Publishing, 2006).

Roediger, David R. *Working Toward Whiteness: How America's Immigrants Became White: The Strange Journey from Ellis Island to the Suburbs* (New York: Basic Books, 2005).

Rolsky, L. Benjamin. *The Rise and Fall of the Religious Left: Politics, Television, and Popular Culture in the 1970s and Beyond* (New York: Columbia University Press, 2019).

Rose, Sheree. "Why Kirby Dick Is a 'Sick' Prick." In *Rated RX: Sheree Rose with and after Bob Flanagan*, edited by Yetta Howard (Columbus: Ohio State University Press, 2020), 60–63.

Rubin, Gayle. "Thinking Sex: Notes for a Radical Theory of the Politics of Sexuality." In *Pleasure and Danger: Exploring Female Sexuality*, edited by Carole S. Vance (Boston: Routledge and Kegan Paul, 1985), 267–319.

Russell, Temperance, Lori Loftin, and Julie Shayne. "The History of San Diego State University's Women's Studies Program." In *Persistence Is Resistance: Celebrating 50 Years of Gender, Women & Sexuality Studies*, edited by Julie Shayne (Seattle: University of Washington Press, 2020). https://uw.pressbooks.pub/happy50thws.

Ryan, Hugh. "The Final Secret of David Wojnarowicz." *Vice.* December 26, 2014. https://www.vice.com.

Ryan, Thomas, and Lawrence Rubin. "By the Numbers: Material Spirituality and the Last Supper." *Spiritus: A Journal of Christian Spirituality* 2, no. 2 (Fall 2002): 147–62.

Saalfield (Gund), Catherine (for Ray Navarro). "On the Make: AIDS Activist Video Collectives." In *Queer Looks: Perspectives on Lesbian and Gay Film and Video*, edited by Martha Gever, John Greyson, and Pratibha Parmar (London: Routledge, 1993), 21–37.

Saalfield (Gund), Catherine, and Ray Navarro. "Shocking Pink Praxis: Race and Gender on the ACT UP Frontlines." In *Inside/Out: Lesbian Theories, Gay Theories*, edited by Diana Fuss (New York: Routledge, 1991), 341–69.

Samuels, Ellen. *Fantasies of Identification: Disability, Gender, Race* (New York: NYU Press, 2014).

Savage, Dan. "*Charlie Hebdo* and *Piss Christ*: On Fear and Self-Censorship and the AP's Dangerous New Precedent." SLOG (*The Stranger*), January 8, 2015. https://www.thestranger.com.

Scarborough, Klare. "Coffins and Cameras: A Conversation with Sheree Rose." *Performance Research* 15, no. 1 (2010): 123–30.

Schaeffer, Frances A. *A Christian Manifesto* (1981; Wheaton, IL: Crossway Books, 2005).

Schapiro, Miriam, and Judy Chicago. "Female Imagery." *Womanspace Journal* 1, no. 3 (Summer 1973): 11–14.

Schmidt, Leigh Eric. *Consumer Rites: The Buying and Selling of American Holidays* (Princeton, NJ: Princeton University Press, 1997).

Schneider, Rebecca. *The Explicit Body in Performance* (New York: Routledge, 1997).

Schulman, Sarah. *Let the Record Show: A Political History of ACT UP New York, 1987–1993* (New York: Macmillan, 2021).

Schulman, Sarah, and Jim Hubbard. ACT UP Oral History Project. Accessed May 6, 2024. https://www.actuporalhistory.org.

Schumm, Darla, and Michael Stoltzfus, eds. *Disability in Judaism, Christianity, and Islam: Sacred Texts, Historical Traditions, and Social Analysis* (New York: Palgrave Macmillan, 2011).

Sedgwick, Eve Kosofsky. *Epistemology of the Closet* (Berkeley: University of California Press, 1990).

Sedgwick, Eve Kosofsky. "Paranoid and Reparative Reading, Or, You're So Paranoid You Probably Think This Essay Is About You." In *Touching Feeling: Affect, Pedagogy, Performativity* (Durham, NC: Duke University Press, 2003), 123–52.

Seitz, John. "Altars of Ammo: Catholic Materiality and the Visual Culture of World War II." *Material Religion* 15, no. 4 (2019): 401–32.

Selcraig, Bruce. "Reverend Wildmon's War on the Arts." *New York Times Magazine,* September 2, 1990. https://www.nytimes.com/1990/09/02/magazine/reverend-wildmons-war-on-the-arts.html.

Self, Robert O. *All in the Family: The Realignment of American Democracy Since the 1960s* (New York: Hill and Wang, 2013).

Shrum, Nicholas. "Mormon American Nationalism and the Religiopolitical Art of Jon McNaughton." *Journal of Mormon History* 50, no. 2 (2024): 43–77.

Silverstein, Jason. "Why the Ashes of People with AIDS on the Whitehouse Lawn Matter." *Vice,* August 29, 2016. https://www.vice.com.

Sisters of Perpetual Indulgence, Inc. "Sistory." Accessed March 7, 2017. https://www.thesisters.org/sistory.

Smith, Leslie Dorrough. *Righteous Rhetoric: Sex, Speech, and the Politics of Concerned Women for America* (New York: Oxford University Press, 2014).

Smith, Wilfred Cantwell. *Belief and History* (Charlottesville: University Press of Virginia, 1977).

Smith, Wilfred Cantwell. *Faith and Belief: The Difference Between Them* (London: Oneworld, 1998).

Smith, Wilfred Cantwell. *The Meaning and End of Religion* (Minneapolis, MN: Fortress, 1991).

Snyder, Carol. "Reading the Language of 'The Dinner Party.'" *Woman's Art Journal* 1, no. 2 (Autumn 1980–Winter 1981): 30–34.

Sontag, Susan. "Notes on 'Camp.'" In *Against Interpretation and Other Essays* (1966; New York: Anchor Books, 1990), 275–92.

Sorett, Josef. *Spirit in the Dark: A Religious History of Racial Aesthetics* (New York: Oxford University Press, 2016).

Spillers, Hortense J. "Interstices: A Small Drama of Words." In *Black, White, and in Color: Essays on American Literature and Culture* (Chicago: University of Chicago Press, 2003), 152–75.

"Statement by John E. Frohnmayer." National Endowment for the Arts. November 9, 1989. https://texts.artistsspace.org/t9wdhfhi.

Steidl, Jason. "The Chicano Movement in the US Catholic Church: Grassroots Activism and Dialogical Ecclesiology" (PhD dissertation, Fordham University, New York, 2018).

Stein, Roger B. *John Ruskin and Aesthetic Thought in America, 1840–1900* (Cambridge, MA: Harvard University Press, 1967).

Steinberg, Leo. *Leonardo's Incessant Last Supper* (New York: Zone Books, 2001).

Steinberg, Leo. *The Sexuality of Christ in Renaissance Art and Modern Oblivion*, 2nd ed. (Chicago: University of Chicago Press, 1996).

Steiner, Wendy. "Introduction: Below Skin-deep." In *Andres Serrano: Works 1983–1993* (Philadelphia: Institute of Contemporary Arts, University of Pennsylvania, 1996), 11–16.

Steiner, Wendy. *The Scandal of Pleasure: Art in an Age of Fundamentalism* (Chicago: University of Chicago Press, 1995).

Steinfels, Margaret O'Brien, ed. *American Catholics, American Culture: Tradition & Resistance* (Lanham, MD: Rowman and Littlefield, 2004).

Stout, Harry S. *The Divine Dramatist: George Whitefield and the Rise of Modern Evangelicalism* (Grand Rapids, MI: William B. Eerdmans Publishing, 1991).

Strub, Whitney. "Lavender, Menaced: Lesbianism, Obscenity Law, and the Feminist Antipornography Movement." *Journal of Women's History* 22, no. 2 (Summer 2010): 83–107.

Strub, Whitney. "Modernizing Decency: Citizens for Decent Literature and Covert Catholic Activism in Cold War America." In *Devotions and Desires: Histories of Sexuality and Religion in the Twentieth-Century United States*, edited by Gillian A. Frank, Bethany Moreton, and Heather R. White (Chapel Hill: University of North Carolina Press, 2018), 133–51.

Strub, Whitney. *Obscenity Rules: Roth v. United States and the Long Struggle over Sexual Expression* (Lawrence: University of Kansas Press, 2013).

Strub, Whitney. *Perversion for Profit: The Politics of Pornography and the Rise of the New Right* (New York: Columbia University Press, 2013).

Stryker, Susan. *Transgender History: The Roots of Today's Revolution* (New York: Seal Press, 2008).

Sullivan, Winnifred. *The Impossibility of Religious Freedom* (Princeton, NJ: Princeton University Press, 2007).

Swarns, Rachel L. *The 272: The Families Who Were Enslaved and Sold to Build the American Catholic Church* (New York: Penguin, 2023).

Takemoto, Tina. "Love Is Still Possible in this Junky World: Conversation with Sheree Rose about Her Life with Bob Flanagan." *Women & Performance* 19, no. 1 (2009): 95–111.

Taves, Ann. *Religious Experience Reconsidered: A Building-Block Approach to the Study of Religion and Other Special Things* (Princeton, NJ: Princeton University Press, 2011).

Taylor, Charles. *Human Agency and Language* (New York: Cambridge University Press, 1985).

Taylor, Clyde. "Empowering the Eye." In *Committed to the Image: Contemporary Black Photographers*, edited by Barbara Head Millstein (New York: Merrell, 2001), 15–25.

Taylor, Diana. *The Archive and the Repertoire: Performing Cultural Memory in the Americas* (Durham, NC: Duke University Press, 2003).

Taylor, Marvin J. "Some Sort of Grace: David Wojnarowicz's Vision." In In *David Wojnarowicz: History Keeps Me Awake at Night,* edited by David Breslin and David Kiehl (New York: Whitney Museum of American Art, 2018), 55–66.

Tillich, Paul. *On Art and Architecture,* edited by Jane Dillenberger and John Dillenberger (New York: Crossroad, 1987).

Tracy, David. *The Analogical Imagination: Christian Theology and the Culture of Pluralism* (1981; New York: Crossroad, 1998).

Treichler, Paula A. *How to Have Theory in an Epidemic: Cultural Chronicles of AIDS* (Durham, NC: Duke University Press, 1999).

Troyer, John Erik. "Technologies of the HIV/AIDS Corpse." *Medical Anthropology* 29, no. 2 (2010): 129–49.

Tweed, Thomas A., ed. *Retelling U.S. Religious History* (Berkeley: University of California Press, 1997).

Tyburczy, Jennifer. "Queer Acts of Recovery and Uncovering: Deciphering Mexico through Ephemera in David Wojnarowicz's *A Fire In My Belly." Text and Performance Quarterly* 35, no. 1 (2015): 4–23.

United States Catholic Conference Administrative Board. "The Many Faces of AIDS: A Gospel Response." *Origins* 17, no. 28 (1987): 481–89.

Vance, Carole S. "The War on Culture." *Art in America,* September 1989, pp. 39–43. Reprinted in *Art Matters: How the Culture Wars Changed America,* edited by Brian Wallis, Marianne Weems, and Philip Yenawine (New York: NYU Press, 1999), 220–31.

Vogel, Shane. "Performing 'Stormy Weather': Ethel Waters, Lena Horne, and Katherine Dunham." *South Central Review* 25, no. 1 (Spring 2008): 93–113.

Walker, Alice. "'One' Child of One's Own: A Meaningful Digression within the Work(s)." In *In Search of Our Mothers' Gardens: Womanist Prose* (San Diego: Harvest/Harcourt, 1983), 361–83.

Walker-Cornetta, Andrew. "Without the Lord: Eliza Suggs, Religion, and the Good Disabled Subject." *American Religion* 5, no. 1 (Fall 2023): 67–92.

Wallace, Michele. "The Culture War within the Culture Wars." In *Dark Designs and Visual Culture* (Durham, NC: Duke University Press, 2004), 202–14.

Wallis, Brian, Marianne Weems, and Philip Yenawine, eds. *Art Matters: How the Culture Wars Changed America* (New York: NYU Press, 1999).

Walsh, Frank. *Sin and Censorship: The Catholic Church and the Motion Picture Industry* (New Haven, CT: Yale University Press, 1996).

Wamsley, Laurel. "What's in the So-Called 'Don't Say Gay' Bill that Could Impact the Whole Country." NPR. October 21, 2022. http://npr.org.

Warner, Michael. "The Rise of 'Secular Humanism.'" Immanent Frame. September 22, 2008. https://tif.ssrc.org/2008/09/22/the-ruse-of-secular-humanism/.

Weigel, George. *Catholicism and the Renewal of Democracy* (Mahwah, NJ: Paulist Press, 1989).

Weigel, George. "The New Anti-Catholicism." *Commentary Magazine*, June 1992, 25–31. https://www.commentary.org/articles/george-weigel-2/the-new-anti-catholicism/.

Weisenfeld, Judith. *New World A-Coming: Black Religion and Racial Identity during the Great Migration* (New York: NYU Press, 2017).

Weston, Kath. *Families We Choose: Lesbians, Gays, and Kinship* (New York: Columbia University Press, 1997).

Wheaton, Deidre Lyniece. "Seeking Salvation: Black Messianism, Racial Formation, and Christian Thought in Late Twentieth Century Black Cultural Texts" (PhD dissertation, University of Michigan, 2008).

White, Artress Bethany. "Fragmented Souls: Call and Response with Renee Cox." In *Soul: Black Power, Politics, and Pleasure*, edited by Monique Guillory and Richard C. Green (New York: NYU Press, 1997), 45–55.

White, Heather R. "How Heterosexuality Became Religious: Judeo-Christian Morality and the Remaking of Sex in Twentieth-Century America." In *Heterosexual Histories*, edited by Rebecca L. Davis and Michele Mitchell (New York: NYU Press, 2021), 331–57.

White, Heather R. *Reforming Sodom: Protestants and the Rise of Gay Rights* (Chapel Hill: University of North Carolina Press, 2015).

Whitehead, Andrew L., and Samuel L. Perry. *Taking America Back for God: Christian Nationalism in the United States* (New York: Oxford University Press, 2022).

Wilbur, Sarah. *Funding Bodies: Five Decades of Dance Making at the National Endowment for the Arts* (Middletown, CT: Wesleyan University Press, 2021).

Wilcox, Melissa M. *Queer Nuns: Religion, Activism, and Serious Parody* (New York: NYU Press, 2018).

Wilcox, Melissa M. *Queer Religiosities: An Introduction to Queer and Transgender Studies in Religion* (Lanham, MD: Rowman and Littlefield, 2021).

Wilcox, Melissa M. "Words Kill: Sex and Definition in US Religion." *American Religion* 1, no. 1 (Fall 2019): 5–26.

Wildmon, Donald E. *The Case Against Pornography* (Wheaton, IL: Victor Books, 1986).

Wildmon, Donald E. *Don Wildmon: The Man the Networks Love to Hate* (Wilmore, KY: Bristol Books, 1989).

Wildmon, Donald E. *The Home Invaders* (Wheaton, IL: Victor Books, 1985).

Williams, Daniel K. *Defenders of the Unborn: The Pro-Life Movement Before Roe v. Wade* (New York: Oxford University Press, 2016).

Williams, Daniel K. *God's Own Party: The Making of the Christian Right* (New York: Oxford University Press, 2010).

Williams, Raymond. *Marxism and Literature* (New York: Oxford University Press, 1977).

Williams, Shannen Dee. *Subversive Habits: Black Catholic Nuns in the Long African American Freedom Struggle* (Durham, NC: Duke University Press, 2022).

Wiltenburg, Joy. "Just When in History Did Men Decide Women Are Not Funny?" *Psyche*, October 24, 2022. https://psyche.co/ideas/just-when-in-history-did-men-decide-that-women-are-not-funny

Winbush, Don, and Donald Wildmon. "Interview with Rev. Donald E. Wildmon: Bringing Satan to Heel." *Time*, June 19, 1989. https://time.com.

Winston, Diane. "Back to the Future: Religion, Politics, and the Media." *American Quarterly* 59, no. 3 (September 2007): 969–89.

Winston, Diane. "News Coverage of Religion, Sexuality, and AIDS." In *The Oxford Handbook of Religion and the American News Media*, edited by Diane Winston (New York: Oxford University Press, 2012), 377–90.

Wojnarowicz, David. "Biographical Dateline." In *David Wojnarowicz: Tongues of Flame*, 2nd ed. (Normal, IL: University Galleries of Illinois State University, 1992), 113–18.

Wojnarowicz, David. *Close to the Knives: A Memoir of Disintegration* (New York: Vintage, 1991).

Wojnarowicz, David. "Postcards from America." In *Close to the Knives* (New York: Vintage, 1991), 111–137.

Wojnarowicz, David. "Postcards from America: X-Rays from Hell." In *Witnesses: Against Our Vanishing* by Artists Space (New York: Artists Space Exhibitions, 1989), 6–11.

Wojnarowicz, David. *Weight of the Earth: The Taped Journals of David Wojnarowicz*, edited by Lisa Darms and David O'Neill (New York: Semiotext(e), 2018).

Wojnarowicz, David, and Cynthia Carr. "Biographical Dateline." In *David Wojnarowicz: History Keeps Me Awake at Night*, edited by David Breslin and David Kiehl (New York: Whitney Museum of American Art, 2018), 285–309.

Wolfe, Tom. *The Painted Word* (New York: Farrar, Straus and Giroux, 1975).

Worley, Taylor. *Memento Mori in Contemporary Art: Theologies of Lament and Hope* (London: Routledge, 2019).

Wright, Joshua. "Comic Belief: Religious Irreverence and Irreverent Religion in Cold War America" (PhD dissertation, Harvard University, 2023).

Wuthnow, Robert. *The Restructuring of American Religion: Society and Faith since World War II* (Princeton, NJ: Princeton University Press, 1990).

Wylder, Viki D. Thompson. "Judy Chicago: Trials and Tributes." In *Judy Chicago: Trials and Tributes*, by Viki D. Thompson Wylder and Lucy R. Lippard (Tallahassee: Florida State University Museum of Fine Arts, 1999), 8–29.

Wylder, Viki D. Thompson. "Judy Chicago's *Dinner Party* and *Birth Project* as Religious Symbol and Visual Theology" (PhD dissertation, Florida State University, Tallahassee, FL, 1993).

Yanagihara, Hanya. "The Burning House." *Paris Review*, July 2, 2018. https://www.theparisrev iew.org/blog/2018/07/02/the-burning-house/.

Young, Neil J. *We Gather Together: The Religious Right and the Problem of Interfaith Politics* (New York: Oxford University Press, 2015).

Zubovich, Gene. "The U.S. Culture Wars Abroad: Liberal-Evangelical Rivalry and Decolonization in Southern Africa, 1968–1994." *Journal of American History* 110, no. 2 (September 2023): 308–32.

Index